HMH SCIENCE DIMENSIONS™

ASSESSMENT GUIDE

Grade 3

Copyright © by Houghton Mifflin Harcourt Publishing Company

All rights reserved. No part of this work may be reproduced or transmitted in any form or by any means, electronic or mechanical, including photocopying or recording, or by any information storage or retrieval system, without the prior written permission of the copyright owner unless such copying is expressly permitted by federal copyright law.

Permission is hereby granted to individuals using the corresponding student's textbook or kit as the major vehicle for regular classroom instruction to photocopy entire pages from this publication in classroom quantities for instructional use and not for resale. Requests for information on other matters regarding duplication of this work should be submitted through our Permissions website at https://customercare.hmhco.com/contactus/Permissions.html or mailed to Houghton Mifflin Harcourt Publishing Company, Attn: Intellectual Property Licensing, 9400 Southpark Center Loop, Orlando, Florida 32819-8647.

Printed in the U.S.A.

ISBN 978-0-544-71331-4

2 3 4 5 6 7 8 9 10 0982 26 25 24 23 22 21 20 19 18 17

4500670536 A B C D E F G

If you have received these materials as examination copies free of charge, Houghton Mifflin Harcourt Publishing Company retains title to the materials and they may not be resold. Resale of examination copies is strictly prohibited.

Possession of this publication in print format does not entitle users to convert this publication, or any portion of it, into electronic format.

Table of Contents

Unit 1: Engineering

Unit 2: Forces

Unit 3: Motion

Unit 4: Life Cycles and Inherited Traits

Unit 5: Organisms and Their Environments

© Houghton Mifflin Harcourt Publishing Company

Introduction

Overview of NGSS Assessment in HMH Science Dimensions™

HMH Science Dimensions assessment has been especially designed to help ensure that your students have the knowledge and skills necessary to achieve the Next Generation Science Standards Performance Expectations.

HMH Science Dimensions assessment has been designed using a scaffolded approach to help you identify how your students are progressing in their ability to apply knowledge to solve problems and explain phenomena.

HMH Science Dimensions assessment options are intended to give you maximum flexibility in assessing what your students know and what they can do. The program's formative and summative assessment categories reflect the understanding that assessment provides a learning opportunity for students.

In an ideal world, all assessment is formative. However, students must also periodically demonstrate mastery of science concepts and science practices in a high-stakes environment. The summative assessments provided in this Assessment Guide can help you ensure that your students are prepared to demonstrate mastery of NGSS Performance Expectations in whatever form future assessments may take, whether print, digital, or performance based.

All *HMH Science Dimensions* tests are available online, in print, and in an editable Word format. All quizzes, tests, and performance-based assessments in this Assessment Guide have a digital component that provides the same interaction online. You may choose to use the digital path, the print path, or a combination of the two.

This Assessment Guide is your directory to assessment in *HMH Science Dimensions*. In it you'll find copy masters for Beginning-of-Year Tests, Unit Pretests, Lesson Quizzes, Unit Tests, Mid-Year and End-of-Year benchmark tests, and Performance-Based Assessments. At the back of this Assessment Guide you will find answers, explanations of most answers, and scoring rubrics for open-ended questions. You will also find information about the Webb's Depth of Knowledge (DOK) for each item, and the NGSS dimensions aligned to each item.

The following pages will provide you with information about the structure and philosophy behind each type of assessment included in this Assessment Guide.

Scaffolding in HMH Science Dimensions *Assessments*

HMH Science Dimensions assessments are designed to increase in difficulty and complexity. Scaffolding occurs both within tests and between tests.

Within each test, scaffolding occurs as assessment begins with lower DOK items to help bolster student confidence. This allows students to build on demonstrated knowledge and understanding throughout the test.

Several of the assessment strategies described below and on the following pages can be used either as formative or as summative instruments, depending on whether you use them primarily for teaching or primarily for evaluation. The choice is yours.

DOK Progression in *HMH Science Dimensions* Assessment

Formative Assessment
Beginning-of-Year Test: DOK 1 and 2; multiple choice and technology-enhanced items
Unit Pretest: DOK 1; multiple choice
Lesson Quiz: mostly DOK 1 and 2; multiple choice and open-ended essay items
Summative Assessment
Unit Test: DOK 1, 2, and 3; multiple choice, technology-enhanced items, open-ended essay items, and interrelated item sets
Mid-Year Test (A and B): mostly DOK 2 and 3; multiple choice, technology-enhanced items, open-ended essay items, and interrelated item sets
End-of-Year Test (A and B): mostly DOK 2 and 3; multiple choice, technology-enhanced items, open-ended essay items, and interrelated item sets
Performance-Based Assessment: DOK 2 and 3; hands-on performance; open-ended activities and assessment

© Houghton Mifflin Harcourt Publishing Company

Skills Measurement in HMH Science Dimensions *Assessments*

The primary skills measurement used in *HMH Science Dimensions* to drive scaffolding is Depth of Knowledge (DOK). In addition, assessment items include Bloom's Traditional and Bloom's Revised process skills information.

Webb's Depth of Knowledge (DOK) for Science

DOK 1 Recall and Reproduction requires recall of information, such as a fact, definition, term, or a simple procedure, as well as performing a simple science process or procedure. DOK 1 keywords include *identify*, *name*, *list*, *label*, and *define*.

DOK 2 Skills and Concepts requires mental processing beyond simple recall. Items require students to make a connection between one concept and another, or recall and use a relationship between concepts. DOK 2 keywords include *predict*, *summarize*, *classify*, *relate*, and *graph*.

DOK 3 Strategic Thinking requires deep knowledge using reasoning, evidence, planning, or analysis of relationships among concepts. These items include tasks that require multiple mental steps to arrive at an answer. DOK 3 keywords include *compare*, *critique*, *revise*, and *explain phenomena*.

DOK 4 Extended Thinking requires high cognitive demand and is very complex. Students are required to relate ideas within or among content areas and to select or devise an approach for designing an experiment or solving a problem. The Performance-Based Assessments provide a DOK 4 level of assessment.

Bloom's Traditional

Bloom's Traditional taxonomy includes six categories of increasingly complex cognitive levels.

Knowledge requires students to recognize and recall facts and data.

Comprehension requires students to interpret, translate, summarize, or paraphrase information.

Application requires students to use information in a different context.

Analysis requires students to separate a whole into parts and show relationships among the parts.

Synthesis requires students to combine elements into a new form.

Evaluation requires students to apply rational criteria to judge or make decisions.

Bloom's Revised

Bloom's Revised taxonomy comprises six categories, some of which are equivalent to those in Bloom's Traditional taxonomy.

Remembering requires students to recall information, facts, procedures, or concepts.

Understanding requires students to explain and recognize the implications of ideas, concepts, methods, or procedures.

Applying requires students to use information or carry out a procedure in a setting similar to the example.

Analyzing requires students to use information or carry out a procedure in a different setting.

Evaluating requires students to justify a decision or a course of action.

Creating requires students to generate new ideas, products, or ways of viewing things, or reorganize elements into a new pattern.

© Houghton Mifflin Harcourt Publishing Company

Formative Assessment

Assessing Prior Knowledge, Addressing Misconceptions, and Informing Remediation

Beginning-of-Year Test
The Beginning-of-Year Test is made up of questions representative of the concepts found in the Performance Expectations from the previous grade year. This test can help you identify areas in which students may require reteaching or additional support throughout the upcoming year.

Unit Pretest
Each of the units begins with a Unit Pretest that assesses prior knowledge related to the upcoming unit content. The Unit Pretest can be used to help you identify gaps in prerequisite knowledge and vocabulary, and ensure that misconceptions are identified and addressed during the course of the lessons.

Lesson Quiz
The Lesson Quizzes are designed to provide short-interval checkpoints to ensure student comprehension of lesson concepts before continuing to the next lesson. They can be used to guide reteaching and remediation.

Classroom Discussion
Discussion offers an organic opportunity to gauge how well students are absorbing the material, and to assess any misconceptions or gaps in their understanding. Students also learn from each other in this informal exchange.

Tips for Classroom Discussion
- Allow students plenty of time to reflect and formulate their answers.
- Call on students if you sense they have something to add but haven't spoken yet.
- At the same time, allow reluctant students not to speak unless they choose to.
- Encourage students to respond to each other as well as to you.

Summative Assessment

Demonstrating Mastery of NGSS Disciplinary Core Ideas, Crosscutting Concepts, and Science and Engineering Practices

Unit Tests

The Unit Tests provide assessment of the specific dimensions of the Performance Expectations that are associated with the unit content. Unit Tests incorporate interrelated item sets centered around one topic that offer a more robust assessment of Performance Expectations. Unit Tests also incorporate three-dimensional rubrics associated with open-ended items. These rubrics can help you determine how students are progressing toward mastery of Disciplinary Core Ideas, Crosscutting Concepts, and Science and Engineering Practices.

Mid-Year and End-of-Year Tests (Test A)

The on-level Mid-Year and End-of-Year Tests (Test A) are designed to help you assess student ability to achieve the Performance Expectations in a format that helps to prepare students for next generation standardized assessments. These tests are primarily made up of technology-enhanced items, interrelated item sets, and incorporate three-dimensional rubrics to help identify mastery of all three dimensions.

Modified Mid-Year and End-of-Year Tests (Test B)

The modified Mid-Year and End-of-Year Tests (Test B) are targeted to help struggling readers and English language learners demonstrate their science mastery with less emphasis on reading ability. These items have a slightly lower difficulty and reading level but are visually identical to the on-level test, and assess the same NGSS dimensions. The digital versions of these tests include audio for added reading support.

Performance-Based Assessments

Performance-Based Assessments (PBAs) provide authentic hands-on assessment of the Performance Expectations. The PBAs are targeted to fully assess Performance Expectations that require a hands-on aspect for full completion. They also combine aspects of multiple Performance Expectations to give students the opportunity to make connections across content areas. The PBAs allow students to demonstrate their ability to perform Science and Engineering Practices and apply Crosscutting Concepts to solve problems, explain phenomena, and make conceptual connections across Disciplinary Core Ideas and Performance Expectations.

Interrelated Item Sets

As specifically called for by the developers of the NGSS, *HMH Science Dimensions* incorporates interrelated sets of assessment items, or item clusters, in Unit Tests, Mid-Year and End-of-Year Tests, and Part 2 of the Performance-Based Assessments. Very rarely can a single question address an entire Performance Expectation. In order to allow students to demonstrate understanding of Disciplinary Core Ideas, use Science and Engineering Practices, and apply Crosscutting Concepts, multiple opportunities must be provided. Clustering items around a single topic provides the opportunity to dive deeper into a concept, and allows students to demonstrate the extent of their progress toward achieving a Performance Expectation.

© Houghton Mifflin Harcourt Publishing Company

Three-Dimensional Rubrics

Evidence-Based Scoring on the NGSS Three Dimensions

Open-ended assessment items in *HMH Science Dimensions* Unit Tests, Mid-Year Tests, End-of-Year Tests, and Part 2 of Performance-Based Assessments use a three-dimensional rubric that allows you to evaluate student responses on all of the NGSS dimensions aligned to the question.

These rubrics rely on an evidence-based approach to assessment that evaluates student responses against claims and evidence of mastery.

Not all questions will be aligned to all three dimensions. Some focus on Science and Engineering Practices (SEPs) in the context of a Disciplinary Core Idea (DCI). Some focus on applying Crosscutting Concepts (CCCs) in the context of a Disciplinary Core Idea (DCI). Still others focus on evaluating student understanding of the Disciplinary Core Ideas (DCI) themselves.

The following example demonstrates a three-dimensional rubric for a question aligned to all three dimensions. The Claims section identifies the knowledge or skill the student should demonstrate related to a particular dimension. The Evidence of Mastery sections provide an explanation for an adequate student response in order for the student to receive full credit for that NGSS dimension.

DCI, SEP, CCC - 3 points	

Claims	The student is able to:
	    1. use past motion to predict future motion (DCI);
	    2. use measurements as the basis for evidence of a phenomenon (SEP); and
	    3. describe the pattern of change used to make the prediction (CCC).

Evidence of Mastery of Disciplinary Core Ideas	1 point for correctly predicting how long it will take to travel 4 laps **Part 1:** One point is earned for identifying that it will take 40 minutes. The following response, or an equivalent, is acceptable. • It will take 40 minutes.
Evidence of Mastery of Science and Engineering Practices	1 point for correctly using the measurements in the table to determine the speed of the car **Part 2:** One point is earned for calculating the speed of the car as 0.1 mile per minute. The following response, or an equivalent, is acceptable. • The cars are going 0.1 mile per minute.
Evidence of Mastery of Crosscutting Concepts	1 point for correctly explaining that each lap takes 10 minutes **Part 3:** One point is earned for explaining that the car takes 10 minutes to travel one lap. The following response, or an equivalent, is acceptable. • Each lap takes 10 minutes.

© Houghton Mifflin Harcourt Publishing Company

Performance-Based Assessment (PBA)

HMH Science Dimensions Performance-Based Assessments (PBAs) provide students with an authentic hands-on opportunity to demonstrate science and engineering practices, to solve complex problems, and to make connections among NGSS Performance Expectations.

Each Performance-Based Assessment consists of two or three performance tasks followed by a summative Part 2 section of questions. The performance tasks include teacher support for materials and preparation, answers, sample models, and support for guiding students through open-ended performance assessment. Each task also includes observational rubrics to help you score student performance. Supplemental Teacher Materials found online provide additional tips for administering these Performance-Based Assessments.

Using Performance-Based Assessment

The key to performance-based assessment is observation. Before beginning a PBA, make a plan for observation that will allow you to observe all students as they are demonstrating skills. Review the rubric in advance so you know what to look for and are well prepared to evaluate student performance. Review the student procedure and make a note of steps in which you would expect to see students demonstrating specific skills identified in the observational rubric.

Administering PBA Tasks

Collaboration: PBA tasks are designed to allow students to interact and to work either collaboratively or independently. You can decide, based on time, materials availability, and classroom dynamics, whether you would like students to work individually or in groups. Additionally, opportunities are provided within certain PBAs for peer assessment and student feedback.

Resources: Many tasks will require student research. Consider in advance whether you will allow students to use their textbooks, library books, or Internet search access. If Internet research is required, be sure to secure time in the computer lab or allow students to bring their own devices as needed. Because these PBAs are also available digitally, you have the option to allow students to use a device such as a computer or tablet to record their progress.

Scoring the Tasks: You may choose to score student performance on the tasks using the observational rubric only, or you may incorporate scores from student answers to procedure and summary items. Alternatively, procedure and summary responses can serve as notes during the summative portion of the PBA.

No Score: If you are unable to observe all students performing all of the rubric criteria, the "no score" option is available to avoid deducting points from students who may have performed the skill well but simply were not seen.

Accommodations: The supplemental materials include some suggestions for accommodating students with special needs, but for each task you'll want to consider ways to allow all students to participate in a manner that is consistent with their abilities.

Administering PBA Part 2

Part 2 of the Performance-Based Assessment is summative and is intended to be completed independently. You can decide whether or not students will be allowed to use their notes from the tasks when completing Part 2. Alternately, you may choose not to assign Part 2 and score only the performance aspect of these PBAs.

PBA as Project-Based Learning

Performance-Based Assessments can also be used as a learning tool. Options for Project-Based Learning are included in the teacher support for each PBA.

© Houghton Mifflin Harcourt Publishing Company

Classroom Observation

Use this checklist to help you observe Science and Engineering Practices

Rating Scale	
3 Outstanding	1 Needs Improvement
2 Satisfactory	0 Did Not Demonstrate Skill
NS Did not have the opportunity to observe	

Teacher Directions:

This rubric allows for performance observation of 12 students. Make copies as needed. If students are working in groups, record the group name.

Group # _____________

Names of Students

Science and Engineering Practices												
Asking Questions												
Defining Problems												
Developing Models												
Using Models												
Planning Investigations												
Carrying Out Investigations												
Analyzing Data												
Interpreting Data												
Using Mathematics and Computational Thinking												
Constructing Explanations												
Designing Solutions												
Engaging in Argument from Evidence												
Obtaining and Evaluating Information												
Communicating Information												
Total												

Portfolio Assessment

Guidelines for Student Evaluation through Portfolio Assessment

A portfolio is a showcase for student work, a place where many types of assignments, projects, reports, and data sheets can be collected. The work samples in the collection provide snapshots of the student's efforts over time, and taken together they reveal the student's growth, attitudes, and understanding. Portfolio assessment involves meeting with each student to discuss the work and to set goals for future performance. In contrast with formal assessments, portfolio assessments have these advantages:

1. They give students a voice in the assessment process.

2. They foster reflection, self-monitoring, and self-evaluation.

3. They provide a comprehensive picture of a student's progress.

Tips for Portfolio Assessment

- Make a basic plan. Decide how many work samples will be included in the portfolios and what period of time they represent.

- Explain the portfolio and its use. Describe the portfolio an artist might put together, showing his or her best or most representative work, as part of an application for school or a job. The student's portfolio is based on this model.

- Together with your class decide on the required work samples that everyone's portfolio will contain.

- Explain that the students will choose additional samples of their work to include. Have students remember how their skills and understanding have grown over the period covered by the portfolio, and review their work with this in mind. The best pieces to choose may not be the longest or neatest.

- Have students record their reasoning as they make their selections and assemble their portfolios.

- Explain to students how you will evaluate the contents of their portfolios.

- Use the portfolios for conferences, grading, and planning. Give students the option of taking their portfolios home to share.

© Houghton Mifflin Harcourt Publishing Company

My Science Portfolio

What Is in My Portfolio	Why I Chose It
1.	
2.	
3.	
4.	
5.	
6.	
7.	

I organized my Science Portfolio this way because ________________________

____

____

____

____

Student Presentation

Guidelines for Evaluating Student Written, Oral, and Visual Presentations

The following guidelines can be used as a starting point for evaluating student presentation of alternative assessments. For each category, use only the criteria that are relevant for the particular format you are evaluating; some criteria will not apply for certain formats.

Written Work

- Matches the assignment in format (essay, journal entry, newspaper report, etc.)
- Begins with a clear statement of the topic and purpose
- Provides information that is essential to the reader's understanding
- Includes supporting details that are precise, related to the topic, and effective
- Follows a logical pattern of organization
- Uses transitions between ideas
- When appropriate, uses diagrams or other visuals
- Uses correct spelling, capitalization, and punctuation
- Uses correct grammar and usage
- Varies sentence structures
- Writes neatly and legibly

Posters and Displays

- Matches the assignment in format (brochure, poster, storyboard, etc.)
- Presents well-researched topic and quality information
- Communicates an obvious, overall message in poster
- Uses large titles on poster, with obvious message or purpose
- Conveys important information by using images that are big and clear
- Gives more important ideas and items more space and uses larger images or text
- Uses colors for a purpose, such as to link words and images
- Uses visual cues, such as arrows, letters, or numbers, to make sequence of presentation easy to follow
- Uses artistic elements that are appropriate and add to the overall presentation
- Uses neat text
- Follows rules for correct spelling, capitalization, and punctuation of captions and labels

Oral Presentations

- Matches the assignment in format (speech, news report, etc.)
- Delivers presentation with enthusiasm for topic
- Pronounces words clearly and can easily be heard
- Presents information in a logical, interesting sequence that the audience can follow
- Uses visual aids that are relative to content, very neat, and artistic
- Often makes eye contact with audience
- Listens carefully to questions from the audience and responds accurately
- Stands straight, facing the audience
- Uses movements appropriate to the presentation; does not fidget
- Covers the topic well in the time allowed
- Gives enough information to clarify the topic, but does not include irrelevant details

Multimedia Presentations

- Researches topic well and presents essential information
- Shows evidence of an original and inventive approach to product
- Conveys an obvious overall message in presentation
- Contains all the required media elements, such as text, graphics, sounds, videos, and animations
- Uses fonts and formatting appropriately to emphasize words; uses color appropriately to enhance the fonts
- Uses logical sequence of presentation and/or easy and understandable navigation
- Uses artistic elements that are appropriate and add to the overall presentation
- Effectively combines multimedia elements with words and ideas
- Follows rules for correct spelling, capitalization, and punctuation of written elements

Next Generation Science Standards

Standards Codes in HMH Science Dimensions *Assessment*

The following tables provide the coding system used in *HMH Science Dimensions* that allow you to track student progress on all three dimensions of the NGSS.

The original NGSS documents provide codes for the Performance Expectations and for the headings for the Disciplinary Core Ideas. These codes are reflected in the following tables of codes.

In addition, we have developed an intuitive coding system for the bulleted standards statements of the Disciplinary Core Ideas (DCI), the Science and Engineering Practices (SEP), and the Crosscutting Concepts (CCC).

These *HMH NGSS Three Dimensions* standards codes are available to download to your learning management system from Academic Benchmarks. The use of the *HMH NGSS Three Dimensions* standards codes will allow you to track student progress toward mastery of all three dimensions of the Next Generation Science Standards.

An important feature of this set of NGSS standards codes is that each SEP and CCC statement is represented by a single code. Across the 3–5 grade band, the same SEP and CCC standards appear repeatedly and are reinforced through the course of student learning. By using the *HMH NGSS Three Dimensions* codes, you can track and report student progress along these dimensions, as well as on Disciplinary Core Ideas, in addition to tracking progress toward the Performance Expectations.

Grade 3 Performance Expectations

PE Title	PE codes	PE Text
Motion and Stability: Forces and Interactions	3-PS2-1	Plan and conduct an investigation to provide evidence of the effects of balanced and unbalanced forces on the motion of an object.
Motion and Stability: Forces and Interactions	3-PS2-2	Make observations and/or measurements of an object's motion to provide evidence that a pattern can be used to predict future motion.
Motion and Stability: Forces and Interactions	3-PS2-3	Ask questions to determine cause and effect relationships of electric or magnetic interactions between two objects not in contact with each other.
Motion and Stability: Forces and Interactions	3-PS2-4	Define a simple design problem that can be solved by applying scientific ideas about magnets.
From Molecules to Organisms: Structures and Processes	3-LS1-1	Develop models to describe that organisms have unique and diverse life cycles but all have in common birth, growth, reproduction, and death.
Ecosystems: Interactions, Energy, and Dynamics	3-LS2-1	Construct an argument that some animals form groups that help members survive.
Heredity: Inheritance and Variation of Traits	3-LS3-1	Analyze and interpret data to provide evidence that plants and animals have traits inherited from parents and that variation of these traits exists in a group of similar organisms.
Heredity: Inheritance and Variation of Traits	3-LS3-2	Use evidence to support the explanation that traits can be influenced by the environment.
Biological Evolution: Unity and Diversity	3-LS4-1	Analyze and interpret data from fossils to provide evidence of the organisms and the environments in which they lived long ago.
Biological Evolution: Unity and Diversity	3-LS4-2	Use evidence to construct an explanation for how the variations in characteristics among individuals of the same species may provide advantages in surviving, finding mates, and reproducing.
Biological Evolution: Unity and Diversity	3-LS4-3	Construct an argument with evidence that in a particular habitat some organisms can survive well, some survive less well, and some cannot survive at all.
Biological Evolution: Unity and Diversity	3-LS4-4	Make a claim about the merit of a solution to a problem caused when the environment changes and the types of plants and animals that live there may change.

© Houghton Mifflin Harcourt Publishing Company

Grade 3 Performance Expectations, cont.

PE Title	PE codes	PE Text
Earth's Systems	3-ESS2-1	Represent data in tables and graphical displays to describe typical weather conditions expected during a particular season.
Earth's Systems	3-ESS2-2	Obtain and combine information to describe climates in different regions of the world.
Earth and Human Activity	3-ESS3-1	Make a claim about the merit of a design solution that reduces the impacts of a weather-related hazard.*
Engineering Design	3-5-ETS1-1	Define a simple design problem reflecting a need or a want that includes specified criteria for success and constraints on materials, time, or cost.
Engineering Design	3-5-ETS1-2	Generate and compare multiple possible solutions to a problem based on how well each is likely to meet the criteria and constraints of the problem.
Engineering Design	3-5-ETS1-3	Plan and carry out fair tests in which variables are controlled and failure points are considered to identify aspects of a model or prototype that can be improved.

* The Performance Expectations marked with an asterisk integrate traditional science content with engineering.

Grade 3 Disciplinary Core Ideas

DCI Title	DCI Code	DCI Text
Forces and Motion	**DCI.3-PS2.A.1**	Each force acts on one particular object and has both strength and a direction. An object at rest typically has multiple forces acting on it, but they add to give zero net force on the object. Forces that do not sum to zero can cause changes in the object's speed or direction of motion. (Boundary: Qualitative and conceptual, but not quantitative addition of forces are used at this level.) (3-PS2-1)
Forces and Motion	**DCI.3-PS2.A.2**	The patterns of an object's motion in various situations can be observed and measured; when that past motion exhibits a regular pattern, future motion can be predicted from it. (Boundary: Technical terms, such as *magnitude*, *velocity*, *momentum*, and *vector quantity*, are not introduced at this level, but the concept that some quantities need both size and direction to be described is developed.) (3-PS2-2)
Types of Interactions	**DCI.3-PS2.B.1**	Objects in contact exert forces on each other. (3-PS2-1)
Types of Interactions	**DCI.3-PS2.B.2**	Electric, and magnetic forces between a pair of objects do not require that the objects be in contact. The sizes of the forces in each situation depend on the properties of the objects and their distances apart and, for forces between two magnets, on their orientation relative to each other. (3-PS2-3),(3-PS2-4)
Growth and Development of Organisms	**DCI.3-LS1.B.1**	Reproduction is essential to the continued existence of every kind of organism. Plants and animals have unique and diverse life cycles. (3-LS1-1)
Ecosystem Dynamics, Functioning, and Resilience	**DCI.3-LS2.C.1**	When the environment changes in ways that affect a place's physical characteristics, temperature, or availability of resources, some organisms survive and reproduce, others move to new locations, yet others move into the transformed environment, and some die. (secondary to 3-LS4-4)
Social Interactions and Group Behavior	**DCI.3-LS2.D.1**	Being part of a group helps animals obtain food, defend themselves, and cope with changes. Groups may serve different functions and vary dramatically in size (Note: Moved from K–2). (3-LS2-1)
Inheritance of Traits	**DCI.3-LS3.A.1**	Many characteristics of organisms are inherited from their parents. (3-LS3-1)
Inheritance of Traits	**DCI.3-LS3.A.2**	Other characteristics result from individuals' interactions with the environment, which can range from diet to learning. Many characteristics involve both inheritance and environment. (3-LS3-2)

© Houghton Mifflin Harcourt Publishing Company

Grade 3 Disciplinary Core Ideas cont.

DCI Title	DCI Code	DCI Text
Variation of Traits	**DCI.3-LS3.B.1**	Different organisms vary in how they look and function because they have different inherited information. (3-LS3-1)
Variation of Traits	**DCI.3-LS3.B.2**	The environment also affects the traits that an organism develops. (3-LS3-2)
Evidence of Common Ancestry and Diversity	**DCI.3-LS4.A.1**	Some kinds of plants and animals that once lived on Earth are no longer found anywhere. (Note: moved from K-2) (3-LS4-1)
Evidence of Common Ancestry and Diversity	**DCI.3-LS4.A.2**	Fossils provide evidence about the types of organisms that lived long ago and also about the nature of their environments. (3-LS4-1)
Natural Selection	**DCI.3-LS4.B.1**	Sometimes the differences in characteristics between individuals of the same species provide advantages in surviving, finding mates, and reproducing. (3-LS4-2)
Adaptation	**DCI.3-LS4.C.1**	For any particular environment, some kinds of organisms survive well, some survive less well, and some cannot survive at all. (3-LS4-3)
Biodiversity and Humans	**DCI.3-LS4.D.1**	Populations live in a variety of habitats, and change in those habitats affects the organisms living there. (3-LS4-4)
Weather and Climate	**DCI.3-ESS2.D.1**	Scientists record patterns of the weather across different times and areas so that they can make predictions about what kind of weather might happen next. (3-ESS2-1)

© Houghton Mifflin Harcourt Publishing Company

Grade 3–5 Science and Engineering Practices

SEP Heading	SEP Code	SEP Text
Asking Questions and Defining Problems	**SEP.3-5.A.1**	Ask questions that can be investigated and predict reasonable outcomes based on patterns such as cause and effect relationships.
Asking Questions and Defining Problems	**SEP.3-5.A.2**	Define a simple design problem that can be solved through the development of an object, tool, process, or system and includes several criteria for success and constraints on materials, time, or cost.
Developing and Using Models	**SEP.3-5.B.1**	Develop a model using an analogy, example, or abstract representation to describe a scientific principle or design solution.
Developing and Using Models	**SEP.3-5.B.2**	Develop and/or use models to describe and/or predict phenomena.
Developing and Using Models	**SEP.3-5.B.3**	Use a model to test cause and effect relationships or interactions concerning the functioning of a natural or designed system.
Planning and Carrying Out Investigations	**SEP.3-5.C.1**	Plan and conduct an investigation collaboratively to produce data to serve as the basis for evidence, using fair tests in which variables are controlled and the number of trials considered.
Planning and Carrying Out Investigations	**SEP.3-5.C.2**	Make observations and/or measurements to produce data to serve as the basis for evidence for an explanation of a phenomenon or test a design solution.
Analyzing and Interpreting Data	**SEP.3-5.D.1**	Represent data in tables and/or various graphical displays (bar graphs, pictographs and/or pie charts) to reveal patterns that indicate relationships.
Analyzing and Interpreting Data	**SEP.3-5.D.2**	Analyze and interpret data to make sense of phenomena, using logical reasoning, mathematics, and/or computation.
Using Mathematics and Computational Thinking	**SEP.3-5.E.1**	Describe, measure, estimate, and/or graph quantities (e.g., area, volume, weight, time) to address scientific and engineering questions and problems.

© Houghton Mifflin Harcourt Publishing Company

Grade 3–5 Science and Engineering Practices, cont.

SEP Heading	SEP Code	SEP Text
Constructing Explanations and Designing Solutions	**SEP.3-5.F.1**	Use evidence (e.g., measurements, observations, patterns) to construct or support an explanation or design a solution to a problem.
Constructing Explanations and Designing Solutions	**SEP.3-5.F.2**	Identify the evidence that supports particular points in an explanation.
Constructing Explanations and Designing Solutions	**SEP.3-5.F.3**	Apply scientific ideas to solve design problems.
Constructing Explanations and Designing Solutions	**SEP.3-5.F.4**	Generate and compare multiple solutions to a problem based on how well they meet the criteria and constraints of the design solution.
Engaging in Argument from Evidence	**SEP.3-5.G.1**	Construct and/or support an argument with evidence, data, and/or a model.
Engaging in Argument from Evidence	**SEP.3-5.G.2**	Make a claim about the merit of a solution to a problem by citing relevant evidence about how it meets the criteria and constraints of the problem.
Obtaining, Evaluating, and Communicating Information	**SEP.3-5.H.1**	Obtain and combine information from books and/or other reliable media to explain phenomena or solutions to a design problem.
Scientific Investigations Use a Variety of Methods	**SEP.NOS.3-5.A.1**	Science investigations use a variety of methods, tools, and techniques.
Scientific Knowledge is Based on Empirical Evidence	**SEP.NOS.3-5.B.1**	Science findings are based on recognizing patterns.
Science Models, Laws, Mechanisms, and Theories Explain Natural Phenomena	**SEP.NOS.3-5.D.1**	Science explanations describe the mechanisms for natural events.

© Houghton Mifflin Harcourt Publishing Company

Grade 3–5 Crosscutting Concepts

CCC heading	CCC Code	CCC Text
Patterns	CCC.3-5.A.1	Similarities and differences in patterns can be used to sort, classify, communicate, and analyze simple rates of change for natural phenomena and designed products.
Patterns	CCC.3-5.A.2	Patterns of change can be used to make predictions.
Patterns	CCC.3-5.A.3	Patterns can be used as evidence to support an explanation.
Cause and Effect	CCC.3-5.B.1	Cause and effect relationships are routinely identified, tested, and used to explain change.
Scale, Proportion, and Quantity	CCC.3-5.C.1	Natural objects and/or observable phenomena exist from the very small to the immensely large or from very short to very long time periods.
Scale, Proportion, and Quantity	CCC.3-5.C.2	Standard units are used to measure and describe physical quantities such as weight, time, temperature, and volume.
Systems and System Models	CCC.3-5.D.1	A system can be described in terms of its components and their interactions.
Energy and Matter	CCC.3-5.E.1	Matter flows and cycles can be tracked in terms of the weight of the substances before and after a process occurs. The total weight of the substances does not change. This is what is meant by conservation of matter. Matter is transported into, out of, and within systems.
Energy and Matter	CCC.3-5.E.2	Energy can be transferred in various ways and between objects.
Scientific Knowledge Assumes an Order and Consistency in Natural Systems	CCC.NOS.3-5.A.1	Science assumes consistent patterns in natural systems.
Science is a Human Endeavor	CCC.NOS.3-5.B.1	Science affects everyday life.
Science is a Human Endeavor	CCC.NOS.3-5.B.2	Most scientists and engineers work in teams.
Science Addresses Questions About the Natural and Material World.	CCC.NOS.3-5.C.1	Science findings are limited to questions that can be answered with empirical evidence.

© Houghton Mifflin Harcourt Publishing Company

Grade 3–5 Crosscutting Concepts, cont.

CCC heading	CCC Code	CCC Text
Interdependence of Science, Engineering, and Technology	**CCC.STSE.3-5.A.2**	Knowledge of relevant scientific concepts and research findings is important in engineering.
Interdependence of Science, Engineering, and Technology	**CCC.STSE.3-5.A.1**	Scientific discoveries about the natural world can often lead to new and improved technologies, which are developed through the engineering design process. (3-PS2-4)
Influence of Engineering, Technology, and Science on Society and the Natural World	**CCC.STSE.3-5.B.2**	People's needs and wants change over time, as do their demands for new and improved technologies.
Influence of Engineering, Technology, and Science on Society and the Natural World	**CCC.STSE.3-5.B.1**	Engineers improve existing technologies or develop new ones to increase their benefits, decrease known risks, and meet societal demands.

© Houghton Mifflin Harcourt Publishing Company

Beginning-of-Year Test

Read each question. Follow the instructions to answer the questions

1. Jaime observes the properties of this plastic spoon. She adds heat to it.

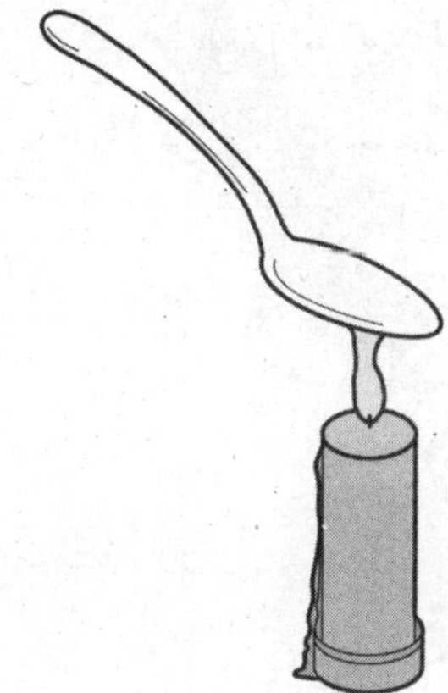

How does the spoon change?

Circle the letter of the correct answer.

A. It melts.

B. It freezes.

C. It becomes stronger.

2. The jump ropes in gym class are tied up.

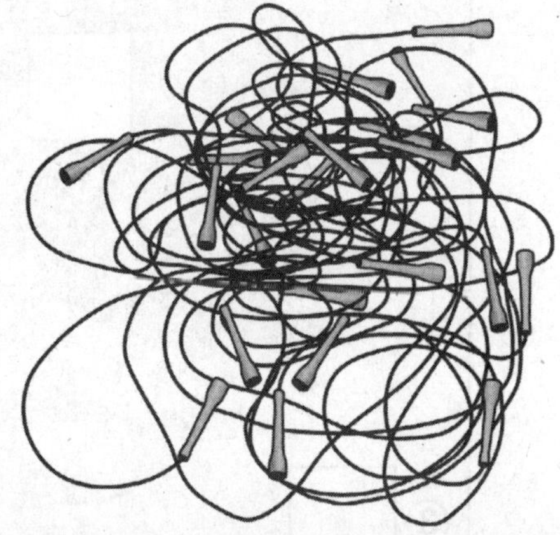

The class will help design a tool to solve this problem. Which questions will help students with their design?

Circle the letters of the 2 correct answers.

A. How many jump ropes are there?

B. How much do the jump ropes cost?

C. Who likes to jump rope?

D. Where are the jump ropes kept?

3. The map shows different kinds of land and water.

Write one letter in each box to match the label with the different kinds of land or water.

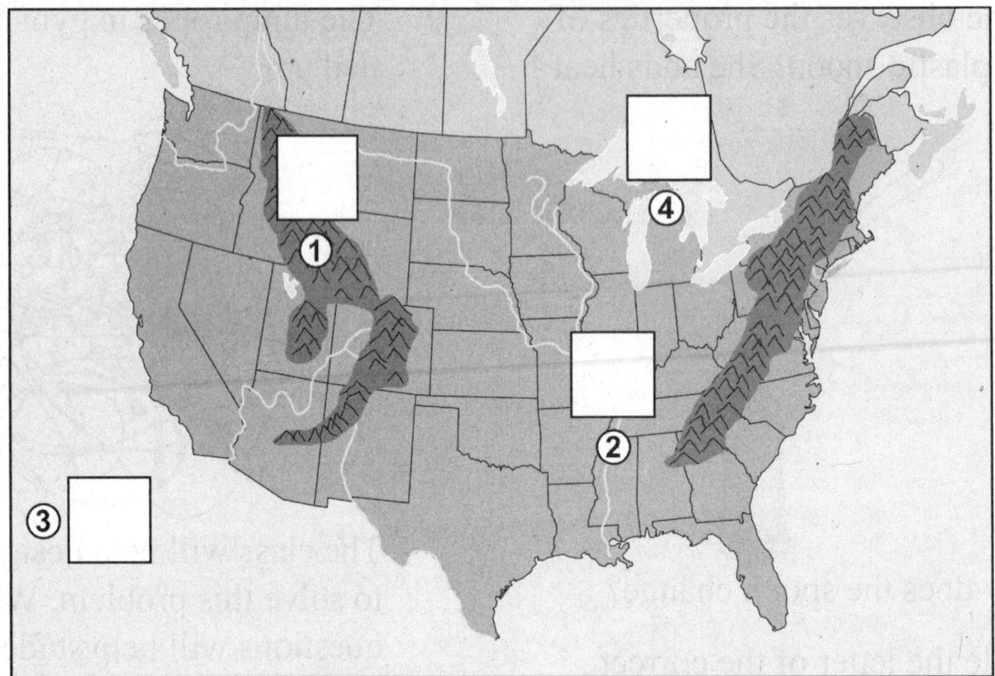

A. plain	**D.** lake
B. pond	**E.** ocean
C. mountain	**F.** river

4. How does a glacier make changes to land?

A. erosion

B. earthquake

C. weathering

5. Liza wants to carry an egg in a basket. She wants to make a cushion for the egg. The cushion should be soft to keep the egg from breaking.

Circle the letters of the best 2 materials.

rocks	leaves	feathers
A.	**B.**	**C.**

6. Micah wants to make a model of a seed that moves by getting stuck to an animal's fur. Which seed should he look at to make his model?

Circle the letter of the correct answer.

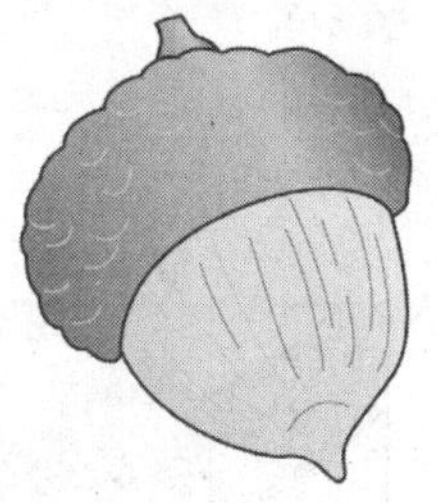 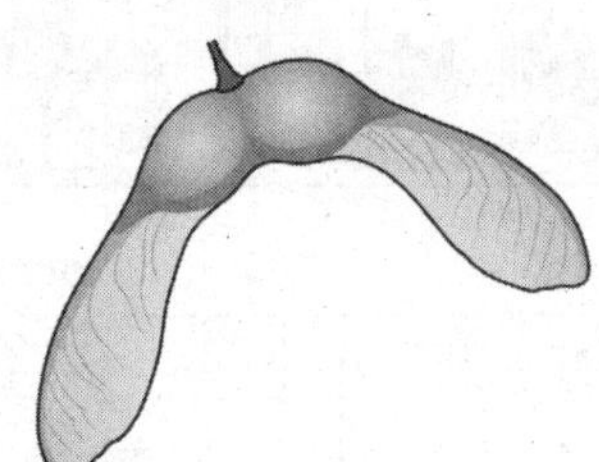 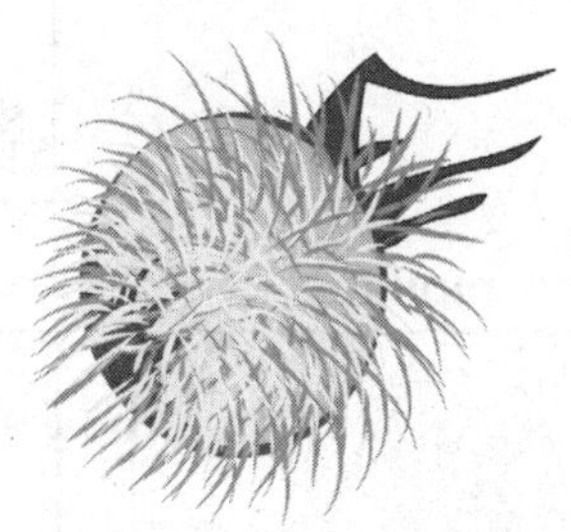

A.	**B.**	**C.**

7. Lara went on a trip. She made a list of the three kinds of water she saw.

Write the letter of the words that tell about the water in the correct box.

ocean		**A.** a flowing body of water
pond		**B.** a large body of salt water
river		**C.** a small body of water with land on all sides

8. Ramon read a book to learn about rainforest habitats. He made a poster to show where different plants and animals live.

Which live in the canopy? Which live in the understory?

Write "C" in the boxes below things that live in the canopy.

Write "U" in the boxes below things that live in the understory.

monkey

uses legs and claws to climb and jump

eagle

uses wings to fly above trees and look for animals to eat

orchid

can grow on a tree to reach the sunlight

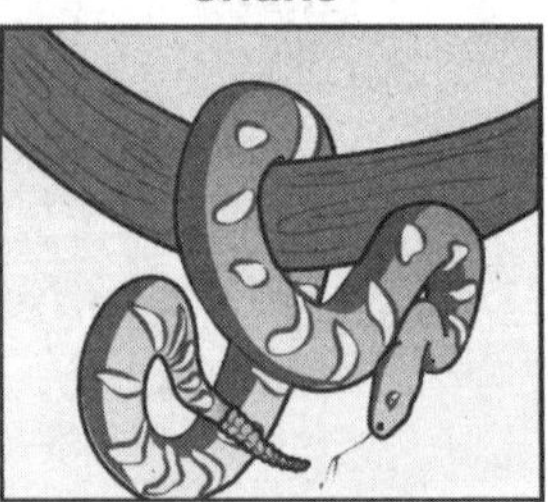

snake

hides in branches and leaves

© Houghton Mifflin Harcourt Publishing Company

9. Char made a water bottle holder. It holds 2 bottles, but they are hard to reach. She will try a new design. Which step in the design process is this?

Draw a circle around the correct step.

Communicate	Test and improve	Plan and build

10. Which bodies of water are the largest on Earth?

Circle the letter of the correct answer.

A. oceans

B. ponds

C. rivers

11. Matter can change in many ways by adding or taking away heat. Some changes to matter are reversible.

Write an X in the correct box in the table for each sentence.

Sentence	Heat was added.	It is reversible.
A. A log becomes ash.		
B. A raw egg becomes a hard-boiled egg.		
C. Liquid cream becomes ice cream.		

12. Anne used the pieces in the first picture to build the larger objects in the second picture.

The houses were made from _____________________ .

Write the correct letter in the blank to complete the sentence.

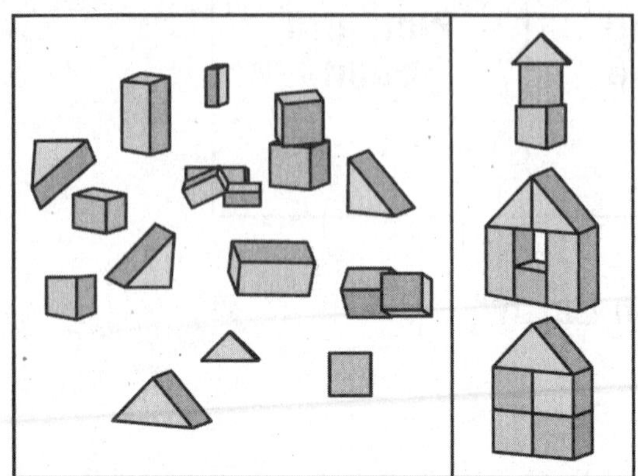

A. one big block

B. many small pieces

C. three large pieces

13. The pictures show land of different shapes that was changed by wind and water. Which picture shows land changed mostly by wind?

Draw a circle around the correct picture.

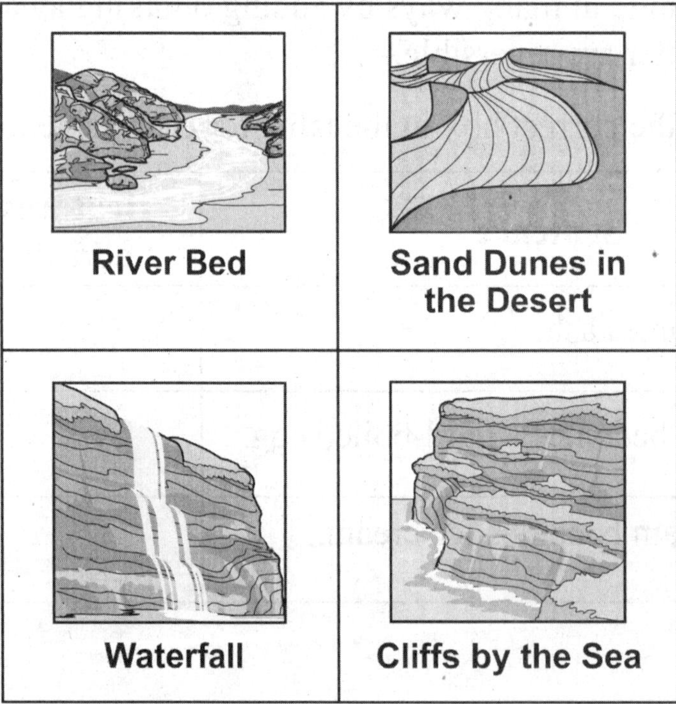

14. Meg classified these objects based on the properties they share.

Write the letter in the box to show which property the materials share.

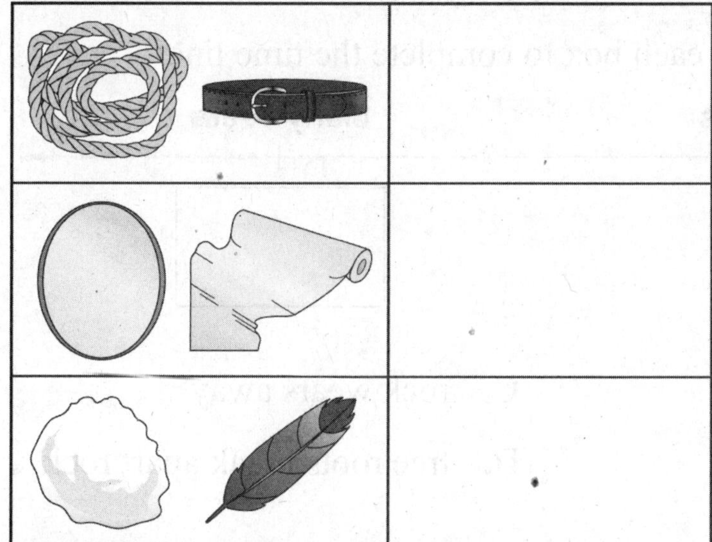

A. soft

B. bendable

C. smooth

15. Antoine decides to design a tool to help his mom in the yard. Which of these things should he do next?

Circle the letter of the correct answer.

A. Dig holes for seeds.

B. Draw pictures of the trees.

C. Ask what jobs need to be done.

16. Abe wants to show that plants need water and air. He will observe plants to gather evidence. Some evidence can be measured, but some cannot.

Circle the letters of the things he should measure.

A. height of plant

C. number of hours in sunlight

B. how dark the soil is

D. amount of water given to plant

17. Some changes to Earth happen quickly and some changes happen slowly. Which changes happen quickly and take only minutes or days? Which changes happen slowly and take many years?

Write the correct letters in each box to complete the time line.

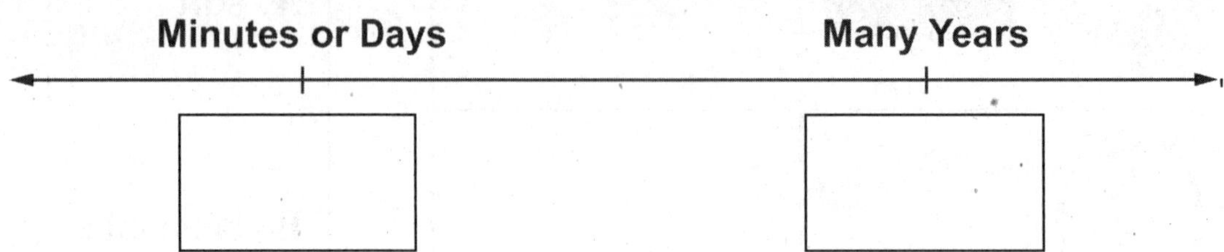

A. flood

B. landslide

C. rock wears away

D. tree roots break apart rock

18. The pictures show a frozen ice treat in a glass bowl.

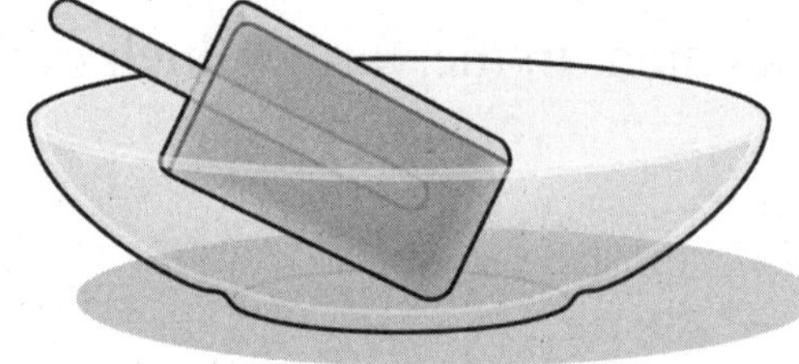

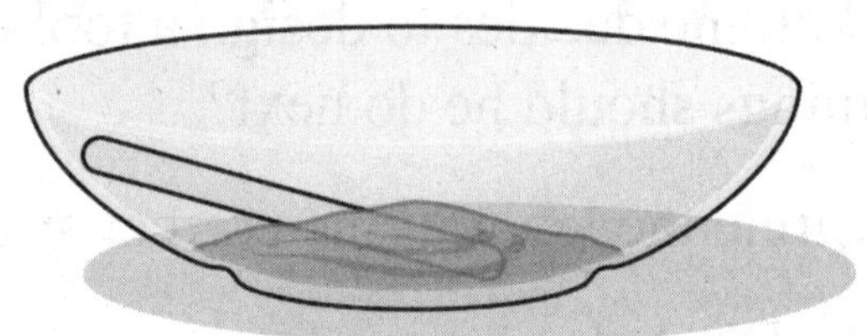

What caused the frozen ice treat to change?

Circle the letter of the correct answer.

A. The stick in the treat broke it apart.

B. The heat in the room melted the treat.

C. The treat did not cook for long enough.

19. Bernie lost a toy under the couch. He will make a tool. The tool needs to be long. It needs to grab his toy. Which part should he add to his tool?

Write the letter of the part Bernie should use in the box.

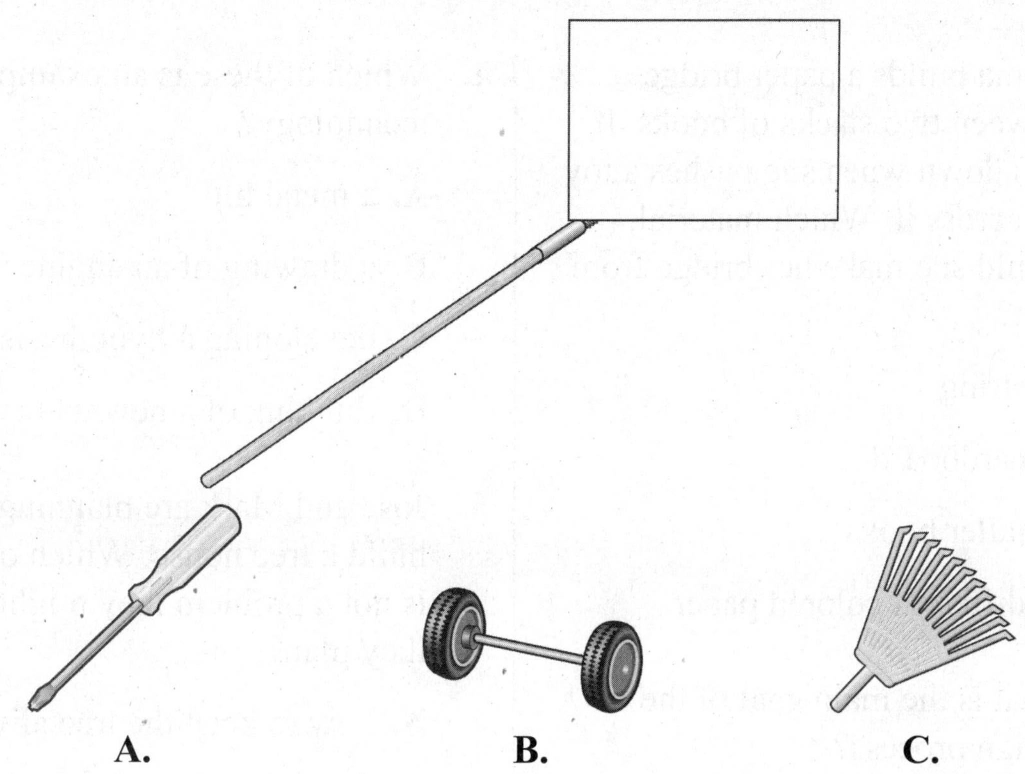

A.   B.   C.

20. Look at the maps.

United States   **Florida**   **My Neighborhood**

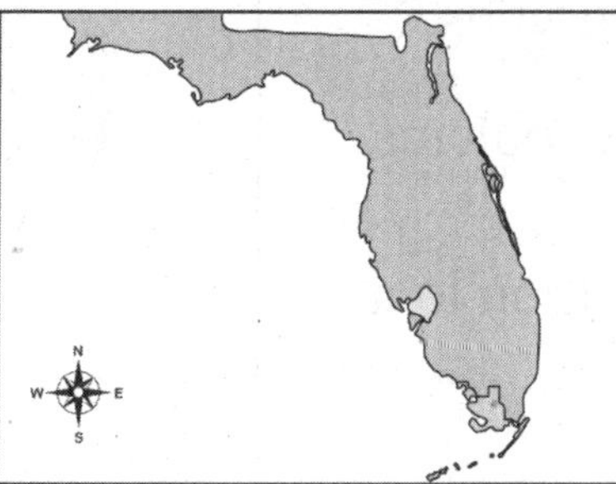

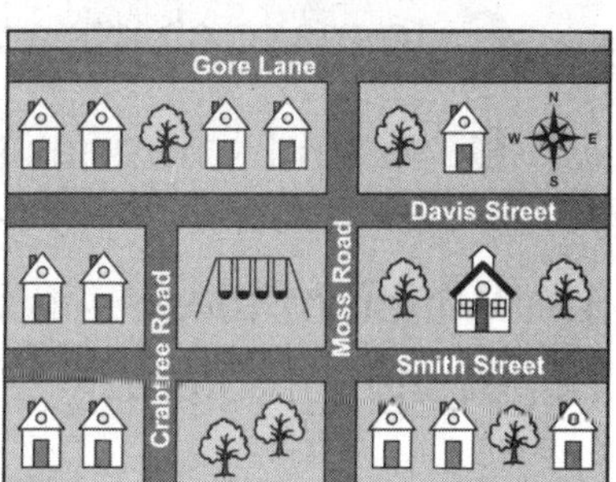

What is missing from each map?

Circle the letter of the correct answer.

A. map key

B. map title

C. compass rose

Pretest: Engineering

Read each question. Circle the letter of the correct answer.

1. Naima builds a paper bridge between two stacks of books. It falls down when she pushes a toy car across it. Which material should she make her bridge from next?

   A. string

   B. cardboard

   C. taller books

   D. different colored paper

2. What is the main goal of the design process?

   A. to write reports

   B. to make prototypes

   C. to make charts and graphs

   D. to find solutions to problems

3. Which of these is a solution to a design problem?

   A. a tornado

   B. a bird's nest

   C. a flooded town

   D. a ringing telephone

4. Which of these is an example of technology?

   A. a metal hip

   B. a drawing of an engine

   C. developing a hypothesis

   D. thinking of a new theory

5. Jose and Mark are planning to build a tree house. Which of these is not a problem they might find as they plan?

   A. how to keep the tree alive

   B. how large to make the tree house

   C. where to put the building in the tree

   D. how to get tools up to the construction site

6. Engineers designed plans to make freezers for food. What main problem did freezing food solve?

    A. how to make ice cubes

    B. how to make ice cream

    C. how to keep food from spoiling

    D. how to make it easier to pack food into trucks

7. Rodrigo made a bird feeder. He placed the feeder in the yard and watched the birds. He saw that the birds could not get through the hole in the feeder. What should Rodrigo do next?

    A. redesign

    B. communicate

    C. plan and build

    D. find a problem

8. A company wants to build a new type of spaceship for transporting astronauts to the moon. Which action should the company take first?

    A. build a model

    B. identify needs

    C. draw the design

    D. test the prototype

9. Computer designs have gotten better over the years. Which example is not a computer improvement?

    A. They are faster.

    B. They are lighter.

    C. They can store more information.

    D. They can be used in only one place at a time.

10. Eva wants to build a doghouse. She lists some steps she should take. Eva forgot about step 3.

    1. Find a problem
    2. Plan and build
    3. ?
    4. Redesign
    5. Communicate

    Which of these should Eva do for step 3?

    A. Keep going

    B. Choose an idea

    C. Test and improve

    D. Think about ideas

© Houghton Mifflin Harcourt Publishing Company

Quiz: Engineer It • How Do We Define a Problem?

Read each question. Circle the letter of the correct answer.

1. Jaya decides to build a bookcase for her bedroom. She draws a plan in which each shelf will be 1 inch tall. Why will she need to improve her design?

   A. Most books are taller than 1 inch.

   B. Most bookcases have at least 2 shelves.

   C. Her design does not have exact measurements.

   D. She will have too many shelves in the bookcase.

2. Sally wants to make a new car engine. The engine will get hotter than 240 degrees Celsius, °C. Sally studies materials that she could use. Her data are in the table.

   Melting Points of Materials

Materials	Melting point (°C)
potassium	64
plastic	120
tin	232
aluminum	660

   Which material should Sally use?

   A. potassium

   B. plastic

   C. tin

   D. aluminum

3. Ed builds a paper bridge. He tests the bridge by rolling toy cars over it. Ed decides to add more paper to the road part of the bridge. Why will adding more layers of paper help the bridge design?

A. makes the bridge heavier

B. makes the bridge stronger

C. makes the bridge hold fewer toy cars

D. makes the bridge attach better at the sides

4. Erik is building a wooden bookcase. He wants to place long plastic tubes on the shelves. Which of these should Erik focus on?

A. wood weight

B. wood type and color

C. shelf length and width

D. shelf strength and durability

5. The picture shows a bridge.

Which problem does building this bridge solve?

A. Roads must be built.

B. People need to drive their cars across water.

C. Drivers of two cars need to drive on the same road.

D. Drivers want their cars to travel farther using the same amount of gas.

Read each statement. Write your answer on the lines.

6. Kenji has to walk around a pond to get to school. The picture shows him thinking like a scientist.

What is the problem Kenji is trying to solve?

____

____

What is one material that Kenji might use to build his solution?

____

____

7. The city council wants to redesign a part of the city. They want many roads for people to drive on. They want the school to have a large park. The picture below shows one design made by engineers.

Does the design meet the two goals the city council wants? Explain.

____

____

____

____

Quiz: Engineer It • How Can We Design a Solution?

Read each question. Circle the letter of the correct answer.

1. Gene built a paper airplane. It does not fly very well. He asked his classmates for ideas on how to improve his paper airplane. Which step in the design process is he using?

   A. redesign

   B. communicate

   C. build a model

   D. find a problem

2. Designers often work with other people. Why is working with others helpful in design?

   A. The partner can do all the work.

   B. All of the ideas belong to one person.

   C. There are more new ideas to think about.

   D. There are fewer new ideas to think about.

3. Eito is building a treehouse. When should Eito research how to build it?

   A. after he designs his plan

   B. after the treehouse fails

   C. after he builds the treehouse

   D. before he begins designing his plan

4. A new type of engine gets too hot after it runs for 10 minutes. What should the engineer who designed the engine do?

   A. research the problem

   B. take the engine apart

   C. evaluate the results of the new engine design

   D. communicate the results of the new engine design

© Houghton Mifflin Harcourt Publishing Company

5. Four groups used materials to build bridges. The table shows the materials and results.

Bridge Materials and Results

Group	Material used	How many cars bridge held
1	paper and tape	1
2	paper, straws, glue	4
3	paper, craft sticks, tape	2
4	paper, craft sticks, glue	3

Why did Group 1's design not work well?

A. The students did not plan a design in advance.

B. The students did not use anything to support the bridge.

C. The students did not communicate with the other groups.

D. The students did not use anything to connect the pieces of the bridge.

Read each statement. Write your answer on the lines.

6. Molly wants to build a paper bridge between two textbooks. Why should Molly use drinking straws in the bridge?

____

____

____

____

____

7. Engineers want to make a machine to wash clothes. They list the things they want the washer to do.

1. use less water
2. clean clothes well
3. cost less than $300

They research the problem and come up with a few designs. How should the engineers decide which designs to build?

____

____

____

____

© Houghton Mifflin Harcourt Publishing Company

Quiz: Engineer It • How Do We Test and Improve a Solution?

Read each question. Circle the letter of the correct answer.

1. Engineers design a plan and then test a prototype. Their data show that the prototype is not working. What will the engineers do next?

   A. start from the beginning

   B. communicate their results

   C. improve the design and test it again

   D. change the data so it looks like the prototype worked

2. Tai designed a box to keep an egg from breaking when dropped from a distance of 2 meters. He made drawings of his design. What should Tai do next?

   A. test the box

   B. build the box

   C. collect and compare the test results

   D. think about how to make the design better

3. An engineer designed and built a prototype. What should the engineer do next?

   A. Test the working prototype.

   B. Make drawings of the prototype.

   C. Collect and compare the test results.

   D. Think of ways to make the design better.

4. Meg has a problem with her soap dish. Water collects in it and slowly dissolves the soap. She designs a soap dish that water can drain from. Then she makes a prototype. When she tests her prototype soap dish, what is the most important result she will watch for?

   A. how large it is

   B. how attractive it is

   C. how quickly water drains from it

   D. how much it looks like the old one

© Houghton Mifflin Harcourt Publishing Company

5. Elena rolled a marble across a paper bridge.

The piece of paper fell off the books. How could Elena improve the paper bridge?

A. make the stacks of books taller

B. make the stacks of books shorter

C. use two marbles to cross the paper

D. tape the paper to each stack of books

Read each statement. Write your answer on the lines.

6. A scientist wants to keep coffee hotter longer. She compared a new material to a foam cup. She put boiling water in each cup and measured the temperature. Her data are in the table.

Does the data show that the new material is better than the foam? Explain.

Cup Results

Cup	Temperature (degrees Celsius)	
	Start	After 1 hour
New material	100	85
Old foam	100	85

____

____

____

____

____

7. Engineers build a prototype for a new car. They test the prototype. What should they do next?

____

____

____

____

____

Unit Test: Engineering

Read each question. Circle the letter of the correct answer.

1. A lamp is bolted to the floor. Lisa and Quinn work together to figure out how to plug the lamp into the outlet that is across the room. Their plans are listed.

   - Quinn's plan: Move the lamp across the room closer to the outlet and plug the lamp into the outlet.
   - Lisa's plan: Drag an extension cord across the room to plug into the outlet.

   Which plan solves the problem based on the criterion?

   A. Quinn's plan because the cord is longer

   B. Lisa's plan because the lamp is heavy

   C. Quinn's plan because the lamp is easily moved

   D. Lisa's plan because the lamp is bolted to the floor

2. Alex wants his door to stay open. He decides to make a doorstop. He does not want the object to scratch the wooden floor. Which material is best for Alex to use?

   A. large brick

   B. folded paper

   C. cotton balls taped together

   D. large rock inside of a sock

3. Ella needs to design a product that will keep the food from going down her drain when she is cleaning dishes in her sink. What is her criterion?

   A. The water must be cold.

   B. The dishes must be clean.

   C. The water must flow slowly.

   D. The food must not go down the drain.

4. Dori lives in an area that gets a lot of snow. She uses a shovel to clear her driveway. The angle of the shovel hurts her back. She plans to design a shovel that will not hurt her back. Which reason best explains why Dori wants to change the shovel?

   A. It will help her meet her needs.

   B. It will earn her fame as an inventor.

   C. It will meet the demands of society.

   D. It will earn her a lot of money when she sells it.

5. Gary wants to use the strongest rope to pull his wagon behind his bike. He tested the strength of two plastic ropes. His data are listed.

Rope	Picture	How many pounds pulled?
brand X		95
brand Y		60

Which rope should Gary use?

   A. brand X, because it is made of plastic

   B. brand Y, because it is thinner than brand X

   C. brand Y, because it is thicker than brand X

   D. brand X, because it pulled the most weight

Read each question. Follow the instructions to answer the questions.

6. Blake needs to partially shade his tomato plant from the late afternoon sun. The pictures show possible designs for a shade with the sun in its later afternoon position. Compare the solutions.

Write the letters of the 2 best solutions in the box.

Meets Criteria

A.
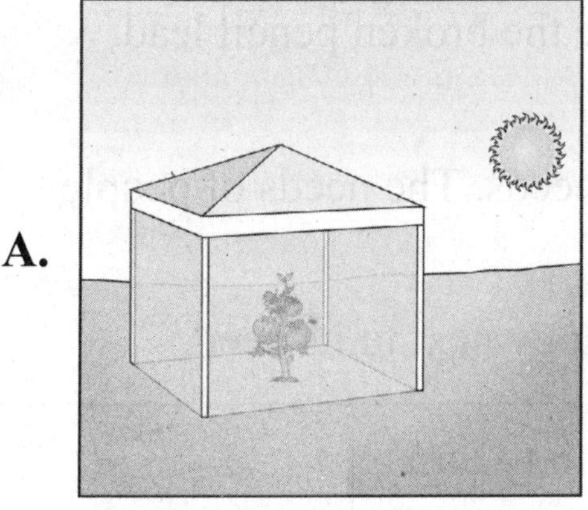

C.
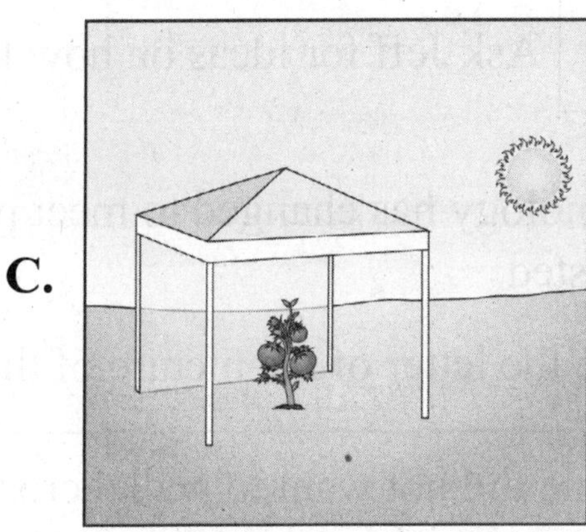

B.

D.
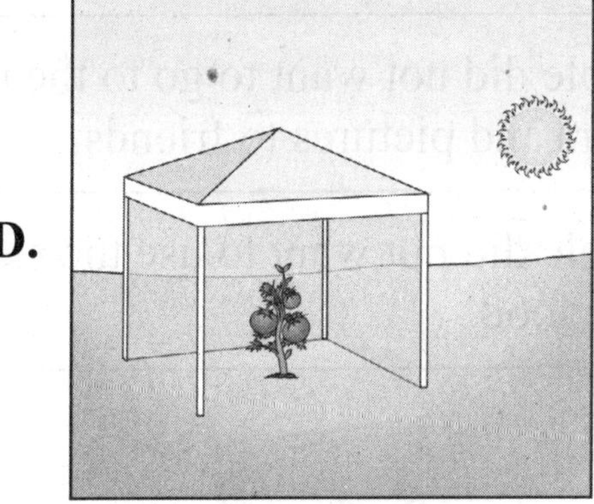

7. Sam is trying to fix the class pencil sharpener that is jammed with lead. He wrote out his plan.

Number the steps from 1 to 5 with 1 as the first step and 5 as the last step.

	Find where the sharpener is broken.
	Redesign and repeat if it doesn't work.
	Test the sharpener to see if it works again.
	Remove the broken pencil lead from the sharpener.
	Ask Jeff for ideas on how to remove the broken pencil lead.

8. Technology has changed to meet people's needs. The needs of people are listed.

Write the letter of the picture of the technology next to its need.

People did not want to walk across the room to turn on the television.	
People did not want to go to the post office to send letters and pictures to friends.	
People did not want to use the stove to heat all of their food.	

A. computer

B. microwave oven

C. remote control

© Houghton Mifflin Harcourt Publishing Company

9. Sara wants to move her wagon easily through sand. She designed two types of tires, type A and type B.

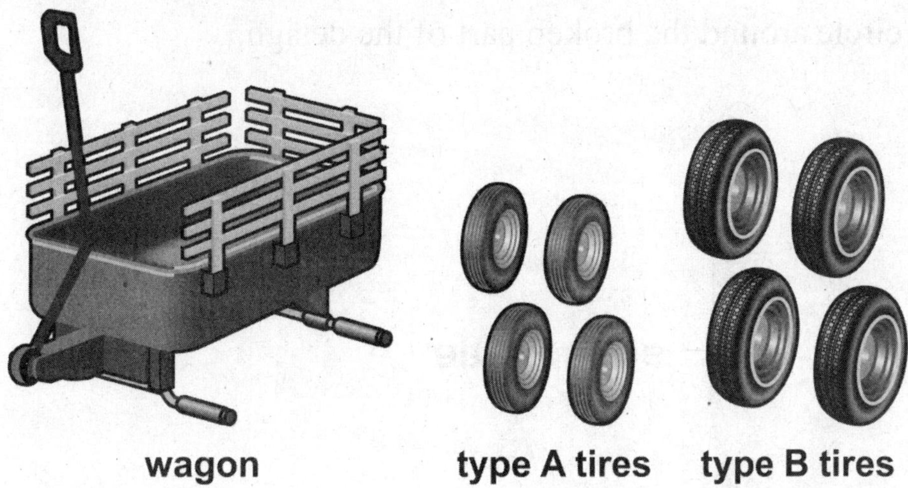

Sara wants to find out which tires work best in sand. What steps should she follow?

Write the steps in the correct order in the table. Some steps will be used more than once.

Step	Action
1	
2	
3	
4	
5	
6	

A. Observe how hard it is to pull the wagon.

B. Put type B tires on the wagon.

C. Put type A tires on the wagon.

D. Pull the wagon through sand.

10. Josh built a watering system for his plants. Water is not reaching plant 3. Where is the watering system broken?

Draw a circle around the broken part of the design.

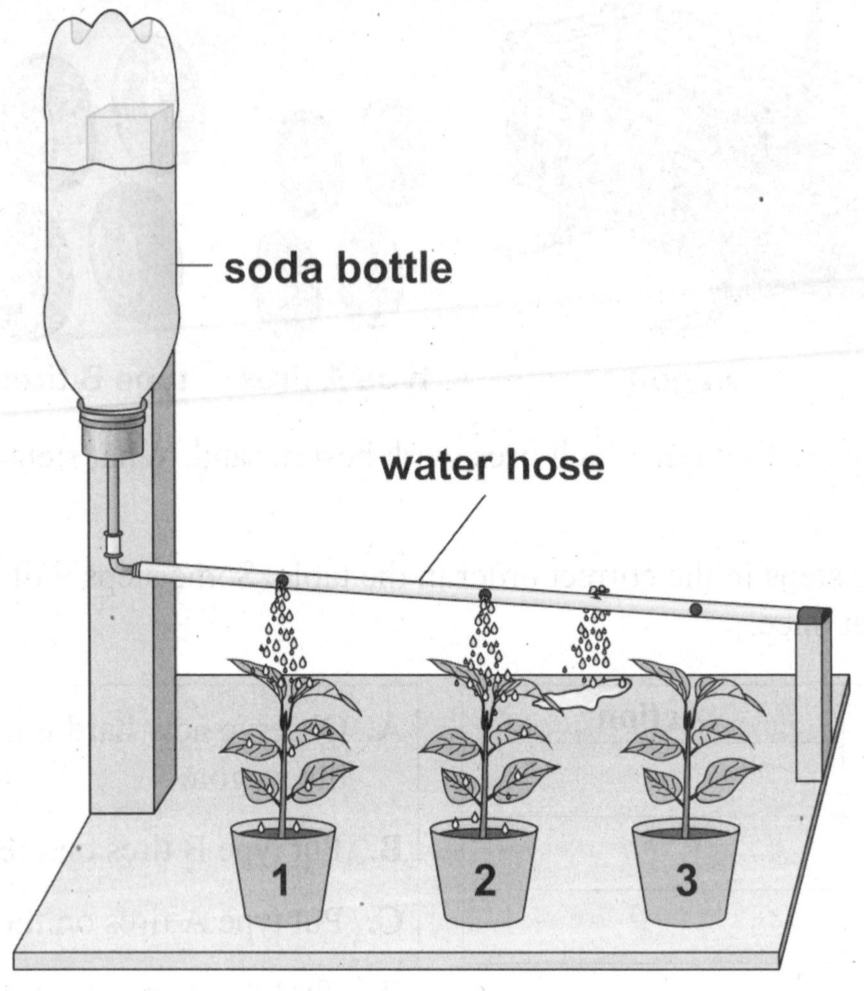

Read each statement. Write your answer on the lines.

11. People in town were having a hard time hearing the tornado siren in the middle of the night. A new siren was designed.

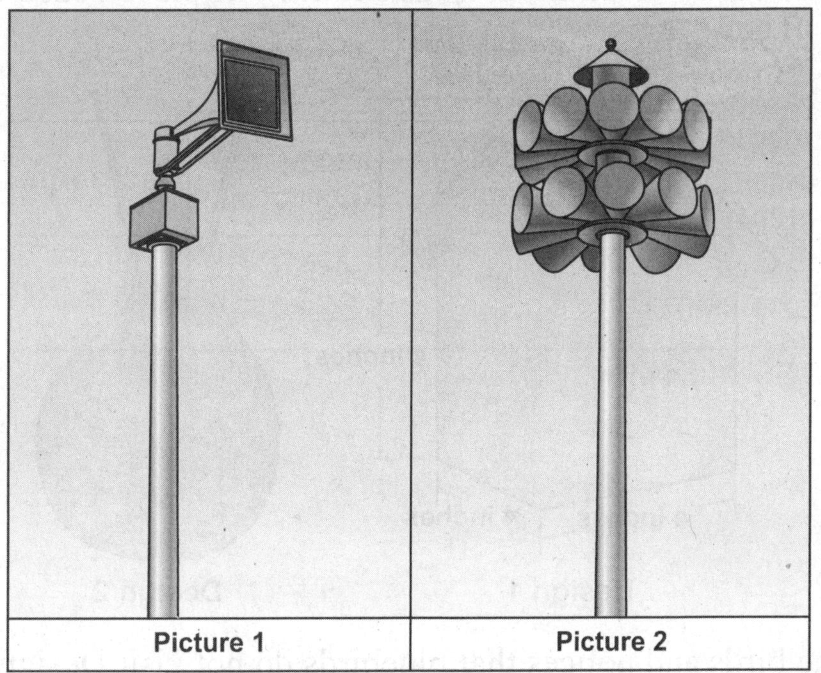

Picture 1 is the type of siren they had before. Picture 2 is the type of siren they have now.

Identify the criterion that was most important when designing the new siren.

____

____

Explain the improvements that were made to the new siren.

____

____

Describe the benefits of the new siren.

____

____

____

Directions: Read the passage, then answer the questions that follow.

Ali's Birdhouses

Ali designed and built two birdhouses, as shown. She placed each 6 feet off the ground.

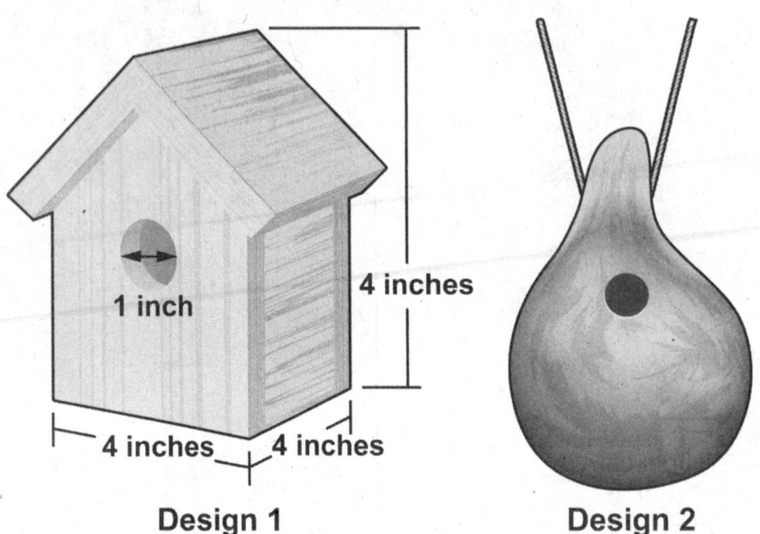

Ali watches the birds and notices that bluebirds do not visit Design 1. She studies the needs of bluebirds. She lists the requirements for their homes.

- houses 4 inches wide by 4 inches deep and 10 inches tall
- one opening that is 1.5 inches wide
- hung 4 to 6 feet off the ground

12. Ali wants to change Design 1 to make it easier to clean. She still wants to keep cats from getting to the birds. Which of these should Ali do to Design 1?

    Circle the letter of the correct answer.

    A. plug the hole in the front

    B. remove the floor of the birdhouse

    C. cut a large hole in the roof of the birdhouse

    D. put a hinged door on the side that latches shut

13. Design 2 is tied to a tree branch with string. The string keeps breaking and the birdhouse falls to the ground. The pictures show ways Ali might improve the design.

Draw a circle around all of the designs that will work for Ali.

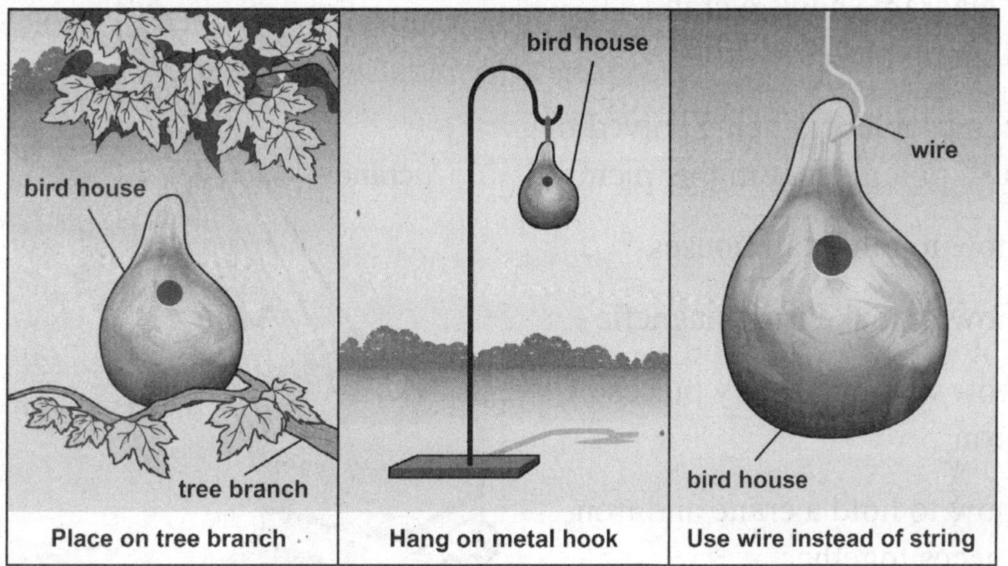

14. Which part of Design 1 meets the needs of the bluebirds?

Circle the letter of the correct answer.

A. the size of the opening

B. the height of the birdhouse

C. how many holes the birdhouse has

D. how far above the ground the birdhouse is hung

15. Describe how Design 1 can be changed to meet the bluebirds' needs.

Write your answer on the lines here.

____

____

____

____

Pretest: Forces

Read each question. Circle the letter of the correct answer.

1. The diagram shows a crane picking up pieces of iron.

   Which problem is being solved by the use of a magnet in this picture?

   A. how to build tall houses

   B. how to make iron magnetic

   C. how to move heavy pieces of iron

   D. how to hold a crane and iron pieces together

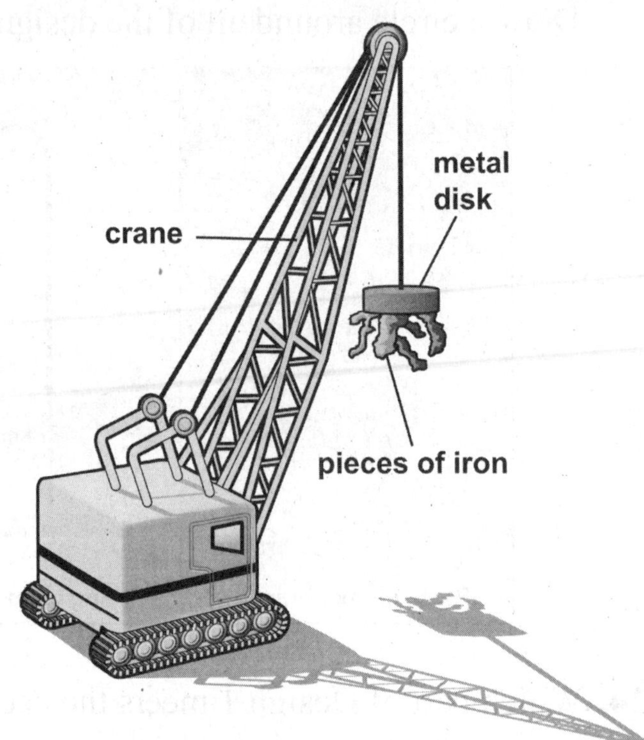

2. Which picture shows a push?

A. 

C. 

B. 

D. 

© Houghton Mifflin Harcourt Publishing Company

3. The pictures show objects that are charged and objects that are not charged. Which picture shows two objects with the same charge?

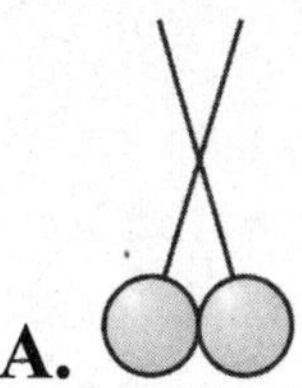

A.

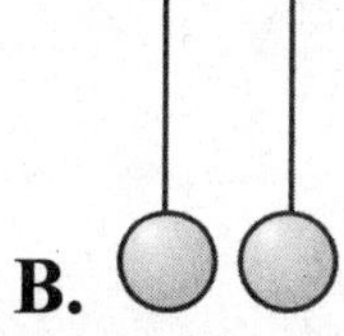

B.

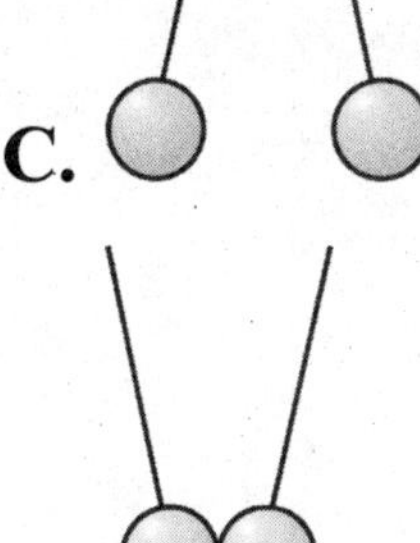

C.

D.

4. What is static electricity?

A. a flow of electrons

B. an electric discharge

C. a repelling between electrons

D. a buildup of electric charge on something

5. Jake hangs two balloons from a desk so that they are close together but not touching. Jake rubs one balloon with a wool cloth. He does nothing to the other balloon. What happens when he lets go of the balloons?

A. They push one another apart.

B. They touch one another and pop.

C. They touch one another and stick together.

D. They are close together but do not touch.

6. Which change in force would make a toy car slow down?

A. kicking it

B. giving it a push

C. pulling it with a string

D. rolling it from cement onto grass

7. Which of these is an example of balanced forces?

A. a book falling from a desk

B. a computer sitting on a table

C. a marble rolling down a ramp

D. a car slowing down at a stop sign

© Houghton Mifflin Harcourt Publishing Company

8. Aisha placed two balloons next to each other.

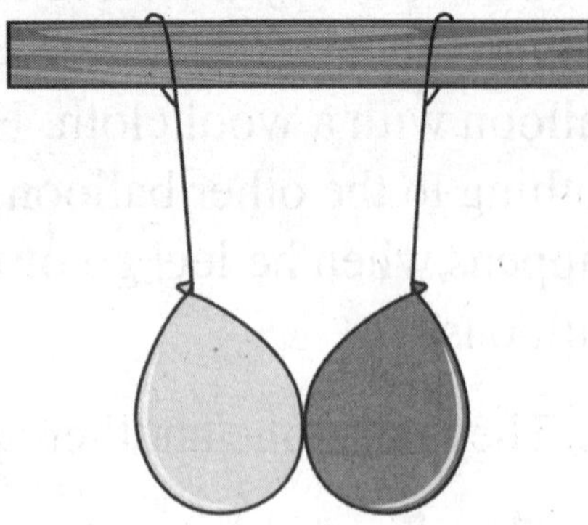

What are the charges on the balloons?

A. They are both positive.

B. They are both uncharged.

C. One is positive and one is negative.

D. One is negative and one is uncharged.

9. Which object does a magnet attract?

A. paper

B. steel nails

C. plastic bottle

D. rubber bands

10. Which object is most likely attracted to a magnet?

A.

B.

C.

D.

Quiz: What Are Forces?

Read each question. Circle the letter of the correct answer.

1. Camryn and her friend are playing outside. Which picture shows Camryn pulling an object?

   A.

   B.

   C.

   D.

2. Erin and Jordan rolled two rubber balls toward each other with the same strength push. The blue ball is larger and heavier than the red ball. What will happen when the red ball and the blue ball hit each other?

   A. both balls will break

   B. both balls will change direction

   C. the red ball will change direction

   D. the blue ball will change direction

3. This picture shows what happened when Jim pushed on a box.

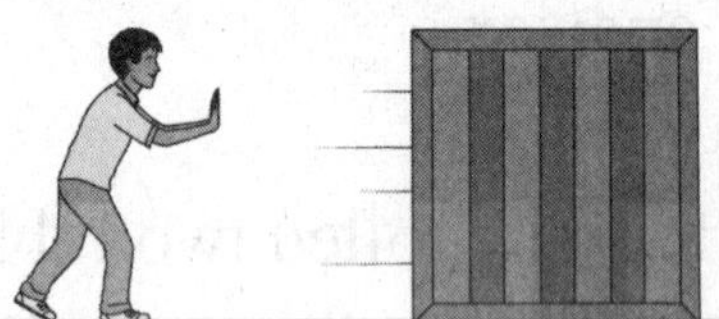

Which picture shows what would happen to the box if Jim pushed with more force?

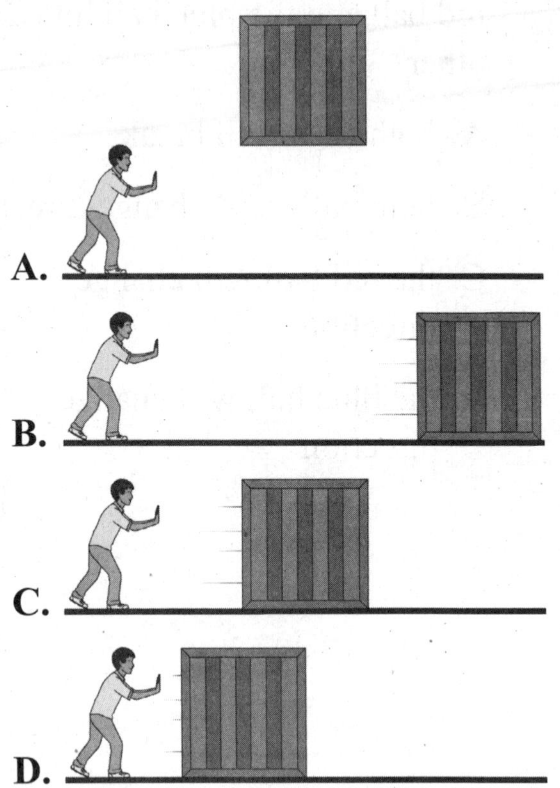

A.

B.

C.

D.

4. Cayden wanted to see what would happen when he kicked his soccer ball. Each time he kicked the ball, he kicked it harder than the last. Cayden measured the distance the ball traveled in meters and recorded his results in the table.

Speed of Ball When Kicked

Strength of kick	Speed of ball
soft	slow
medium	medium
hard	fast

What happened when Cayden kicked the ball harder?

A. Less force made the ball move faster.

B. Less weight made the ball move faster.

C. More weight made the ball move faster.

D. More force made the ball move faster.

5. Mike hits a moving tennis ball, as shown in the picture.

Which sentence describes the force of the ball when hit with the tennis racquet?

A. The force changes the speed and direction of the ball.

B. The force changes the speed, but the direction is the same.

C. The force does not change the speed, but the direction of the ball changes.

D. The force does not change the speed, and it does not change the direction of the ball.

Read each statement. Write your answer on the lines.

6. What does a spring scale measure?

____

____

____

____

____

7. Grant wondered what would happen if he held a book with both hands and let go.

Describe the forces on the book when Grant is holding it.

____

____

Explain what will happen to the book when Grant lets go of it.

____

____

Describe the forces on the book when Grant lets go of it.

____

____

Quiz: What Are Some Types of Forces?

Read each question. Circle the letter of the correct answer.

1. Forces can change the motion of an object. Which of these is a force?

   A. time

   B. speed

   C. gravity

   D. distance

2. When Josh hits the baseball with a bat, it changes the direction of the ball. Which is a true statement about the forces on the bat and ball?

   A. The forces are not balanced; the bat pushes with more force.

   B. The forces are not balanced; the ball pushes with more force.

   C. The forces are balanced; the ball and bat push with the same force.

   D. The forces are not balanced; the ball and bat push with the same force.

3. What force pulls objects toward Earth?

   A. a kick

   B. a push

   C. gravity

   D. magnetism

4. The picture shows a bird, a tree, a cloud, and a dog.

   Which objects are pushing or pulling each other?

   A. the tree and the dog

   B. the bird and the tree

   C. the dog and the cloud

   D. the bird and the cloud

© Houghton Mifflin Harcourt Publishing Company

5. Two race cars with the same mass started moving on a race track at the same time. One car reached the finish line of the track in 15 seconds, and the other car reached the finish line in 20 seconds. Why did the cars take different amounts of time to reach the finish line?

A. The force of gravity slowed one car but not the other car.

B. There were no forces on the second car, so it moved more slowly.

C. The forces were balanced on one car and unbalanced on the other car.

D. The engine of the faster car pushed with more force than the engine of the other car.

Read each statement. Write your answer on the lines.

6. Zoe puts a pencil on the desk. The pencil does not roll. Explain whether the forces on the pencil are balanced or unbalanced.

____

____

____

____

____

7. Mr. Leins' class is doing an experiment. They set up these two ramps of equal length. They will measure the force needed to pull each car up its ramp.

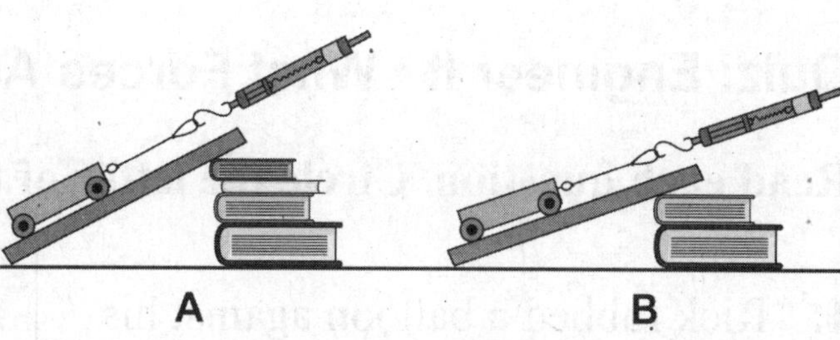

Explain which car will take less force to pull up the ramp.

____

____

____

____

Quiz: Engineer It • What Forces Act from a Distance?

Read each question. Circle the letter of the correct answer.

1. Rick rubbed a balloon against his head. He put the balloon near a wall. The balloon stuck to the wall. Which diagram shows the forces of the wall and balloon?

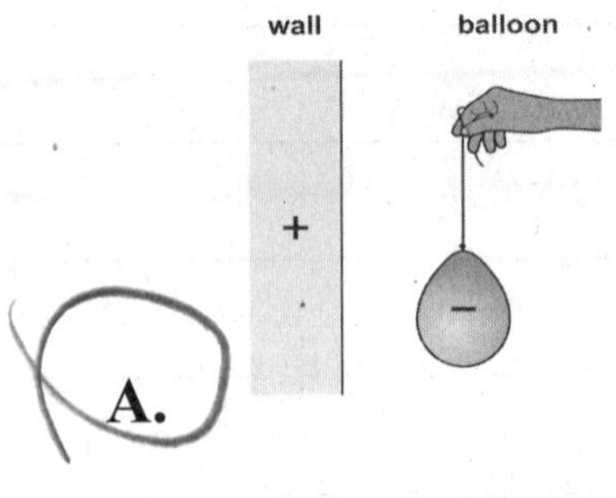

A.

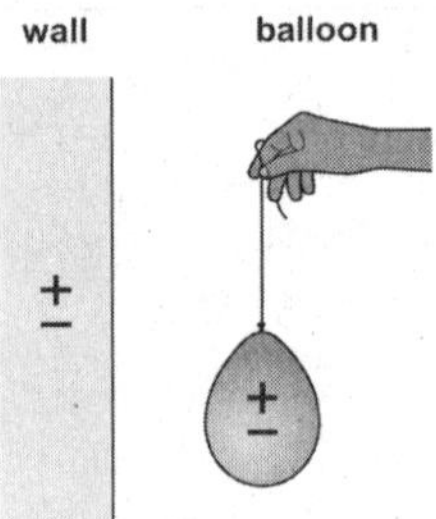

B.

C.

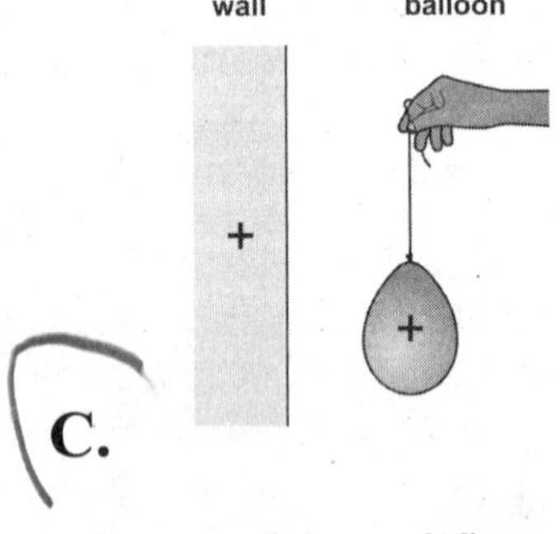

D.

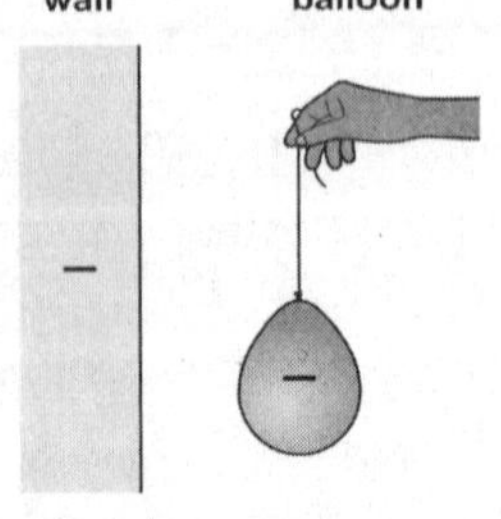

2. What happens if you put the same poles of two magnets together?

   A. Nothing happens.

   B. The magnets repel each other.

   C. The magnets attract each other.

   D. The two magnets become one magnet.

3. Mary made a metal game board and put it on her wall. She made wooden game pieces to put on the game board. She wants the game pieces to stay on the board without falling off. The game pieces should be easy to remove so she can play the game again. How should she attach the game pieces to the board?

   A. buttons

   B. glue

   C. magnets

   D. nails

4. Which magnets will attract each other?

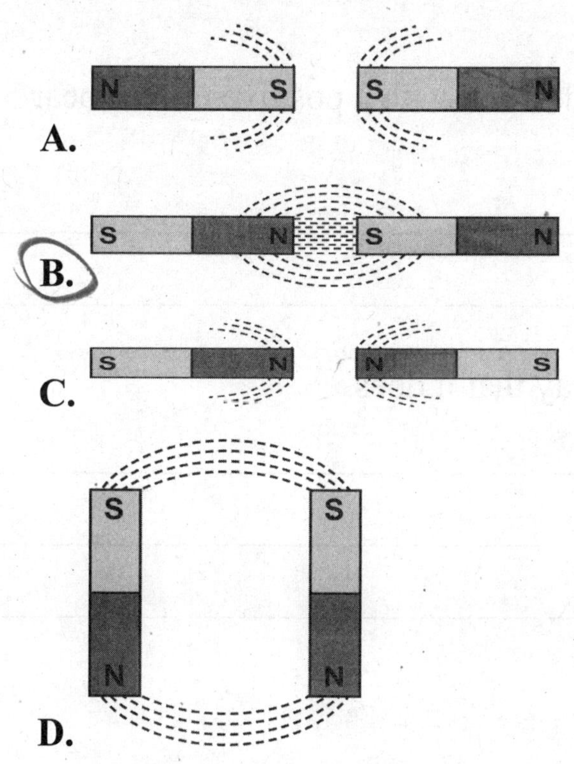

A.

B.

C.

D.

5. Hector rubs a comb with a wool cloth. Next, he holds the comb near, but not touching, some bits of paper on a plate. Which of these is most likely to happen?

A. The paper bits will move away from the comb.

B. The paper bits will not be attracted to the comb.

C. A spark will jump between the paper bits and the comb.

D. The paper bits will be attracted to the comb and will stick to it.

Read each statement. Write your answer on the lines.

6. The picture shows two pairs of magnets.

Identify the pair of magnets that will repel each other.

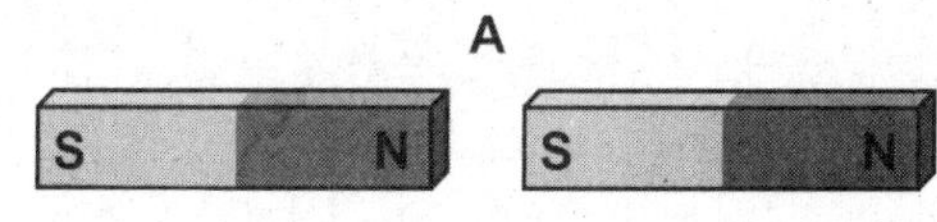

_______ B _______

Explain your answer.

Because it is S-S together and that makes it repel

7. Fran hangs three balloons from strings. She gives the first balloon a positive charge. She gives the second balloon a negative charge. She does not give the third balloon a charge.

Describe what will happen if Fran holds a rod with a positive charge near each balloon.

It will repel.

Explain why each balloon reacts the way that it does.

It is positive no

Unit Test: Forces

Read each question. Circle the letter of the correct answer.

1. Which sentence describes zero net force?

   A. a book sitting on a desk

   B. a leaf falling from a branch on a tree

   C. a girl putting on the brakes on her bike

   D. a truck speeding up to get on the highway

2. Gina is studying static electricity. Which question will help her the most?

   A. Which materials are attracted to magnets?

   B. How big should magnets be to attract each other?

   C. Do objects have to touch to transfer static electricity?

   D. Is static electricity the buildup of electricity in an object?

3. Which picture shows Car 1 having the greater force?

   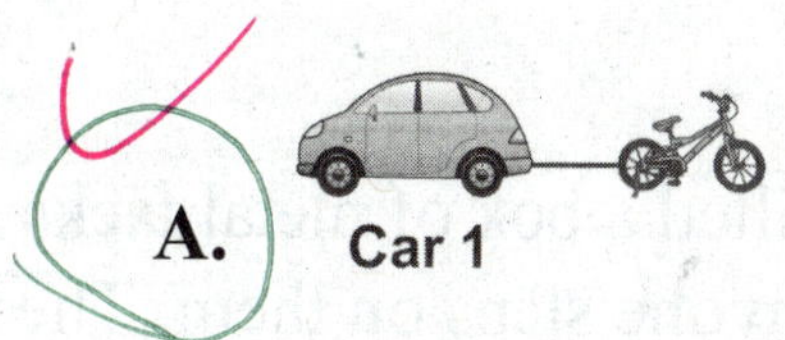
   A. Car 1

   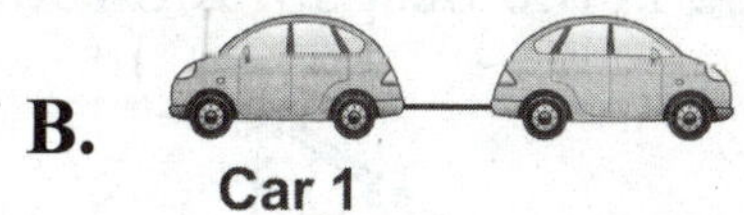
   B. Car 1

   C. Car 1

   D. Car 1

4. Which picture shows the strongest magnetic attraction?

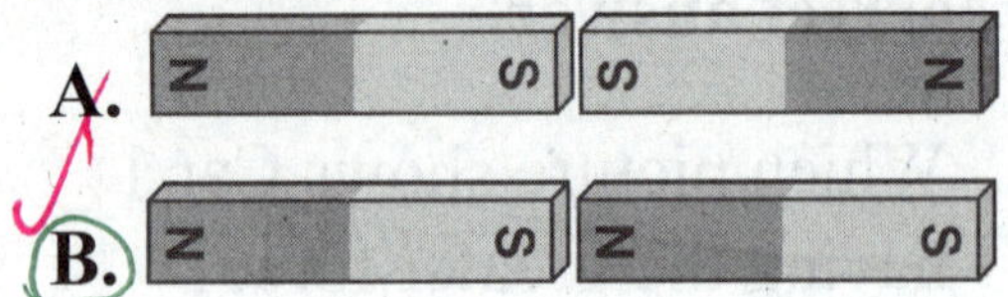

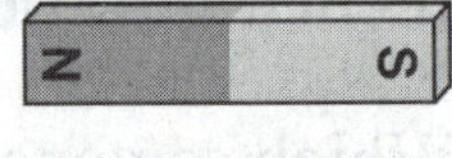

5. Larry spilled a box of metal tacks in the tall grass. He wants to pick them up before anyone steps on them. The solution should cost less than $20. Which of these is the best solution for Larry's problem?

A. magnet tied to broom-$15

C. picking up tacks by hand-$0

B. mowing tall grass-$150

D. shining light on grass-$10

6. Which picture shows movement by pulling?

A.

C.

B.

D.

7. Kori wants to show an unbalanced force. Her friend will sit on a chair. Kori will push the chair. Which questions should Kori ask herself before she sets up her experiment?

Write one letter in each blank to show which questions Kori should ask.

1. Does the chair have wheels? __________

2. What color should the chair be? __________

3. Should the friend weigh less than Kori? __________

> **A.** Yes, Kori should ask this question.
>
> **B.** No, this question does not help with the experiment.

8. Jim wants to show his classmates balanced and unbalanced forces. He will use a small seesaw and wooden blocks made of the same type of wood.

   Write the correct letters in the boxes to show the steps Jim should follow. Not all of the letters will be used.

Step 1: Balanced forces without blocks	C
Step 2: Unbalanced forces	D
Step 3: Balanced forces with blocks	A

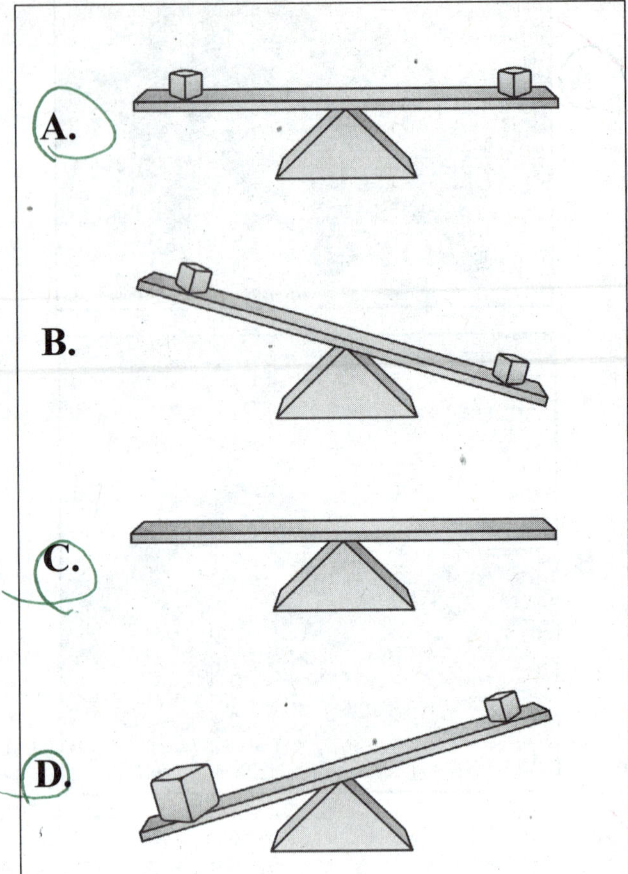

9. The picture shows a simple discovery.

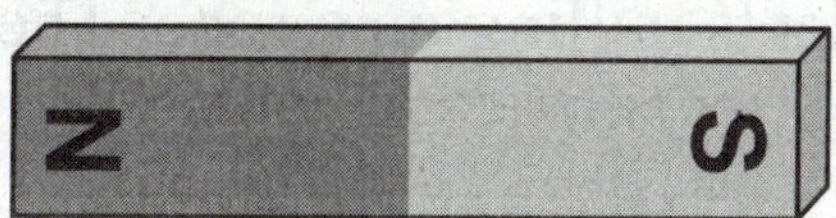

Which technologies work because of this discovery?

Circle the letters of the 2 correct answers.

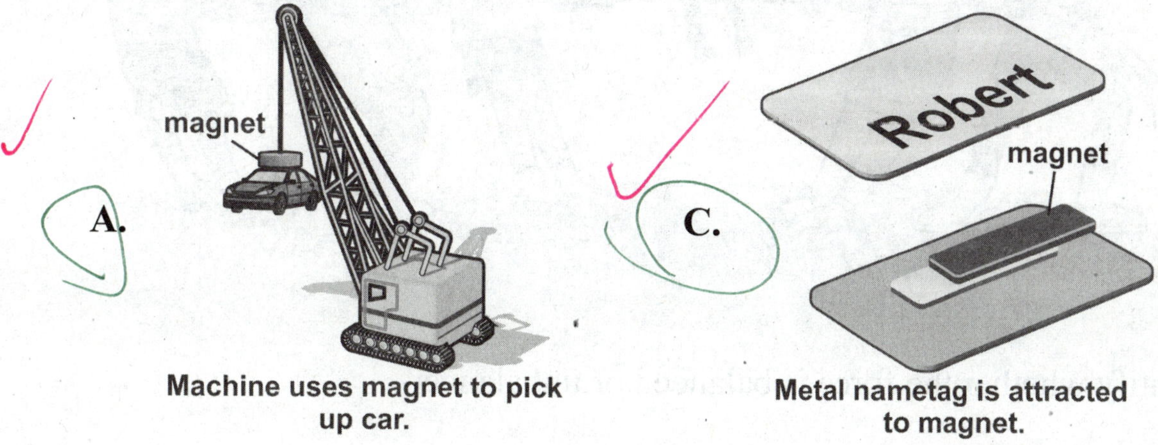

A. Machine uses magnet to pick up car.

C. Metal nametag is attracted to magnet.

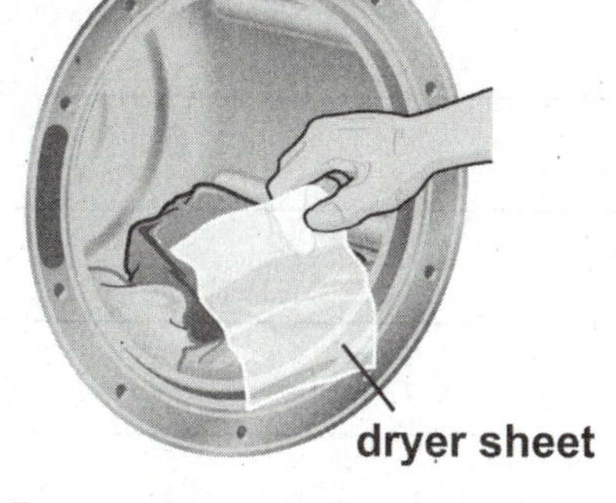

B. Dryer sheet prevents static cling in clothes.

D. Machine makes static.

© Houghton Mifflin Harcourt Publishing Company

Read each statement. Write your answer on the lines.

10. The picture shows students pulling on a rope. The arrow shows the direction the rope is moving.

Identify whether the force is balanced or unbalanced.

____

Explain your answer.

____

____

____

____

Directions: Read the passage, then answer the questions that follow.

Rolling Cars

Kate used bricks to build 3 ramps. She rolled identical cars down each ramp. The picture shows her setup. The car on Ramp C rolled the farthest.

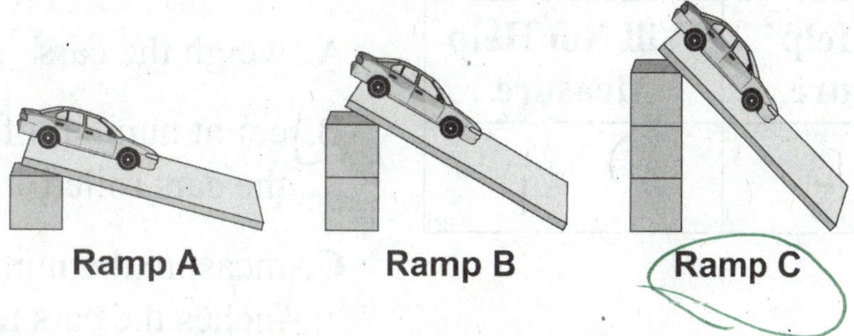

11. Kate will make a fourth ramp with 4 bricks. She will use the same type of car to roll down this new ramp. What will happen to the toy car rolled down the new ramp?

   Circle the letter of the correct answer.

   A. It will weigh more than the other cars.

   B. It will be taller than the other ramps.

   C. It will not roll as far as the cars on the other ramps.

   D. It will have more force pushed on it than the cars on the other ramps.

12. Kate added magnets to the bottom of two toy cars. Car 1 has a positive magnet. Car 2 has a negative magnet.

   Write one X in the correct box for each statement

Statement	True	False
A. Car 1 will be attracted to car 2.	X	
B. Car 2 will be attracted to car 1.	X	
C. Car 1 and car 2 will repel each other.		X
D. Car 1 will be attracted to car 2, but car 2 will repel car 1.		X

13. Kate set up an experiment with toy cars and ramps. She wants to know which car moved more than the others. Which types of measurements will help Kate?

Write the letters of the sentences in the correct boxes.

Will Help Measure	Will Not Help Measure
C B	D A

A. weigh the cars

B. count number of seconds the cars rolled

C. measure the number of inches the cars rolled

D. take pictures of the cars before being rolled

14. Kate placed a ball at the end of Ramp A. She rolled the toy car down the ramp. In which picture are the arrows showing the actions of the toy car and ball?

Circle the letter of the correct answer.

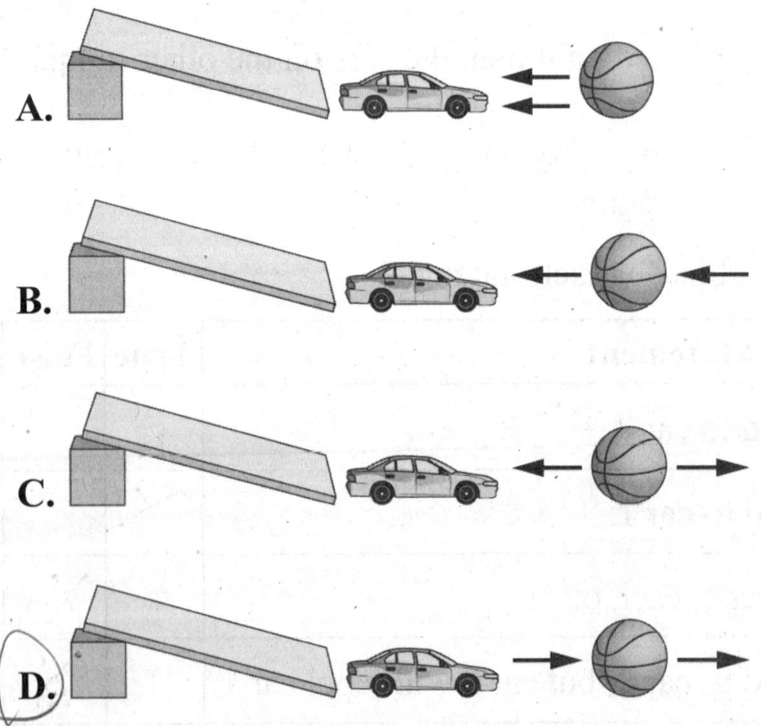

© Houghton Mifflin Harcourt Publishing Company

15. Kate set up an experiment with toy cars and ramps.

Read each statement. Write your answer on the lines.

Identify which car had the most force pushing it down the ramp.

____

____

Explain why this car had the greatest force.

____

____

____

____

© Houghton Mifflin Harcourt Publishing Company

Pretest: Motion

Read each question. Circle the letter of the correct answer.

1. Four balls are on a hill. The table shows where the balls are at different times.

Where on Hill

Type of ball	After 1 minute	After 2 minutes	After 3 minutes
Basketball	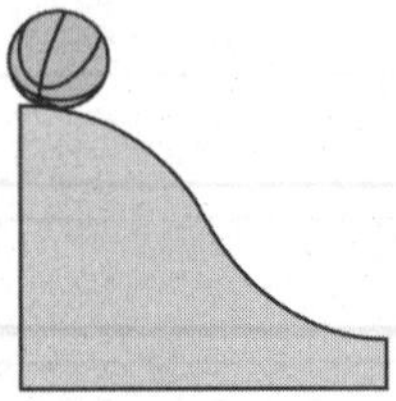	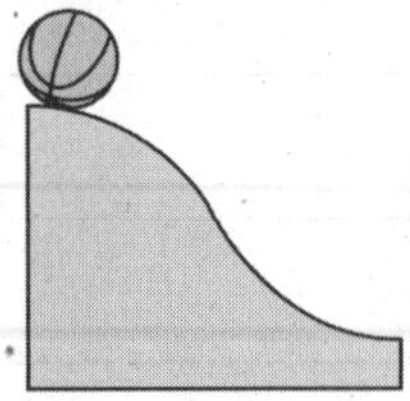	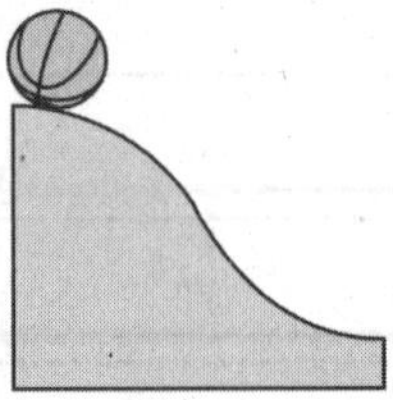
Tennis ball	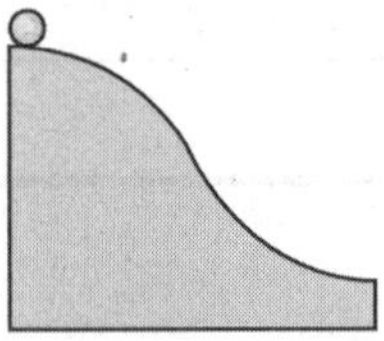	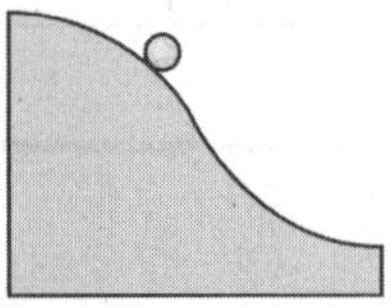	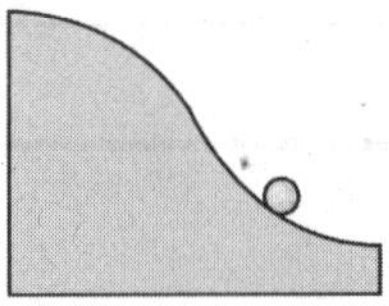
Soccer ball	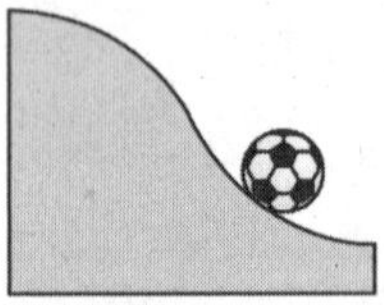	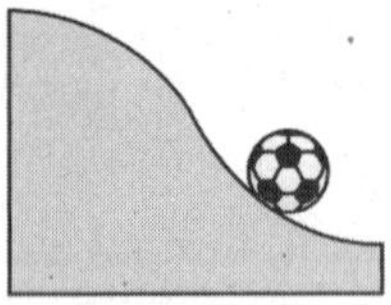	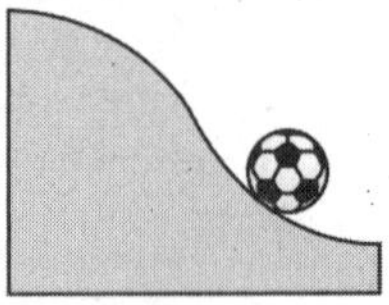
Bowling ball	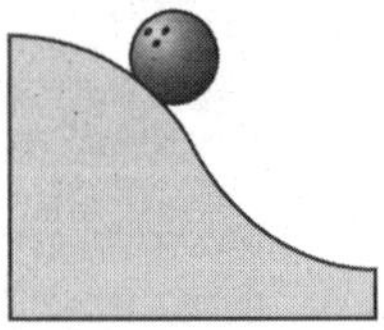	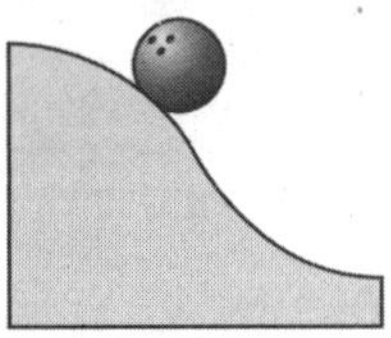	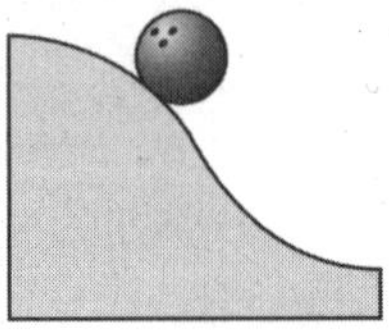

Which ball is moving?

A. basketball

B. soccer ball

C. bowling ball

D. tennis ball

2. Desmond kicks a football toward a goal. Which two measurements does he need to know the speed of the ball?

A. weight and time

B. time and distance

C. direction and weight

D. distance and direction

3. The picture shows how a seesaw moves.

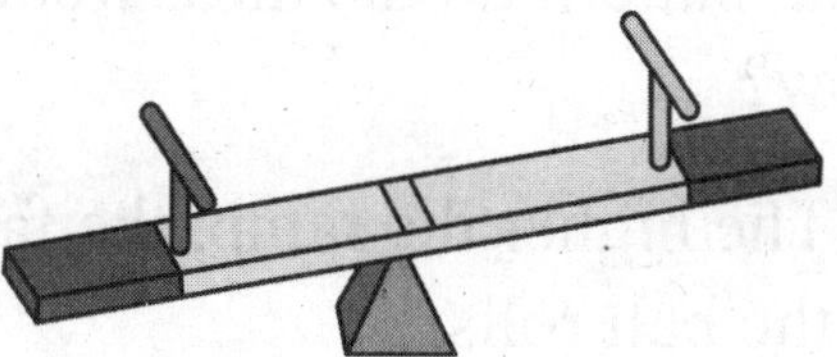

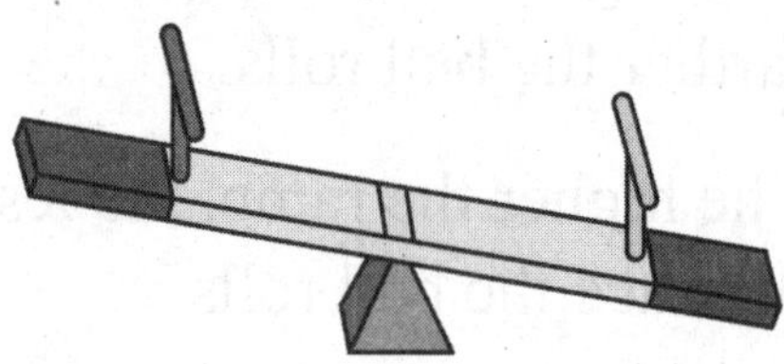

What is the pattern of movement of the seesaw?

A. Both sides stay at equal heights.

B. The left goes up when the right goes up.

C. The left goes up when the right goes down.

D. The left goes down when the right goes down.

4. A man pushes a heavy box on a skateboard.

What will happen to the box and the skateboard?

A. The skateboard and box will both fall over.

B. The skateboard and box will move together.

C. The skateboard will move, but the box will stay still.

D. The skateboard will not move, but the box will move.

5. Two toy cars hit each other. What will most likely happen to the cars?

A. The cars will stop moving.

B. One car will go over the top of the other car.

C. The cars will change the directions they were moving.

D. One car will lose force and the other car will gain force.

6. The picture shows a parent and a child on a swing set.

Two boys are about to use the same force to push the parent and the child. Which describes what will happen?

A. The child will move faster.

B. The parent will move faster.

C. The parent will swing backward.

D. The child will change directions.

7. Sheldon rolled a ball down three different ramps. Each ramp is a different height. He measured how far the ball rolled each time. His measurements are in the table.

Distance Ball Rolled

Height of ramp (inches)	Distance ball rolled (inches)
3	10
2	7
1	4

What pattern do the measurements show?

A. The higher the ramp, the faster the ball rolls.

B. The higher the ramp, the farther the ball rolls.

C. The higher the ramp, the less distance the ball rolls.

D. The ramp height does not affect how far the ball rolls.

8. Karla is watching cars race around a track. She wants to know when her favorite car will come around the track again.

Which observation should she record to figure out when the car will pass her again?

A. how many cars are on the track

B. how many cars pass her each minute

C. how many times the cars go around the track

D. how many minutes it takes for a car to go around the track

9. Benny drops a ball off a bridge. The ball drops straight down, as shown in the diagram.

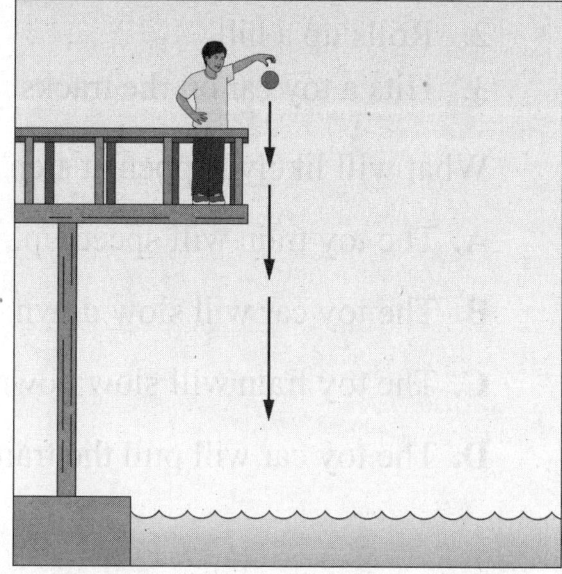

What happens to the ball as it falls?

A. It speeds up.

B. It slows down.

C. It changes direction.

D. Its speed stays the same.

© Houghton Mifflin Harcourt Publishing Company

10. A student pushes a toy train on a straight train track. The train follows these steps.

1. Rolls down a hill
2. Rolls up a hill
3. Hits a toy car on the tracks

What will likely happen at step 4?

A. The toy train will speed up.

B. The toy car will slow down.

C. The toy train will slow down until it stops.

D. The toy car will pull the train off the tracks.

Quiz: What Is Motion?

Read each question. Circle the letter of the correct answer.

1. Which of these is an example of balanced forces?

   A. an apple falling from a tree

   B. a bird sitting on a fence post

   C. a boy speeding up on his bike

   D. a girl changing direction in a swing

2. Which of these is an example of unbalanced forces?

   A. Twelve children push against one wall.

   B. A satellite orbits Earth at a constant speed.

   C. A bus moves along a highway in a straight line at 65 miles per hour.

   D. Two tug-of-war teams move an inch in one direction and then an inch in thc other direction.

3. Four students are playing baseball. The table shows the speeds for the fastest pitch of each student in meters per second, m/s.

   Speed of Fastest Pitch

Student	Speed (m/s)
Will	19
Kyle	16
Corey	15
Teri	9

   Which player pitched the ball with the greatest force?

   A. Will

   B. Kyle

   C. Corey

   D. Teri

4. Jevon pulls on the handle of a wagon filled with 50 pounds of soil. The wagon does not move. Which action would be most likely to move the wagon?

  A. pushing instead of pulling

  B. pulling harder on the handle

  C. pulling with the same force on the handle

  D. increasing the weight of the soil in the wagon

5. Students measure the speed of a toy car moving down a ramp. They know the time it takes for the car to reach the bottom. What else do they need to know to find the average speed of the car?

  A. the mass of the car

  B. the force on the car

  C. the distance the car traveled

  D. the direction the car moved

Read each statement. Write your answer on the lines.

6. Ken pulls his little brother in a wagon. Next, Ken tries to pull his dad in the wagon. He cannot get the wagon moving. Explain why this could be happening. Use the words *force* and *weight* in the answer.

____

____

____

____

7. The picture shows two cars connected together. They are both trying to drive away, but neither car is moving.

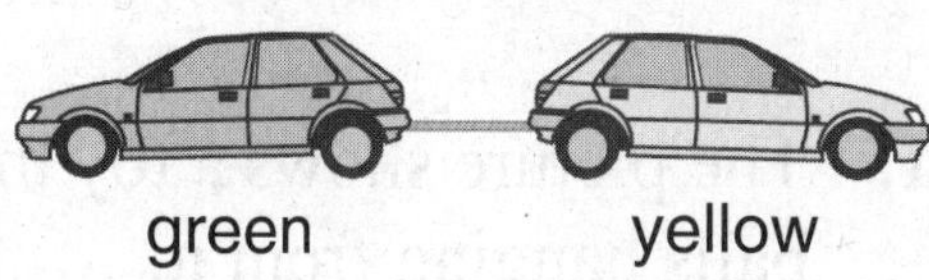

Identify why neither car is moving.

____

____

Explain what would happen if the engine of the green car was turned off.

____

____

Quiz: What Are Some Patterns in Motion?

Read each question. Circle the letter of the correct answer.

1. The picture shows a toy that has balls hanging from it.

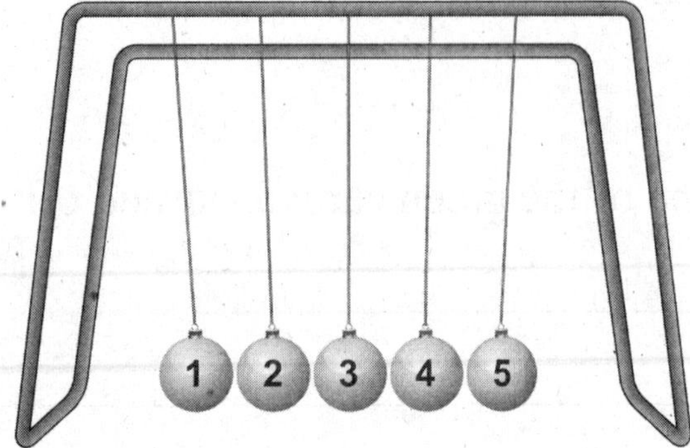

Shaunn pulls ball 5 up and to the right and lets go. Ball 5 swings down and hits ball 4. The force transfers across the balls and ball 1 swings up in the air to the left.

What will happen next?

A. Ball 2 will break.

B. Ball 1 will fly off the toy.

C. Ball 2 will swing up in the air to the left.

D. Ball 1 will swing back down and hit ball 2.

2. Matt watched the animals on a small carousel go around in a circle. There are only four animals on the carousel. He writes down what he sees.

- lion
- bear
- horse
- duck

What animal will Matt likely see next?

A. lion

B. bear

C. duck

D. seal

3. Delilah wants to test how pulling a spring back affects how far a ball moves. She pulls the spring back a little and lets go.

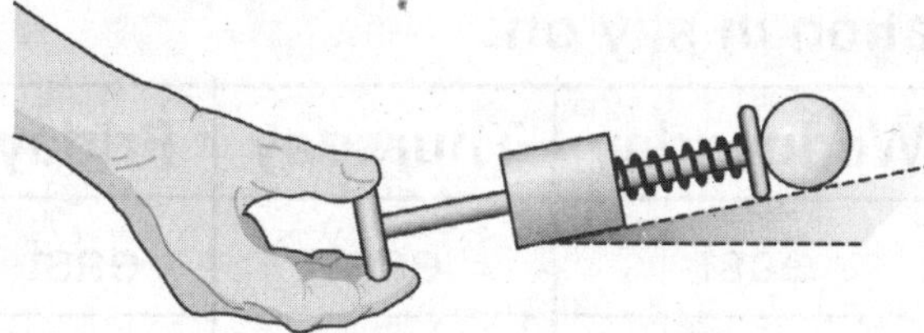

What should she measure?

A. the length of the spring and the size of the ball

B. the distance she pulls the spring back and the weight of the ball

C. the distance she pulls the spring back and the distance the ball flies

D. the time it takes to pull the spring back and the time it takes for the spring to release

4. Jose is playing on a merry-go-round. He writes down the time when the merry-go-round turns once. Jose's data are in the table.

Merry-go-round Data

Turn	Time (seconds)
1	2
2	4
3	6
4	8

At what time will the merry-go-round make its fifth turn?

A. 2 seconds

B. 5 seconds

C. 10 seconds

D. 20 seconds

5. Qin writes down where in the sky he sees the sun. He does this twice every day for a week. The table shows his data.

Where is the Sun?

Time	Location in sky on:				
	Monday	**Tuesday**	**Wednesday**	**Thursday**	**Friday**
7:00 a.m.	east	east	east	east	east
7:00 p.m.	west	west	west	west	west

What pattern does Qin's data show?

A. The sun comes up in the west.

B. The sun goes down in the west.

C. The sun goes back and forth across the sky each day.

D. The sun is cooler in the morning and hottest at night each day.

Read each statement. Write your answer on the lines.

6. Javier dropped a tennis ball from a height of 100 centimeters, cm. He wrote down how high the ball bounced each time.

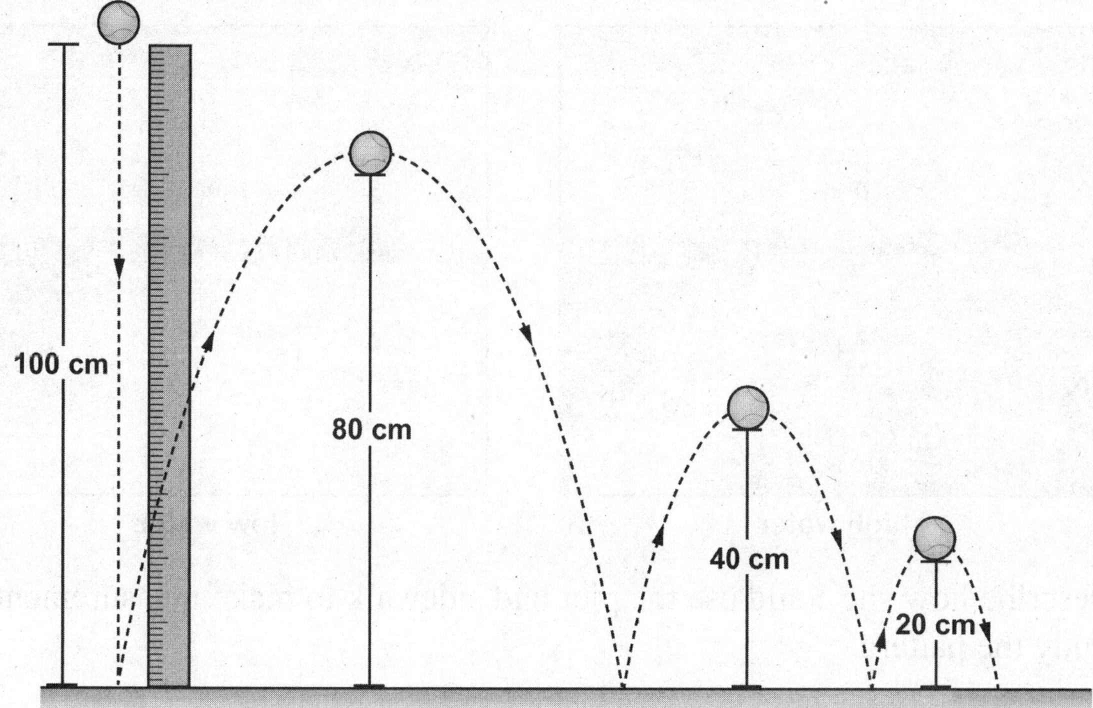

Predict the height of the next bounce.

____

____

____

____

____

7. Gabby lives by the ocean. She notices that sometimes the water comes up high. It gets close to the sidewalk, and there is very little beach. Sometimes the water is low. It is much farther from the sidewalk, and there is a big beach.

high water

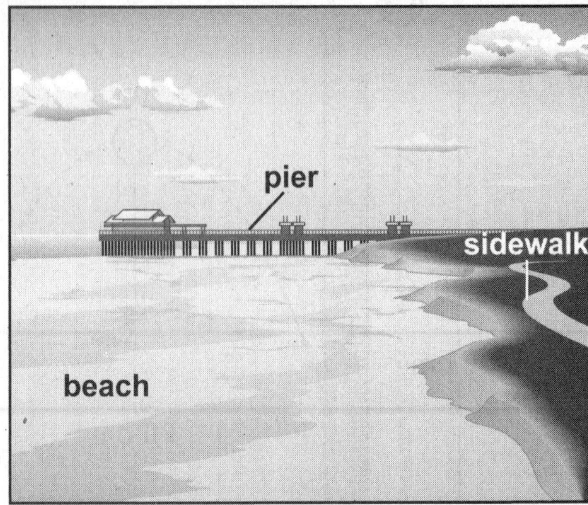

low water

Describe how she could use the pier and sidewalk to make measurements to study the pattern.

____

____

____

____

____

Unit Test: Motion

Read each question. Circle the letter of the correct answer.

1. Jake used a seesaw to show a balanced force. He placed a brick on Side 1, as shown.

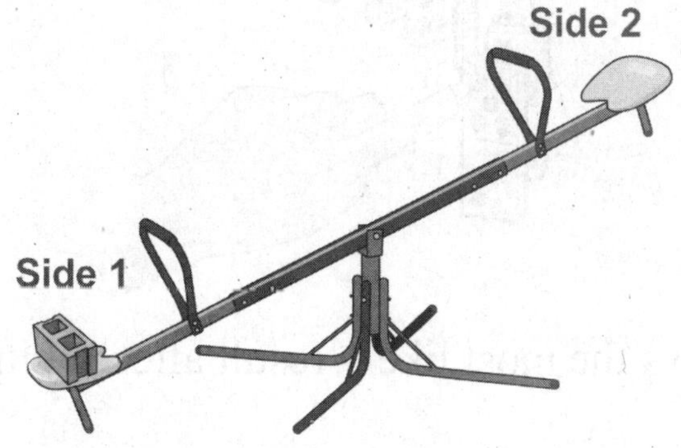

   What was likely his second step?

   A. Place two larger bricks on Side 2.

   B. Add a smaller brick to both sides.

   C. Place an identical brick on Side 2.

   D. Add a second identical brick on Side 1.

2. Jack was riding his bike up a hill. When he started riding down the hill he noticed that he did not have to pedal as many times. Why did Jack not have to pedal as many times?

   A. He sped up as he went down the hill.

   B. He slowed down as he went down the hill.

   C. His speed stayed the same as he rode down the hill.

   D. He started shaking side to side as he rode down the hill.

3. Whitney wants to know what would happen to her domino set after she pushes over the first domino.

Which picture shows the most likely result after Whitney pushes over the first domino?

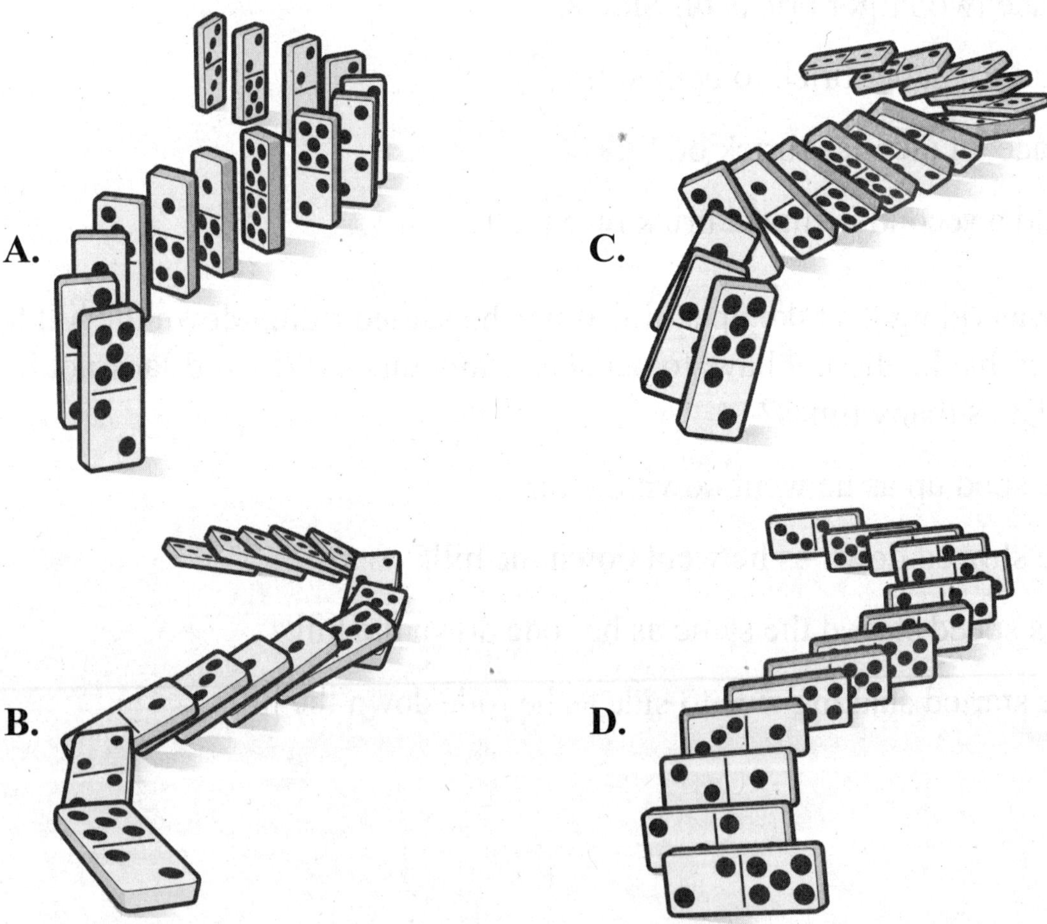

A.

C.

B.

D.

4. Which picture shows an object moving in an unpredictable pattern?

A. 

C. 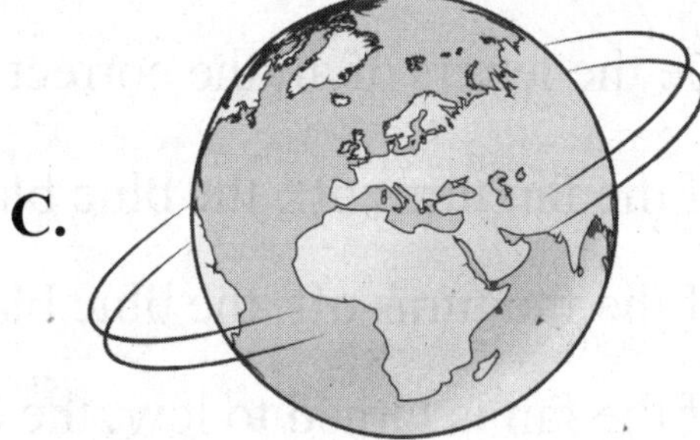

B. 

D. 

Read each question. Follow the instructions to answer the questions.

5. Which picture shows a pattern of back-and-forth motion?

Draw a circle around the correct picture.

6. Stacy observed the blades of a fan spinning. She noticed one blue blade on the fan each time it went around. What are some other observations that Stacy likely made about the fan?

   Circle the letters of all the correct responses.

   A. If the fan turns off, the blue blade will stop moving.

   B. If the fan turns off, the blue blade will keep spinning.

   C. If the fan is turned to low, the blue blade will go around faster.

   D. If the fan is turned to low, the blue blade will go around slower.

7. The picture shows a person about to kick a ball.

   Draw an arrow in the picture to show the direction the ball will move.

© Houghton Mifflin Harcourt Publishing Company

8. John drew a picture of objects with different patterns of motion in his notebook and labeled the pattern.

Write one letter in each blank to correctly describe the pattern of motion.

Patterns

Drawing	Pattern of motion
	1.
	2.
	3.

A. circular	**B.** zigzag	**C.** up and down

9. Ana did an experiment with a pendulum. She changed the length of the string and counted the number of swings. She wrote down the number of times the rope swung. Finish her table.

Write one letter in each box to correctly complete the table.

Length of rope (centimeters, cm)	15 cm	30 cm	60 cm	90 cm
Number of swings	60 swings		30 swings	

A. 0 swings	**B.** 15 swings	**C.** 45 swings

10. Bob rolled a skateboard down a short ramp and then down a tall ramp. The skateboard rolled 5 meters with the tall ramp. It rolled 1 meter with the short ramp.

Graph his data. Use your pencil to draw lines to show the skateboard data.

Skateboard Data

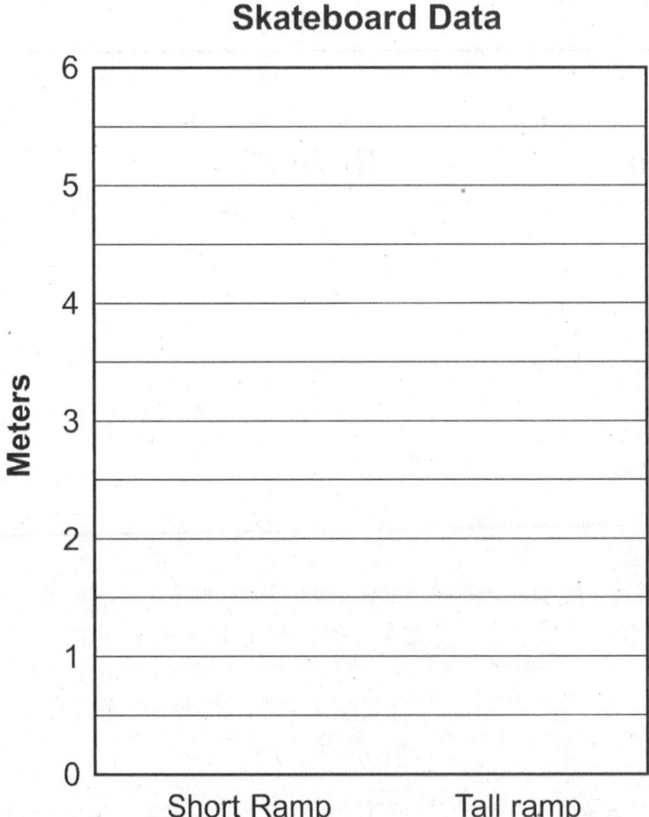

© Houghton Mifflin Harcourt Publishing Company

11. Eric raced his car on a track. He drove the same speed each time around the track. His data are in the table.

Car Data

Laps	Time (minutes)
1	10
2	20
3	30
4	*

Read each statement. Write your answer on the lines.

Predict how long it will take Eric to travel 4 laps.

____

Describe the pattern in the data.

____

____

The track is 1 mile long. Calculate how fast the car is going in miles per minute.

____

____

Directions: Read the passage, then answer the questions that follow.

Rope Activities

A group of students has a long rope at recess. The students do different activities with the rope to make it move in different patterns. The pictures show their activities.

Students Playing with Rope

Activity 1

Activity 2

Activity 3

12. Which pattern of motion did the students see in Activity 1?

Circle the letter of the correct answer.

A. zigzag

B. circular

C. up and down

D. back and forth

13. Which models best show the motion of Activity 2?

Draw circles around the 2 correct models.

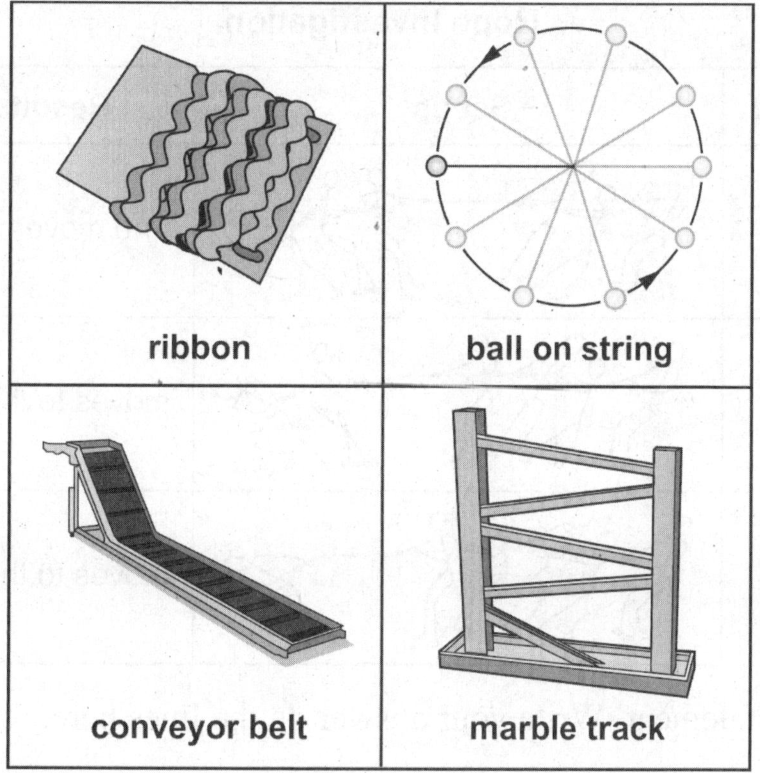

14. The rope moves or does not move because of the forces on the rope. In the student activities, were the forces balanced or unbalanced?

Write one X in the correct box for each activity.

Activity	Balanced	Unbalanced
A. Activity 1		
B. Activity 2		
C. Activity 3		

15. The students decide to turn Activity 3 into an investigation to test forces and motion. Their results are shown in the table.

Rope Investigation

Trial	Set up	Results
1		no movement
2		moves to the left
3		moves to the left

Read each statement. Write your answer on the lines here.

Explain the cause and effect that led to the results the students saw.

____

____

Describe how the speed of the motion likely changed from trial 2 to 3.

____

____

Explain what the student should do next to check their results.

____

____

Pretest: Life Cycles and Inherited Traits

Read each question. Circle the letter of the correct answer.

1. The young grasshopper hatches from its egg. It looks like an adult, only smaller. What is the name of this kind of young insect?

   A. larva

   B. nymph

   C. pupa

   D. seed

2. A butterfly starts its life as a caterpillar. It goes through a different type of life cycle. What is the name of this life cycle?

   A. complete life cycle

   B. incomplete life cycle

   C. complete metamorphosis

   D. incomplete metamorphosis

3. A bird lays an egg. What is the next stage in the egg's life cycle?

   A. flying

   B. growing

   C. hatching

   D. reproducing

4. Some insects go through different life cycles, but all insect life cycles start the same. What is the starting stage of insects' life cycles?

   A. egg

   B. larvae

   C. nymph

   D. pupa

5. What is the first stage in plant reproduction?

   A. egg

   B. seed

   C. growth

   D. pollination

6. How do insects reproduce?

   A. by growing

   B. by developing

   C. by laying eggs

   D. by giving birth

© Houghton Mifflin Harcourt Publishing Company

7. A grasshopper has three stages in its life cycle. Which kind of metamorphosis does a grasshopper go through?

   A. complete life cycle

   B. incomplete life cycle

   C. complete metamorphosis

   D. incomplete metamorphosis

8. A manatee is a water animal that lives off the coast of Florida. Female manatees usually have only one baby at a time.

Which word best describes this part of the life cycle?

   A. death

   B. growth

   C. adulthood

   D. reproduction

9. The picture shows the life cycle of a fly. An arrow is pointing to one stage of life.

Life Cycle of a Fly

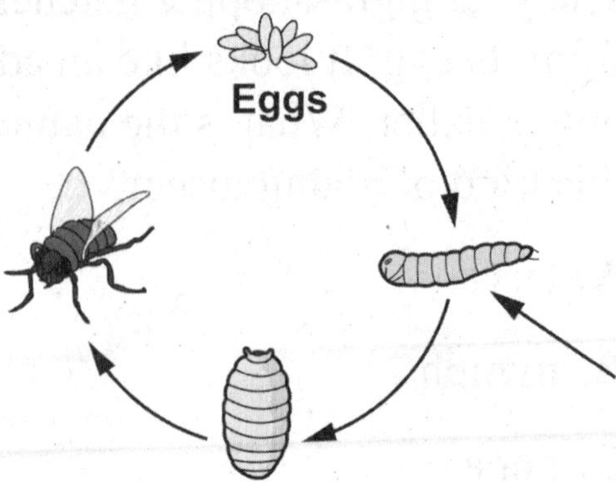

What is the name of the stage?

   A. adult

   B. larva

   C. nymph

   D. pupa

10. Which animal goes through complete metamorphosis?

   A. frog

   B. turtle

   C. shark

   D. chicken

© Houghton Mifflin Harcourt Publishing Company

Quiz: What Are Some Plant Life Cycles?

Read each question. Circle the letter of the correct answer.

1. The life cycle of a flower is shown in the picture.

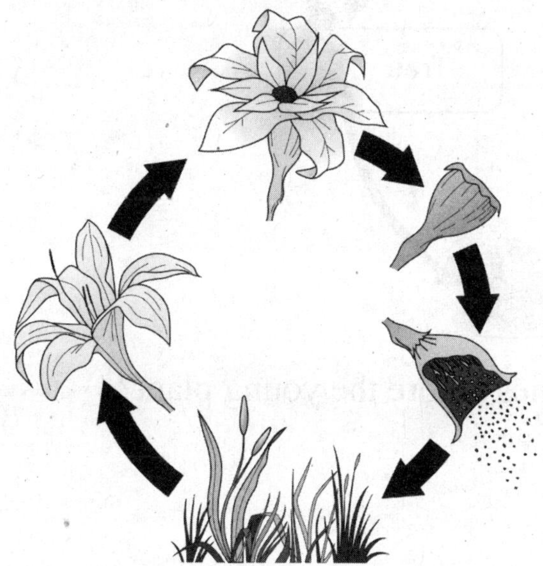

   Which stage of the plant life cycle is not shown?

   A. birth

   B. death

   C. growth

   D. reproduction

2. Which is not part of plant reproduction?

   A. larvae

   B. pollen

   C. seed

   D. spore

3. These living things go through a life cycle.

   1. butterfly
   2. frog
   3. grasshopper
   4. rosebush

   Which living things go through a complete metamorphosis?

   A. 1 and 2

   B. 2 and 3

   C. 1, 2, and 3

   D. 2, 3, and 4

4. Which of these best describes the life cycle of an insect?

   A. the structures that it makes

   B. the steps in its reproduction

   C. the parts of it that form as it grows

   D. the stages it goes through in its life

5. The picture shows the life cycle of a pine tree.

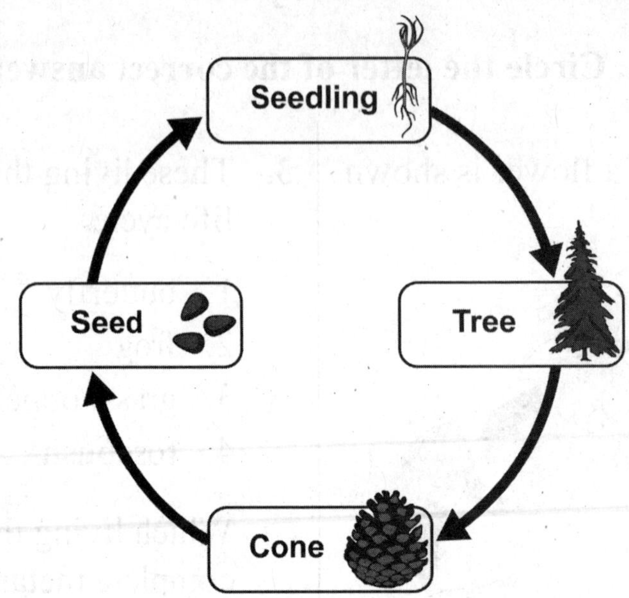

Which part of the plant's life cycle comes before the young plant?

A. tree

B. cone

C. seed

D. seedling

Read each statement. Write your answer on the lines.

6. Jared found a young plant growing in his backyard. Describe how he could find out how the plant will reproduce.

____

____

____

____

7. Julie made this drawing of the stages of growth of a bean seed.

The order shown is incorrect. Describe how the order should be changed to show how a bean seed changes as it grows.

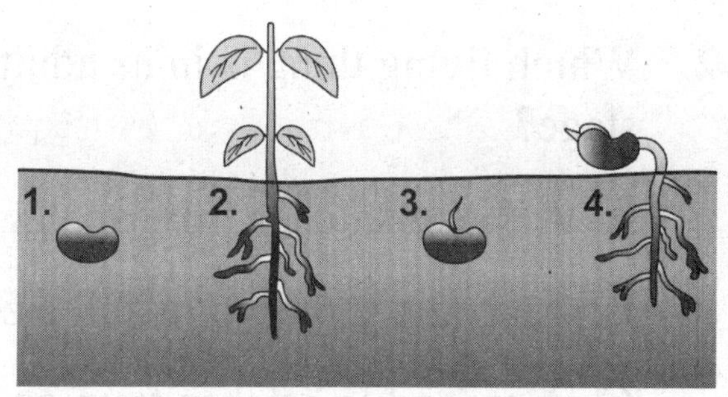

____

____

____

____

Quiz: What Are Some Animal Life Cycles?

Read each question. Circle the letter of the correct answer.

1. What is the first stage in the life cycle of an animal?

   A. birth

   B. seed

   C. adult

   D. growth

2. Which living thing is in its adult stage?

   A. A snake hatches from an egg.

   B. An eagle grows to its full size.

   C. A crocodile hatches from an egg.

   D. A tree stops growing and falls over.

3. Which pair contains an adult animal with its offspring?

   A. frog, pupa

   B. robin, chick

   C. ladybug, tadpole

   D. butterfly, nymph

4. Chickens are birds. Which of these describes the first stage in a chicken's life cycle?

   A. born alive from parent

   B. growing from chick to adult

   C. changing from egg into chick

   D. hatched from an egg laid by parent

5. The picture shows a stage in the life cycle of many animals.

   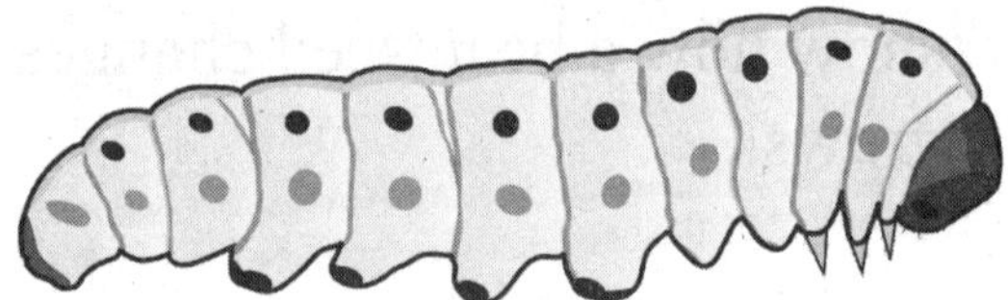

   Which kind of animal can have this stage in its life cycle?

   A. bird

   B. dog

   C. insect

   D. frog

Read each statement. Write your answer on the lines.

6. Identify the four parts of every animal's life cycle.

____

____

____

____

7. Leah found the eggs of an insect on a blade of grass. She brought the blade of grass home and made a container for it to keep the young insects safe when they hatch. Explain how she can tell what kind of insect eggs she found.

____

____

____

____

Quiz: What Are Inherited Plant and Animal Traits?

Read each question. Circle the letter of the correct answer.

1. Which term describes a behavior that an animal knows without being taught?

   A. error

   B. fact

   C. learned

   D. inherited

2. Sally listed what she thought were inherited behaviors. Which should Sally remove from the list?

   A. dog barking at stranger

   B. bird making nest for eggs

   C. horse letting person ride on back

   D. fish swimming away from danger

3. Bob listed different animal families. Which family has members that look different from each other?

   A. Rabbit Family: all have long ears

   B. Turtle Family: all have hard shells

   C. Cow Family: some eat grass, some eat hay

   D. Bird Family: some have grey feathers, some have white feathers

4. The picture shows a mother dog with her puppies.

Which of these statements is most likely correct?

A. The father dog is a different shape.

B. The father dog is a different color.

C. The father dog has a different owner.

D. The father dog wears a different collar.

5. Which behavior that happens during migration is inherited?

A. knowing when to leave

B. traveling on a learned path

C. traveling thousands of miles

D. stopping to rest while traveling

Read each statement. Write your answer on the lines.

6. Animals inherit behaviors from their parents. Describe an example of an inherited behavior of a bird.

____

____

____

____

7. A black cat with a large body and a white cat with a small body have kittens. Describe what the kittens will look like.

____

____

____

____

Unit Test: Life Cycles and Inherited Traits

Read each question. Circle the letter of the correct answer.

1. The image shows an adult tomato plant.

Which image shows what the tomato plant offspring might look like at the beginning stages of growth?

A. 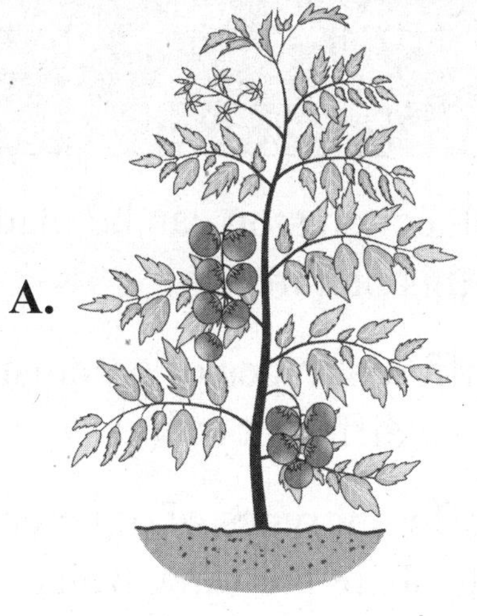

C. 

B. 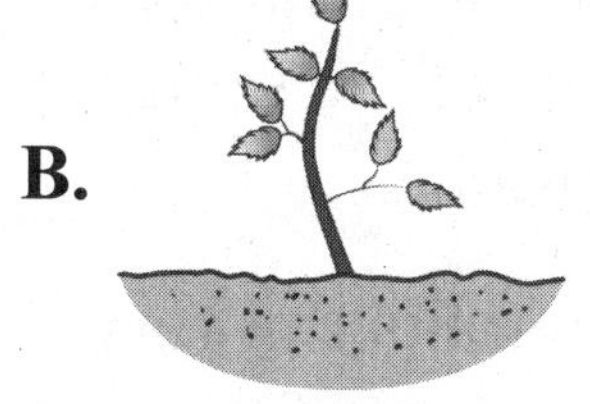

D. 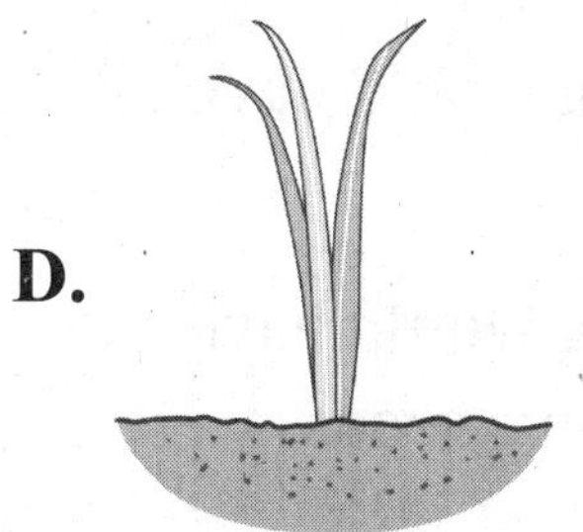

© Houghton Mifflin Harcourt Publishing Company

2. The picture shows a butterfly in one of its life stages.

Which life stage is this butterfly in?

A. adult

B. egg

C. larva

D. pupa

3. Dale is growing corn in his field. He has corn with two different colors of seeds. The offspring of the two yellow-seeded corn plants was also yellow. The offspring of one blue-seed corn plant and one yellow-seed corn plant resulted in a plant that had both yellow and blue seeds. What outcome should he expect from the offspring of two blue-seeded corn plants?

A. The offspring would have all blue seeds.

B. The offspring would have all yellow seeds.

C. The offspring would have yellow and blue seeds.

D. The offspring would have yellow, blue, and green seeds.

4. Which trait of a pine tree is inherited?

A. type of leaves

B. where it is planted

C. how much light it gets

D. how many branches it has

5. The picture shows pea plants.

Which conclusion can be made from this picture?

A. Different types of organisms have different traits.

B. Different types of organisms can share the same traits.

C. Inherited traits cause all organisms of the same type to look the same.

D. Inherited traits can vary within a group of the same type of organism.

6. Which picture shows the stages of a sunflower's life in the correct order?

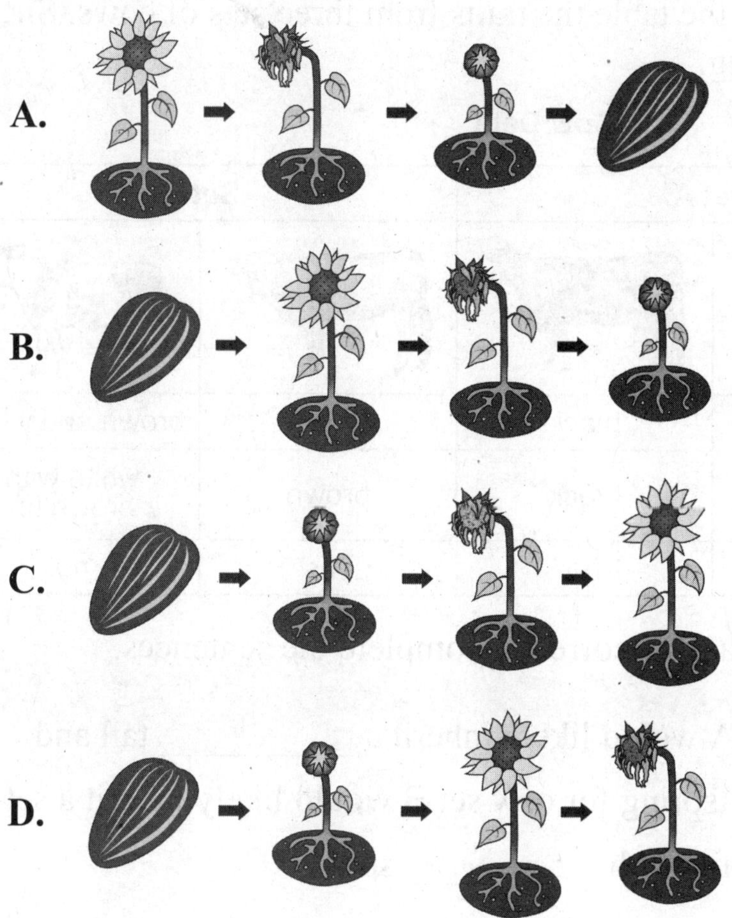

Read each question. Follow the instructions to answer the questions.

7. Clown fish live in the ocean in coral reefs. They are orange, white, and black and have three white stripes. They grow to be two to five inches long. They can live about ten years. Predict the traits of a young clown fish.

Circle the 2 correct answers.

A. will live ten years

B. has two white stripes

C. is orange, white, and black

D. is less than two inches long

8. Layla is reading about inherited traits passed from animal parents to their offspring. She recorded in the table the traits from three sets of cows. She then described the offspring.

Cow Data

Traits	Set A		Set B	
Color	black and white	black	brown	brown and white
Tail color	black	black	brown	white with brown tip
Horns	no	no	yes	no

Write one letter in each blank to correctly complete the sentences.

The offspring for cow set A would likely inherit a ___________ tail and black ___________. The offspring for cow set B would likely inherit a set of ___________ and white fur with ___________ spots.

A. spots	B. black	C. horns	D. brown

9. Match the offspring to the parent. Draw one line from the adult falcon to its young. Then draw one line from the adult sparrow to its young.

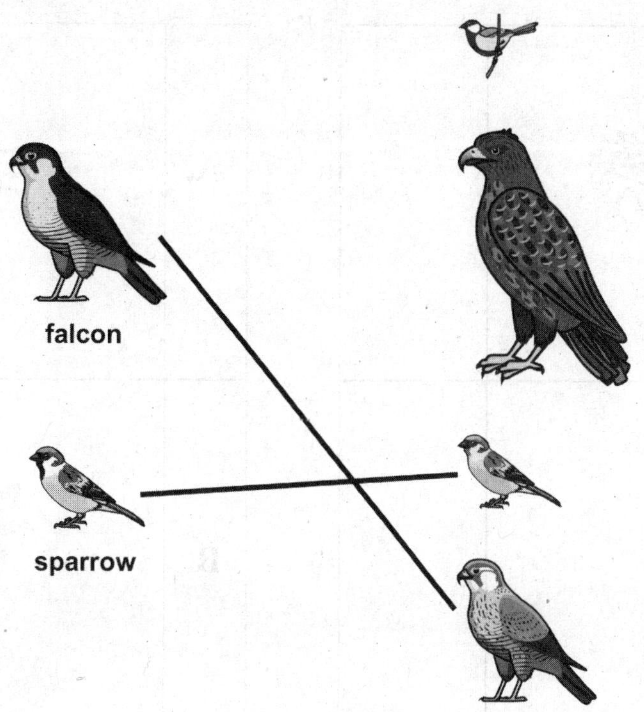

10. Match the offspring to the parent tree by looking at inherited traits.

Write the letter of the offspring in the box next to the correct parent tree.

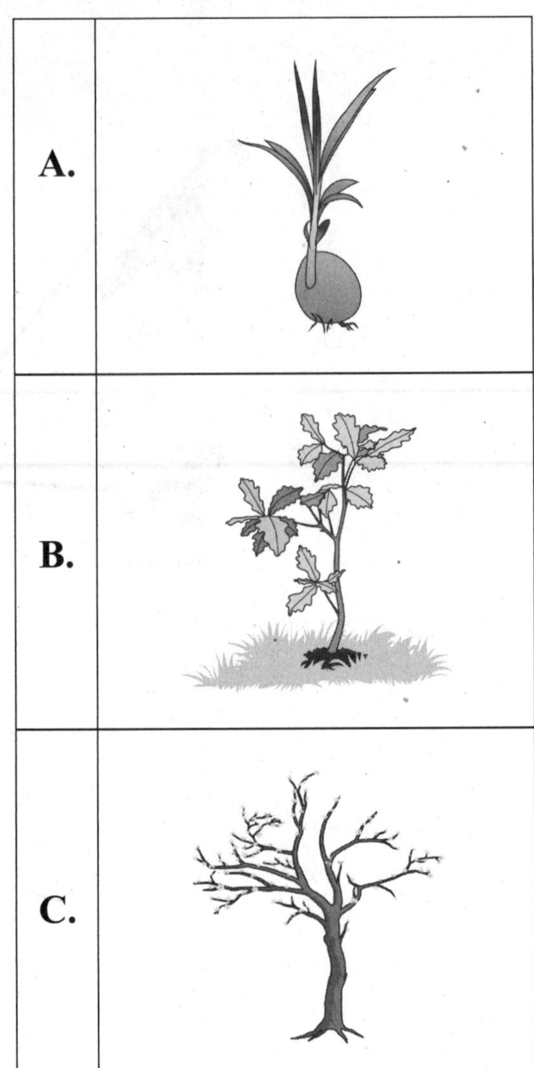

Read each statement. Write your answer on the lines.

11. The table shows data from three different types of oak trees.

Oak Data

Type	Willow oak	White oak	Chestnut oak
Height	50 to 80 feet	80 to 100 feet	50 to 70 feet
Trunk diameter	1 to 2.5 feet	2 to 4 feet	2 to 3 feet
Acorn shape	round	oval	oval with pointed end
Acorn height	0.5 inches	0.75 inches	1 inch
Leaf shape			

Blaine finds an oak tree that is 50 feet tall, and its trunk is one foot in diameter. It does not have any acorns. The leaves are rounded with smooth edges.

Explain which type of oak tree the offspring belongs to.

____

____

Describe how Blaine knows the tree is not yet full grown.

____

____

Describe the possible similarities and differences you might see if there were a sibling tree.

____

____

Directions: Read the passage, then answer the questions that follow.

It's a Frog's Life

Ramon draws the life cycles of a frog and a turtle.

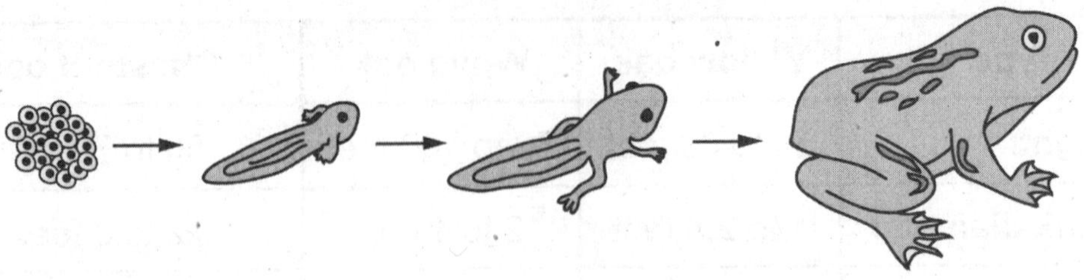

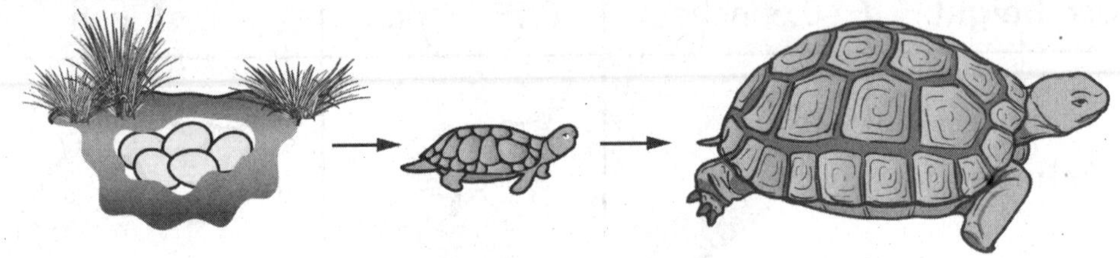

12. Which sentence describes an inherited trait of the turtle but not of the frog?

Circle the letter of the correct answer.

A. The young have a tail.

B. The young have a shell.

C. The young live in water.

D. The young do not have legs.

13. Look at the life cycles of the fish and the turtle.

Write an X in the correct boxes for each statement. Each statement could have an X for the frog, the turtle, or both.

Statement	Frog	Turtle
A. They started the life cycle as eggs.		
B. The life cycle includes a larval stage.		
C. The young are born looking like the adults.		

14. The life-cycle diagrams Ramon found are not labeled.

Write the letter of the life cycle stage in the correct box.

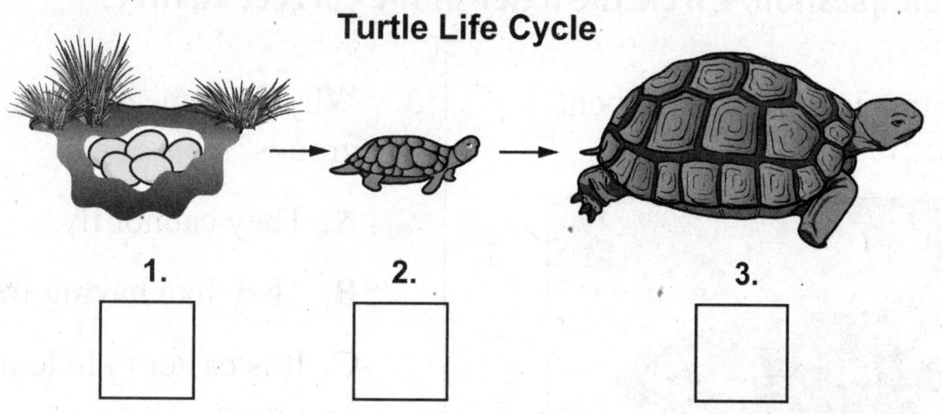

| | A. adulthood | B. birth | C. growth |

15. Ramon finds a bird's egg in the park.

Identify whether the bird's life cycle is more like the turtle or frog life cycle.

____

Explain what stage of the life cycle the bird is likely to enter next.

____

____

Explain why it is necessary for birds to lay eggs.

____

____

____

____

Pretest: Organisms and Their Environments

Read each question. Circle the letter of the correct answer.

1. This tree is growing in a bent shape.

   What caused this tree to grow this way?

   A. all trees of this type are bent

   B. strong winds caused it to bend

   C. too much water caused it to bend

   D. too much sunlight caused it to bend

2. Which trait did a mouse most likely learn?

   A. It has big ears.

   B. It lives in a field.

   C. It can complete a maze.

   D. It eats plants and meat.

3. Why do some animals live in groups?

   A. They cannot fly.

   B. They like having friends.

   C. It is easier to hide in a large group.

   D. More animals mean more protection.

4. A toucan is a bird that lives in a tropical rain forest. Which change would affect the toucan population the most?

   A. A tree is cut down.

   B. There is no rain for a week.

   C. A fire burns down the rain forest.

   D. A piece of trash is thrown onto the forest ground.

5. The two lizards shown in the picture live in different environments.

How are their environments most likely different?

A. The color is different.

B. The amount of food is different.

C. The amount of rain is different.

D. The number of hours of light is different.

6. Where would an animal with large ears and thin fur most likely live?

A. desert

B. stream

C. underground

D. cold, snowy area

7. A forest catches fire. What do animals in the forest do?

A. change their diet to eat burned trees

B. hide in the burning forest to stay safe

C. live in the burned area until a new forest grows

D. escape the fire to find new homes in other places

8. Which of these is an example of group behavior?

A. birds build nests

B. rabbits dig holes

C. squirrels collect nuts

D. swans fly to warmer areas in winter

9. The picture shows a flowering plant.

A Flowering Plant

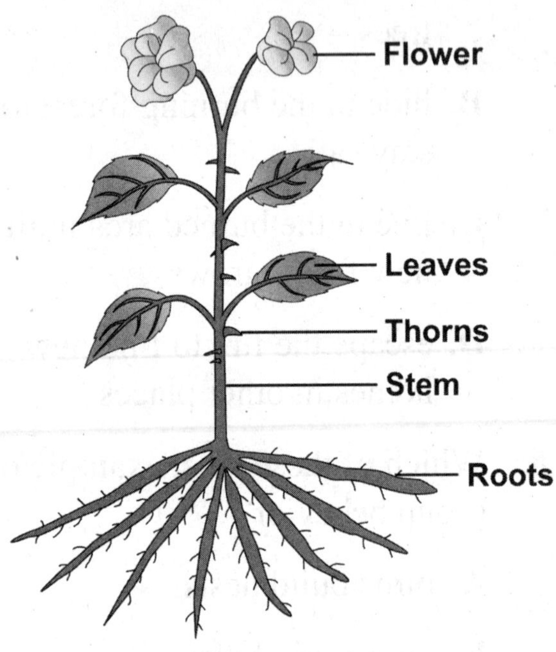

Which adaptation keeps the plant from being eaten?

A. stem

B. roots

C. thorns

D. flower

10. Which adaptation allows a cactus to live in the desert?

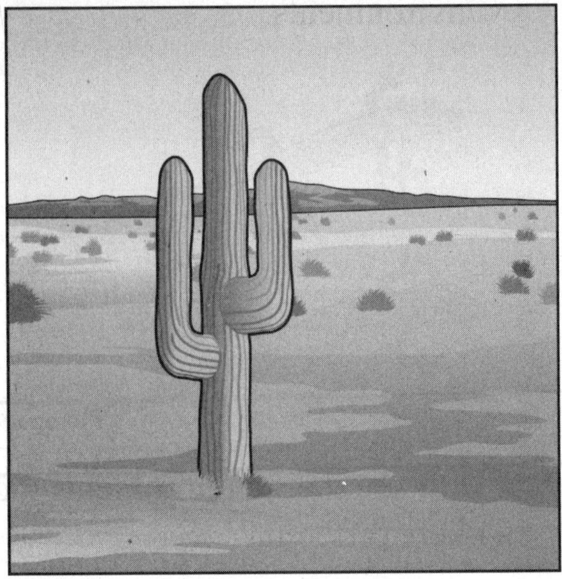

A. large stems that store water

B. tall limbs that reach the sunlight

C. large leaves that capture the rainfall

D. green tissue that blends into the environment

Quiz: How Does the Environment Affect Traits?

Read each question. Circle the letter of the correct answer.

1. This reptile changes color each day.

   In the morning when the weather is cool, it turns dark brown. When it is hot out, the reptile turns light brown. What type of a trait is the reptile color?

   A. It is an environmental trait that is learned.

   B. It is an environmental trait that is not inherited.

   C. It is an inherited trait that changes with the environment.

   D. It is an inherited trait that does not change with the environment.

2. Which spider trait is due to the environment?

   A. It eats insects.

   B. It has a broken leg.

   C. It spins a web.

   D. It has a black body.

3. Which of these plant traits is due to the environment?

   A. It has thorns.

   B. It has a hard stem.

   C. It has red flowers.

   D. It has a missing branch.

© Houghton Mifflin Harcourt Publishing Company

4. Some goldfish live in a lake. Some goldfish live in a fishbowl.

Why is there a size difference between the goldfish in the lake and the goldfish in the bowl?

A. The lake hides the growing goldfish.

B. The lake has other fish chasing the goldfish.

C. The fishbowl limits the goldfish from growing large.

D. The fishbowl is the better environment for the goldfish.

5. The picture shows the same plant in two different years. The chemicals added to the soil each year were different.

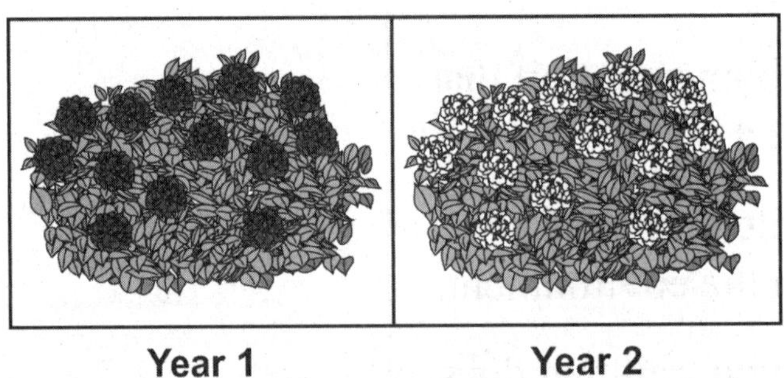

How did the plant change?

A. The environment changed the color of the flowers.

B. The environment changed the type of the plant.

C. The plant inherited different-colored flowers.

D. The plant inherited different chemicals.

Read each statement. Write your answer on the lines.

6. The pictures show an Arctic fox at different times of the year.

Explain how the environment changes the Arctic fox.

____

____

____

____

7. A cardinal is a red bird that eats berries and seeds that contain a special chemical. When a cardinal eats foods with that chemical its feathers get very bright. Cardinals that eat only food without the chemical have dull red feathers.

Explain how the color of the cardinal is an inherited trait.

Explain how the color of the cardinal is a trait linked to the environment.

____

____

____

____

Quiz: What Are Adaptations?

Read each question. Circle the letter of the correct answer.

1. Look at the bird beak in the picture.

   Which activity does a beak like this help a bird do?

   A. eat fruit

   B. tear meat

   C. crack nuts

   D. chew grass

2. A hedgehog is a small mammal with many spines. What is most likely the reason for the spines?

   A. to eat its food

   B. to find a new home

   C. to attack its enemies

   D. to scare predators away

3. Snakes are predators that catch their food by surprise. Which snake is most likely able to catch its food by surprise?

   A. a yellow corn snake on grass

   B. a brown snake on white desert sand

   C. a green snake on a leafy tree branch

   D. a red and black king snake on a white rock

4. A skunk can spray a foul smelling liquid. Why would a skunk spray a barking dog?

   A. to scare away the dog

   B. to alert other skunks to danger

   C. to become friends with the dog

   D. to help the dog blend into the area

5. A bat lives in a cave. Which of these helps a bat find insects in the cave?

   A. white fur

   B. large ears

   C. small nose

   D. short tongue

Read each statement. Write your answer on the lines.

6. A wolf walks near a possum and a turtle. The possum plays dead. The turtle hides in its shell.

Describe how playing dead helps the possum.

____

____

Describe how hiding in its shell helps the turtle.

____

____

7. Animals have body parts that help them live in a habitat. List two ways that desert rabbits and arctic rabbits might be different.

____

____

____

____

Quiz: How Can Organisms Succeed in Their Environments?

Read each question. Circle the letter of the correct answer.

1. The security camera shown in the figure is placed in a store to take digital pictures. The images are sent by phone line to a computer in the security office for processing and storage. The dashed line in the diagram represents the information being sent through the phone line.

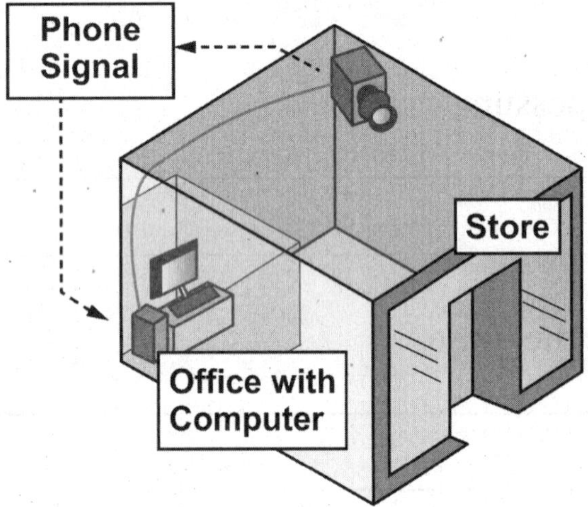

Which organ serves the same purpose in the human body that the phone line serves in the security system?

A. brain

B. eyes

C. nose

D. nerves

2. Which set of organs most helps people know if something is cold?

A. brain and skin

B. heart and tongue

C. nose and muscles

D. eyes and stomach

3. Children are playing near a fence. The fence blocks the view, but they know that food is cooking on the other side.

Which sense lets them know this?

A. hearing

B. smell

C. taste

D. touch

4. A Venus flytrap has hairs that can sense when an insect lands on its leaves. How is this different from the sense of touch in animals?

  A. Animals do not have hairs that can sense things.

  B. Most animals do not use their sense of touch to catch food.

  C. The Venus flytrap does not have a brain to process the information.

  D. Animals also use sensory hairs to taste the food but the Venus flytrap does not.

5. Rasheed accidentally bumped his leg on a desk. What is the first thing that happened within Rasheed's nervous system?

  A. He yelled, "Ow!"

  B. The nerves in his leg sensed pain.

  C. The leg nerves sent a message to the brain.

  D. The brain sent a message to the skin in his leg.

Read each statement. Write your answer on the lines.

6. Animals use their senses for defense. Explain how animals use two of their senses to help defend themselves.

____

____

____

____

7. Tamra is the goalie for her soccer team. The goalie blocks the ball from going into the net. She uses her brain, eyes, nerves, and muscles to play the sport. Explain how these four parts of her nervous system work together to coordinate Tamra's muscle movements as she tries to block the ball.

____

____

____

____

Quiz: Engineer It • What Happens when Environments Change?

Read each question. Circle the letter of the correct answer.

1. A landslide may happen if too much rain falls on a mountainside. Which living things would not survive a large landslide?

   A. fish

   B. birds

   C. worms

   D. plants

2. Buffalo eat grass. The grass in one area burned. What most likely will happen to the buffalo?

   A. There will be fewer buffalo.

   B. There will be more buffalo.

   C. The number of buffalo will stay the same.

   D. The buffalo will learn to eat something else.

3. Jill has a flower garden. She added nutrients to the soil. What most likely will happen?

   A. The soil will be poisoned.

   B. The plants will grow bigger.

   C. The soil will get more water.

   D. The plants will stop growing.

4. A group of people camp in the woods. Which activity would be harmful to organisms living in the woods?

   A. using a rowboat in the river

   B. leaving the area exactly as they found it

   C. cutting down a tree to burn in a campfire

   D. keeping trash off the land and away from the river

5. A population of insects lives in a meadow. The insect can only eat plant P. What will happen if people remove plant P?

A. The insect will die out.

B. The plant will grow taller.

C. The plant population will die out.

D. The insect population will grow larger.

Read each statement. Write your answer on the lines.

6. What are two ways that a flood can harm animals?

____

____

____

____

7. A blizzard is a big snowstorm. What does a blizzard do to living things?

____

____

____

____

Unit Test: Organisms and Their Environments

Read each question. Circle the letter of the correct answer.

1. The picture shows some plants and animals.

   Which nonliving factor most likely controls where the plants in this environment live?

   A. air

   B. birds

   C. shade

   D. soil

2. After a volcano erupts, the temperature in the area increases because of the extremely hot lava. How does the lava affect plants?

   A. All of the nearby plants are destroyed.

   B. The plants move to a different habitat.

   C. The volcanoes release oxygen, and the plants grow better than before.

   D. The heat causes the plants to release their seeds, and many new plants grow right away.

3. Some animals travel together. What is most likely the reason they do this.

   A. They are friends.

   B. They work together to hunt.

   C. They work together to grow food.

   D. They move in so that they blend in with the land.

4. A katydid is a type of plant-eating insect. Most of these insects are green, but a few are pink. What is the most likely reason for this?

   A. Pink katydids have an advantage because they look like flowers.

   B. Green katydids have an advantage because they can sneak up on their prey.

   C. Green katydids have an advantage because they blend in with their environment.

   D. Pink katydids have an advantage because they are more attractive to their mates.

5. The picture shows an Antarctic Ocean food chain.

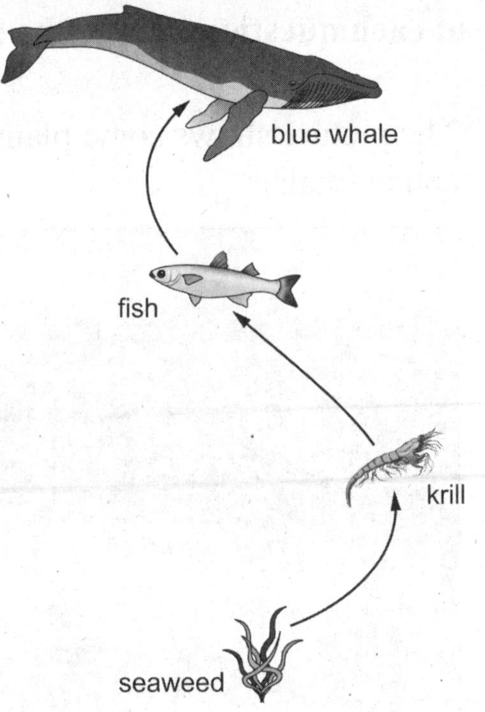

The krill depend on having winter sea ice for reproduction. When the water temperatures are too warm, the krill do not produce as much. Which effect could this have on the other organisms in the food chain?

   A. The seaweed would stop growing.

   B. The fish population would increase.

   C. The whale population would increase.

   D. The fish and whale populations would decrease.

6. The picture shows two of the same type of bird.

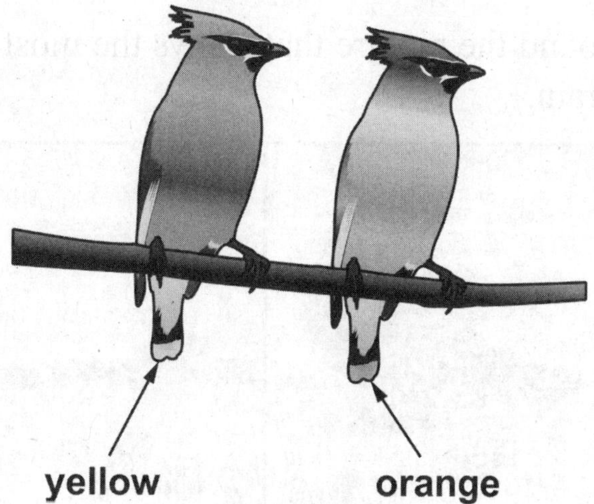

How do you think the environment affected these birds?

Circle the letter of the correct answer.

A. One bird gets more water than the other.

B. One bird eats more food than the other.

C. One bird eats different colored berries than the other.

D. One bird lives where it is hot, and the other lives where it is cold.

Read each question. Follow the instructions to answer the questions.

7. Which characteristics help an animal survive, and which help an animal find a mate?

Write the letter of each characteristic in the table.

Advantage for Surviving	Advantage for Attracting a Mate

A. is very good at hiding

B. has pretty colored feathers

C. sings a loud, beautiful song

D. runs faster than others in its group

8. The pictures show a pond over a four-year period.

Draw a circle around the picture that shows the most change to the habitat due to a lack of rain.

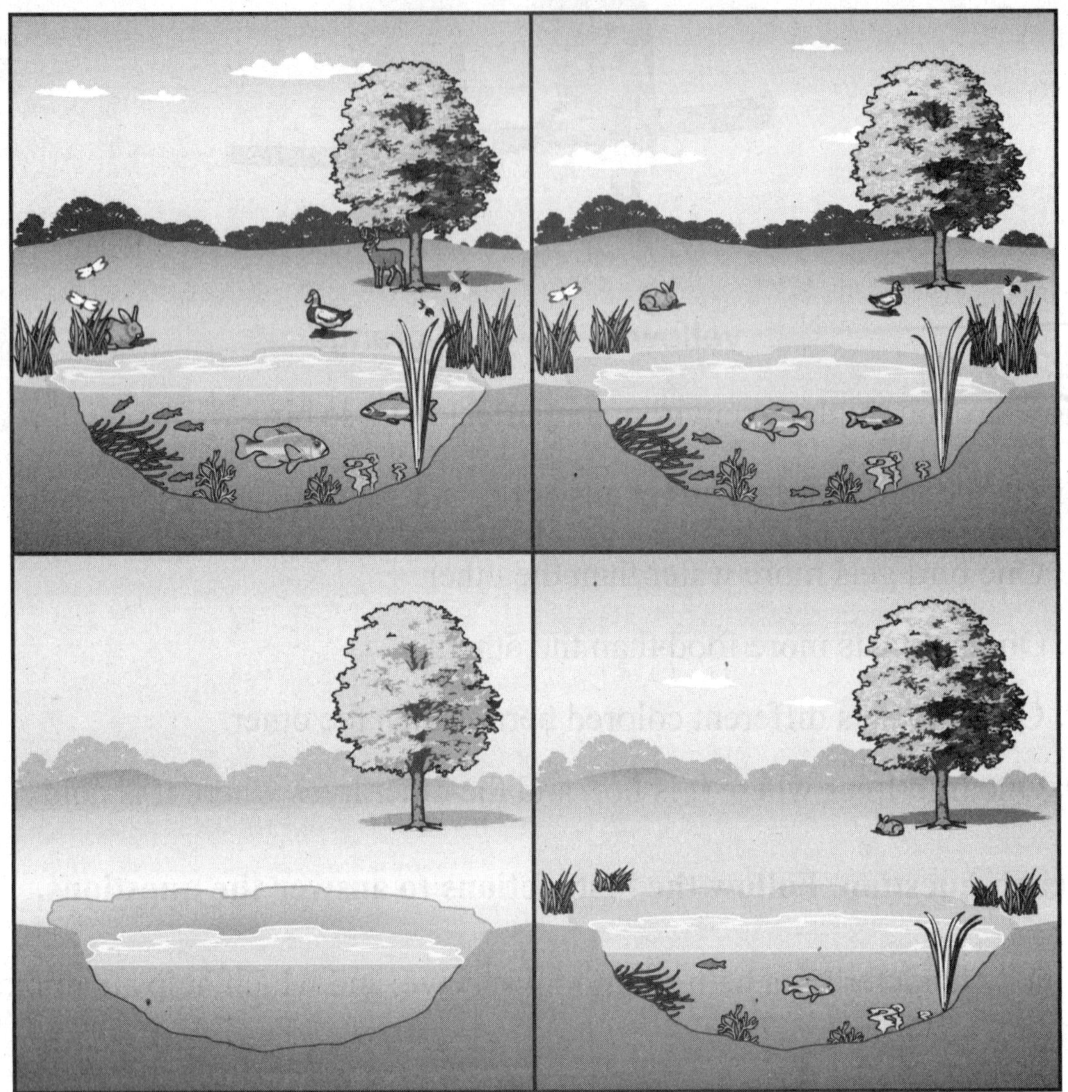

© Houghton Mifflin Harcourt Publishing Company

9. Noah is studying different types of bears. He writes his data in a table.

Type of bear	Florida black bear	Polar bear
Habitat	forest with warm, humid climate	Arctic with sea and ice
Fur	thick and smooth	thick, dense, water repellent
Special features	shed their underfur during the summer months hibernate for a short time during the winter	thick layer of black skin to keep warm in the water paws have back claws for gripping

Write one letter in each blank to correctly complete the sentences. Some letters will not be used.

Polar bears are more likely to survive in a __________ environment. Their claws help them __________. Black bears can live in a __________ environment.

A. warmer	**C.** climb trees	**E.** cold, harsh
B. cool off	**D.** grip the ice	

© Houghton Mifflin Harcourt Publishing Company

10. Animals live in groups for many reasons. Match the cause-and-effect relationships.

Write the letters of the effects in the correct boxes next to the causes.

Sperm whales travel in large pods.		**A.**	More infants reach adulthood.
Antelope travel together to have more eyes looking for predators.		**C.**	A lion sneaks through the grass stalking its prey.

Read each question. Write your answer on the lines.

11. The skin of an octopus changes as it moves over different surfaces of the ocean floor.

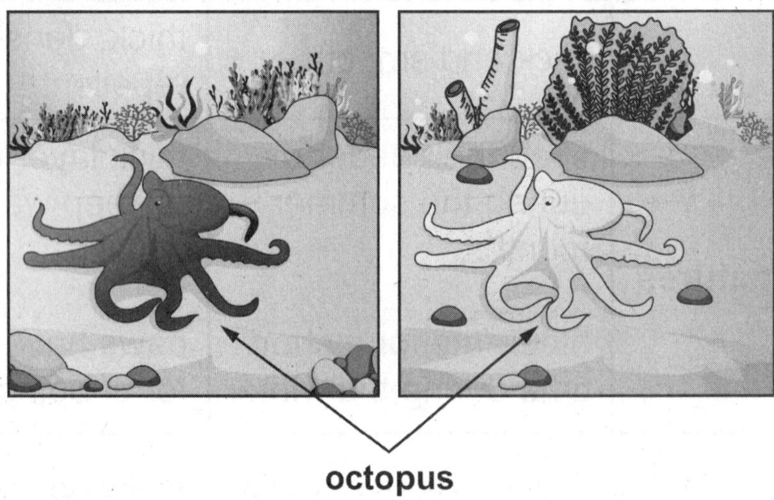

How did the octopus change?

____

How did this change help the octopus from predators?

____

____

What might happen if the octopus could not change?

____

Directions: Read the passage, then answer the questions that follow.

Different Roots

Plants have roots and leaves that help them survive in their environment. Plants have either a taproot or fibrous roots. A taproot has one central larger root and many smaller roots that come out from it. Fibrous roots are all about the same length and size.

Plants that have small leaves or needles do not lose much water to the air. Plants that have large leaves can capture more sunlight, but loose more water.

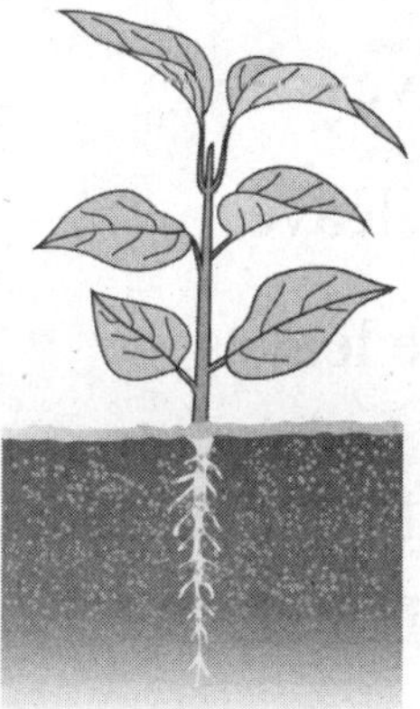

This plant has a taproot. It gets most of its water from deep underground.

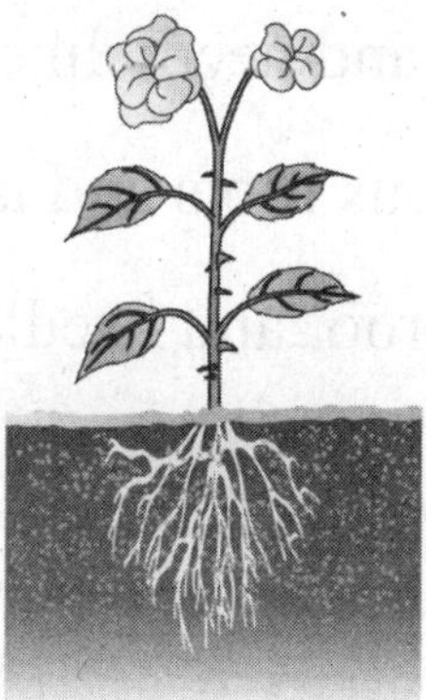

This plant has fibrous roots. It gets its water both from near the surface and deep underground.

This plant has fibrous roots that mostly get water from near the surface.

12. How could moving a plant to a warm, wet environment change a plant?

Circle the letter of the 2 correct sentences.

A. The roots will stop growing.

B. The plant will lose all its leaves.

C. The plant's leaves will become larger.

D. Its roots will spread more on the surface.

E. The plant will grow needles instead of leaves.

13. Look at the pictures. Describe how a plant will look after a long period without rain. Write your answer on the lines.

____

____

14. Which plant would be most likely to survive in a desert environment?

Circle the letter of the correct answer.

A. a plant with short fibrous roots and large leaves

B. a plant with a short taproot and needlelike leaves

C. a plant with very long, fibrous roots and large leaves

D. a plant with a very long taproot and needlelike leaves

15. Jan's farm has grass with fibrous roots her cows like to eat. Jan is worried because the weather is getting hotter and there isn't much rain.

Read each statement. Write your answer on the lines.

Explain how the change in rain and temperature could affect the grass.

____

____

Explain how that would affect the cows.

____

____

Describe a solution that might solve Jan's problem.

____

____

Pretest: Fossils

Read each question. Circle the letter of the correct answer.

1. What is a dinosaur?

   A. a plant that is extinct

   B. an animal that lives in the ocean

   C. an animal that gives birth to live young

   D. an animal that lived on Earth millions of years ago

2. What does the word *extinct* mean?

   A. found in a fossil

   B. made of soft body parts

   C. no longer living anywhere

   D. buried in clay, sand, or mud

3. What can scientists study to learn the most about animals that are extinct?

   A. fossils

   B. erosion

   C. ecosystems

   D. living things

4. The picture shows a mastodon fossil.

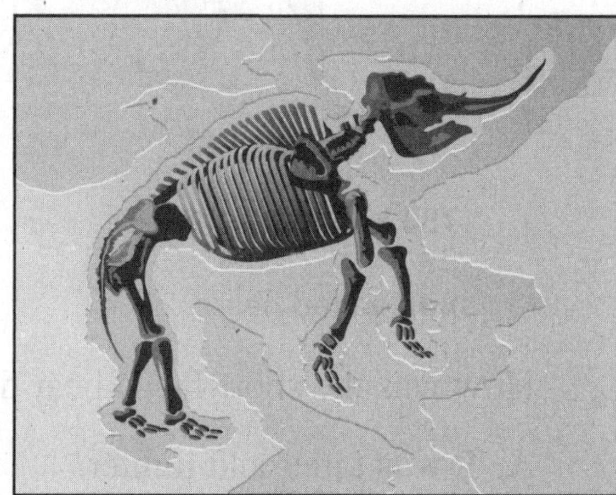

   Which of these animals is most likely related to the mastodon?

   A. pig

   B. bear

   C. tiger

   D. elephant

5. The picture shows a fossil of a short-faced bear next to a living grizzly bear.

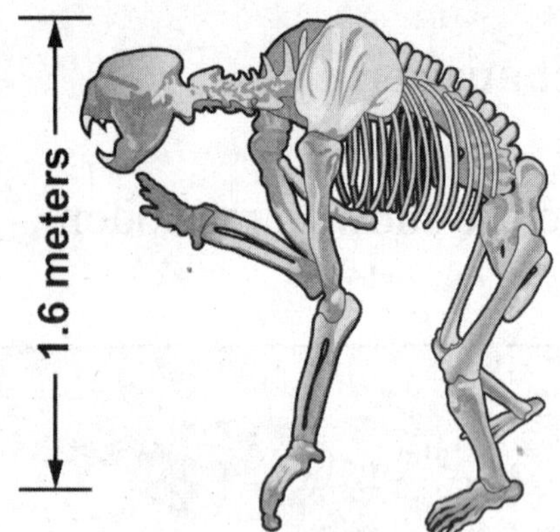

How was the short-faced bear different from the grizzly bear?

A. It was taller and lighter.

B. It was taller and heavier.

C. It was shorter and lighter.

D. It was shorter and heavier.

6. The picture shows a woolly mammoth fossil.

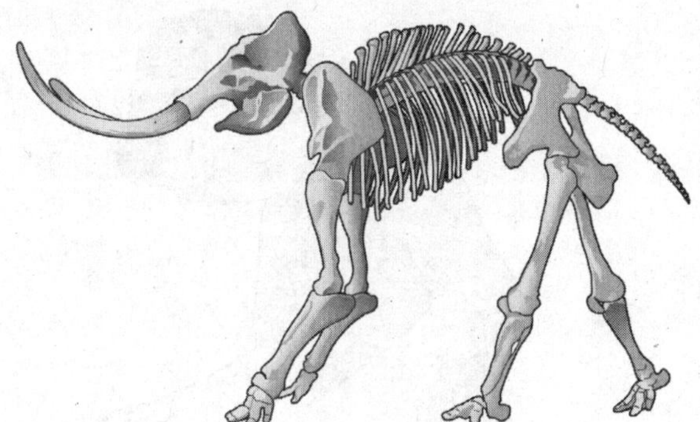

Where did the woolly mammoth most likely live?

A. sea

B. trees

C. grassland

D. underground

7. The picture shows a fossil.

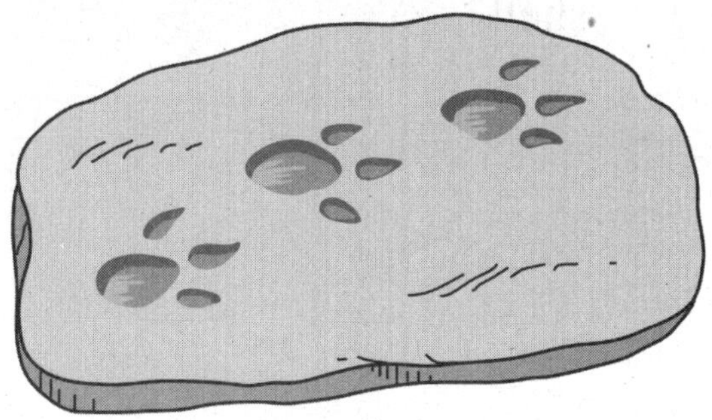

Which of these could be learned by studying this fossil?

A. what the animal ate

B. how the animal walked

C. how old the animal was

D. what color the animal was

8. Sandy is studying the fossils of dinosaurs. She makes this graph.

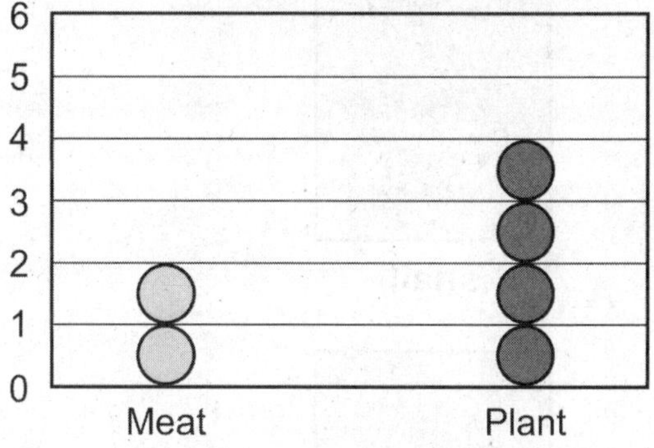

How is Sandy sorting the dinosaurs?

A. by what they ate

B. by where they lived

C. by how they walked

D. by how big they were

9. A scientist is studying an extinct bird. Which fossil would best help him learn more about the bird?

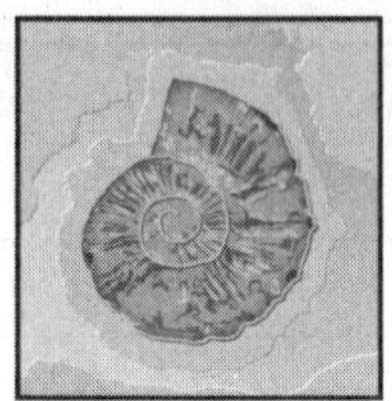

A. snail

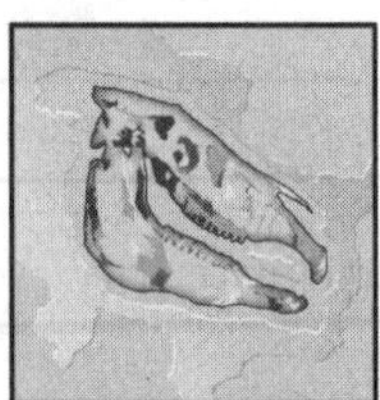

B. horse skull

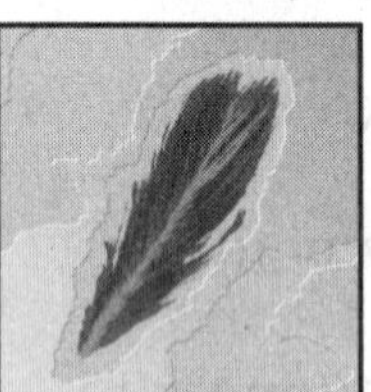

C. feather

D. dinosaur skull

10. This girl is making a model fossil by pressing a shell into clay.

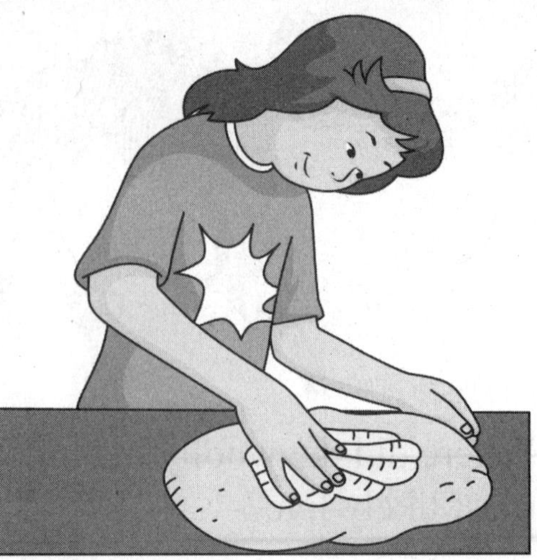

What should she do next?

A. fill the shell with glue

B. take the shell out of the clay

C. observe the imprint in the clay

D. add more clay on top of the shell

© Houghton Mifflin Harcourt Publishing Company

Quiz: What Is a Fossil?

Read each question. Circle the letter of the correct answer.

1. Which fossil shows an animal that is extinct?

A.   **camel**

B.   **dinosaur**

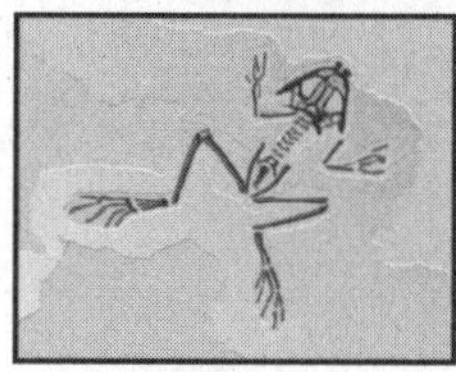

C.   **frog**

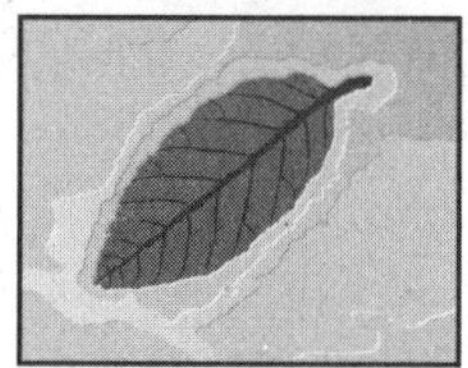

D.   **tree**

2. Which part of an animal is most likely to become a fossil?

A. fur

B. skin

C. teeth

D. heart

3. Which of these happens first when a fossil forms?

A. A living thing dies and is buried by mud.

B. The soft parts of a living thing break down.

C. The hard parts of a living thing turn to rock.

D. Erosion wears away rock around the living thing.

4. Which statement is true about fossils?

A. Fossils form very quickly.

B. Fossils are made from only animals.

C. Fossils are made from only the soft parts of animals.

D. Fossils can show what once-living things looked like.

5. The picture shows a fossil.

Which animal made the fossil?

A. fish

B. snake

C. insect

D. reptile

Read each statement. Write your answer on the lines.

6. The pictures show fossils, a living plant, and a living animal.

   Which pictures are of fossils? Explain.

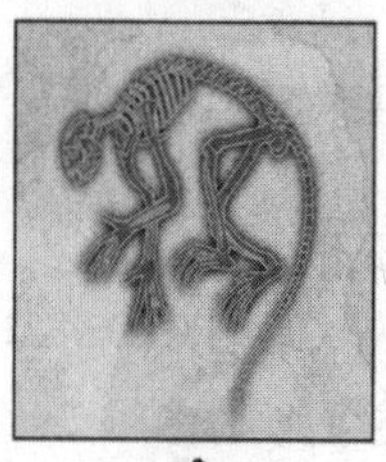

____

____

____

7. Some parts of animals are frequently found as fossils, while other body parts are only rarely found as fossils. Explain why this is true.

____

____

____

Quiz: What Do Fossils Tell Us About the Past?

Read each question. Circle the letter of the correct answer.

1. What might a scientist learn from a dinosaur fossil?

   A. what year the dinosaur was born

   B. what things the dinosaur ate when it was living

   C. what things the dinosaur saw when it was living

   D. what the dinosaur thought about when it was living

2. Kyle found a rock with a fossil shaped like a clam shell. Which conclusion can Kyle make from the find?

   A. Clams are now extinct.

   B. Clams used to live on land.

   C. The rock formed underwater.

   D. The rock was eaten by a clam.

3. Fossils of woolly mammoths and saber-toothed cats have been found in the same rock layer. Which conclusion can be made from these fossils?

   A. Both animals lived in caves.

   B. Both animals lived to be very old.

   C. These types of animals lived in large groups.

   D. These types of animals lived at the same time in history.

4. A scientist visits an area. She finds a flat rock covered with fossils. She lists things she can learn from the fossils.

   1. the current weather
   2. the color of the animals' fur
   3. the plants that lived in the area
   4. the animals that lived in the area

   Which numbers should she remove from the list?

   A. 1 and 2 only

   B. 2 and 3 only

   C. 1, 3, and 4

   D. 2, 3, and 4

© Houghton Mifflin Harcourt Publishing Company

5. Scientists found many large-animal fossils in one area. The table shows what they found.

Number of Fossils Found

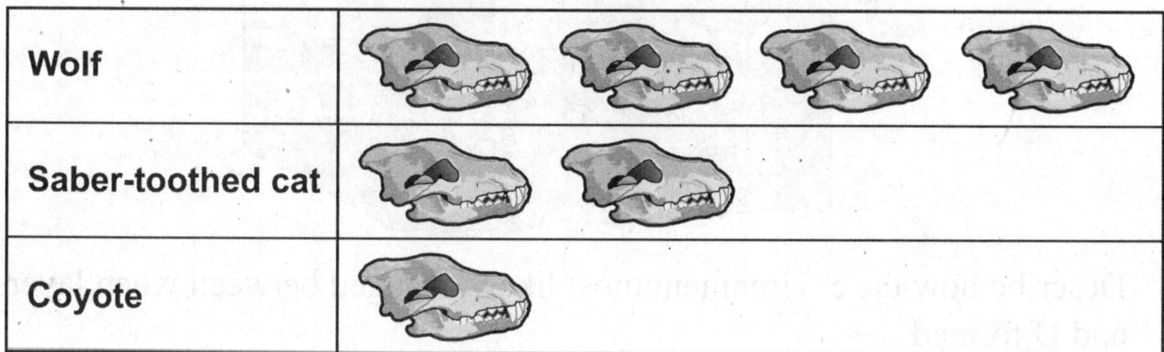

How many of each fossil type did the scientists find?

Choose the correct answer.

A. 1 wolf; 4 saber-toothed cats; 2 coyotes

B. 1 wolf; 2 saber-toothed cats; 4 coyotes

C. 2 wolves; 4 saber-toothed cats; 1 coyote

D. 4 wolves; 2 saber-toothed cats; 1 coyote

Read each statement. Write your answer on the lines.

6. Scientists found many plant fossils in one area. The area is now a desert. Write a conclusion about how the area changed.

____

____

____

____

© Houghton Mifflin Harcourt Publishing Company

7. The picture shows some fossils found in different layers of rock.

Describe how the environment most likely changed between when layers C and D formed.

____

____

____

____

____

Unit Test: Fossils

Read each question. Circle the letter of the correct answer.

1. A scientist compares a megalodon tooth to a great white shark tooth.

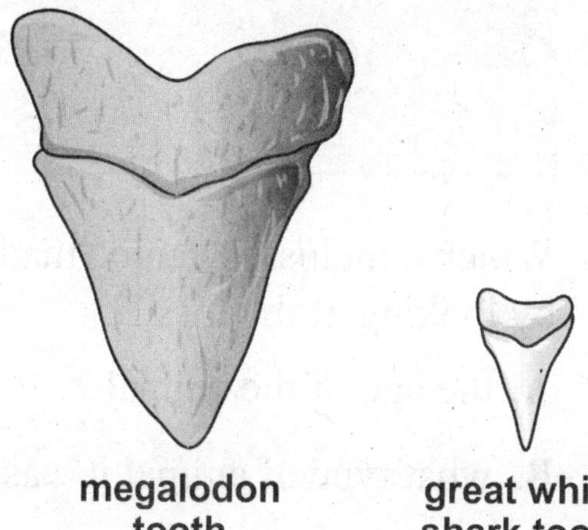

   Which conclusion can she make from studying the different teeth?

   A. The megalodon and great white shark both only ate plants.

   B. The megalodon was bigger than the great white shark.

   C. The megalodon ate meat, but the great white shark did not.

   D. The megalodon was smaller than the great white shark.

2. Which is not a way that fossils are formed?

   A. An organism is frozen in ice.

   B. An organism is trapped in amber.

   C. An organism is covered in hot lava.

   D. An organism is buried in sediments.

3. The picture shows a fish fossil next to a quarter. Quarters are about 24 millimeters wide.

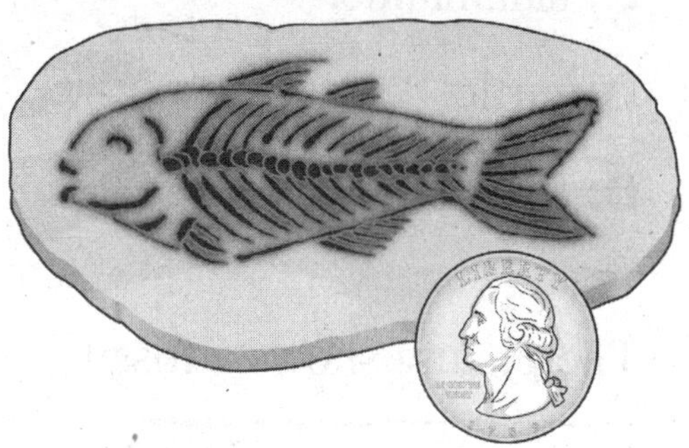

   About how big was the fish?

   A. 8 millimeters

   B. 24 millimeters

   C. 72 millimeters

   D. 96 millimeters

4. A paleontologist was studying different fossils found at a digging site.

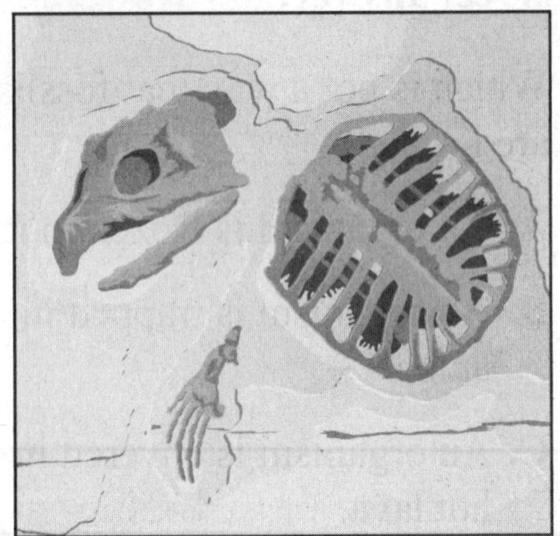

Which modern-day animal do these fossils look most like?

A. fish

B. snail

C. salamander

D. turtle

D. 96 millimeters

5. The picture shows a fossil.

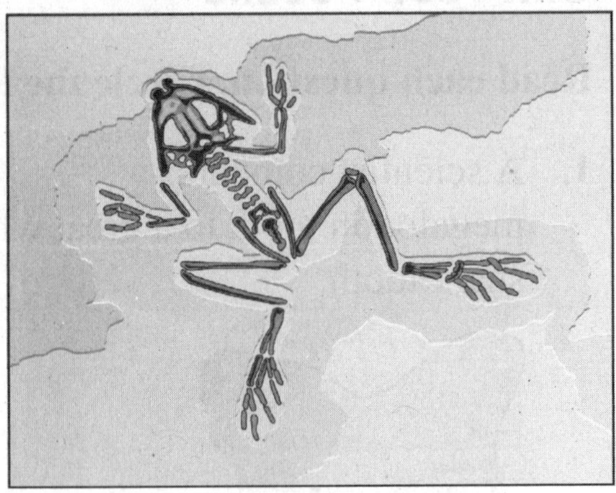

Which conclusion can be made by looking at the fossil?

A. the age of the animal

B. what type of animal it was

C. the color of the animal's skin

D. what kind of sounds the animal made

6. The picture shows a fossil.

Which sentences describe the picture?
Circle the letter of all the true statements.

A. This animal had a tail.

B. This kind of animal is alive today.

C. The animal that makes this fossil is now extinct.

D. This animal lived on Earth millions of years ago.

Read each question. Follow the instructions to answer the questions.

7. The diagram shows that fossils of different types of organisms can be found in different layers of rock.

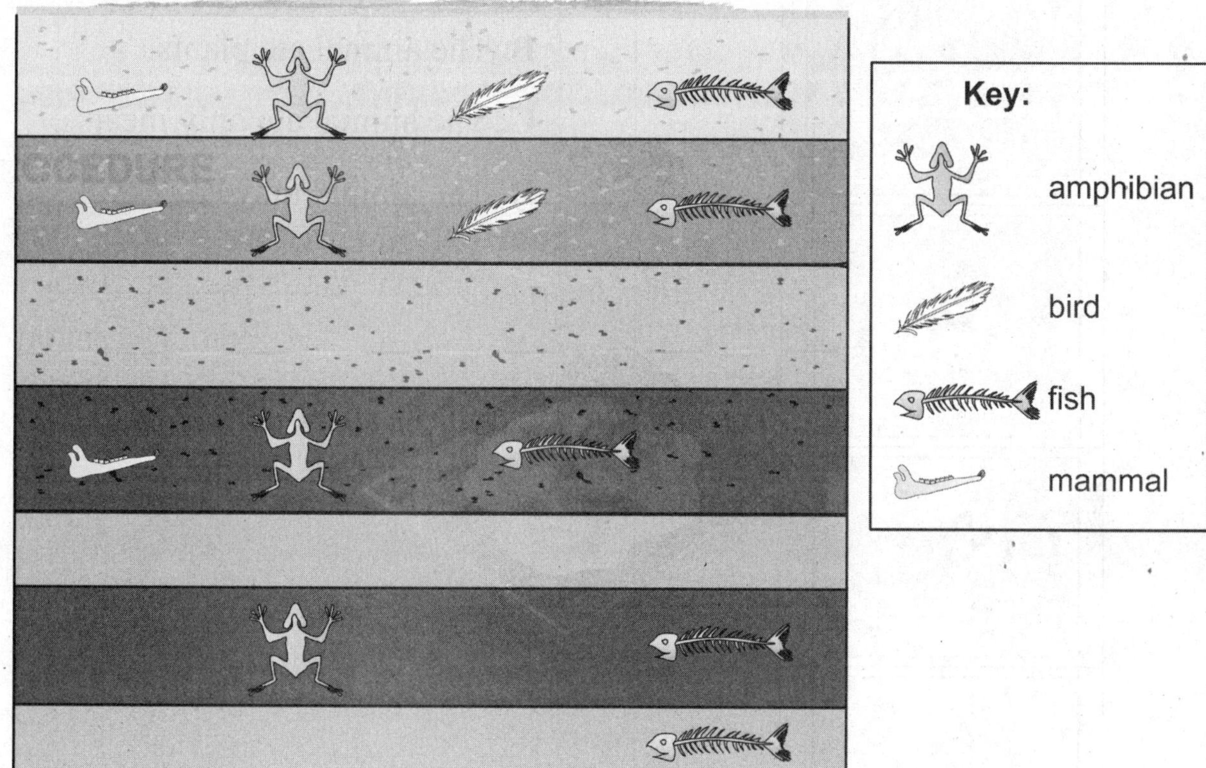

Draw a circle around the type of organism that has been found on Earth for the longest time period.

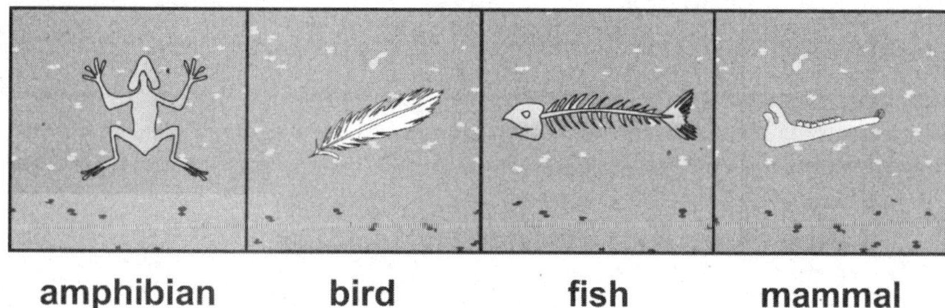

8. The pictures show different fossils. What can be learned about each fossil?

Write the letters of the descriptions in the boxes next to the correct pictures.

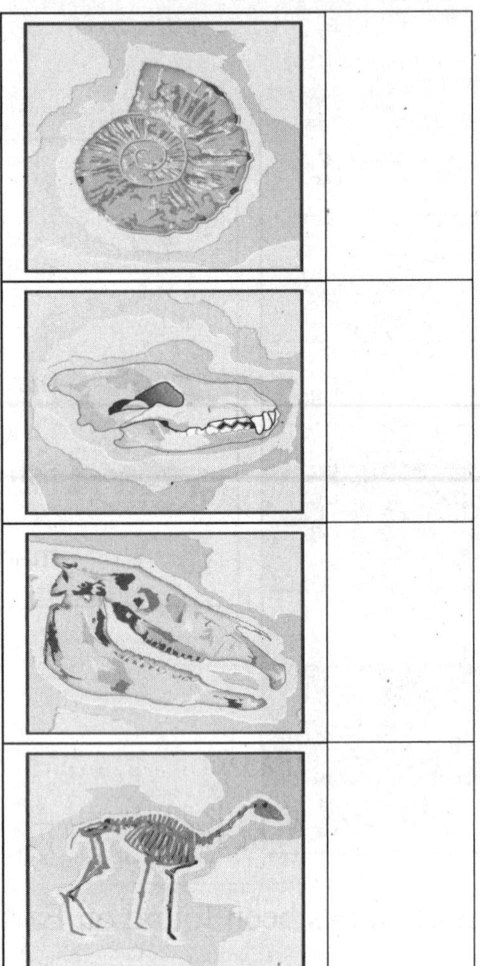

A. The animal had a tail.

B. The animal ate plants.

C. The animal ate only meat.

D. The animal may have lived in water.

© Houghton Mifflin Harcourt Publishing Company

9. A scientist was studying trace fossils. Match the trace fossil to the animal that most likely formed it.

Write one letter of the type animal in the box next to the trace fossil it formed.

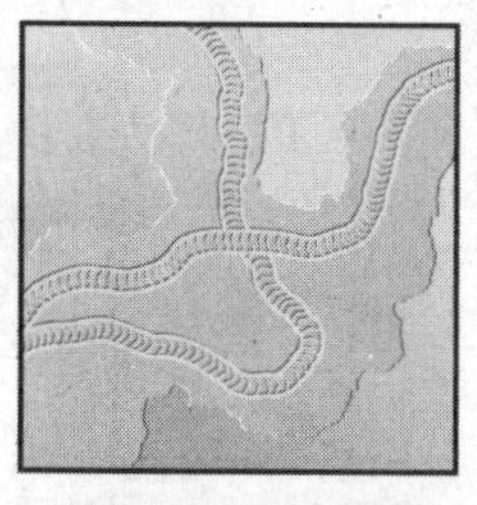

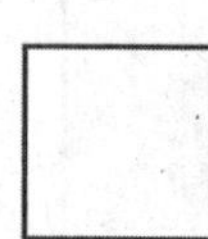

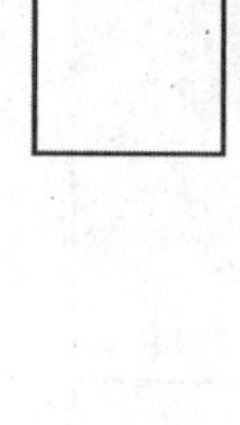

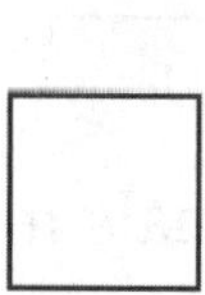

A. a starfish

B. a slug or snail

C. a four-legged land animal

10. Cara was taking a nature hike and found several items. She recorded what she found in her science journal.

Draw a circle around each drawing in Cara's journal that is a fossil.

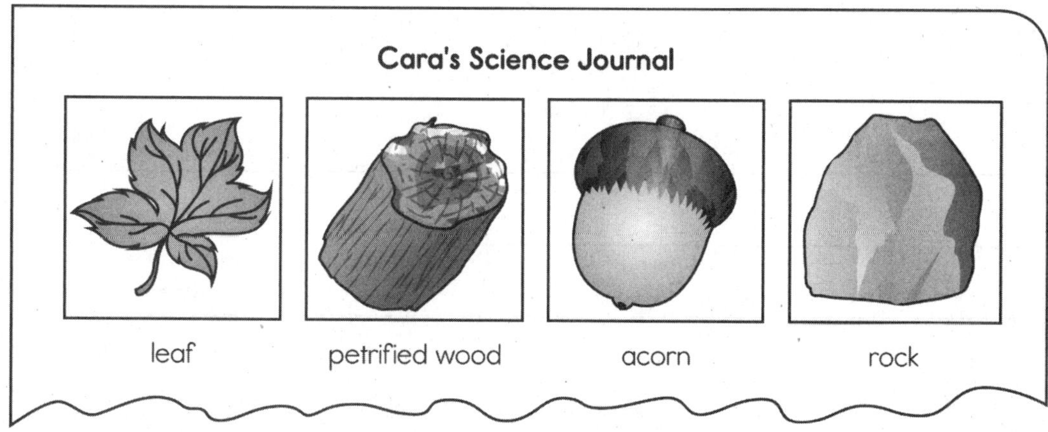

Read each statement. Write your answer on the lines.

11. Scientists found three fossils in an area that is now a forest.

Fossils Found in Area 1

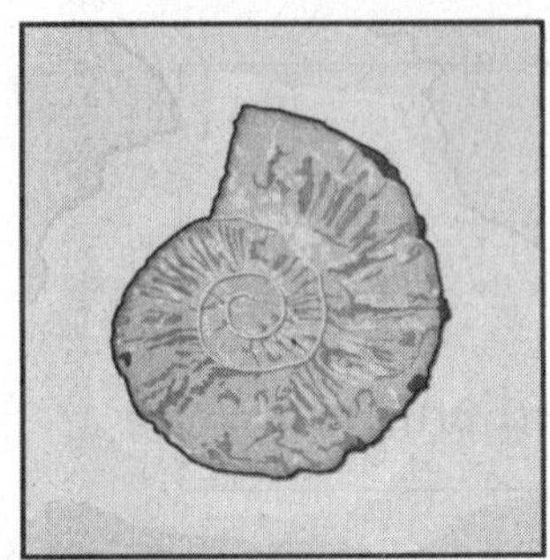

Fossil A

Fossil B

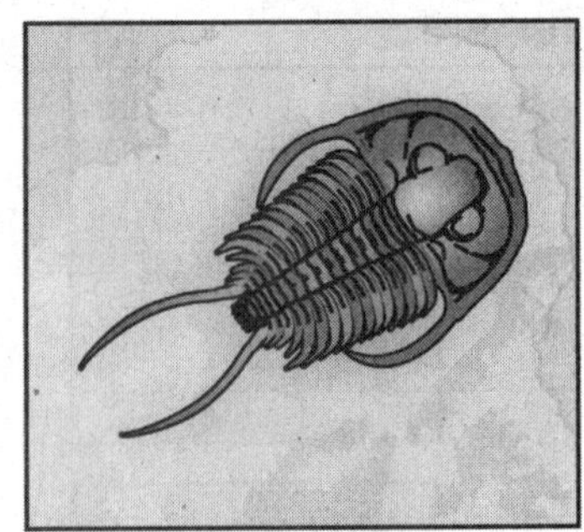

Fossil C

Identify in which type of environment the animals most likely lived.

____

Explain a likely reason why all three fossils were found in the same layer of rock.

____

____

____

____

Describe how the environment changed from the time these animals lived to today.

____

____

____

____

Directions: Read the passage, then answer the questions that follow.

Digging for Fossils

Jane is digging for fossils. The diagram shows the fossils she found in different rock layers.

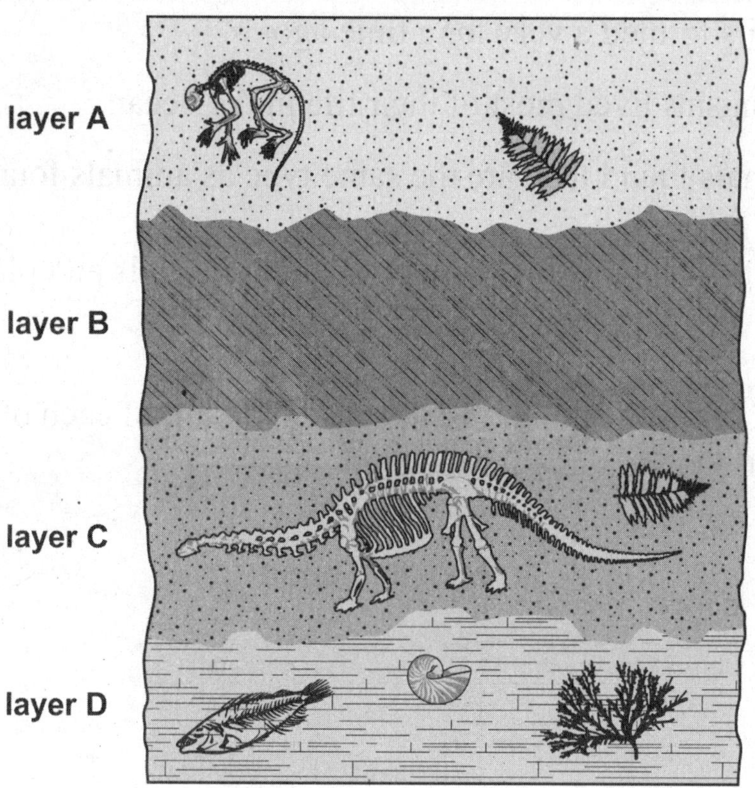

12. Which type of organism Jane found was present on Earth for the longest time period?

Choose the correct answer.

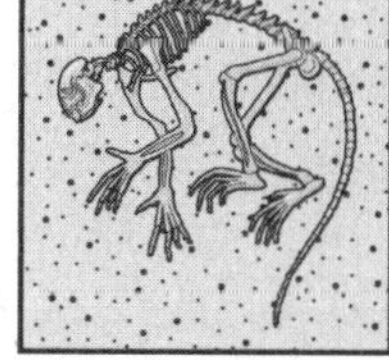

A.

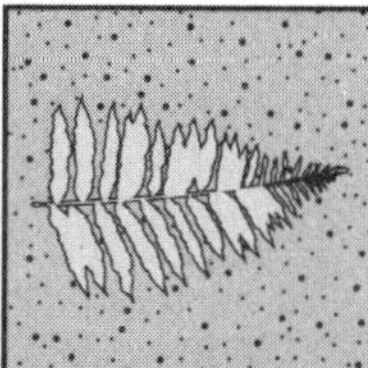

B.

C.

D.

© Houghton Mifflin Harcourt Publishing Company

13. Which statements describe the fossils in layer C?

Circle the letters of the 2 correct answers.

A. One was a very large land animal.

B. The fossils formed in the last few years.

C. The fossils formed a very long time ago.

D. The organisms lived most of their life in the ocean.

E. The animals found then are the same type as animals found today.

14. Use your pencil to show the number of animal fossils and plant fossils Jane found.

Draw one X for each animal fossil, stacked on top of each other to show the total number. Do the same for the plant fossils.

Fossils Found

animal   plant
Type of fossil

15. The fossils Jane finds indicate how Earth has changed over millions of years.

Read each statement. Write your answer on the lines.

Describe the environment of layer D millions of years ago.

____

____

____

____

Explain why Jane will find the oldest fossils in layer D.

____

____

____

____

Explain why most animals in layers C and D are no longer found on Earth.

____

____

____

____

Pretest: Weather and Patterns

Read each question. Circle the letter of the correct answer.

1. Which sentence best describes a flood?

   A. It does not rain for a long time.

   B. Earth wears down and breaks apart.

   C. A fire makes space for new plant growth.

   D. A large amount of water covers normally dry land.

2. Which climate is most likely to be hot and wet?

   A. polar

   B. tropical

   C. temperate

   D. mid-continental

3. Which of these describes *climate* best?

   A. number of floods in a year

   B. amount of rain in one month

   C. type of weather over many years

   D. where an area is located on Earth

4. This house was designed to reduce the impact of a certain type of weather hazard.

   Which type of weather hazard is this house designed for?

   A. flooding

   B. blizzards

   C. tornadoes

   D. ice storms

5. Which tool measures precipitation?

   A. wind vane

   B. rain gauge

   C. anemometer

   D. thermometer

6. What causes a drought?

   A. hot weather

   B. moving water

   C. less rainfall than normal

   D. more rainfall than normal

7. Which word describes dangerous weather?

   A. severe

   B. snowy

   C. strong

   D. sunny

8. Which weather describes a blizzard?

   A. strong wind and lots of rain

   B. strong wind and lots of snow

   C. light rain and cold temperatures

   D. light snow and mild temperatures

9. Isaiah made a graph of the average low temperature in his city every other month. The temperatures are in degrees Fahrenheit, °F.

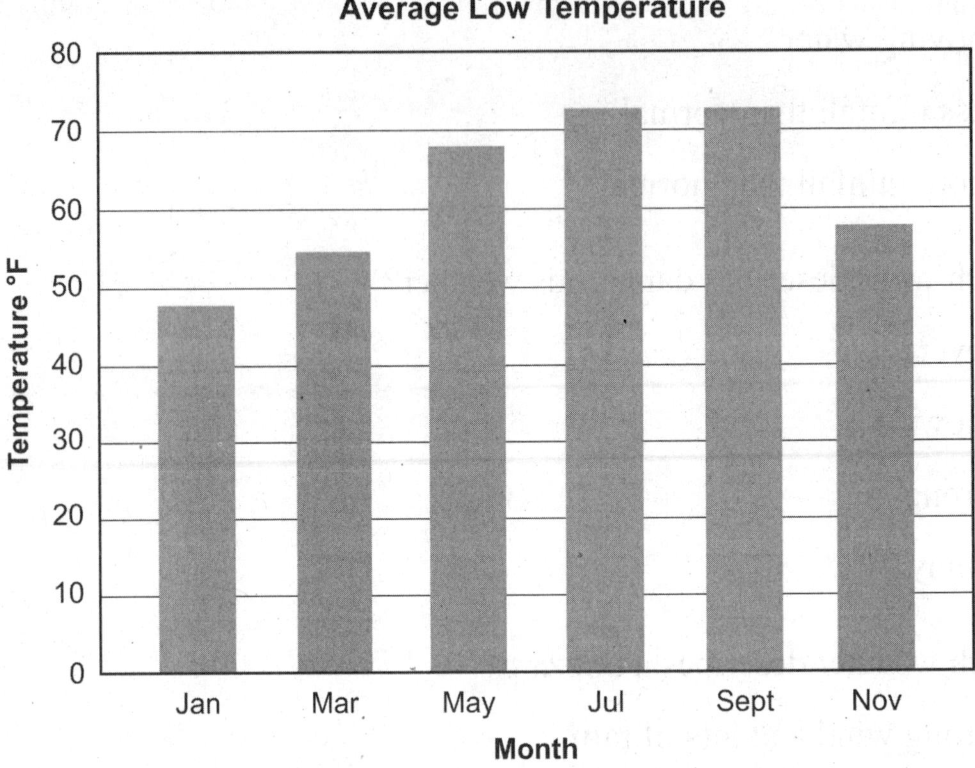

Which low temperature is most likely for a day in January?

A. 46 °F

B. 56 °F

C. 65 °F

D. 72 °F

10. The picture shows weather over a mountain range.

Which kind of weather is happening?

A. dry

B. fair

C. sunny

D. rainy

Quiz: How Is Weather Measured?

Read each question. Circle the letter of the correct answer.

1. Four tools that measure weather are shown.

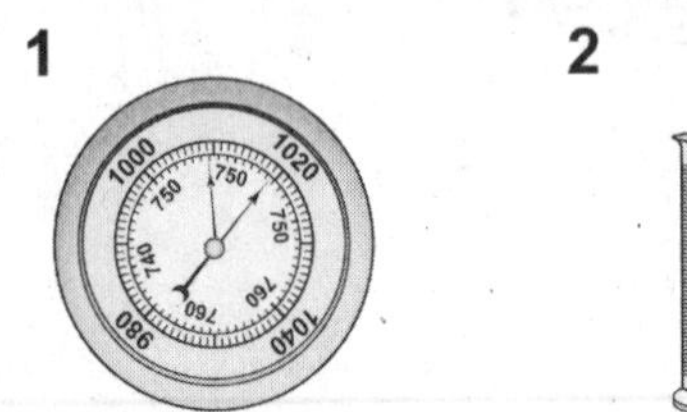
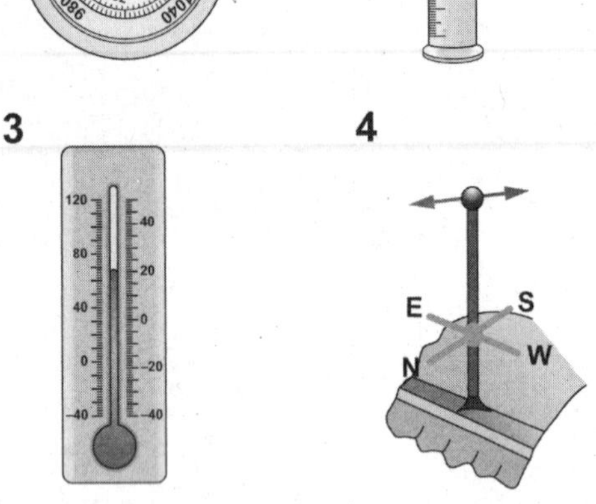

Which tool measures wind direction?

A. 1

B. 2

C. 3

D. 4

2. Which weather instrument is used to measure air temperature?

A. rain gauge

B. anemometer

C. thermometer

D. weathervane

3. The temperature in Mainville has been 0 °C for a week. Precipitation is expected soon. What type of weather is likely to happen in Mainville?

A. snow and sleet

B. high winds and rain

C. some wind and sunshine

D. warmer temperatures and tornadoes

4. A section of a thermometer is shown.

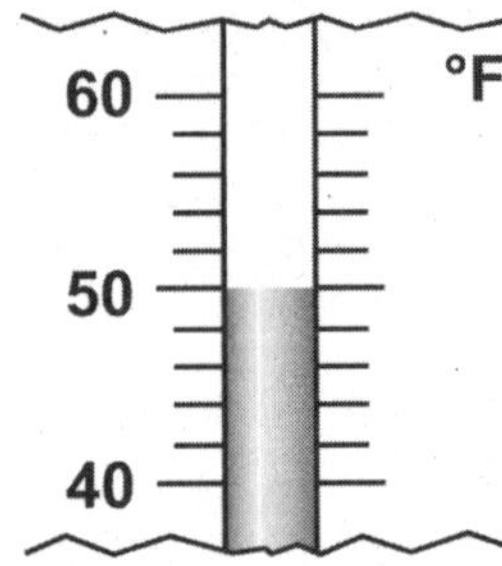

What does this instrument show about the weather?

A. There is 50 feet of snow.

B. The temperature is 50 °F.

C. There is 50 centimeters of rain.

D. The wind speed is 50 miles per hour.

5. The picture shows boys playing outside.

What is the weather like in this picture?

A. windy and hot

B. rainy and cold

C. snowy and cold

D. sunny and warm

Read each statement. Write your answer on the lines.

6. Jen made a graph of the rain that collected in her rain gauge.

Identify how much more rain fell each hour. Include units in the answer.

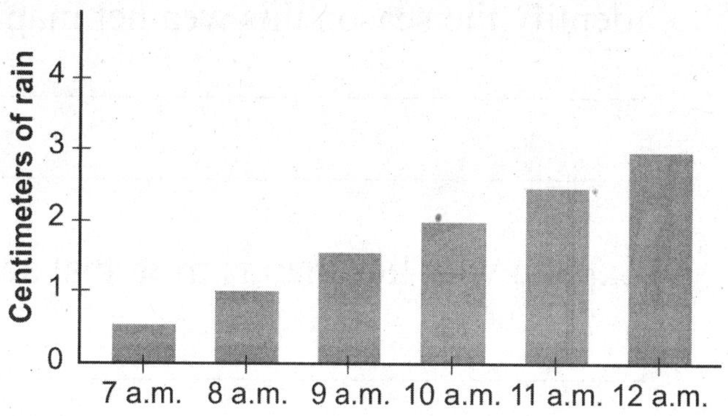

____

____

____

____

7. A weather map for the United States is shown. It shows the high and low temperatures for the day in degrees Fahrenheit, °F.

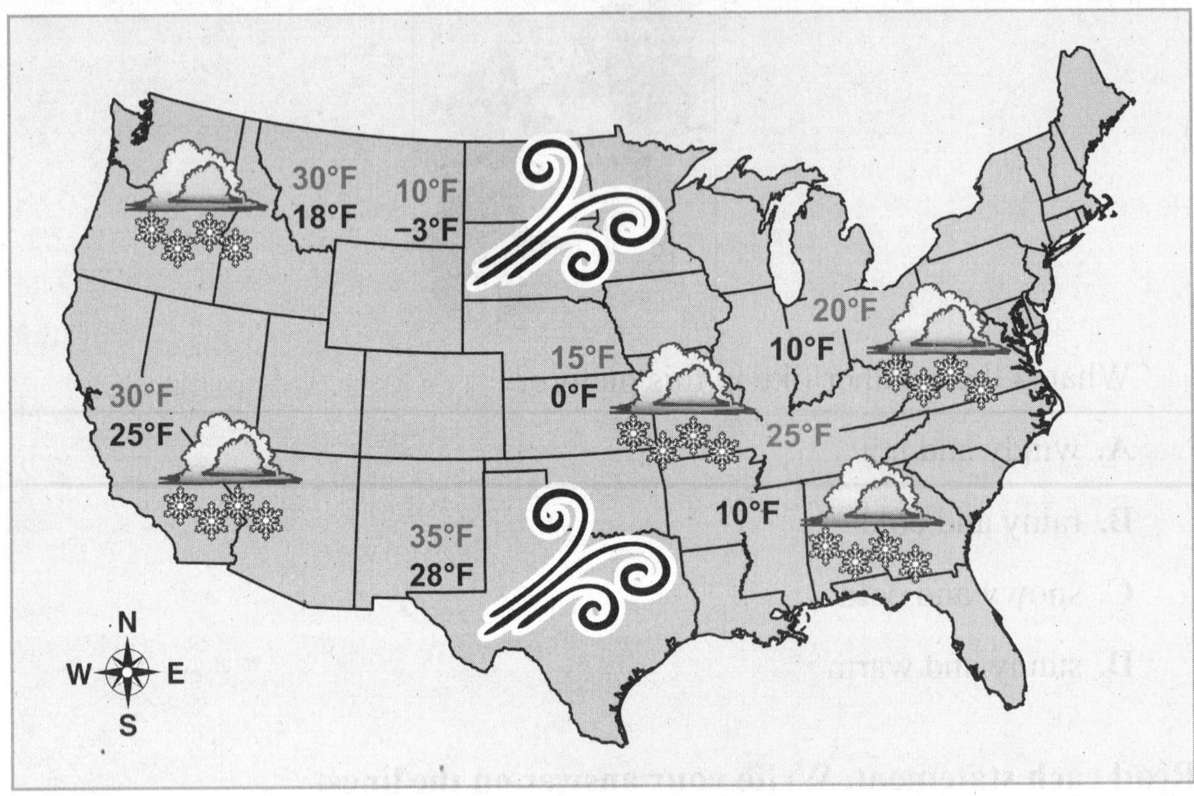

Identify the season this weather map is most likely from.

____

____

Explain why this map is from that season.

____

____

____

Quiz: How Can We Predict Weather?

Read each question. Circle the letter of the correct answer.

1. This table shows the average temperature for four months in one town. The temperature is given in degrees Fahrenheit, °F.

Average Temperature (°F)

February	May	September	December
35	65	70	37

Which conclusion matches the data?

A. May has the coldest average temperature.

B. December has the coldest average temperature.

C. February has the warmest average temperature.

D. September has the warmest average temperature.

2. This table shows weather data for three days in degrees Fahrenheit, °F.

Asheville's Weather

January 1		January 2		January 3	
High	Low	High	Low	High	Low
57 °F	39 °F	53 °F	37 °F	49 °F	35 °F

How did the weather change from January 1 to January 3?

A. It became drier.

B. It became cooler.

C. It became hotter.

D. It became wetter.

3. Tandi recorded the number of sunny days each season for five years.

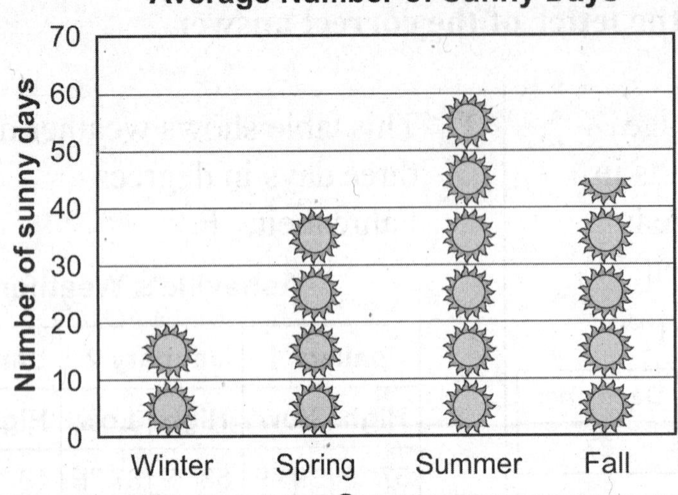

Which season has the fewest sunny days?

A. winter

B. spring

C. summer

D. fall

4. Shalani observed the weather for five days and made this table.

Weather Observations

Day	Monday	Tuesday	Wednesday	Thursday	Friday
Weather	cloudy	rainy	sunny	cloudy	rainy

Which conclusion matches the table?

A. On Saturday, the weather will be rainy.

B. It was sunny on more days than it was cloudy.

C. The weather on Sunday must have been cloudy.

D. On days when it rained, the day before was cloudy.

5. Alejandro observed the weather for five days and made a table. He measured temperature in degrees Fahrenheit, °F.

Weather Observations

Day	Monday	Tuesday	Wednesday	Thursday	Friday
Weather	rain	sunny	mostly cloudy	rain	snow
Temperature (°F)	36	40	38	34	30

Which observation is shown in the table?

A. It was coldest during sunny weather.

B. The temperature was the same on the two rainy days.

C. The temperature was lower on the days that it rained.

D. The temperature increased each day from Monday through Friday.

Read each statement. Write your answer on the lines.

6. Deepak hears a rumble of thunder and sees dark clouds in the sky. Describe what kind of weather is likely to happen next.

____

____

____

____

7. The graph shows the average rainfall for a coastal city for a year.

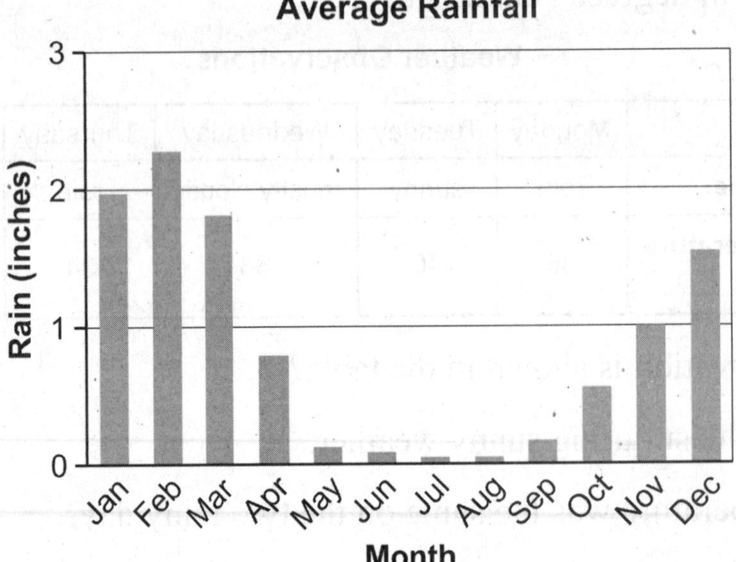

Identify which season the weather is most likely to be rainy.

____

____

Explain the answer.

____

____

Quiz: Engineer It • What Are Some Severe Weather Impacts?

Read each question. Circle the letter of the correct answer.

1. This picture shows weather that is hazardous.

Which part of the weather shown in the picture is most dangerous?

A. cloud

B. lightning

C. rain

D. thunder

2. Which of these should someone do to be safe during a blizzard?

A. go outdoors

B. stay indoors

C. wear rainwear

D. wear sunglasses

3. This picture shows a symbol for a type of severe weather.

What does this symbol represent?

A. tornado

B. blizzard

C. hurricane

D. thunderstorm

4. This boat is being affected by a severe storm.

Which type of severe storm is shown?

A. tornado

B. drought

C. blizzard

D. hurricane

5. A large area is flooded after a storm. What likely caused the flood?

A. large hail

B. heavy rains

C. low temperatures

D. high temperatures

Read each statement. Write your answer on the lines.

6. Describe four things a family can do to be safe in a flood.

____

____

____

____

7. Meteorologists study the weather.

Explain how meteorologists use technology to predict severe storms such as hurricanes.

____

____

Explain how accurate weather prediction can help save lives.

____

____

Quiz: What Are Some Types of Climates?

Read each question. Circle the letter of the correct answer.

1. The graphs show weather for each season in Capital City. The first graph shows average temperature in degrees Fahrenheit, °F. The second graph shows average precipitation in inches.

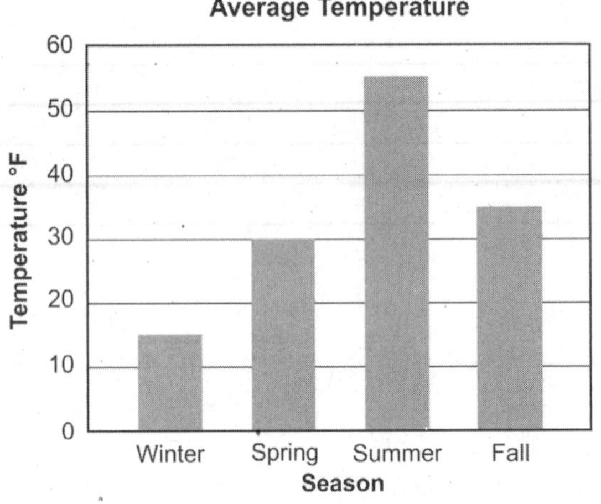

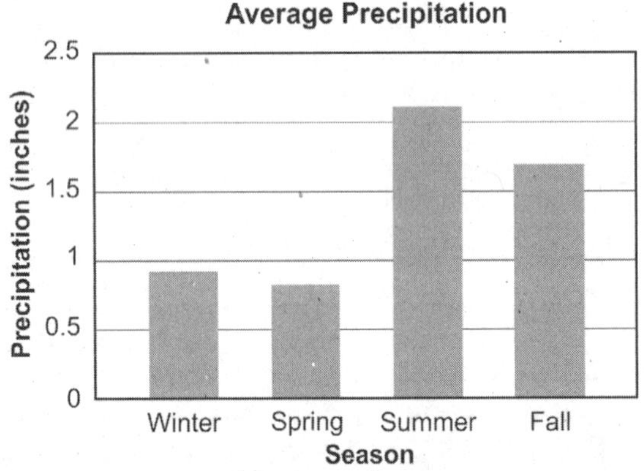

   Which type of climate does Capital City experience?

   A. hot and dry

   B. hot and wet

   C. cold and dry

   D. cold and wet

2. Which weather is most likely in a tropical climate near the equator?

   A. dry and hot

   B. dry and cold

   C. rainy and hot

   D. rainy and cold

3. City 1 is located on the coast. City 2 is not near water. How does the climate of City 1 differ from the climate of City 2 in the summer?

   A. City 1 is drier and colder.

   B. City 1 is wetter and colder.

   C. City 1 is drier and has fewer windy days.

   D. City 1 is wetter and has milder temperatures.

4. The table shows average precipitation in inches for one city for four months.

Average Precipitation (inches)

December	January	February	March
11.6	9.3	9.6	13.4

One year the total precipitation for January and February was less than 1 inch. Which event happened from January to February?

A. flood

B. tornado

C. drought

D. hurricane

5. The table shows the average wind direction and wind speed in miles per hour, mph, for a city.

Average Wind Direction and Speed

Month	January	March	April	June	August	October	December
Wind direction	northwest	northwest	northwest	southeast	southeast	west	northwest
Wind speed (mph)	12	10	12	9	7	9	9

Which month would this city be most likely to have a 7 mph southeast wind?

A. January

B. April

C. August

D. December

Read each statement. Write your answer on the lines.

6. The map shows the three main climate zones on Earth.

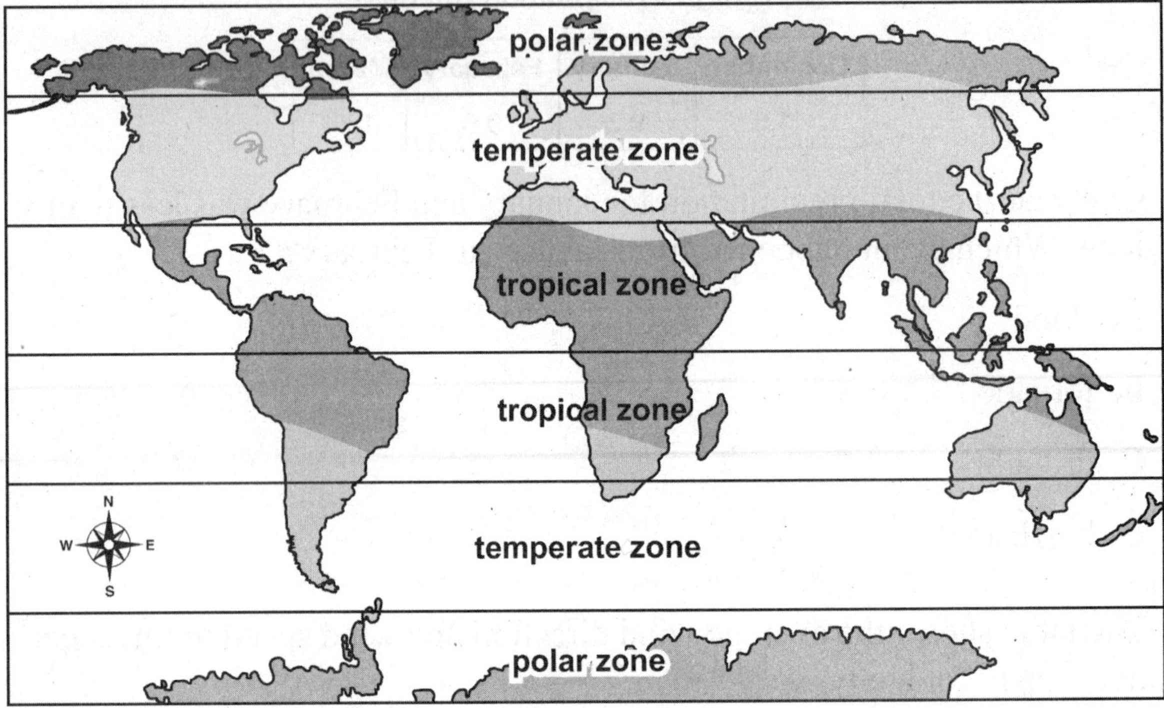

Describe the climate of each of these two zones.

polar

____

____

temperate

____

____

____

7. Dena and Abram recorded the high and low temperatures and the rainfall for a month. Dena's data was very different from Abram's data. Identify one reason that data for the same period of time can be very different.

____

____

____

____

Unit Test: Weather and Patterns

Read each question. Circle the letter of the correct answer.

1. The chart shows the average monthly rain in a county.

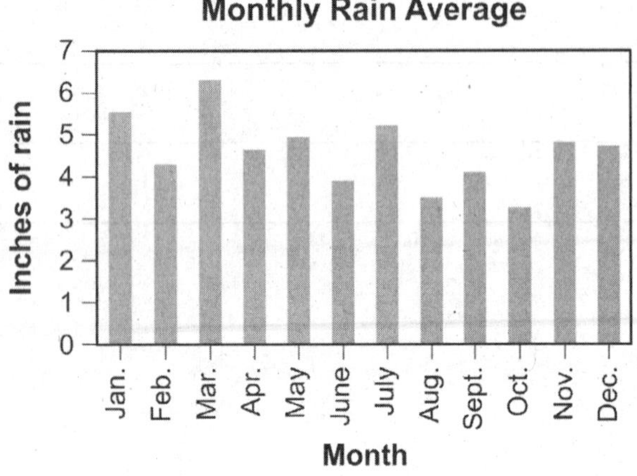

Which month is typically the wettest?

A. August

B. July

C. March

D. September

2. Which type of weather might cause a family to have to leave its home and move away from the ocean?

A. hurricane

B. thunderstorm

C. sunny day

D. winter storm

3. Lofton looked at the weather forecast online. She found this table. The temperature is given in degrees Fahrenheit (°F).

Weather Forecast

Day	Thursday
Weather	
Low night temperature (°F)	28

Which weather conditions are most likely in Lofton's town Thursday night?

A. clear and cool

B. foggy and cold

C. snowing and cold

D. raining and warm

4. The table shows the average daytime temperature and the amount it rained each season in one city. The temperature is given in degrees Fahrenheit (°F). The rainfall is measured in inches (in.).

Seasonal Averages

Season	winter	spring	summer	fall
Average daytime temperature (°F)	54	70	91	70
Rainfall (in.)	4	14	27	9

Which conclusion matches the data?

A. There is more rain during the colder months.

B. There is more rain during the warmer months.

C. It rains more at the beginning of the year.

D. The city gets less than 40 inches of rain a year.

© Houghton Mifflin Harcourt Publishing Company

5. Noah recorded the average rainfall for two different cities.

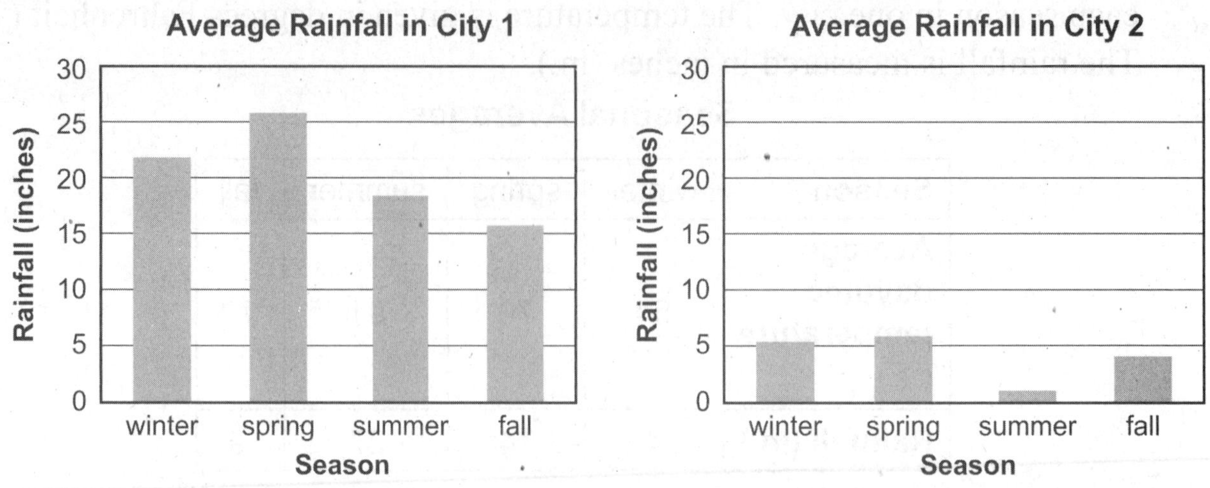

Which prediction can Noah make about next year by looking at his data?

A. It will rain less during the spring in City 1 than during the spring in City 2.

B. It will rain more during the summer in City 2 than during any other season.

C. It will rain the same amount in both cities during the winter months.

D. It will rain more during the spring in City 1 than it will rain all year long in City 2.

Read each question. Follow the instructions to answer the questions.

6. Mrs. Kerry teaches swimming lessons. For the safety of her students she needs to know when there is lightning detected in the area so she can get her students out of the pool safely. In what order do the steps take place that help protect Mrs. Kerry and her students from lightning while swimming?

Number the steps in the correct order from 1 to 4 with 1 being the first step and 4 being the last step.

	Kerry hears the alert.
	Meteorologists study the weather.
	Everyone gets out of the pool safely.
	Meteorologists alert the weather center of lightning in the area and send out an alert.

7. The map shows the climates around the world.

Draw a circle around at one area on the map that includes mostly hot, wet climate.

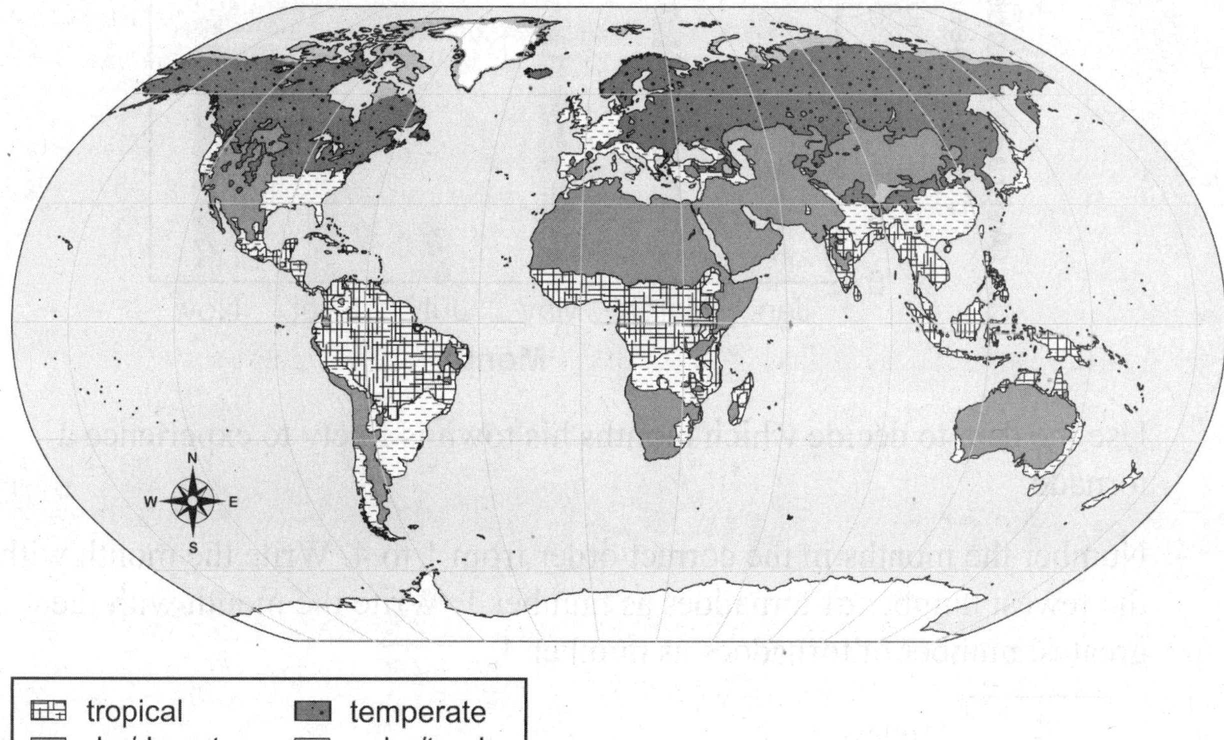

8. There are many weather events that humans need to take steps to be ready for. Match the weather event to how to get prepared.

Write the letter of the weather event in the correct box.

Ashley's family went into an underground shelter for a day.	
Steve wore rubber boots and took an umbrella to school.	
Jason put on a big coat, gloves, a scarf, boots, and a hat to go outside.	

A. tornado

B. snowstorm

C. heavy rain

9. Elton made a chart of the average number of tornadoes in certain state during some months.

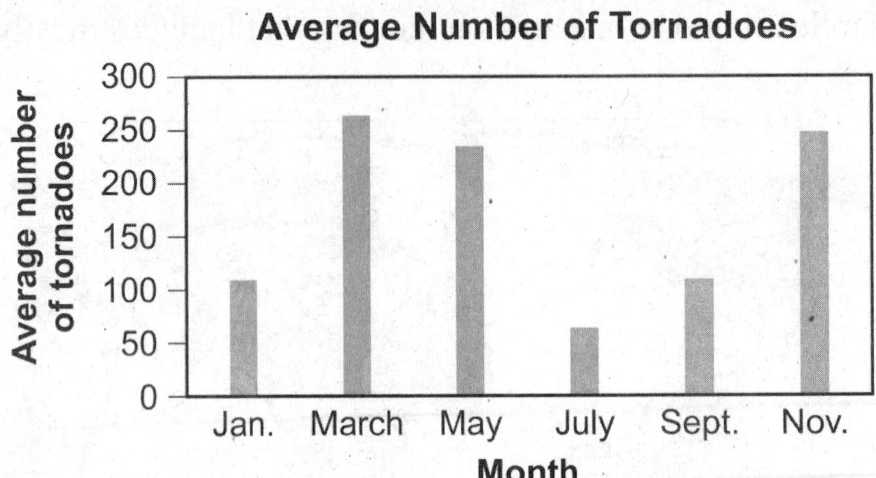

Use the data to decide which months his town is likely to experience a tornado.

Number the months in the correct order from 1 to 4. Write the month with the fewest number of tornadoes as number 1. Write the month with the greatest number of tornadoes as number 4.

	January
	March
	July
	November

10. Ryan is studying Bactrian camels. The camels live in an area that is very hot in the summer. It is very cold in the winter. There is little water in the area. What helps the camel live in this area?

Circle the letter of the correct answer.

A. They grow a thicker coat of hair before summer.

B. They live in a tropical area that is warm and wet.

C. They store fat in their humps to use for energy and water.

Read each statement. Write your answer on the lines.

11. Mary and Frank live in different states. The table shows the typical weather for a week in winter in their states. The high temperature for each location is given in degrees Fahrenheit, °F.

	Monday	Tuesday	Wednesday	Thursday	Friday
Mary	36 °F	40 °F	38 °F	34 °F	30 °F
Frank	68 °F	69 °F	67 °F	65 °F	70 °F

Describe how the climate is different for these two locations.

____

____

____

____

Explain how you used the table to make your conclusion about the climates.

____

____

____

____

Directions: Read the passage, then answer the questions that follow.

Climate of Four Cities

The table shows climate data for four cities. The temperature is given in degrees Fahrenheit, °F.

Climate Data

Location	Average precipitation (inches)	Average low temperature (°F)	Average high temperature (°F)	Description of climate	Common severe weather
City 1	43.8	44	59	wet with warm summers and cold snowy winters	blizzards
City 2	14.8	56	71	year-round moderate-to-warm weather with a dry summer and a winter rainy season	drought
City 3	62.7	61	78	wet with very hot humid summers and mild short winters	tornados
City 4	16.1	46	63	cold snowy winter and hot dry summer	severe thunderstorms

12. Which city has the most desert-like climate?

Circle the letter of the correct answer.

A. City 1

B. City 2

C. City 3

D. City 4

13. Which of these cities will most likely have the highest average temperature next year?

Circle the letter of the correct answer.

A. City 1

B. City 2

C. City 3

D. City 4

14. The different cities in the passage have different types of severe weather. Match the letter of the technology to the city that it will help.

Write each letter in the correct box.

City	Technology
City 1	
City 2	
City 3	
City 4	

A. lightning rods

B. tornado sirens

C. irrigation systems

D. roofs that hold heavy snow

15. City 3 is next to a large river and gets large amounts of rain. People use water gauges to help provide a warning of when the water levels are getting too high. A water gauge is a tool that measures the height of water in a river or lake.

Describe a common hazard people are worried about.

____

Explain how this type of hazard can affect people near the river.

____

____

____

Explain how a water gauge would meet people's needs in this type of hazard.

____

____

____

____

Push Me, Pull You

Task 1: Magnetic Personality

The student will use magnets to investigate balanced and unbalanced forces.

Performance Expectations and 3D Learning:

3-PS2-1 Plan and conduct an investigation to provide evidence of the effects of balanced and unbalanced forces on the motion of an object.

3-PS2-2 Make observations and/or measurements of an object's motion to provide evidence that a pattern can be used to predict future motion.

3-PS2-3 Ask questions to determine cause-and-effect relationships of electric or magnetic interactions between two objects not in contact with each other.

3-PS2-4 Define a simple design problem that can be solved by applying scientific ideas about magnets.

Additional SEP.3-5.C.1 and **C.2** Planning and Carrying Out Investigations

Safety:

- Use caution when handling the wooden sticks, bamboo skewers.
- Remove sharp tips of bamboo skewers before providing to students.
- Instruct students to use materials only as directed.
- Instruct students to use caution when using sharp tools, such as the bamboo skewers.
- Instruct students to wash their hands thoroughly after the investigation.

Tip **Preparation Quick Tips:**

- Use bamboo skewers for the wooden sticks.
- Prepare the magnet stand in advance for less dexterous or less patient students or groups.
- Substituting string for the yarn or twine is not advised; the friction of the yarn or twine helps keep the ring magnet from swinging too fast or too long for students to count.
- Students may notice that if they keep their bar magnets too close to the magnet stand that they cause unintended motion of the hanging magnet.
- Organize and group materials in advance so as to allow for a smooth transition between the end of one class and the start of the next.

Options for Project-Based Learning:

- Students can plan their own investigation with the magnets before starting their lessons on forces.
- Students can give, receive, and use feedback on their answers to the guiding questions in the task.

Time Rating:

1 = less time; 4 = more time
Teacher Prep: 1
Student Prep: 1
Student Cleanup: 1
Time on Task: 45 min

Materials:

For each group
- 2 magnets, bar
- 1 magnet, ring
- masking tape, 1 ft
- pencil
- 6 rubber bands, small
- 1 stopwatch
- 6 wooden sticks, 12 in.
- yarn or twine, 10 in.

For each student
- pencil

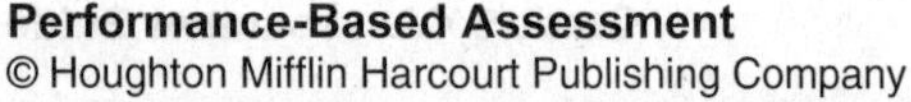

Task 1 – Procedure Answers:

4. a second magnet, one of the bar magnets

8. 6

10. What happens when I put the north poles of the bar magnets together? How close do I have to put the bar magnet to the ring magnet before it moves away?

12. Answers will vary but show that the student used the like poles to repel the magnets. Recorded observations should resemble the sample data table shown.

Data Table

Answers will vary but should show that the number of swings is the same or similar for a low, medium, and high height. Recorded observations should resemble the sample data table shown.

Data Table

Height	Number of swings in 5 seconds
Low	6
Medium	6
High	6

Task 1 – Summary Answers:

1. balanced

Task 1 Performance Rubric

Rating Scale

3 Outstanding	1 Needs Improvement
2 Satisfactory	0 Did Not Demonstrate Skill

Teacher Directions:
This rubric allows for performance observation of 10 students. Make copies as needed. If students are working in groups, record the group name.

Group Name ___________

Names of Students

Skills										
DCI.3-PS2.A.1 Forces and Motion The student demonstrates that an object at rest has zero net force, and forces that do not sum to zero cause changes in speed or direction.										
SEP.3-5.C.1 Planning and Carrying Out investigation The student plans and carries out steps in an investigation to test magnets.										
CCC.3-5.B.1 Cause and Effect The student identifies cause and effect relationships with the magnets.										
DCI.3.PS2.B.2 Types of Interactions The student uses various orientations of magnets to move objects from a distance.										
SEP.3-5.A.1 Asking Questions and Defining Problems The student asks questions that can be investigated using the magnets.										
Overall Achievement of Performance Expectation The student plans and conducts an investigation to provide evidence of the effects of balanced and unbalanced forces on the motion of the magnet.										
Total										

Push Me, Pull You

Task 1: Magnetic Personality

In this task, you will use magnets to investigate balanced and unbalanced forces.

PROCEDURE

Make the magnet stand.

1. Arrange 3 wooden sticks to form a triangle. Connect the wooden sticks together using 3 rubber bands. This is the base of the stand.

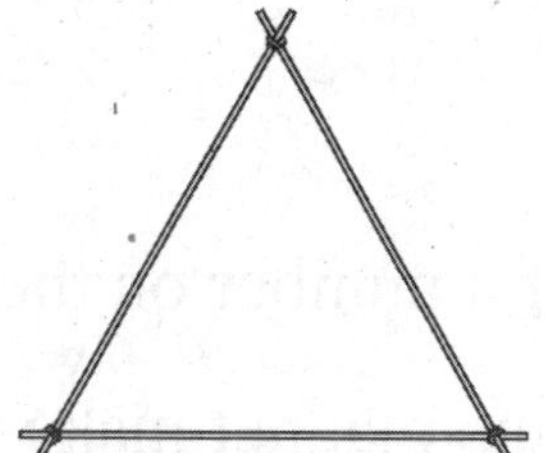

2. Use the other wooden sticks and rubber bands to form a pyramid. Tape the stand to the table.

3. Tie one end of the yarn to the ring magnet. Tie the other end of the yarn to the top of the pyramid stand.

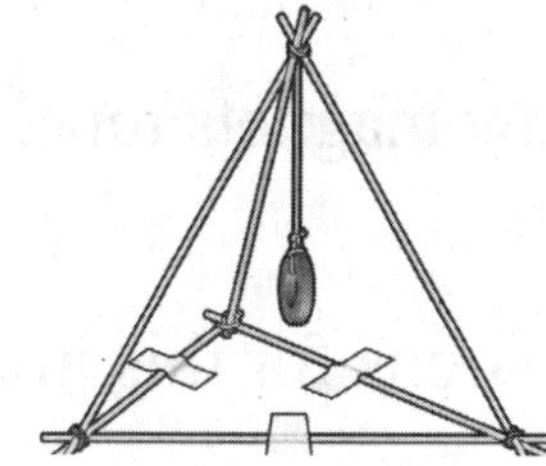

Investigate magnetic forces.

4. What material do you have that will move the magnet without touching it?

   Write your answer on the lines.

---

5. Without touching the ring magnet or the pyramid, make the magnet change directions.

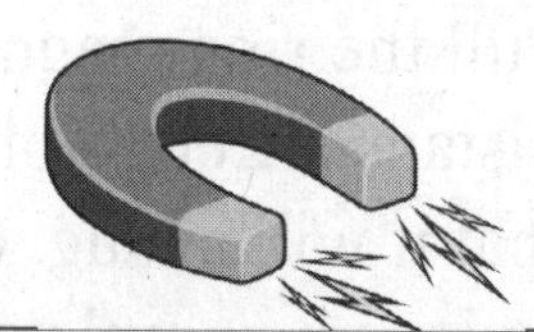

OBJECTIVE

Investigate magnetic force.

SAFETY

MATERIALS

For each group
- 2 magnets, bar
- 1 magnet, ring
- masking tape, 1 foot
- 6 wooden sticks, 12 inches
- 6 rubber bands, small
- stopwatch
- yarn or twine, 10 inches

For each student
- pencil

© Houghton Mifflin Harcourt Publishing Company

6. Pull the ring magnet to the right a short distance. Let go of the ring magnet so that it will swing. Count the number of swings it completes in 5 seconds. Record your data in the *Data Table*.

7. Pull the hanging magnet up higher than in step 6. Count how many times it swings in 5 seconds. Record your data in the *Data Table*.

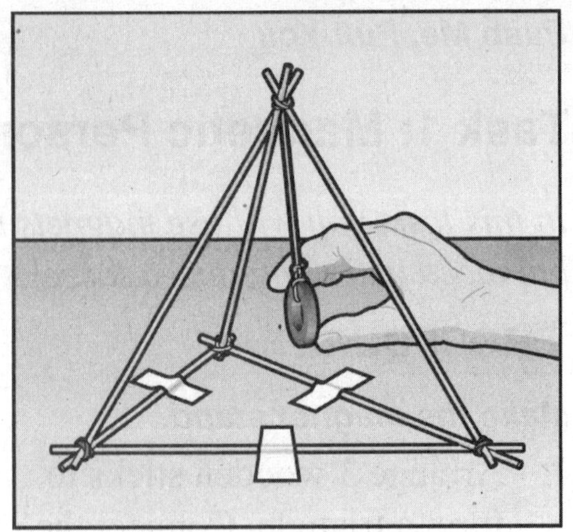

Make a prediction.

8. Make a prediction. Enter a number on the line.

   How many swings will the magnet make in 5 seconds? _______________

9. Pull the ring magnet up higher than in step 7. Count how many times it swings in 5 seconds. Record your data in the *Data Table*.

Repel two magnets.

10. You are going to show how magnets repel each other. Investigations start with a question.

    Circle the letters of 2 questions for this investigation.

    A. Why is the ring magnet attracted to the bar magnet?

    B. What happens when I put the north poles of the bar magnets together?

    C. Does the south pole of a bar magnet move the north pole of another bar magnet?

    D. How close do I have to put the bar magnet to the ring magnet before it moves away?

11. Test your question using the materials available.

12. Explain what you did to show that magnets repel.

Write your answers on the lines.

____

____

____

____

Data Table

How many times did the magnet swing? Complete the data table based on steps 6, 7, and 9.

Write the number of swings in the table.

Height	Number of Swings in 5 seconds
low	
medium	
high	

TASK SUMMARY

1. Look at the setup in step 3. Are the forces balanced or unbalanced?

Write your answers on the lines.

____

____

____

____

© Houghton Mifflin Harcourt Publishing Company

Push Me, Pull You

Task 2: Making a Compass

The student will design a compass using magnets.

Performance Expectations and 3D Learning:

3-PS2-4 Define a simple design problem that can be solved by applying scientific ideas about magnets.

3-5-ETS1-1 Define a simple design problem reflecting a need or a want that includes specified criteria for success and constraints on materials, time, or cost.

Additional SEP.3-5.C.2 Planning and Carrying Out Investigations

Safety:

- Strong magnets should not be used near computers, or ingested.
- Instruct students to avoid water spills on floor and alert the teacher of a water spill.
- Instruct students to wash their hands thoroughly after task.

Tip **Preparation Quick Tips:**

- Review what a compass is and how it relates to Earth's magnetic field.
- Organize materials into groups.

Time Rating:

1 = less time; 4 = more time
Teacher Prep = 1
Student Prep = 1
Student Cleanup = 1
Time on Task: 30 min

Materials:

For each student
- bottle lid, plastic
- bowl
- magnet, bar or ring
- paper clip, metal
- paper clip, plastic
- pencil
- penny
- sand, 1 cup
- water, 1 cup

Options for Project-Based Learning:

- Students can research how to induce magnets and design their own compass.
- Students can work with a compass to follow directions to a location — enabling them to better create their own criteria and constraints for a compass design.
- Students can discuss how people's needs have changed since compasses were first invented and how the smart phone has typically replaced the compass, but there are limitations to smart phone use that using a compass does not have.

Task 2 − Procedure Answers:

2. A compass can help you know where to go if you are lost. It tells you which direction is north.

3. The answers for criteria will vary but could be any two of these: (1) The material in the bowl should allow the compass needle to turn and to float. (2) The needle should float. (3) The needle should be made of metal.

4. The answers for the constraints will vary but could be any one of these: (1) The compass should be completed in a class period. (2) The compass can only be made of the provided materials.

Task 2 Performance Rubric

Rating Scale

3 Outstanding	1 Needs Improvement
2 Satisfactory	0 Did Not Demonstrate Skill

Teacher Directions:
This rubric allows for performance observation of 10 students. Make copies as needed. If students are working in groups, record the group name.

Group Name __________

Names of Students

Skills										
DCI.3-PS2.B.2 Types of Interactions The student demonstrates that magnetic force between the magnet (compass) and Earth's magnetic force do not have to be in contact.										
SEP.3-5.A.2 Asking Questions and Defining Problems The student defines the design problem that is solved through the development of a compass.										
DCI.3-5-ETS1.A.1 Defining and Delimiting Engineering Problems The student defines the criteria and constraints of building the compass.										
Additional: SEP.3-5.C.2 Planning and Carrying Out Investigations The student makes observations to serve as the basis for an explanation of a phenomenon (Earth's magnetic force).										
Overall Achievement of Performance Expectation The student defines the criteria and constraints of a compass and evaluates their compass on those criteria and constraints.										
Total										

Push Me, Pull You

Task 2: Making a Compass

In this task, you will define the problem that can be solved by use of a compass. You will make your own compass.

OBJECTIVE
Make a compass.

PROCEDURE

Make your plan.

1. Watch the demonstration on how to make a compass.

2. Describe the problem that can be solved by using a compass.

   Write your answer on the lines.

   ____

   ____

   ____

   ____

3. Identify two criteria for the materials that will allow your compass to work.

   Write your answer on the lines.

   ____

   ____

   ____

   ____

SAFETY

MATERIALS

For each student
- bottle lid, plastic
- bowl
- magnet
- paper clip, metal
- paper clip, plastic
- pencil
- penny
- sand, 1cup
- water, 1 cup

© Houghton Mifflin Harcourt Publishing Company

4. Identify one constraint that limits the design for building your compass. Write your answer on the lines.

____

____

____

____

Make Your Compass.

5. Choose the materials for your compass. Choose one from each group.

   - Material in the bowl: sand or water
   - Material the needle sits on: bottle lid or penny
   - Needle material: plastic paper clip or metal paper clip

6. Place the material you choose in the bowl. Place the material the needle sits on in the bowl.

7. Rub the magnet along the paper clip you chose 50 times in the same direction.

8. Place the needle on the penny or bottle lid in the bowl.

9. Does your compass work like the one your teacher showed you? If not, refine your design. Go back to step 5 and reconsider your choices.

© Houghton Mifflin Harcourt Publishing Company

Push me, Pull You

Part 2: A Tale of Three Scales

Read the passage. Then follow the instructions to answer the questions.

Mr. Roberts assigned students to build scales. Each group can use up to $25 to build the scale. The scale should measure objects that weigh from 1 to 5 pounds. It should hold blocks and balls. The scale should be easy to use.

Each group built a scale. The pictures show each group's design.

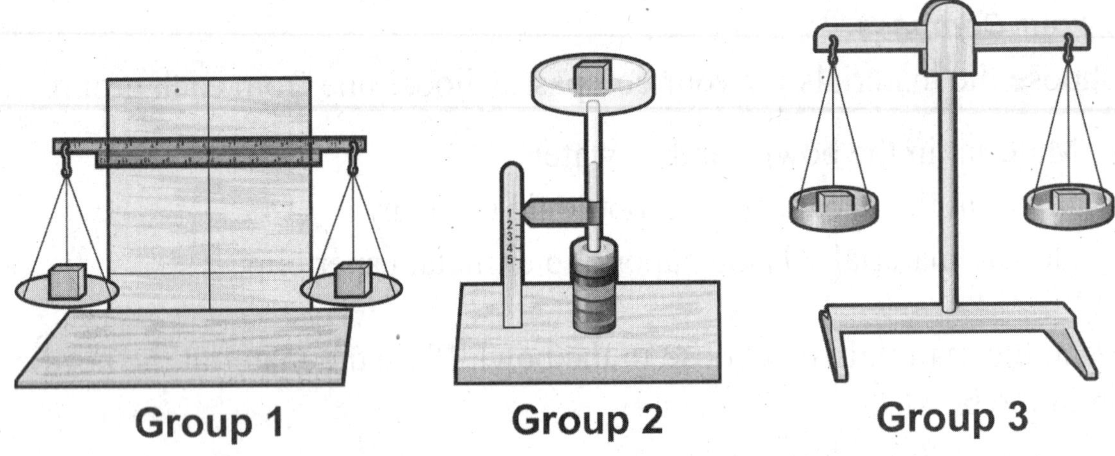

Each group tested its scale. The strings of Group 1's scale broke. Group 2's scale measures to only four pounds. The results of all 3 groups are shown in the table.

Scale Results

Group	Cost (dollars)	Time (days)	Hold blocks and balls	Measures 1–5 pounds	Easy to use
1	11	2	no	no	No, the objects slide off the trays.
2	25	1.5	yes	no	Yes, the pan moves down and the arrow points to the weight.
3	25	2	yes	yes	Yes, the pans hold the objects without sliding and the scales do not tip over.

1. Mr. Roberts gave some criteria and constraints for building the scale. Decide if each statement describes criteria or constraints.

   Write one X in the correct box in the table for each statement.

Statement	Criteria	Constraints
A. The scale should be easy to use.		
B. Each group had 2 days and $25 to design its scale.		
C. The scale should hold both blocks and balls that weigh from 1 to 5 pounds.		

2. Group 2 made its scale using magnets. When the magnets are placed on the stand one way, they touch. When they are placed a different way, they push apart from each other.

   Write the letter of the magnet in order so they would all push apart from each other. The letters can be used more than once or not at all.

	Magnet stack
Magnet 1	
Magnet 2	
Magnet 3	

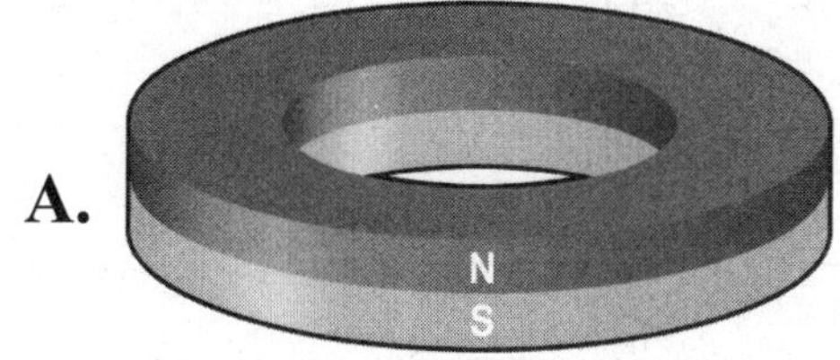

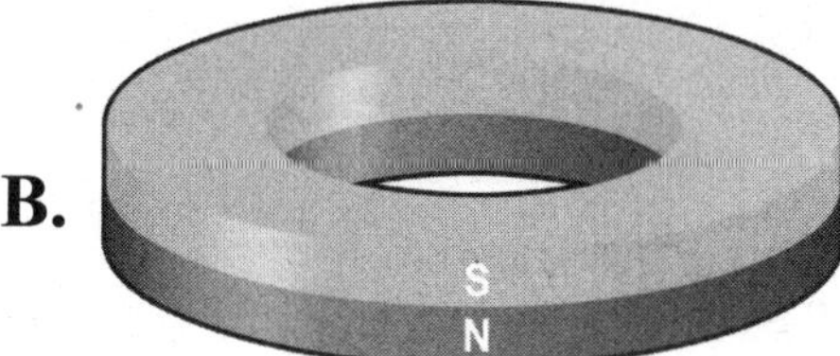

3. The table shows how the scales move when different weights are placed on them.

Write the letter of the pictures in the empty boxes to complete the patterns.

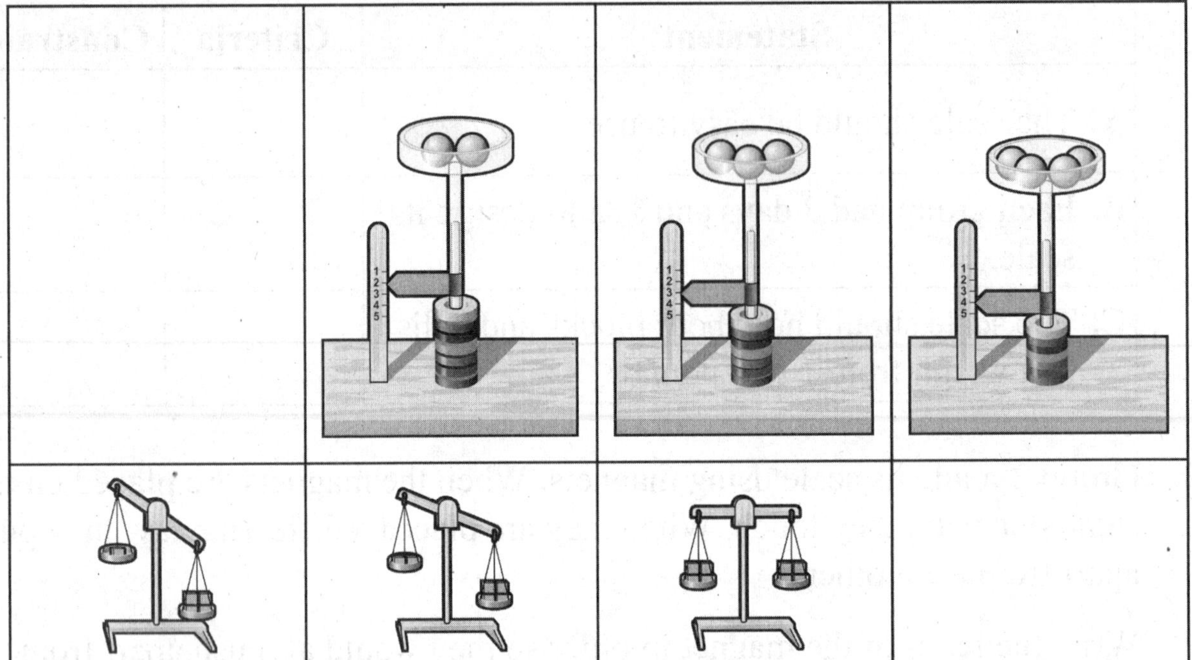

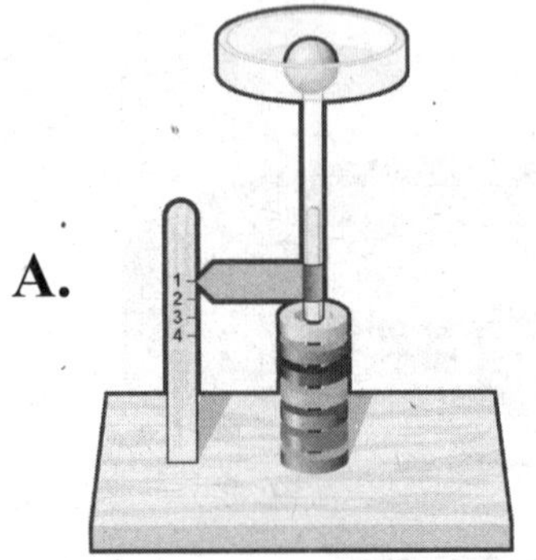

A.

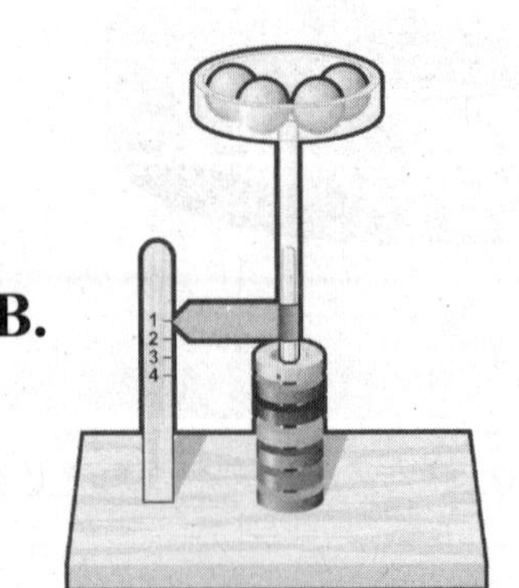

B.

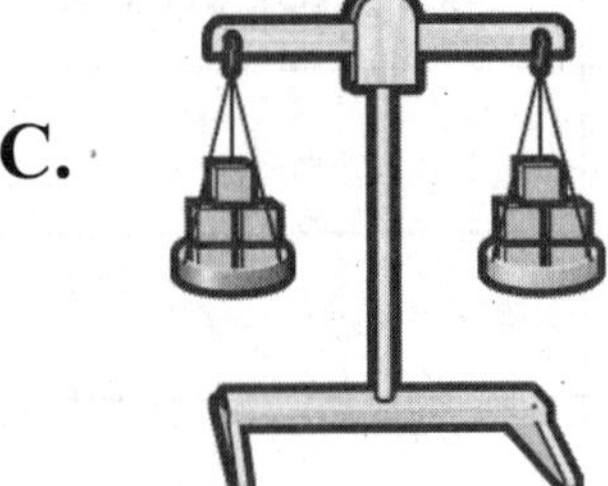

C.

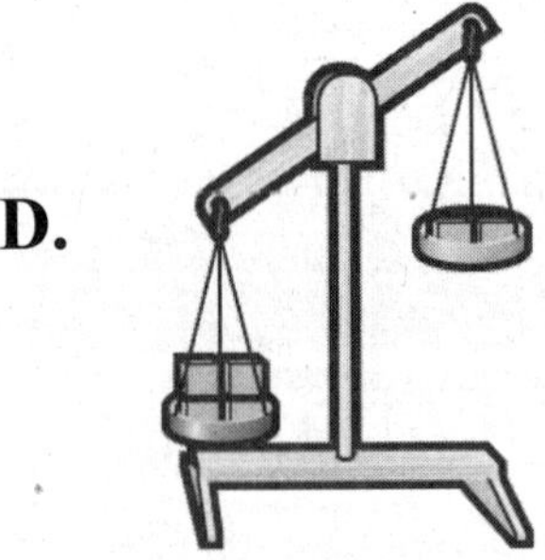

D.

4. Not all of the designs met the requirements Mr. Roberts provided.

Identify the design that was least successful.

____

Describe one change that could be made to that design so that it better meets Mr. Roberts' requirements.

____

____

5. Group 2 wants to make its scale hold more weight. Students in the group make a second scale using different magnetic rings. The pictures show their first and second scales.

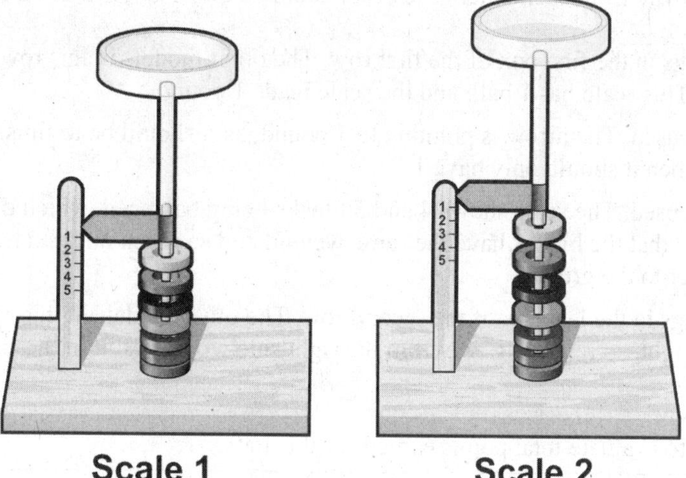

Identify what is most likely different about the magnets in the second scale.

____

____

Explain how this would allow their scale to hold more weight.

____

____

____

Push Me, Pull You

Item Analysis		
Item #	**Standards**	**DOK**
1	3-5-ETS1-1, DCI.3-5-ETS1.A.1, SEP.3-5.A.2	2
2	3-PS2-3, DCI.3-PS2.B.2, CCC.3-5.B.1	3
3	3-5-ETS1-1, DCI.3-PS2.A.2, CCC.3-5.A.2	3
4	3-5-ETS1-3, DCI.3-5-.ETS1.C.1	3
5	3-PS2-4, DCI.3-PS2.B.2, CCC.STSE.3-5.A.1	3

1. **A.** This is a criterion given by Mr. Roberts. It is a desired feature of the scale.

   B. These are constraints given by Mr. Roberts. They set a limit on the time and money resources available to the students to make their scales.

   C. This is a constraint given by Mr. Roberts. It is a desired feature of the scale.

2. The student should place the magnets so that they have like poles facing each other. This would result in all of the magnets pushing away from each other. The order could be either B, A, B or A, B, A.

3. **A.** This model belongs in the first box of the first row. The other models in this row show that that each ball weighs 1 pound. This scale has 1 ball, and the scale reads 1 pound.

   B. This model is not used. The arrow is pointing to 1 pound, as it should be to finish the pattern, but the scale has 4 balls in it when it should only have 1.

   C. This model is not used. The scale shows 4 and 5 blocks being balanced, which does not follow the pattern. The pattern shows that the blocks have the same weight, and so when one pan has more blocks, that side is pulled down closer to the ground.

   D. This model belongs in the last box of the second row. The other models in this row show that the blocks have the same weight, so removing two from the right side would result in the right pan being higher than the left pan.

4. Use the rubric below to evaluate total points earned for this item.   *[max point: 3]*

DCI Only - 3 Points	
Claims	The student is able to determine how well the scales perform against the criteria and the constraints, and identify aspects of the prototype that can be improved to better meet the criteria and constraints (DCI).
Evidence of Mastery of Disciplinary Core Ideas	1 point for the correctly identifying the design that meets fewest requirements **Part 1:** One point is earned for identifying that design 1 meets the fewest requirements. The following, or an equivalent, is acceptable. • design 1 2 points for correctly describing how design 1 could be improved **Part 2:** Two points are earned for describing that design 1 could be adjusted to hold balls, measure 1 to 5 pounds, or make it easier to use. One of the following, or an equivalent, is acceptable. • Instead of using flat circles to hold the weight, they could use bowls. • They could build it using something stronger than strings.

© Houghton Mifflin Harcourt Publishing Company

5. Use the rubric below to evaluate total points earned for this item.   *[max point: 2]*

DCI, CCC - 2 Points	
Claims	The student is able to: 1. explain that the size of the forces in the two prototypes depend on the properties of the magnets and their distances apart (DCI); and 2. explain how to use the engineering design process to build an improved technology (CCC).
Evidence of Mastery of Disciplinary Core Ideas	1 point for correctly explaining why difference allow scale to hold more weight **Part 2:** One point is earned for explaining the stronger magnets would have greater forces to push the magnets farther apart. The following response, or an equivalent, is acceptable. It has more force.
Evidence of Mastery of Crosscutting Concepts	1 point for correctly identifying what is most likely different **Part 1:** One point is earned for explaining that the magnet in the revised design is most likely a stronger magnet. The following response, or an equivalent, is acceptable. It has bigger/stronger magnets.

© Houghton Mifflin Harcourt Publishing Company

Luck of the Trait

Teacher Resource Task 1: Designing a Life-Cycle Model

The student will review inherited and environmentally influenced traits in a plant and then make a model of a plant's life cycle.

Performance Expectations and 3D Learning:

3-LS1-1 Develop models to describe that organisms have unique and diverse life cycles but all have in common birth, growth, reproduction, and death.

3-LS3-1 Analyze and interpret data to provide evidence that plants and animals have traits inherited from parents and that variation of these traits exists in a group of similar organisms.

Safety:

- Instruct students to use materials only as directed.
- Instruct students to use caution when using sharp tools.
- Instruct students to wash their hands thoroughly after the investigation.

Tip **Preparation Quick Tips:**

- Prepare materials in advance for each group.
- Print enough copies of *Class Inventory* for each student.
- This task requires that the student read about the chosen plant (pine tree, pumpkin, sunflower, tomato). Work with the school librarian to collect books. Or, locate reliable online resources for print or for students to read on the Internet.
- Prepare an example life cycle on a paper plate in advance of task.
- Students will select a plant from which to make a model of the life cycle. Be sure to encourage an even distribution of each type of plant as this will be helpful in *Task 2.*

Options for Project-Based Learning:

- Students can make models of all the plants.
- Students can rate each other's models and make recommendations for improvement.

Task 1 – Model Requirements:

- name of student (on masking tape)
- type of plant labeled as one of these: pine tree, pumpkin, sunflower, tomato (on masking tape)
- parts of the plant life cycle labeled in order: seed or birth, sprout or growing, seedling or growing, adult plant
- arrows indicating stages from start to finish

Time Rating:

1 = less time; 4 = more time
Teacher Prep: 1
Student Prep: 4
Student Cleanup: 1
Time on Task: 1.5 hours

Materials:

For each group
- masking tape, 6 inches

For each student
- colored pencils or crayons
- paper plate, 9 inches
- pencil

Sample Model

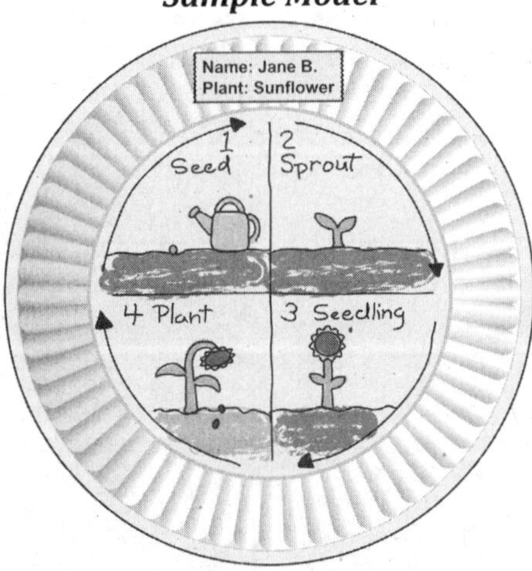

Task 1 − Procedure Answers:

1. The number of students, the tally, will vary. The inherited traits are: green/blue eyes, brown eyes, straight hair, curly hair, dimples, short legs, and long legs. The traits determined by learning or the environment are: can do cartwheel, wears jewelry, and plays piano.

2. Answers will vary, but students should recognize if there were more inherited traits or more traits influenced by the environment.

3. Answers will vary based on which plant the students chose. The options include pine tree, pumpkin plant, sunflower plant, or tomato plant.

5. Answers will vary, but students should identify five traits about their plant. Traits could include stem color or size, flower petal color or size, height of the plant, seed size, or any other possible answer.

6. Models will be similar and should include the four main stages: seed, seed with root, young plant, and adult plant.

Task 1 − Summary Answers:

1. Answers will vary, but students should be able to identify that writing with their left hand, learning to whistle, batting with their right hand, or any other possible answer are traits they have learned from their environment.

2. Yes, plants do have traits that are influenced by their environment. Examples include but are not limited to, drought, fertilizer changing the color of a flower petal, or any other acceptable answer.

3. No, plants do not get to pick their traits; however, traits are predictable based on the parent plant, or any other acceptable answer.

4. Answers will vary but should indicate that a plant reproduces and then the plant no longer lives; it dies.

© Houghton Mifflin Harcourt Publishing Company

Task 1 Performance Rubric

Rating Scale

3 Outstanding	1 Needs Improvement
2 Satisfactory	0 Did Not Demonstrate Skill
NS Did not have the opportunity to observe	

Teacher Directions:

This rubric allows for performance observation of 10 students. Make copies as needed. If students are working in groups, record the group name.

Group Name ___________

Names of Students

Skills										
DCI.3-LS1.B.1 Growth and Development of Organisms The student recognizes the cycle a plant moves through: birth, growth, reproduction, death.										
SEP.3-5.B.2 Developing and Using Models The student develops a model of a plant's life cycle and labels the seed, sprout, seedling, and plant.										
CCC.3-5.A.2 Patterns The student identifies the pattern a plant cycles through: seed, sprout, seedling, and plant.										
DCI.3-LS3.A.1 Inheritance of Traits The student identifies which traits an offspring inherits from a parent.										
CCC.3-5.A.1 Patterns The student identifies the patterns of inherited traits to help classify data.										
SEP.3-5.A. 1 Asking Questions and Defining Problems The student asks questions that can be investigated using the magnets.										
Overall Performance Expectation The student identifies inherited traits and builds a model of a plant's life cycle and appropriately labels the seed, sprout, seedling, and plant										
Total										

Luck of the Trait

Task 1: Designing a Life-Cycle Model

In this task, you will survey your classmates' traits. Then you will pick one of the plant choices and make a life-cycle model.

PROCEDURE

Review traits.

1. Follow your teacher's directions for surveying your classmates. Record the data on the *Class Inventory* table.

2. Analyze the data with your partner. Discuss the difference between inherited traits and those influenced by the environment. Were there more inherited traits, or more traits influenced by the environment?

   Write your answer on the lines here.

   ____

   ____

   ____

OBJECTIVE

Design a model of a plant's life cycle in order to study inherited and environmentally

SAFETY

MATERIALS

For each group
- masking tape, 6 inches

For each student
- colored pencils or crayons
- paper plate, 9 inches

Research plants.

3. Pretend you are a botanist at a new research facility.

   Circle the letter of one type of plant to study.

   A. pine tree

   B. pumpkin plant

   C. sunflower plant

   D. tomato plant

4. Follow your teacher's instructions on how to research the plant you chose.

5. List 5 traits about your plant.

    Write your answer on the lines.

    ____

    ____

    ____

    ____

Create the model.

6. Using the information you gathered about what your plant looks like and the provided materials, create a paper-plate life cycle of the plant you are studying. Divide your plate into four sections. Be sure to label all parts of the plant.

7. Meet with other botanists that are studying the same plants to compare your life cycles. Discuss how your life cycle models are the same and different.

    Follow your teacher's instructions for showing your life cycle model with the class.

Class Inventory Table

Determine the number of students with each trait. Decide if the trait is something inherited or something the environment causes.

Write the numbers in the table.

Trait	Number of students	Inherited? (yes/no)	Environmental? (yes/no)
green or blue eyes			
brown eyes			
straight hair			
curly hair			
can do cartwheel			
right handed			
can roll tongue			
dimples			
wears jewelry			
plays the piano			
short legs			
long legs			

TASK SUMMARY

1. List three things that you have learned from your environment.

   Write your answer on the lines.

   ____

   ____

   ____

   ____

2. Do plants have traits that are influenced by the environment?

Write your answer on the lines.

____

____

____

____

3. Do plants get to choose which traits they have?

Write your answer on the lines.

____

____

____

____

4. What happens in the life cycle of a plant when the plant becomes an adult?

Write your answer on the lines.

____

____

____

____

© Houghton Mifflin Harcourt Publishing Company

Luck of the Trait

Task 2: New Plant Species

The student will create a new plant species with a partner using the life-cycle model he or she created during *Task 1*.

Performance Expectations and 3D Learning:

3-LS3-1 Analyze and interpret data to provide evidence that plants and animals have traits inherited from parents and that variation of these traits exists in a group of similar organisms.

Safety:

- Instruct students to use materials only as directed.
- Instruct students to wash their hands thoroughly after the investigation.

Tip **Preparation Quick Tips:**

- The intent of this task is for students to generate a new plant species using the traits from their plant and their partner's plant. They need to recognize what an inherited trait is.
- Prepare materials in advance and consider how to group students so that each group represents two plants.
- Demonstrate how to roll the die for each student to pick a trait. Partner 1 picks when an even number is rolled. Partner 2 picks when an odd number is rolled. Explain that each trait that is picked should come from the parent plant of either partner 1 or partner 2

Options for Project-Based Learning:

- Students can research different environmental influences that could change the way their plant grows and reproduces.
- Students can build their new plant species with a variety of material provided by the teacher.
- Students can rate each other's models and make recommendations for improvement.
- Students can present their new plant species.
- Students can group with other members of the class who have the same two parent plants. They can compare their new plants. What is alike and different?

Task 2 − Model Requirements:

- name of student
- traits of the student's parent plant
- Identify which traits the new species plant will have.

Time Rating:

1 = less time; 4 = more time
Teacher Prep: 1
Student Prep: 3
Student Cleanup: 1
Time on Task: 45 min

Materials:

For each group
- die
- each student's plant life-cycle models from *Task 1*

For each student
- colored markers or pencils
- pencil
- scissors

Sample Model

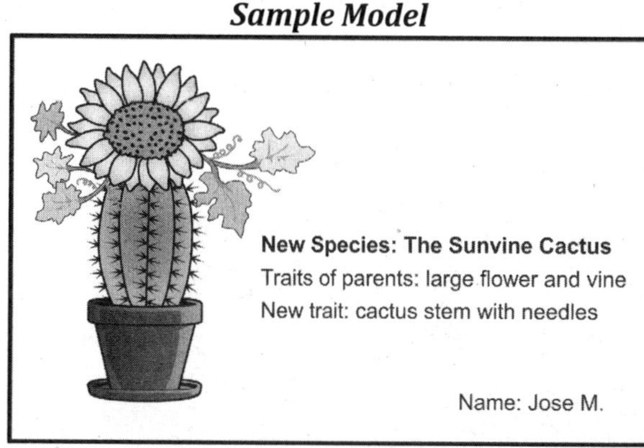

Task 2 – Procedure Answers:

1. Answers will vary but students should identify different inherited traits in plants such as color, height, thickness, flower, or fruit.

3. Answers will vary and will be dependent upon the student's plant *Task 1*.

7. Recorded traits will vary depending on the traits of the parent plants, the two plant models from *Task 1*. The table should match the sketch drawn in procedure 8.

8. Sketches will vary but should include the student's name, the traits of the parents, and which traits the offspring has. Refer to the sample model shown in the "Model Requirements" section.

Task 2 – Summary Answers:

1. Answers will vary but should indicate the traits or characteristic of the new plant species that was like their original parent plant. Color, size, shape, and thickness are all possible answer. They should do the same for how their new plant is different.

2. Yes, it is possible for the plants of two groups to resemble each other. Just as siblings resemble each other, there could be similar traits in two plants.

3. Inherited traits include: color of the leaf, shape of the roots, shape of the petal, spines on a cactus, and thorns on a rose. Traits influenced by the environment include: direction the flower grows and plants dying due to a lack of water.

Task 1 Performance Rubric	
Rating Scale	
3 Outstanding	1 Needs Improvement
2 Satisfactory	0 Did Not Demonstrate Skill
NS Did not have the opportunity to observe	

Teacher Directions:
This rubric allows for performance observation of 10 students. Make copies as needed. If students are working in groups, record the group name.

GroupName ___________

Names of Students

Skills										
DCI.3-LS3.A.1 Inheritance of Traits The student identifies inherited traits in plant offspring.										
DCI.3-LS3.B.1 Variation of Traits The student identifies that plants' functions vary based on the traits that were inherited.										
SEP.3-5.D.2 Analyzing and Interpreting Data The student sorts through data and determines which traits were inherited.										
CCC 3-5.A.1 Patterns The student recognizes similarities and differences in the plants.										
Overall Performance Expectation The student creates a new species of plants using the data he or she analyzed from the adult parent plants.										
Total										

Luck of the Trait

Task 2: New Plant Species

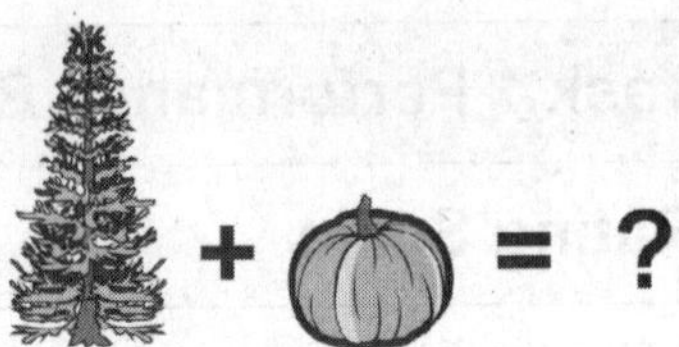

In this task, you and your partner will use your plant models from Task 1 to invent a new plant species.

PROCEDURE

Brainstorm with your partner.

1. Discuss with your partner what a trait is. What is one example of an inherited trait in plants?

   Write your answer on the lines.

   ____

   ____

2. Look at your life-cycle model from *Task 1*.

3. Which traits does your plant life-cycle model have? Complete the table based on your own plant model from *Task 1*.

Parent Traits Table

Type of Trait	Yes or No?
Stem thickness (thick or thin)	
Stem color	
Leaf color	
Leaf size (small or large)	
Leaf shape (smooth or rough edges)	
Petal color	
Petal size (small or large)	
Fruit color (if present)	
Overall plant size (small or large)	
Any other trait?	

OBJECTIVE

Invent a new species of plant.

SAFETY

MATERIALS

For each group
- colored markers or pencils
- die
- each student's plant life-cycle model from *Task 1*

For each student
- pencil
- scissors

© Houghton Mifflin Harcourt Publishing Company

Pick the traits.

The new species of plant will be made from traits from your plant model and your partner's plant model. The new species of plant cannot have both traits. For example, it cannot have a thick stem and a thin stem. You will decide which traits from the two plant models will be given to the new species by rolling a die.

4. You will be botanist 1. When the die lands on an odd number, whatever trait your plant model has will be given to, or inherited by, the new species.

5. Your partner will be botanist 2. When the die lands on an even number, whatever trait your plant model has will be given to the new species.

6. Look at the first trait, stem thickness. Roll the die. If the number is odd, botanist 1 will look at their *Parent Traits Table* and 'give' the new species that trait. If the number is even, botanist 2 looks at their *Parent Traits Table* and 'gives' the new species that trait.

7. For each trait, roll the die, determine the trait, and complete the *New Species Traits Table*.

New Species Traits Table

Type of Trait	Trait New Species Will Have (Yes or No?)
Stem thickness (thick or thin)	
Stem color	
Leaf color	
Leaf size (small or large)	
Leaf shape (smooth or rough edges)	
Petal color	
Petal size (small or large)	
Fruit color (if present)	
Overall plant size (small or large)	
Any other trait?	

Draw the new plant.

8. Look at the completed *New Species Traits Table*. Use these traits to draw a
    sketch of what the new species plant will look like.

TASK SUMMARY

1. List two ways the new plant is like your original plant.

   Write your answers on the lines.

   ____

   ____

   ____

   ____

2. Is it possible for another group's plant to look like yours? Why or why not?

   Write your answers on the lines.

   ____

   ____

   ____

   ____

3. Group these plant traits into two categories: traits that were inherited or traits that were influenced by the environment.

   Write the letters of the traits in the correct boxes.

Inherited	Influenced by environment

A. color of the leaf
B. direction the flower grows
C. dying plant due to a lack of water
D. shape of the roots
E. shape of the petal
F. spines on a cactus
G. thorns on a rose

Luck of the Trait

Part 2: Husky Traits

Read the passage, then answer the questions that follow.

Hudson adopted a three-year old dog from the pound. He named him Sparky.

Hudson made a list of things he noticed about the dog.

	Traits about Sparky
○	
	Has fluffy, dark grey fur
	Chases after balls
	Has fluffy, white fur
	Rolls over on command
	Sits on command
	Has large blue eyes
○	Has a pink tongue
	Has dark grey ears
	Barks at people
	Sleeps on sofa
	Weighs 45 pounds
○	

1. Classify some of the items on Hudson's list into two categories: inherited or learned.

    Write the letters in the correct boxes.

Inherited	Learned

A. sleeps on sofa	**D.** sits on command
B. has a pink tongue	**E.** has dark grey ears
C. has fluffy, white fur	**F.** has large blue eyes

2. Hudson wondered about Sparky's parents. What information on his list could he use to predict what Sparky's parents looked like?

    Circle the letters of all the correct responses.

A. barks at people	**E.** has a pink tongue
B. sits on command	**F.** has dark grey ears
C. chases after balls	**G.** has large blue eyes
D. has fluffy, white fur	**H.** rolls over on command

Name: _______________________ Date: _______________________

3. After having the new dog home for several months, Hudson noticed that Sparky's weight changed. Sparky has been eating a lot and not exercising.

Circle the picture that most likely shows what Sparky looks like now.

4. Write the letter of the word in each blank to correctly complete the sentences. Some letters may be used more than once or not at all.

Sparky looks the way he does because of the traits he ____________. These traits are ____________ from his parents. Some traits are ____________ by the environment, such as having too much food to eat.

A. behavior	**C.** influenced	**E.** learned
B. was born with	**D.** inherited	**F.** offspring

5. Why did the change in Sparky's diet and the lack of exercise change the way he looked? Identify whether that is an inherited trait or a learned behavior.

Write your answers on the lines.

____

____

____

© Houghton Mifflin Harcourt Publishing Company

Luck of the Trait

Item Analysis		
Item #	**Standards**	**DOK**
1	3-LS3-2, DCI.3-LS3.B.2	2
2	3-LS3-2, DCI.3-LS3.B.2	2
3	3-LS3-2, DCI.3-LS3.B.2	2
4	3-LS3-2, DCI.3-LS3.B.2	2
5	3-LS3-1, DCI.3-LS3.B.1	2

1. **A.** *Has pink tongue* is a trait that is inherited. A dog cannot be taught to have a certain tongue color.

   B. *Sleeps on sofa* is a trait that is learned. A dog learns that a sofa is comfortable.

   C. *Has fluffy, white fur* is a trait that is inherited. A dog cannot be taught to have a particular fur color.

   D. *Has dark grey ears* is a trait that is inherited. A dog cannot be taught to have a particular fur color.

   E. *Sits on command* is a trait that is taught. A dog can be taught to sit and move as requested by a person.

   F. *Has dark blue eyes* is a trait that is *inherited*. A dog cannot be taught to have a particular eye color.

2. **A.** *Barks at the people* could not be used to predict what Sparky's parents looked like. It is an environmentally influenced trait, not inherited.

   B. *Sits on command* could not be used to predict what Sparky's parents looked like. It is an environmentally influenced trait, not inherited.

   C. *Chases after balls* could not be used to predict what Sparky's parents looked like. It is an environmentally influenced trait, not inherited.

   D. *Has fluffy, white fur* could be used to predict what Sparky's parents look like because it is an inherited trait.

   E. *Has pink tongue* could be used to predict what Sparky's parents look like because it is an inherited trait.

   F. *Has dark grey ears* could be used to predict what Sparky's parents look like because it is an inherited trait.

   G. *Has large blue eyes* could be used to predict what Sparky's parents look like because it is an inherited trait.

   H. *Rolls over on command* could not be used to predict what Sparky's parents looked like. It is an environmentally influenced trait, not inherited.

3. The picture of the left of the fatter dog is correct. If a dog eats a lot of food and does not exercise, that dog will gain weight.

4. **A.** *Behavior* does not belong in any of the blanks.

   B. *Was born with* belongs in the first blank. Sparky, and other living things, inherits traits from parents.

   C. *Influenced* belongs in the third blank. Some traits were influenced by the environment, such as over-eating can cause some animals to gain weight.

   D. *Inherited* belongs in the first or second blank. Inherited traits are traits a living thing is born with, such as appearance.

   E. *Learned* does not belong in any blank.

5. Use the rubric below to evaluate total points earned for this item.   *[max point: 2]*

	DCI, CCC - 2 Points	
Claims	The student is able to: 1. identify that the trait is influenced by environment (DCI); and 2. explain the effect that not exercising and excessive eating had on the dog (CCC).	
Evidence of Mastery of Disciplinary Core Ideas	1 point for correctly identifying that the trait is influenced by environment **Part 2:** One point is earned for correctly identifying that the excessive eating and a lack of exercise is brought on and learned by the environment. • The dog learned to excessively eat and not exercise in his environment, it was not inherited.	
Evidence of Mastery of Crosscutting Concepts	1 point for correctly explaining the effect that not exercising and excessive eating had on the dog **Part 1:** One point is earned for explaining that because the dog ate too much and didn't exercise he gained too much weight. • The dog gained weight because he did not exercise and he ate too much.	

© Houghton Mifflin Harcourt Publishing Company

Creature Creation

Task 1: Adaptive Puppet

The student will make a puppet of an animal with characteristics that allow it to survive in a particular environment.

Performance Expectations and 3D Learning:

3-LS4-2 Use evidence to construct an explanation for how the variations in characteristics among individuals of the same species may provide advantages in surviving, finding mates, and reproducing.

Additional SEP 3-5.B.2 Develop or use models to describe and/or predict phenomena.

Safety:

- Instruct students to use materials only as directed.
- Instruct students to wash their hands thoroughly after the investigation.
- Instruct students to use caution when using sharp tools, working with chemicals

Tip ▸ **Preparation Quick Tips:**

- Ask parents to collect and donate listed materials.
- Collect scrap pieces of art supplies from other activities and from other teachers.
- Prepare materials in advance for each group to allow for a smooth transition into task.
- Make environment cards in advance. Hand write the names of environments on index cards, one environment on one card. Each student in the class will get an environment card. Organize the cards so that there are at least two of the same environments. Environments may include arctic, alpine, desert, deciduous forest, grassland, marine, tropical rainforest. Students will be organized according to the environment card they select or are assigned.

Time Rating:

1 = less time; 4 = more time
Teacher Prep: 4
Student Prep: 1
Student Cleanup: 2
Time on Task: 1 h

Materials:

For each group
- buttons, assorted colors
- chenille sticks
- construction paper, assorted colors
- environment cards
- feathers, assorted colors
- felt material, assorted colors
- glue
- tape
- unlined white paper
- yarn, assorted colors

For each student
- colored markers
- paper bag, white, 5 in. x 3 in. x 9.4 in.
- pencil
- scissors

Options for Project-Based Learning:
- Students can research the different environments and prepare model designs in advance and use the models while working through the concepts of their lessons.
- Students can select and collect their own materials instead of the teacher providing materials.
- Students can rate each other's models and make recommendations for improvement.

Task 1 – Model Requirements:
- name of student
- name of the animal or fictional creature
- two labeled physical adaptations

Sample Model

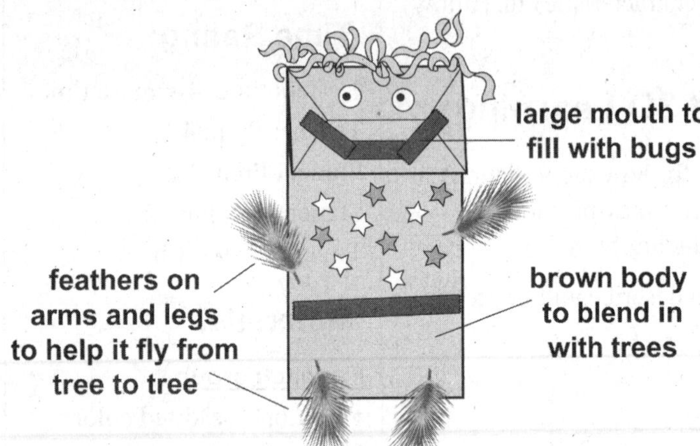

Task 1 – Procedure Answers:

2. Answers will vary but should include some type of physical features an animal would need to survive in an environment. Examples include, but are not limited to, thick fur or hair for warmth, camouflage into the ocean floor, webbed feet, mimic a tree trunk, or any other acceptable adaptation for their specific environment.

4. Students' sketches will vary but should have two labeled physical features that correspond with the environment.

7. Answers will vary but students should be able to identify the physical features of the two animals that are alike and different. Answers could include feathers, fur, beaks, coloring, shape, size, or any other acceptable response.

Task 1 – Summary Answers:

1. The student identifies which animal would have a higher chance of surviving in its environment when comparing their animal to their partner's.

2. Animals have parts that allow them to <u>survive</u> in their environment. The <u>physical</u> parts that an animal has might include its size, shape, and/or <u>color</u>. The animal may also <u>behave</u> in a particular way in order to survive.

Task 1 Performance Rubric

Rating Scale

3 Outstanding	1 Needs Improvement
2 Satisfactory	0 Did Not Demonstrate Skill

NS Did not have the opportunity to observe

Teacher Directions:
This rubric allows for performance observation of 10 students. Make copies as needed. If students are working in groups, record the group name.

Group Name ___________

Names of Students

Skills										
DCI.3-LS4.B.1 Natural Selection The student explains advantageous characteristics of an animal that allow it to survive in its environment.										
SEP.3-5.F.1 Constructing Explanations and Designing Solutions The student explains how a particular characteristic provides an advantage to an animal.										
CCC.3-5.B.1 Cause and Effect The student identifies connections between changes in environments and the consequential effect of the change.										
Additional SEP.3-5.B.2 Developing and Using Models The student makes a model of an organism with specific features that provides an advantage to surviving in its environment.										
Overall Achievement of Performance Expectation The student compares models of an organism and explains how variations in the models would allow one or both to have an advantage in surviving their environment.										
Total										

Creature Creation

Task 1: Adaptive Puppet

*In this task, you will make a puppet to represent an
animal that could survive in a specific environment*

PROCEDURE

Think about the environment.

1. Pick an environment card from the teacher. You
   will be partnered with someone with the same
   environment card.

2. Think about the environment listed on the card.
   Discuss this environment with your partner. What
   physical features would an animal need to survive
   in your selected environment?

   Write your answer on the lines.

   ____

   ____

   ____

   ____

   ____

Sketch your idea for the puppet.

3. Look at the materials available. Talk with your
   partner about two animals that could survive in
   the environment. The animals can be real or from
   your imagination.

OBJECTIVE

Make a puppet based
on a made-up animal.

SAFETY

MATERIALS

For each group
- buttons
- chenille sticks
- construction paper
- glue
- environment cards
- feathers
- felt material
- tape
- unlined white paper
- yarn

For each student
- colored markers
- paper bag
- pencil
- scissors

4. Sketch your idea for the puppet. Label two physical features your animal needs to survive in its environment. The features for each animal should be different.

NOTE: Your puppet must be a different animal than that of your partner.

5. Show your sketch to your partner. Explain how the puppet represents an animal that lives in the environment.

Make the puppet.

6. Make the puppet based off your sketch. Write your name and the name of the animal on the puppet.

7. Compare your creature to your partner's. What physical features are alike? What physical features are different?

Write your answer on the lines.

____

____

____

____

TASK SUMMARY

1. Which animal would be more likely to survive in the environment, yours or your partner's? Explain your reasoning.

Write your answer on the lines.

____

____

____

____

2. Write the letter of the word in each blank to correctly complete the sentences.

Animals have parts that allow them to __________ in their environment.

The __________ parts that an animal has might include its size, shape,

and/or __________. The animal may also __________ in a particular way in

order to survive.

A. behave	C. physical
B. color	D. survive

Creature Creation

Task 2: Home Sweet Home

The student will build an environment and work in pairs to develop two animal models/puppets featuring different adaptations to demonstrate how animals survive in a particular environment.

Performance Expectations and 3D Learning:

3-LS4-3 Construct an argument with evidence that in a particular habitat some organisms can survive well, some survive less well, and some cannot survive at all.

Additional DCI.3-LS4.D.1 The student identifies changes in an environment and how those changes will affect their fictional creature.

Additional SEP 3-5.B.1 Develop or use models to describe and/or predict phenomena.

Safety:

- Instruct students to use materials only as directed.
- Instruct students to wash their hands thoroughly after the investigation.
- Instruct students to use caution when using sharp tools, working with chemicals

Tip Preparation Quick Tips:

- Ask parents to donate listed materials.
- Collect scrap pieces of art supplies from other activities and from other teachers.
- Prepare materials in advance for each group to allow for a smooth transition into the task.
- Assign students to design their habitat in advance and to work on their sketches in advance of the task.

Options for Project-Based Learning:

- Students can research the different environments, prepare model designs in advance, and use the models while working through the concepts of their lessons.
- Students can select and collect their own materials instead of the teacher providing materials.
- Students can rate each other's models and make recommendations for improvement.
- Students can present their animals, habitats, and changes to the class.

Time Rating:

1 = less time; 4 = more time
Teacher Prep: 1
Student Prep: 3
Student Cleanup: 1
Time on Task: 1 h

Materials:

For each group
- construction paper, assorted colors
- cotton balls
- feathers, assorted colors
- felt material, assorted colors
- foam packaging pieces
- pebbles
- plastic plants
- sand
- tape
- unlined white paper

For each student
- cardboard shoebox
- colored markers
- glue
- index card
- pencil
- scissors

Task 2 – Model Requirements:
- names of students
- name of environment
- features of the environment: food, water, shelter, natural elements

Sample Model

Task 2 – Procedure Answers:

2. Answers will vary but should include several features about their environment. The features should include vegetation, climate, temperature, water sources, food sources, and any other acceptable answer.

4. Models will vary but should include features associated with the habitat, such as sand for a desert or water for a marine habitat.

8. Answers will vary but should demonstrate an understanding that some animals survive better in some environments over other environments.

9. Answers will vary but could include any of these three factors: drought, fire, or human causes such as building a highway or clearing a forest.

10. Answers will vary but should describe logical changes due to a flood, a fire, an earthquake, clearing of land, a hurricane, or a mudslide. For example, a fire will affect the animal because the tree it lives in may be burned down.

Task 2 – Summary Answers:

1. Changes quickly: fire, flood, mudslide, volcanic eruption; Changes slowly: drought, forest clearing

© Houghton Mifflin Harcourt Publishing Company

Task 2 Performance Rubric	
Rating Scale	
3 Outstanding	1 Needs Improvement
2 Satisfactory	0 Did Not Demonstrate Skill
NS Did not have the opportunity to observe	

Teacher Directions:
This rubric allows for performance observation of 10 students. Make copies as needed. If students are working in groups, record the group name.

Group Name __________

Names of Students

Skills										
DCI.3-LS4.C.1 Adaptation The student evaluates organism models to identify which would survive well, less well, and or would not survive in particular environments.										
SEP 3-5.G.2. Engaging in Argument from Evidence The student describes which part(s) of an environment better allow for an organism to survive.										
CCC. 3-5 B.1 Cause and Effect The student observes cause and effect relationships between the changing environment and their fictional creature.										
Additional DCI.3-LS4.D.1 Biodiversity and Humans The student identifies changes in an environment and how those changes will affect their fictional creature.										
Additional SEP 3-5.B.1 Developing and Using Models The student creates a model that meets the needs of their fictional creature.										
Overall Achievement of Performance Expectation The student will determine what features their fictional creature needs to survive an environmental change.										
Total										

Creature Creation

Task 2: Home Sweet Home

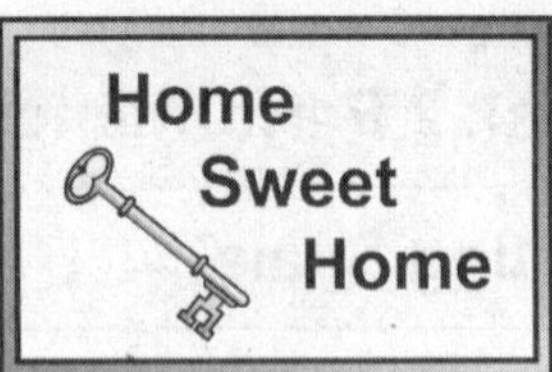

In this task, you and your partner will use all or portions of the provided materials to create a habitat for the puppets you made in Task 1.

PROCEDURE

Design and construct the environment model.

1. You selected an environment card in *Task 1*. Think about that environment that your puppet animal survives in best. Discuss with your partner the features found in that environment. Think about how the puppet animal would have food, water, and shelter.

2. What specific features are found in the environment for your puppet animal from *Task 1*?

   Write your answer on the lines.

   ____

   ____

   ____

   ____

3. Plan the appearance of the puppet animal's environment, its home. Consider only those materials available.

4. Use the available materials to make your environment model.

5. Place your puppet in the box.

6. Write on the index card three features about the environment.

OBJECTIVE

Create an environment for your puppet animal.

SAFETY

MATERIALS

For each group
- construction paper
- cotton balls
- feathers
- foam pieces
- pebbles
- sand
- tape
- unlined white paper

For each student
- cardboard shoebox
- colored markers
- glue
- index card
- pencil
- scissors

© Houghton Mifflin Harcourt Publishing Company

Share your habitat.

7. Put your environment model in the location directed by your teacher. View each classmate's environment model.

8. In which of your classmates' models could your puppet animal survive well, survive less well, and not survive at all? Record your answers in the table. Write your answers of well, less well, or will not survive.

Names of students	Name of environment	How well will your puppet animal survive?

© Houghton Mifflin Harcourt Publishing Company

9. Think about the changes that might affect the plants and animals in your environment. Make a list of three different changes.

   Write your answer on the lines.

   ____

   ____

   ____

Change the environment.

10. There are many factors that can change an environment. Make a list of three different changes that could affect your environment, and the plants and animals that live there.

    Which environmental change did you select? _______________________

    List two ways the environmental change will affect the puppet animal you made.

    ____

    ____

11. Make any necessary changes to your puppet animal. Add new features to your animal that will help it survive the change.

TASK SUMMARY

1. Some environmental changes occur quickly, and some occur slowly.

   Write the letter in the correct boxes.

Changes quickly	Changes slowly

A. drought
B. fire
C. flood
D. forest clearing
E. mudslide
F. volcanic eruption

Creature Creation

Part 2: Fire in the Forest

Read the passage, then answer the questions that follow.

Picture A shows a forest in the spring. Picture B shows the same forest after a fire. Many animals and plants were affected.

A

B

1. How were the plants and animals most likely affected by the fire?

    Write the correct letters that describe how the monkeys and trees were affected.

monkeys	
trees	

    A. burned down

    B. found food under ash

    C. lost their homes

© Houghton Mifflin Harcourt Publishing Company

2. What can people do to help rebuild the forest?

   Circle the letters of all the correct answers.

   A. plant more native trees

   B. spread seeds for plants

   C. bring food to the animals

   D. find a new place for the animals to live

3. Write the letter of the word in each blank to correctly complete the sentences. Some answers may be used more than once or not at all.

   The forest was home to a troop of monkeys. Several monkeys __________ their homes in the fire. Many monkeys lost their __________.

   Shelters were __________.

A. lost	**C.** created	**E.** source of food
B. found	**D.** destroyed	**F.** source of water

4. Which animals would most likely survive the fire?

   Circle the letters of all the correct responses.

   A. animals that live alone

   B. animals that have thick fur

   C. animals that sleep at night

   D. animals that can find shelter elsewhere

   E. animals that don't eat the trees for food

5. The plants and animals were affected by the forest fire.

Describe how the monkey family was likely affected by the fire.

____

____

____

____

____

Identify how humans may have started the fire.

____

____

Explain how humans can help restore the forest.

____

____

____

____

____

© Houghton Mifflin Harcourt Publishing Company

Creature Creation

Item Analysis		
Item #	**Standards**	**DOK**
1	3-LS4-4, DCI.3-LS4.D.1, CCC.3-5.B.1	2
2	3-LS4-4, DCI.3-LS4.D.1	2
3	3-LS4-4, DCI.3-LS4.D.1	3
4	3-LS4-4, DCI.3-LS4.D.1	2
5	3-LS4-4, DCI.3-LS4.D.1	3

1. **A.** *Burned down* matches with the trees because that is how the trees will be affected.

   B. *Found food under ash* does not match any of the answers because ash means something burned. Any food would have been destroyed.

   C. *Lost their homes* matches monkeys because that is what will happen to the monkeys after the fire.

2. **A.** *Plant more native trees* is correct because it would help rebuild the forest.

   B. *Spread seeds for plants* is correct because it would help rebuild the forest.

   C. *Bring food to the animals* is incorrect. Though animals need food, this action will not result in regrowth of the plants in the forest.

   D. *Find a new place for the animals to live* is incorrect. Though this is would offer alternative homes to many animals, it will not allow for regrowth of plants in the forest.

3. **A.** *Lost* belongs in the first space. The monkeys lost their homes in the fire.

   B. *Found* does not belong in any space. A fire does not usually help monkeys locate anything. The opposite is often true; they lost their homes and food source to a fire.

   C. *Created* does not belong in any space. A fire does not usually create anything but ash.

   D. *Destroyed* belongs in the fourth space. The fire burned the trees that the monkeys lived in.

   E. *Source of food source* belongs in the third space. The fire burned vegetation, killed many insects, and relocated many animals, thus causing the monkeys to lose their food source.

   F. *Source of water* does not belong in any box. Fires turn vegetation into ash, which may blow into existing water; however, fire does not in itself provide a source of water.

4. **A.** This is incorrect because living alone will not help the animals survive the fire.

   B. This is incorrect because having thick fur will not help the animals survive.

   C. This is incorrect because animals that sleep at night are not more likely to survive.

   D. This is correct because animals that find shelter elsewhere are more likely to survive.

   E. This is correct because animals that do not eat the trees as their main source of food are more likely to survive.

5. Use the rubric below to evaluate total points earned for this item.   *[max point: 3]*

DCI, SEP, CCC - 3 points	
Claims	The student is able to: • describe how the monkey family was likely affected by the fire (DCI); and • explain how humans can help restore the forest (SEP); and • identify how humans played a role in the fire starting (CCC).
Evidence of Mastery of Disciplinary Core Ideas	1 point for correctly describing how fire likely affected monkeys **Part 1:** One point is earned for describing that the monkeys would lose their source of food, water, and shelter in the fire. Therefore, the monkeys would either have to find a new home or they would perish. One of the following responses, or an equivalent, is acceptable. • The monkeys' shelter, food, and water would be destroyed in the fire. • The monkeys would have no place to live and nothing left to eat. • The monkeys would need to find a new place to live or they wouldn't make it very long.
Evidence of Mastery of Science and Engineering Practices	1 point for correctly explaining how humans can help **Part 3:** One point is earned for correctly explaining that humans can help restore the forest by planting new native trees to the area. They can spread seeds of different bushes and trees. The following response, or an equivalent, is acceptable. • Humans can help plant new trees and plants that used to be in the area.
Evidence of Mastery of Crosscutting Concepts	1 point for correctly identifying the role of humans in fire **Part 2:** One point is earned for explaining that human action may have started the fire many different ways. One of the following responses, or an equivalent, is acceptable. • People built a campfire that burned out of control. • Humans burned wood during a drought and it caught other dry plants on fire. • They could have thrown burning trash.

© Houghton Mifflin Harcourt Publishing Company

Winding Down

Task 1: Here Comes the Flood

The student will investigate methods to prevent flooding.

Performance Expectations and 3D Learning:

PE.3-ESS3-1 Make a claim about the merit of a design solution that reduces the impacts of a weather-related hazard.

PE.3-5-ETS1-2 Generate and compare multiple possible solutions to a problem based on how well each is likely to meet the criteria and constraints of the problem.

Safety:

- Provide towels on hand to clean up any water messes immediately.
- Instruct students to use materials only as directed. Dough should not be ingested.
- Instruct students to wash their hands thoroughly after the investigation.

Tip Preparation Quick Tips:

- Prepare the riverbed or model houses for any students needing assistance.
- Make modeling dough in advance and separate into two 1-pound balls—approximately the size of a very large grapefruit.
- If completing *Task 2*, consider having the students build the model trees and craft stick houses on day 1 to allow the glue to dry.
- Keep the clay riverbed and paper houses for *Task 2*.
- Organize and group materials in advance so as to allow for a smooth transition between the end of one class and the start of the next.

Options for Project-Based Learning:
- Students can test different river patterns or other land forms on their model.
- Students can research other flood-prevention techniques and model them.

Task 1 − Procedure Answers:

6. and **7.** Regular river flow and flooding. The water stayed in the river, and the houses were dry when a little water was used. When there was a lot of water fast, it went everywhere and the houses all got wet.

9. Answers will vary but may include the following. *I made levees out of clay. I put them between the river and the house. I made sandbags out of plastic bags and sand, I put them next to the house. I put my house on toothpick stilts.*

Time Rating:

1 = less time, 4 = more time
Teacher Prep: 4
Student Prep: 1
Student Cleanup: 1
Time on Task: 45 min

Materials:

For each group
- baking pan or tub
- book or board, thick
- cardstock
- house pattern
- measuring cup, 2-cup size
- modeling clay or dough, 2 pounds
- 2 plastic sandwich bags
- sand, 2 cups
- tape, 1 ft
- 2 toothpicks, cut in half
- 2 towels
- water, 2 cups

For each group
- *All About Flood Safety* document
- pencil

Data Table
Data will vary but should resemble the sample data table shown.

Design idea	Flood solution	Describe what happened when it flooded
1	build levee	Water went around levee and houses stayed dry.
2	use sandbags	Water mostly went around sandbags. Some of the houses got a little wet when water went under or around the sandbags.
3	built house on stilts	The floodwater went under the house and the house stayed dry.

Task 1 – Summary Answers:

1. People who live where it floods a lot, like right by a river or lake, probably have to worry about it a lot. Sometimes streets are closed, or houses are ruined, or it can cause landslides and erosion.

2. a house on stilts, because it kept the house dry, and you could build it right by the river

3. the levee because you need space to build the levee between the river and the house

4. the sandbags because you might not ever need to protect the house from flooding, so you can put them up and take them down when you need to

Print and distribute information in the textbox, All about Flood Safety. Enlarge as needed.

All about Flood Safety

There are many ways that people try to prevent flooding of homes.

Levee
A levee is a natural or human-made wall that blocks water. Levees are usually made of dirt. Rivers make natural levees by pushing the dirt to the side of the river. Natural levees run in the same direction of the flow of water. Human-made levees are built by piling up a hill of soil, sand, or rocks. Sometimes they are made using wood or concrete.

Homes on Stilts
Some people build their houses on top of wooden or cement posts. The house does not touch the ground! This is usually done to keep the house from getting wet in a flood. The floodwater can rise up under the house and the house stays dry.

Sandbags
A canvas or plastic bag is filled with sand. Sand is very heavy and is cheap. Sand is easy to put in bags. Sand is easier to clean up than clay. Gravel can also be used but does not work as well. People put the sand in bags that are small enough that they can lift and stack the bags. They put the bags next to the river, or pile them up around a house. Sandbags can be placed around a house quickly.

© Houghton Mifflin Harcourt Publishing Company

Task 1 Performance Rubric

Rating Scale

3 Outstanding	1 Needs Improvement
2 Satisfactory	0 Did Not Demonstrate Skill

NS Did not have the opportunity to observe

Teacher Directions:
This rubric allows for performance observation of 10 students. Make copies as needed. If students are working in groups, record the group name.

Group Name ___________

Names of Students

Skills										
DCI.3-ESS3-1.B Natural Hazards The student takes steps to reduce the impact of the flood.										
SEP.3-5.G.1 Engaging in Argument from Evidence The student makes a valid claim about the merit of the design solution that reduces the impacts of flooding.										
CCC.3-5.B.1 Cause and Effect The student identifies cause-and-effect relationships between the design solution and the impact of the flooding.										
CCC.NOS.3-5.B.1 Science is a Human Endeavor The student describes how the design solution can affect everyday life.										
DCI.3-5-ETS1-2.B.2 Developing Possible Solutions The student researches flood prevention, and bases the solution on his or her research.										
SEP.3-5.F.4 Constructing Explanation and Designing Solutions The student compares multiple solutions to the flooding problem based on how well the solutions meet the criteria and constraints of the problem.										
Overall Achievement of Performance Expectation The student uses a model to generate and compare multiple possible solutions to reduce the impact of a weather-related hazard.										
Total										

© Houghton Mifflin Harcourt Publishing Company

Winding Down

Task 1: Here Comes the Flood

In this task, you will make a model of a flooding river. You will model different options to reduce the effects of the flood on houses.

PROCEDURE

Make the models.

1. Press clay into an even layer in the top center of pan.

2. Make a riverbed in the clay that looks like the picture.

3. Place the board under one end of the pan to make the river slope downhill.

4. Follow the directions on the house template to build 4 paper houses. One of the houses is an extra.

5. Put 3 houses next to the river like what is shown in the picture below. Use a toothpick to mark where the houses go on the clay. Draw around the house with a pencil or a toothpick. This way you can put the houses back in the same place.

OBJECTIVE

Design a way to reduce flooding.

SAFETY

MATERIALS

For each group

- baking pan
- book or board, thick
- cardstock
- house pattern
- measuring cup
- modeling clay
- 2 plastic sandwich bags
- sand
- tape, 1 foot
- 2 toothpicks, cut in half
- 2 towels
- water

For each student

- *All about Flood Safety* document
- pencil
- scissors

© Houghton Mifflin Harcourt Publishing Company

Investigate and read.

6. Pour 1/2 cup of water slowly down the river. Record your observations. Carefully pour the water from the tub or pan back into the measuring cup or into the sink. Clean up any spilled water with the towel.

7. Pour 2 cups of water quickly down the river.

   Think about steps 6 and 7. What is being modeled in these steps? What did you observe in steps 6 and 7?

   Write your answer on the lines.

   ____

   ____

   ____

   ____

8. Think about what you learned about floods in class. Read *All about Flood Safety*.

Build a design.

9. Each person in your group should build one of the flood safety designs from the *All about Flood Safety*.

   Describe your flood solution. Include a description of where you placed your solution.

   Write your answer on the lines.

   ____

   ____

   ____

   ____

© Houghton Mifflin Harcourt Publishing Company

10. Place undamaged houses on the riverbed in the spots you marked with a toothpick.

11. Place the flood safety design you built on the riverbed.

12. Pour 2 cups of water quickly down the river. Record your observations in the *Data Table*. Carefully pour the water from the tub or pan back into the measuring cup or into the sink. Clean up any spilled water with the towel.

13. Repeat steps 10 through 12 to test each of the designs your group made.

Data Table

Record your observations for the three flood solutions.

Design Idea	Flood Solution	Describe what happened when it flooded
1	build levee	
2	use sandbags	
3	built house on stilts	

TASK SUMMARY

1. How does flooding affect everyday life?

Write your answer on the lines.

____

____

____

____

____

2. Which flood solution would be best for a house right next to a river that
floods often?

Write your answer on the lines.

____

____

____

____

3. Which flood solution would be best for a house that is close to, but not right
next to, a river that floods often?

Write your answer on the lines.

____

____

____

____

____

4. Which flood solution would be best for a house that is in an area that does
not flood often?

Write your answer on the lines.

____

____

____

____

____

Winding Down

Task 2: Huff and Puff and Blow Your House Down

The student will investigate methods to prevent damage due to wind.

Performance Expectations and 3D Learning:

PE.3-ESS3-1 Make a claim about the merit of a design solution that reduces the impacts of a weather-related hazard.

PE.3-5-ETS1-2 Generate and compare multiple possible solutions to a problem based on how well each is likely to meet the criteria and constraints of the problem.

Safety:

- Instruct students to use materials only as directed.
- Instruct students to wash their hands thoroughly after the investigation.
- Instruct students to use caution when using sharp tools and the electric fan.

Tip **Preparation Quick Tips:**

- Prepare the model houses and trees for any students needing assistance.
- If an electric fan is not available, paper or cardboard can be used as a fan, or students can blow on the houses.
- If only one fan is available for the whole class, students can take turns with the fan by moving their model to the fan.
- Keeping the clay in the pan from *Task 1* is not advised, because the lip of the pan will cause a wind block for the fan. It is best to place the clay on a flat surface such as a board or piece of cardboard for this task.
- Consider making the model trees and craft-stick house a day in advance to allow the glue to dry.
- Cut craft sticks and toothpicks in half. This makes them the right size for the scale of other houses and the thickness of clay they have to push the toothpicks into.
- The paper houses should not be pressed into the clay or dough, just placed gently on top.
- Students could be organized into groups of four and each assigned a different house design to build (House 1 requires no modifications).
- Organize and group materials in advance. Build an example log cabin for student reference.

Time Rating:

1 = less time; 4 = more time
Teacher Prep: 2
Student Prep: 1
Student Cleanup: 1
Time on Task: 45 min

Materials:

For each group

- cardboard, small piece
- cardstock
- 6 cotton balls
- 16 craft sticks
- 6 craft sticks, cut in half
- fan
- flat surface for riverbed
- glue
- house pattern, from *Task 1*
- riverbed model, from *Task 1*
- tape
- 2 toothpicks, cut in half

For each student

- pencil
- scissors

- **Build the walls of the log cabin.** Cut one craft stick in half so that you have two pieces. Make a frame by gluing the two smaller pieces to two regular-sized craft sticks. Repeat this four times so that you have four rectangular frames. Glue the frames on top of each other to build the walls of the cabin.

- **Build the roof of the log cabin.** Cut a craft stick in half. Place the craft sticks parallel to each other. Glue four craft sticks to the two cut pieces. This makes half of a roof. Repeat this step to make the other half of the roof.

- Refer to *Task 2* of *Supplemental Teacher Materials: Winding Down* for specific directions.

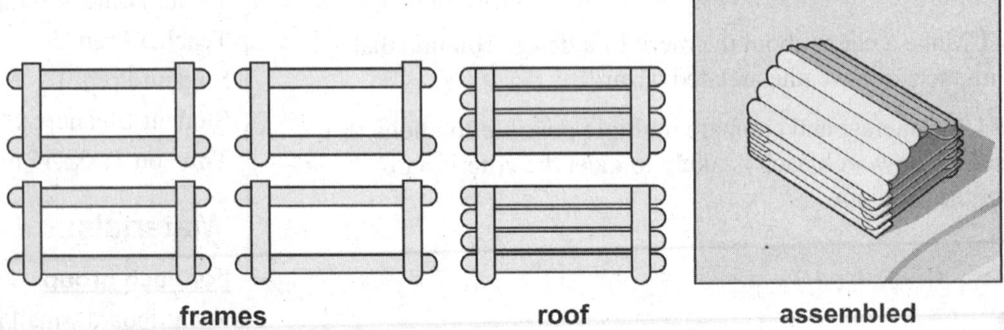

Options for Project-Based Learning:

- Students can come up with their own ways of designing solutions to test.
- Students can think of other natural hazards that could affect the houses and model those natural hazards using the materials provided.

Task 2 – Procedure Answers:

9, 10, and **11.** Observations will vary but should show that House 1, the house without any adjustments, blew away, while the other houses may not have blown away so easily. Houses 4 and 5 likely did not blow away. The observations should resemble the sample data table shown.

Data Table

Data will vary but should resemble the sample data table shown.

House	Fan on low	Fan on medium	Fan on high
1 paper house	blew away	blew away	blew away
2 toothpick anchors	stayed where it was	stayed where it was	shook some, but stayed where it was
3 trees	stayed where it was	stayed where it was	blew away, tree fell down
4 cardboard	stayed where it was	stayed where it was	blew away
5 craft sticks	stayed where it was	stayed where it was	stayed where it was

Task 2 – Summary Answers:

1. So we could compare the solutions to the original (as a control).

2. It blocks the wind.

3. House 5, the one of blocks/craft sticks. It stayed where it was even in strong winds.

4. Answers will vary, but the following or an equivalent is acceptable. *I would put the toothpicks with the cardboard, so the house would be stronger, and stay where it is.*

Print and distribute the house patterns; two patterns are shown below.

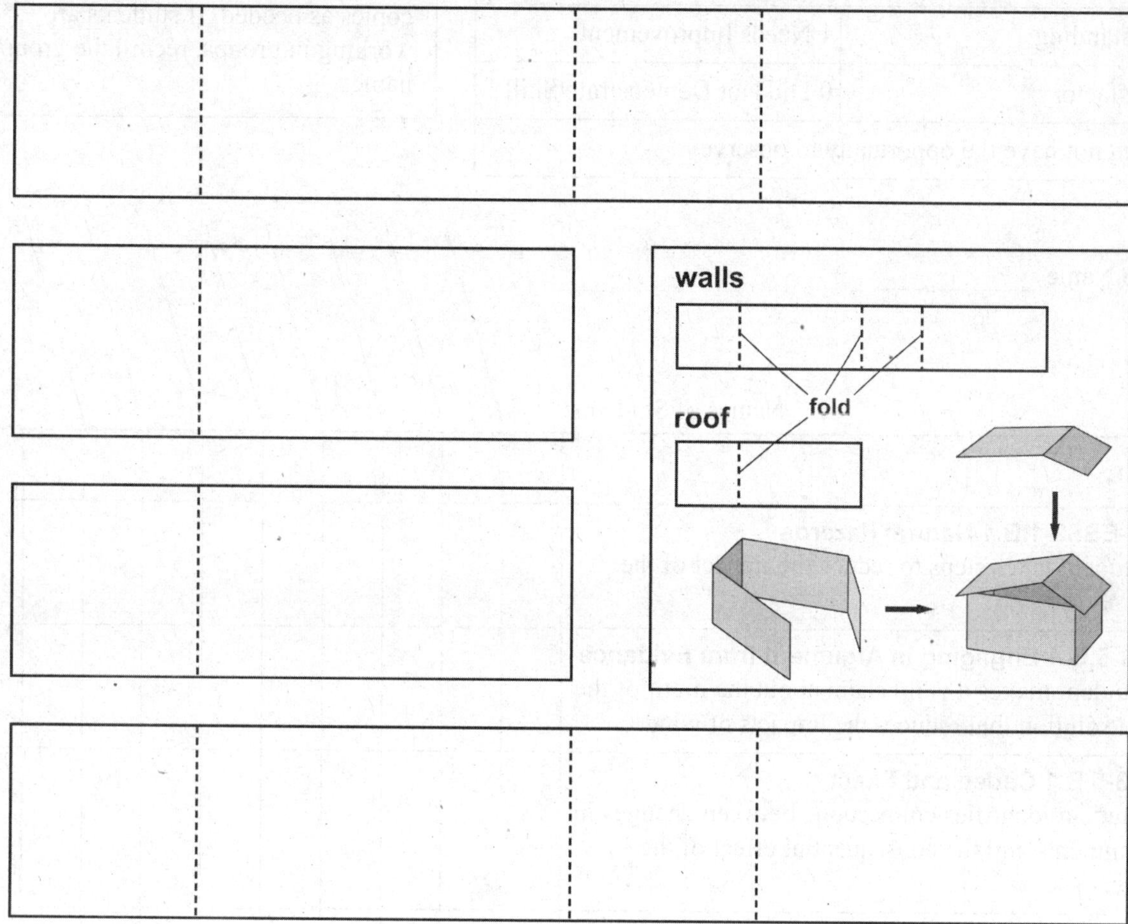

Task 2 Performance Rubric

Rating Scale

3 Outstanding	1 Needs Improvement
2 Satisfactory	0 Did Not Demonstrate Skill

NS Did not have the opportunity to observe

Teacher Directions:
This rubric allows for performance observation of 10 students. Make copies as needed. If students are working in groups, record the group name.

Group Name ___________

Names of Students

Skills										
DCI.3-ESS3-1.B.1 Natural Hazards The student takes steps to reduce the impact of the wind.										
SEP.3-5.G.1 Engaging in Argument from Evidence The student makes a valid claim about the merit of the design solution that reduces the impacts of wind.										
CCC.3-5.B.1 Cause and Effect The student identifies connections between changes in environments and the consequential effect of the change.										
DCI.3-5-ETS1-2.B.2 Developing Possible Solutions The student tests how the solutions work under a range of likely conditions.										
SEP.3-5.F.4 Constructing Explanation and Designing Solutions The student compares multiple solutions to the wind problem based on how well they meet the criteria and constraints of the problem.										
Overall Achievement of Performance Expectation The student uses a model to generate and compare multiple possible solutions to reduce the impact of a weather-related hazard.										
Total										

Winding Down

Task 2: Huff and Puff and Blow Your House Down

In this task, you will model the effects of wind on a house. You will model different solutions to reduce the impacts of the wind on houses.

PROCEDURE

Build the houses and prepare the land.

1. Use the house pattern to make three paper houses. Number the houses 1, 2, and 3.

2. Put the clay riverbed model from *Task 1* on a flat board or table.

Set up the houses.

3. House 1 stays as it is with no changes.

4. Adjust House 2 so that it is on stilts.

   Use toothpicks to anchor the paper house to the clay on the board. Put the toothpicks inside the walls of the house, and then press the toothpicks into the clay.

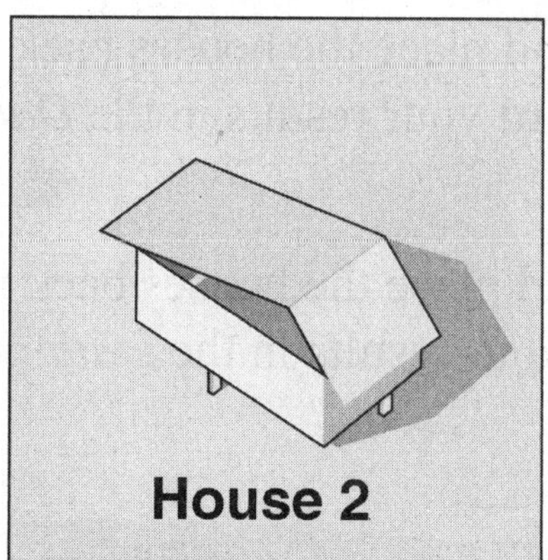

OBJECTIVE

Design solutions to reduce the impact of high winds.

SAFETY

MATERIALS

For each group

- cardboard
- cardstock
- 6 cotton balls
- 16 craft sticks
- 6 craft sticks, cut in half
- fan
- flat surface for riverbed
- glue
- house pattern
- riverbed model
- tape
- 2 toothpicks, cut in half

For each student

- pencil
- scissors

5. Add trees next to House 3. Glue a cotton ball to the end of a craft stick to make a model tree. Make a second tree. Put the model trees in the clay between House 3 and where the fan will be.

House 3

House 4

6. Make House 4. Trace the house pattern on to cardboard. Carefully cut the cardboard and tape it to make the cardboard house.

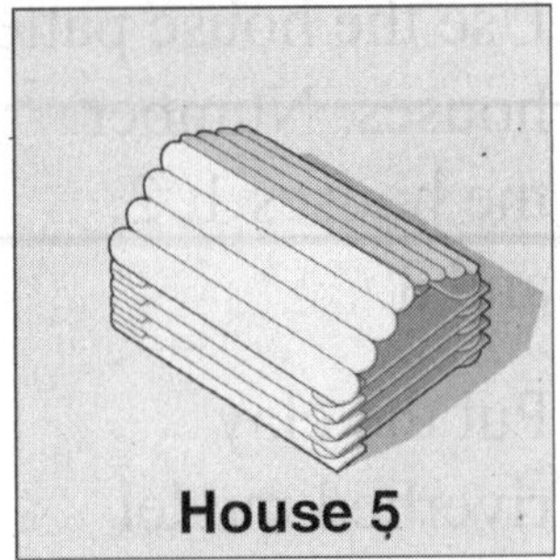

House 5

7. Look at the teacher model of a log cabin. Make House 5 a log cabin out of craft sticks and glue.

8. Place all five houses in a row on the board, like that shown in the picture of the five houses.

Test the houses.

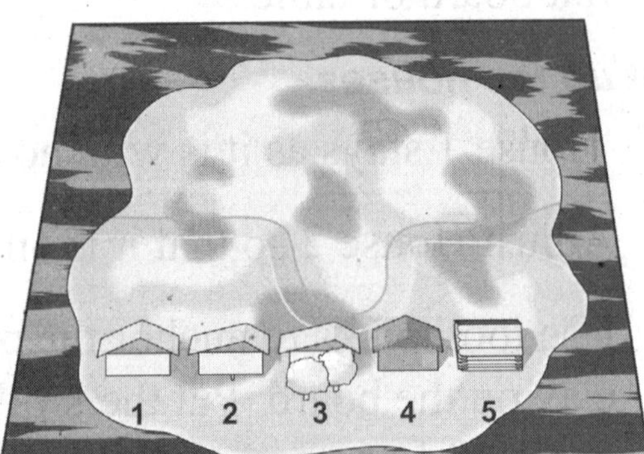

9. Follow your teacher's directions for using the fan. Put the model in front of the fan. Turn the fan on low. Record your results in the *Data Table*.

10. Fix or replace any houses that were damaged, and place the houses back in their same spots. Turn the fan on medium. Record your results in the *Data Table*.

11. Fix or replace any houses that were damaged and place the houses back in their same spots. Turn the fan on high. Record your results in the *Data Table*.

Data Table

Did the houses from steps 9–11 blow away or stay in place?

Write the "blew away" or "stayed in place" for each house in the table.

House Number	Fan on low speed	Fan on medium speed	Fan on high speed
1			
2			
3			
4			
5			

TASK SUMMARY

1. Explain why you kept one house the same as the teacher's, without making changes to it. Write your answer on the lines.

____

____

____

____

____

2. Explain how planting trees next to the house helps in windy conditions. Write your answer on the lines.

____

____

____

____

____

3. Identify which house is the best for strong winds. Explain your answer. Use results from your experiment to provide support for your answer.

Write your answer on the lines.

____

____

____

____

____

4. Sometimes even better designs can be made by combining solutions.

Describe how you could combine solutions to make a better design.

____

____

____

____

____

Explain how you chose to combine those solutions.

____

____

____

____

____

Winding Down

Task 3: Weather Wise

The student will research typical weather conditions.

Performance Expectations and 3D Learning

PE.3-ESS2-1 Represent data in tables and graphical displays to describe typical weather conditions expected during a particular season.

 **Preparation Quick Tips:**

- Fill out parts of the graph and table for those needing additional assistance.
- Organize and group materials in advance so as to allow for a smooth transition between the end of one class and the start of the next.

Options for Project-Based Learning:

- Students can research weather affecting their town.
- Students can research when flooding and wind damage is most likely in their town.

Task 3 – Procedure Answers:

2. Answers will vary but should resemble the sample table shown.

Kuni's Wind Data

Season	Wind speed (mph)	Wind direction
Winter	10.5	east
Spring	11	east
Summer	8	southeast
Fall	10	east

Task 3 – Summary Answers:

1. winter
2. summer
3. melting snow, broken dams, how close you are to river
4. The trees should be placed on the east side of the house.

Time Rating:

1 = less time, 4 = more time
Teacher Prep: 1
Student Prep: 1
Student Cleanup: 1
Time on Task: 30 min

Materials:

For each student
- *Kuni's Weather Journal*
- pencil

3. Answers will vary but should resemble the sample graph shown.

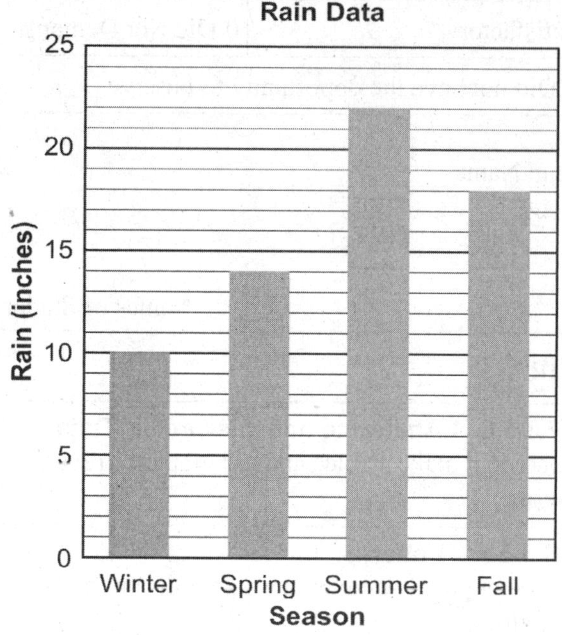

Print and distribute information in the textbox, Kuni's Weather Journal. Enlarge as needed.

Kuni's Weather Journal

My name is Kuni, and I live in Florida. I have been taking notes on the weather every year in my journal. This is a summary of my notes over the years.

Winter

Winter is chilly! Brrr! We get about 10 inches of rain in winter. Usually we get light rain, and it almost never snows. There is always a nice breeze here. The wind speed is usually 10.5 miles per hour (mph). It blows from the east most of the time.

Spring

The wind usually comes from the southeast or east. The wind is a little faster in spring, 11 mph. We usually get about 14 inches of rain.

Summer

The wind is mostly from the southeast and is around 8 mph. We get lots of big thunderstorms in summer. We get about 22 inches of rain. It is hot and humid here.

Fall

There are not as many thunderstorms in fall. We still get around 18 inches of rain, though. The wind is about 10 mph again and comes from the east.

Task 3 Performance Rubric

Rating Scale

3 Outstanding	1 Needs Improvement
2 Satisfactory	0 Did Not Demonstrate Skill

NS Did not have the opportunity to observe

Teacher Directions:
This rubric allows for performance observation of 10 students. Make copies as needed. If students are working in groups, record the group name.

Group Name ___________

Names of Students

Skills										
SEP.3-5.D. 1 Analyzing and Interpreting Data The student makes tables and bar graphs to reveal patterns.										
CCC.3-5.A.2 Patterns The student uses patterns in weather data to make predictions.										
Overall Achievement of Performance Expectation The student represents data in tables and graphical displays to describe typical weather.										
Total										

Winding Down

Task 3: Weather Wise

In this task, you research weather patterns and organize your data into tables and graphs. You will make predictions based on patterns.

PROCEDURE

1. Read Kuni's weather journal.

2. Finish the data table showing the wind speed and direction in Kuni's town.

OBJECTIVE

Research weather condition

MATERIALS

For each student

- *Kuni's Weather Journal*
- pencil

Kuni's Wind Data

Season	Wind speed (mph)	Wind direction
winter		
spring		
summer		
fall		

3. Make a bar graph of Kuni's rain data.

   Draw a bar for each season's rain data.

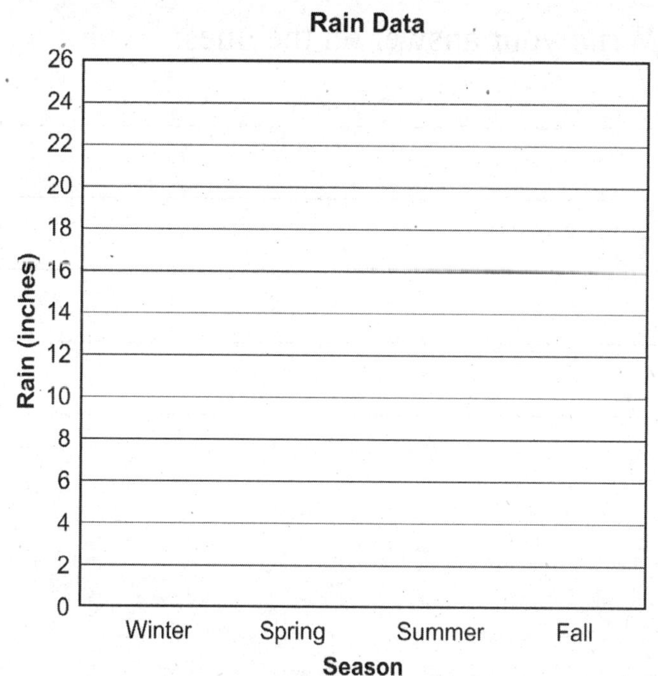

Rain Data

TASK SUMMARY

1. Write the letter of the season to correctly complete the sentence.

    Kuni's town gets the least amount of rain in __________.

    A. spring

    B. summer

    C. fall

    D. winter

2. Write the letter of the season to correctly complete the sentence.

    Flooding is most likely to happen in Kuni's town in the __________.

    A. spring

    B. summer

    C. fall

    D. winter

3. Which factors, other than rain, can cause flooding?

    Write your answer on the lines.

    ____

    ____

    ____

    ____

    ____

4 Kuni's family wants to plant trees to block the wind from his house. Where should they put the trees to best protect his house?

Draw trees next to Kuni's house.

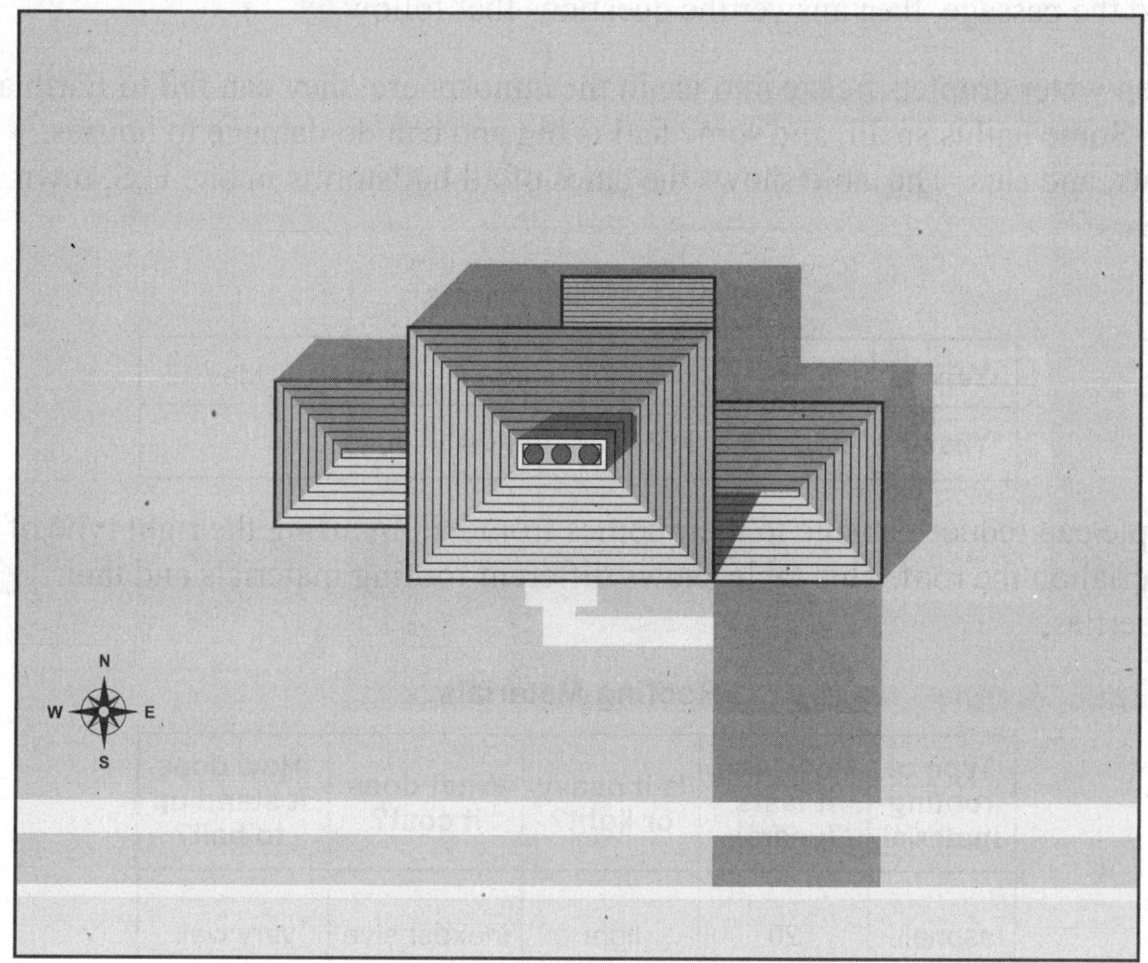

© Houghton Mifflin Harcourt Publishing Company

Winding Down

Part 2: Hail, a Natural Hazard

Read the passage, then answer the questions that follow.

When water droplets freeze into ice in the atmosphere, they can fall to Earth as hail. Some hail is small, and some hail is big and can do damage to houses, plants, and cars. The table shows the dates of all hailstorms in one U.S. town in 2 years.

Dates of Hailstorms

Year 1	July 9	June 27	June 25	June 24	May 17
Year 2	August 4	July 26	July 24	July 20	

People can reduce damage to their homes from hail by using the right type of material on the roof. This table shows different roofing materials and their properties.

Roofing Materials

Type of roofing material	How long it lasts (years)	Is it heavy or light?	What does it cost?	How does it stand up to hail?
asphalt	20	light	inexpensive	very well
clay tile	15	heavy	expensive	brittle and breaks easily
metal	40	light	middle	gets dents, but does not break
slate	10	very heavy	expensive	can chip and break

1. Tobias needs a roof that is light, inexpensive, and stands up well to hail. Rank the roofing materials by how well they meet his criteria and constraints.

    Number the materials in order from 1 to 4 with 1 as the best option and 4 as the worst option.

	asphalt
	clay tile
	metal
	slate

2. The map shows the frequency of hailstorms across the United States.

    Circle the region of the United States that is most likely to have hailstorms.

    Hail Storms in the United States Over 10 Years

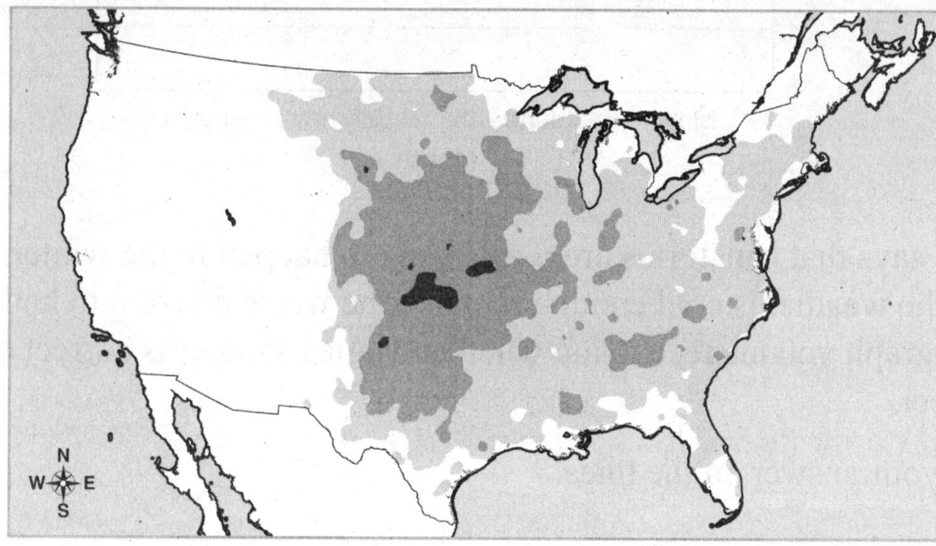

3. Complete the graph to show in which months the hailstorms happened.

Draw a bar for the number of hailstorms each month.

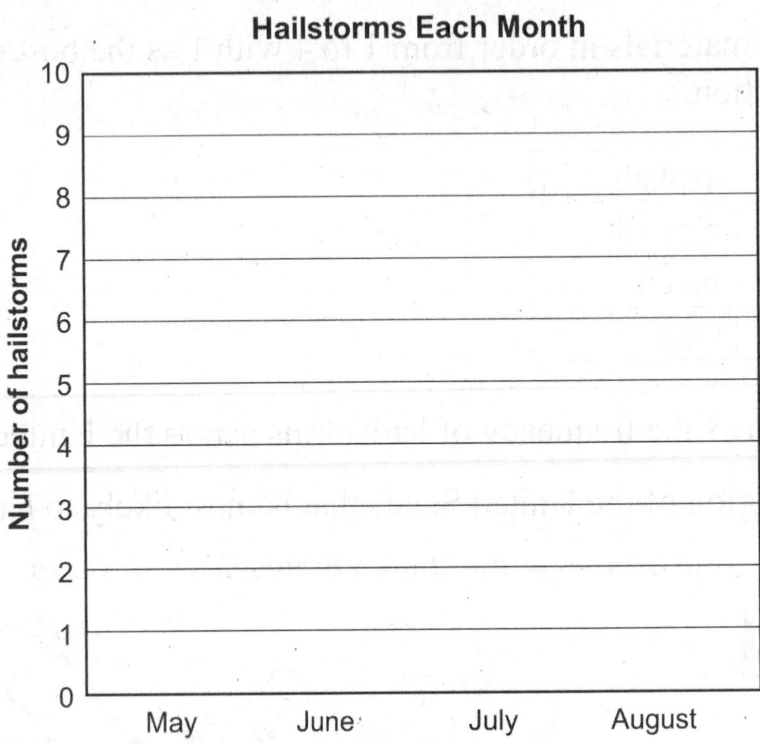

4. Matias says that hailstorms are most likely to happen in the winter. That is when the weather is cold enough to make the water freeze into hail. Based on the graph you made, explain whether Matias's claim is correct or incorrect.

Write your answer on the lines.

____

____

____

____

____

5. Katrin wants a roof that lasts at least 30 years. She does not really care how much the material costs, but she wants the material to be light. She lives in an area that has occasional hailstorms.

Identify which material Katrin should use. Explain your answer.

____

____

____

____

Explain whether this solution will stop hail from hitting her house.

____

____

____

____

Explain how researching the technology available can help Katrin.

____

____

____

____

Winding Down

Item Analysis		
Item #	**Standards**	**DOK**
1	3-5-ETS1-2, DCI.3-5.ETS1.B.2, SEP.3-5.F.4	3
2	3-ESS2-1, DCI.3-ESS2.D.1, CCC.NOS.3-5.A.1	2
3	3-ESS2-1, DCI.3-ESS2.D.1, SEP.3-5.D.1	3
4	3-ESS2-1, DCI.3-ESS2.D.1, CCC.3-5.A.2	3
5	3-ESS3-1, DCI.3-ESS3.B.1, SEP.3-5.G.2, CCC.NOS.3-5.B.1	3

1. The numbers are 1, 3, 2, and 4. Asphalt meets all of the criteria and constraints. Metal meets the criteria of being light, and it stands up okay to hail. It is the second least expensive option. Clay tile comes next because it is expensive and it breaks but is lighter than the slate. Slate meets none of the criteria or constraints.

2. Central U.S. that is shaded to show 8+ hailstorms is correct.

3. May had 1 hailstorm. June had 3 hailstorms. July had 1 hailstorm, and August had 1 hailstorm.

4. Use the rubric below to evaluate total points earned for this item.   *[max point: 1]*

CCC - 1 point	
Claims	The student is able to use patterns to make predictions (CCC).
Evidence of Mastery of Crosscutting Concepts	1 point for correctly using the data to make a prediction **Part 1:** One point is earned for explaining that Matias is incorrect because the hailstorms occurred in the summer. The following response, or an equivalent, is acceptable. • Matias is incorrect. All of the hailstorms happened in the summertime, so they are not more likely in the winter.

5. Use the rubric below to evaluate total points earned for this item.   *[max point: 3]*

DCI, SEP, CCC - 3 points	
Claims	The student is able to: 1. explain that humans cannot eliminate hazards but can take steps to reduce their impacts (DCI); and 2. make a claim about the merit of a solution by citing evidence about how it meets the criteria and constraints (SEP); and 3. explain how science affects everyday life (CCC).
Evidence of Mastery of Disciplinary Core Ideas	1 point for correctly explaining that the solution will not stop hail from hitting the house **Part 2:** One point is earned for explaining that the solution will not stop hail from hitting the house; however, it will likely reduce the amount of damage. The following answer, or an equivalent, is acceptable. • No, the hail will still hit the house, but it will do less damage.

Evidence of Mastery of Science and Engineering Practices	1 point for correctly identifying the best material to use **Part 1:** One point is earned for identifying that metal should be selected because it meets all of the criteria and constraints. The following answer, or an equivalent, is acceptable. • metal
Evidence of Mastery of Crosscutting Concepts	1 point for correctly explaining how doing research can help Katrin **Part 3:** One point is earned for explaining that research helps Katrin know what to choose to fit her needs. The following answer, or an equivalent, is acceptable. • Knowing what options are available help her make better choices for her needs.

© Houghton Mifflin Harcourt Publishing Company

Mid-Year Test

Read each question. Follow the instructions to answer the questions.

1. Tim designs a wagon that waters the grass.

   Tim tests the wagon. He finds that the water drains out too quickly. How could Tim improve his design?

   Circle the letter of the correct answer.

   A. make the holes smaller

   B. make the handle longer

   C. make the wheels larger

   D. make the wagon smaller

2. The picture shows some stages of a chicken's life cycle. Some stages are not shown.

   Birth is the first stage of a chicken's life cycle.

   Number the other stages in the correct order, starting with "2" for the second stage.

1	birth
	death
	reproduction
	growth

3. Jo started to group pictures of animals. She did not finish.
Complete the grouping of pictures.

Write one letter in each box. Some letters may not be used.

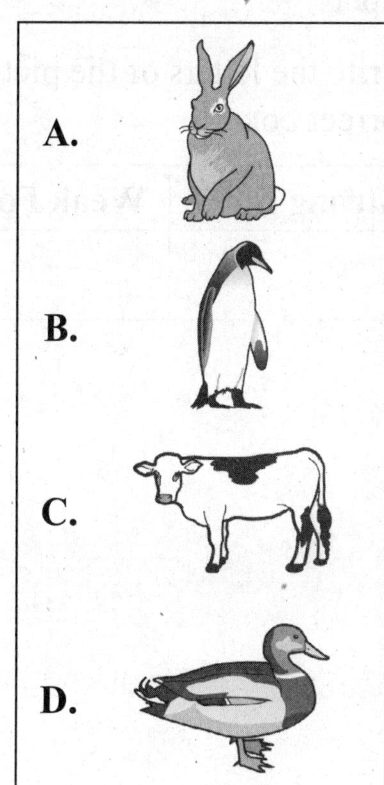

A.

B.

C.

D.

4. Sam wants to show how magnets attract each other. How should
she set up the magnets?

Write the letters of the pictures and words in the correct boxes.

	Magnet 1	Magnet 2	Reason
Attract			
Repel			

C. Poles are alike.

D. Poles are different.

5. Bob is studying static electricity. He held a glass rod over pieces of paper. What happened with the rod and paper?

Write the letters of the pictures in the correct boxes.

Strong Force	Weak Force

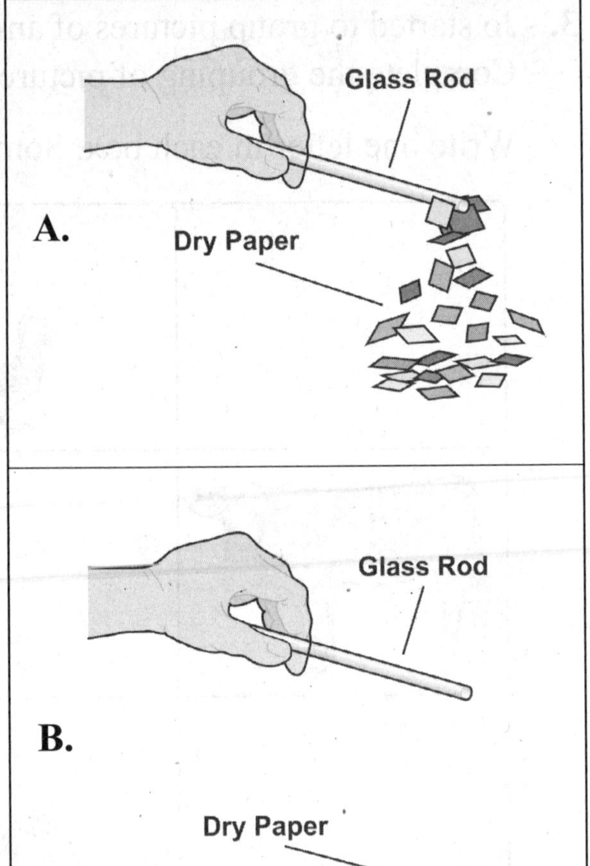

6. Heath saw two adult dogs and their puppies. He wrote down the color of the puppies' fur.

Which statements are true about how the dogs look?

Circle the letters of the 2 correct sentences.

Puppy Number	Color of Fur
1	Black
2	Brown
3	Black
4	Black
5	Brown
6	Brown

A. The puppies look like their mother but not like their father.

B. Some of the puppies have the same fur color as their father.

C. One parent has brown fur because some of the puppies have brown fur.

7. Jen tied the same weight onto strings of different lengths. She counted the number of swings until the weight stopped moving.

The 5-centimeter, cm, string made 10 swings. The 10-centimeter string made 45 swings.

Make a bar graph of Jen's data. Use your pencil to draw each bar up to the correct number.

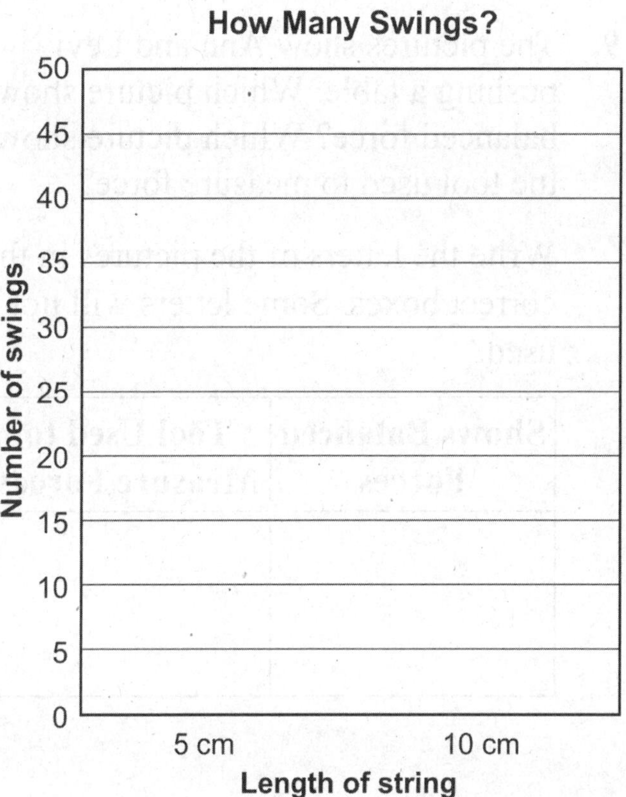

8. The stages of life for a frog and a lizard are listed.

Life Cycle Data for Two Animals

Stage in Life Cycle	Frog	Lizard
Birth	Eggs hatch tadpoles in water	Eggs hatch on land
Growth	Lives in water and on land; adults breathe air	Lives on land; adults breathe air
Reproduction	Happens in water	Happens on land

How are the life cycles of the frog and the lizard alike?

Circle the letter of the correct answer.

A. adults breathe air

B. reproduce on land

C. lay eggs that hatch in water

D. born on land and move to water

© Houghton Mifflin Harcourt Publishing Company

9. The pictures show Ann and Levi pushing a table. Which picture shows a balanced force? Which picture shows the tool used to measure force?

Write the letters of the pictures in the correct boxes. Some letters will not be used.

Shows Balanced Forces	Tool Used to Measure Forces

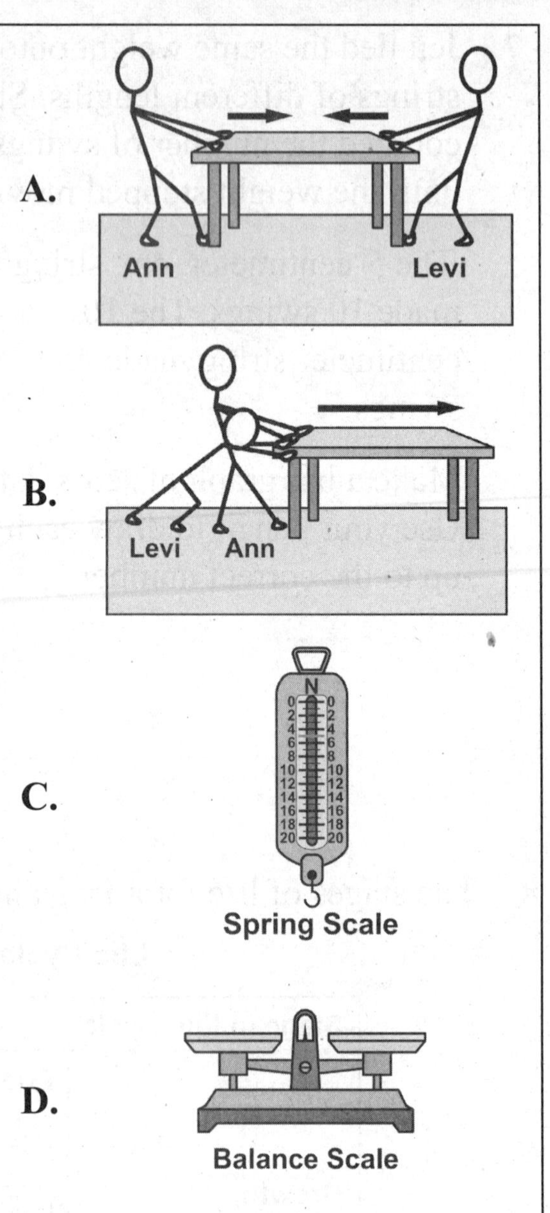

10. Some of the first car tires were very thin. Cars with these thin tires would slide off the road in rainstorms. New, bigger tires were made, as shown in the picture.

What are the likely reasons for the change in the tire design?

Early Design Thin Tire   Recent Design Thick Tire

Write one X in the correct box to show whether each statement is a likely reason or not.

Reason	Likely	Not Likely
A. People wanted safer tires.		
B. People wanted tires that could stay on wet roads.		
C. Car companies wanted nicer-looking tires on the cars.		

11. The pictures show the same plant.

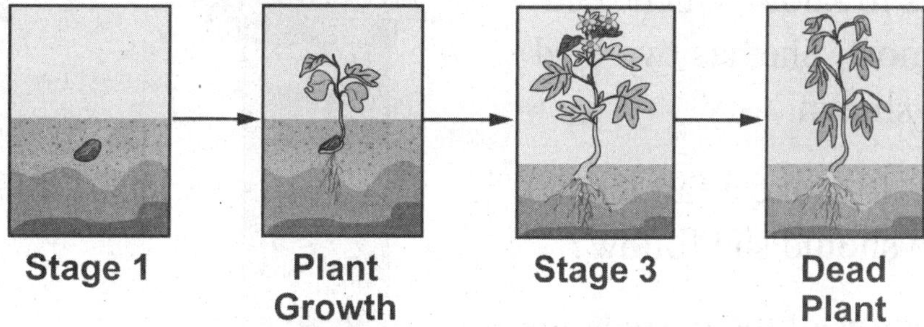

Stage 1   Plant Growth   Stage 3   Dead Plant

Read each question. Write your answer on the lines.

What is the name of the process shown?

____

What is the name of stage 1?

____

What is the name of stage 3?

____

© Houghton Mifflin Harcourt Publishing Company

12. Kim is studying magnets. She wrote down some of what she learned. Complete her table.

Write the letters in the empty boxes to correctly complete the table. Some letters will not be used.

Kim's Data Table

Picture of Magnet and Nail	Distance	Force
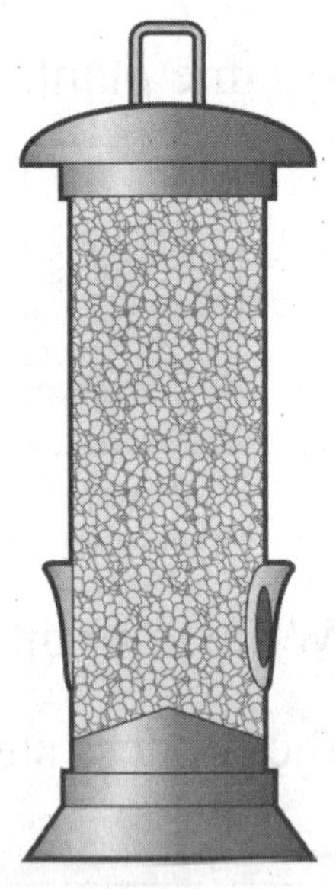		Strongest
	Far apart	

A. Weakest

B. Far apart

C. Close together

D. 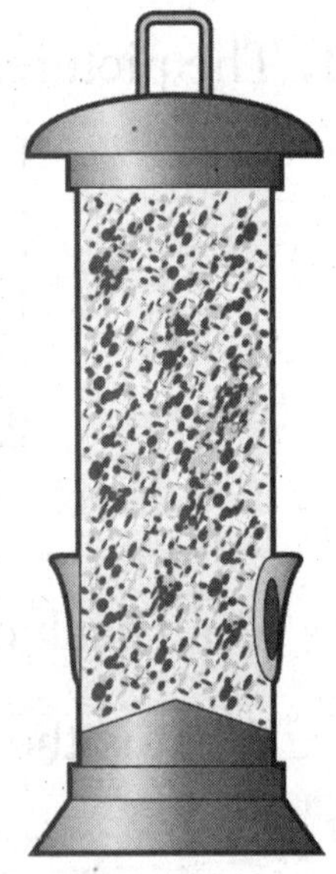

E.

13. Mina wants to know which seed birds like most. She has two bird feeders, as shown.

Mina wants to make a fair test. Which step should she follow?

Circle the letter of the correct answer.

A. Look at one feeder only in the morning.

B. Place the feeders far apart from each other.

Bird Feeder 1   **Bird Feeder 2**

C. Watch the feeders for the same amount of time.

D. Put one feeder on the ground and the other in a tree above it.

14. The pictures show the life cycles of a butterfly and a tree.

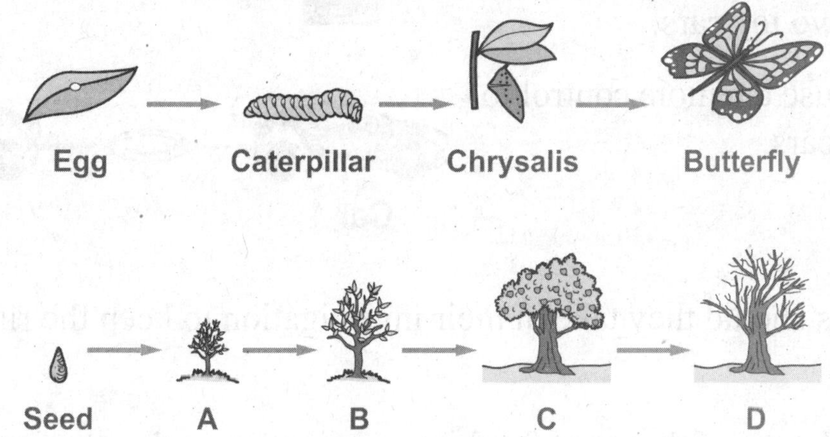

Decide if each sentence is true or false.

Write one X in the box to show whether each statement is true or false.

Statement	True	False
A. The life cycles of the butterfly and tree are the same.		
B. The caterpillar lays the egg that becomes the butterfly.		
C. The tree grows larger and the caterpillar changes into a butterfly.		

15. Walt put different weights on springs. He measured how far a spring stretched in centimeters, cm. The lengths the springs stretched were:

weight A, 22 cm; weight B, 18 cm; weight C, 20 cm; and weight D, 16 cm.

Write the letter of the weight in the box next to the length that the spring stretched.

Length of Spring	Letter of Weight
16 cm	
18 cm	
20 cm	
22 cm	

A. weight A

B. weight B

C. weight C

D. weight D

© Houghton Mifflin Harcourt Publishing Company

16. Leo and Mary want to show that forces can keep an object still. They connect a plastic ring between two toy cars.

Each will use a remote control to move the cars.

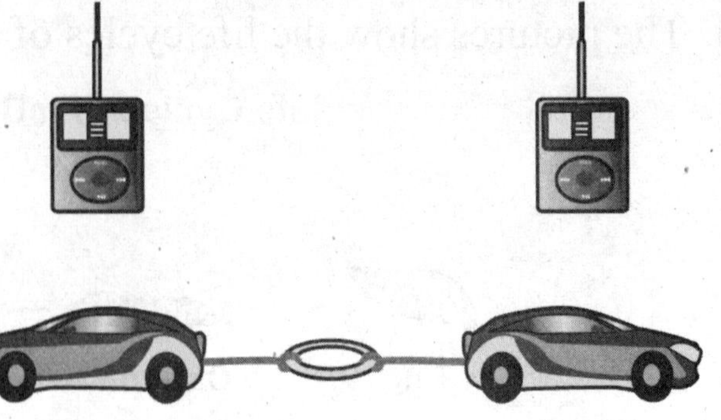

What steps should they take in their investigation to keep the ring from moving?

Write the letters of the steps for this investigation in the correct order. Some letters will not be used.

Step	Letters for the Step
1	
2	
3	

A. Move Car 1 forward but keep Car 2 still.

B. Move Cars 1 and 2 forward at the same time and at the same speed.

C. Watch that the ring remains still.

D. Write down that the ring moved in the same direction that Car 1 moved.

E. Write down that both cars had equal forces on the ring.

17. The pictures show how some living things are grouped.

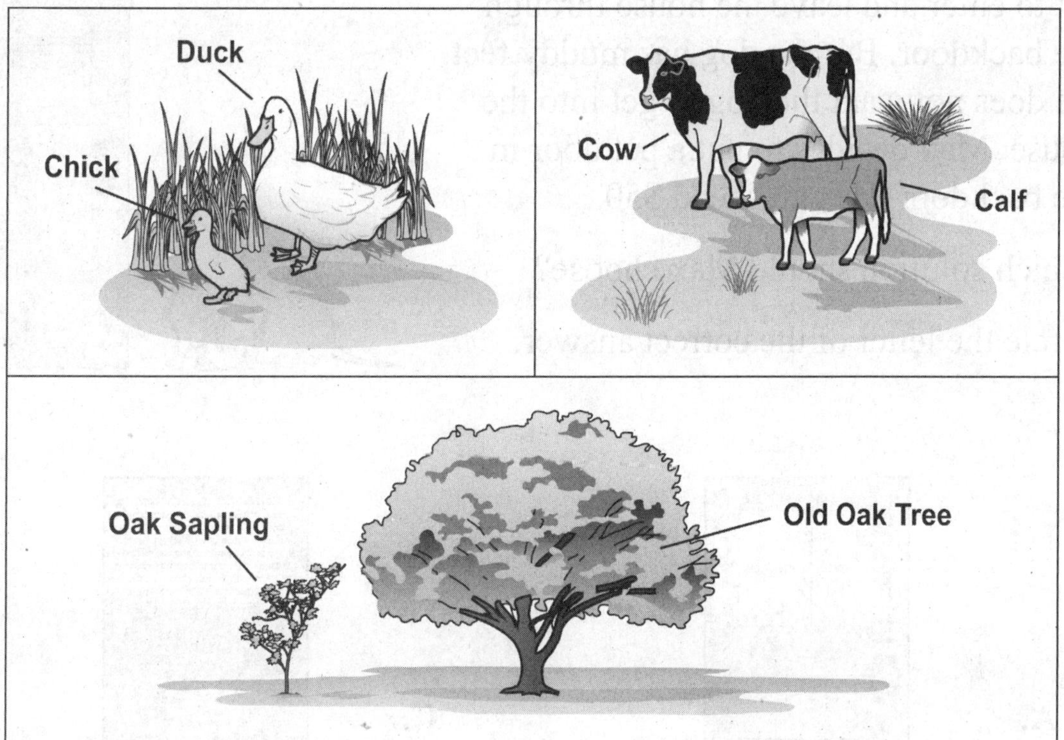

In which way are the pictures grouped?

Circle the letter of the correct answer.

A. by size

B. by how much they eat each day

C. by how similar the babies look to the adults

D. by how different the babies look from the adults

18. Max has a cat and a dog. He wants his cat to enter and leave the house through the backdoor. But the dog has muddy feet. He does not want the dog to get into the house. Max decides to put a pet door in the backdoor. He can spend $50.

Which solution should Max choose?

Circle the letter of the correct answer.

A.

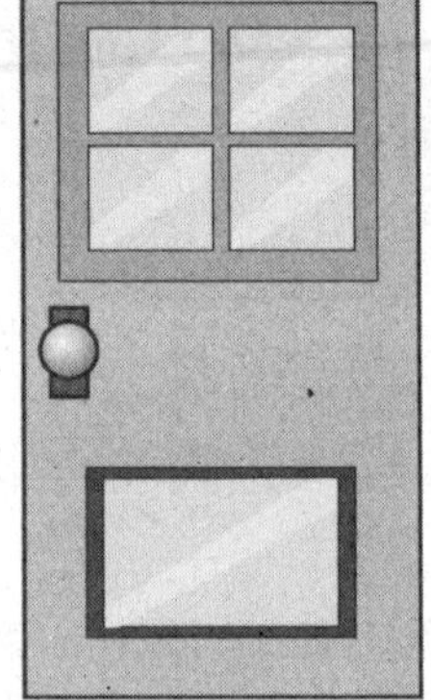

Cost of Cutting Large Hole in Door = $0

C.

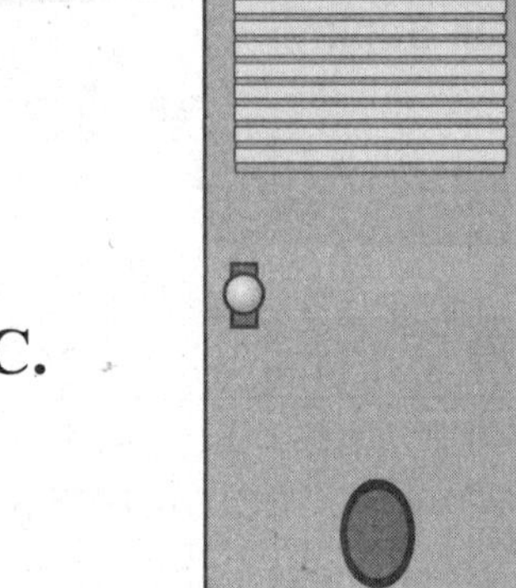

Cost of Buying New Door with Built-In Cat Door = $150

B.

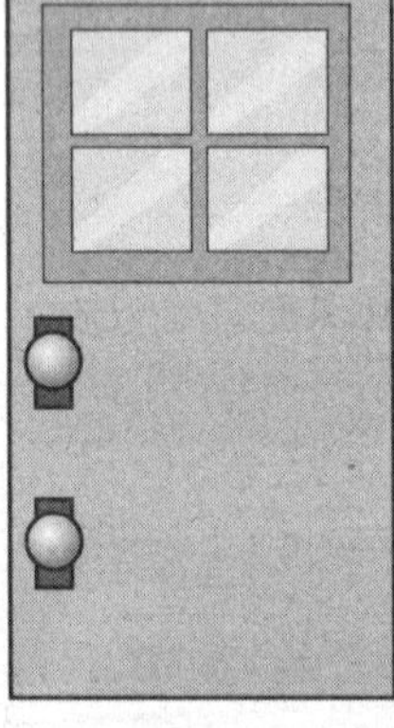

Cost of Installing New Doorknob Closer to Ground = $10

D.

Cost of Installing Small Plastic Flap with Magnetic Closure = $40

Directions: Read the passage, then answer the questions that follow.

Making the Shade

The sun shines on Dunia's porch. The heat hurts the plants on her porch. She put cloth curtains in the doorway of the porch.

The curtains block the sunlight. But there are downsides. The wind blows the curtains open, letting sunlight into the porch area. Dunia wants to fix the problem but has some requirements.

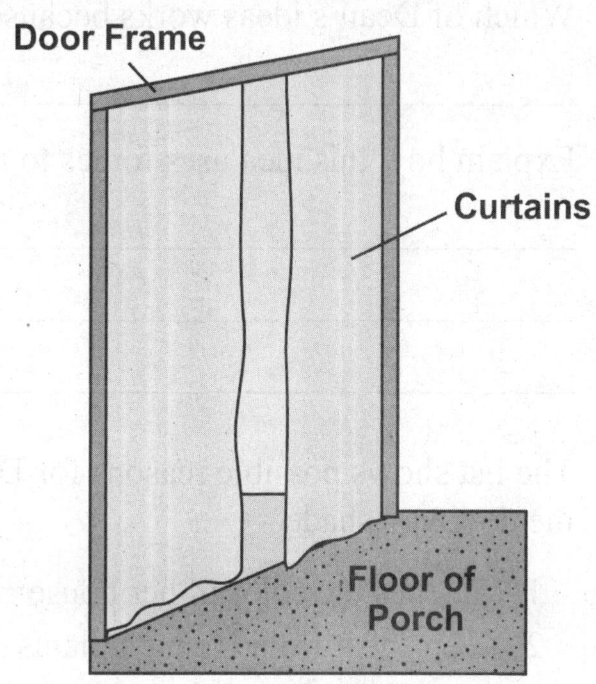

1. She must be able to walk through the doorway.
2. Her dogs must be able to walk through the doorway on their own.
3. The total cost must be $50 or less.

Dunia's friend Dean has helped other people with the same problem. He drew sketches of ideas that have worked for others. Dean wrote down the cost of each idea in a table.

Dean's Idea	Cost
1. Hang doors in doorway.	$100
2. Tie the curtains to the doorframe posts.	$10
3. Put magnets on the curtains to keep the wind from opening.	$5
4. Tie a string in the doorway and twist growing vines on the string.	$20

19. Look at Dean's ideas listed in the passage.

Read each statement. Write your answer on the lines.

Which of Dean's ideas works because of forces at different distances?

____

Explain how this idea uses forces to meet Dunia's requirements.

____

____

____

20. The list shows possible reasons for Dunia to make changes to the doorway shade.

1. Matches the color of her house
2. Keeps heat from Dunia's plants
3. Keeps people from breaking into Dunia's house

Which reasons match Dunia's requirements?

Circle the letter of the correct answer.

A. 1 only   **B.** 2 only   **C.** 1 and 3   **D.** 2 and 3

21. Dean's third idea uses magnets. What facts and discoveries about magnetic force were used in Dean's idea?

Circle the letters of all of the sentences that are correct.

A. Magnets can attract or repel each other.

B. The force of a magnet can move through fabrics.

C. A magnet must touch an object in order to move it.

22. Dunia wants to walk through the porch doorway. She wants her dogs to walk through the doorway on their own. She does not want to spend more than $50. Which of Dean's ideas best fits Dunia's needs?

Circle the letter around the idea Dunia should select.

<table>
<tr><td>

A. Idea 1:

- blocks sunlight and will not blow open
- keeps the dogs on the porch

B. Idea 2:

- blocks the sunlight
- will not blow open if kept tied down

</td><td>

C. Idea 3:

- a person or a dog can open the curtains
- the magnets will close the curtains behind a person or dog

D. Idea 4:

- blocks sunlight
- dogs cannot open

</td></tr>
</table>

23. Dean's third idea uses magnets. The diagram shows the positions of the magnets on the bottom part of the curtain.

What is the position of two magnets when the force is the strongest?

Circle the letter that shows the magnet position when the force is the strongest.

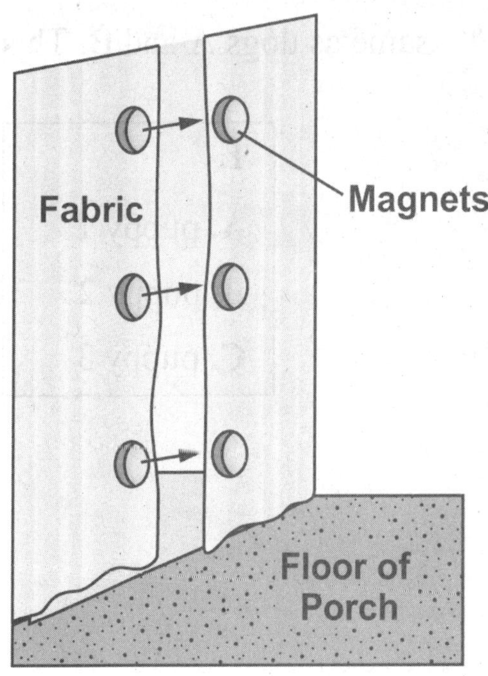

Magnet Positions

A	〇 〇
B	〇 〇
C	〇〇〇

24. The picture shows two dogs that are parents to one of the puppies.

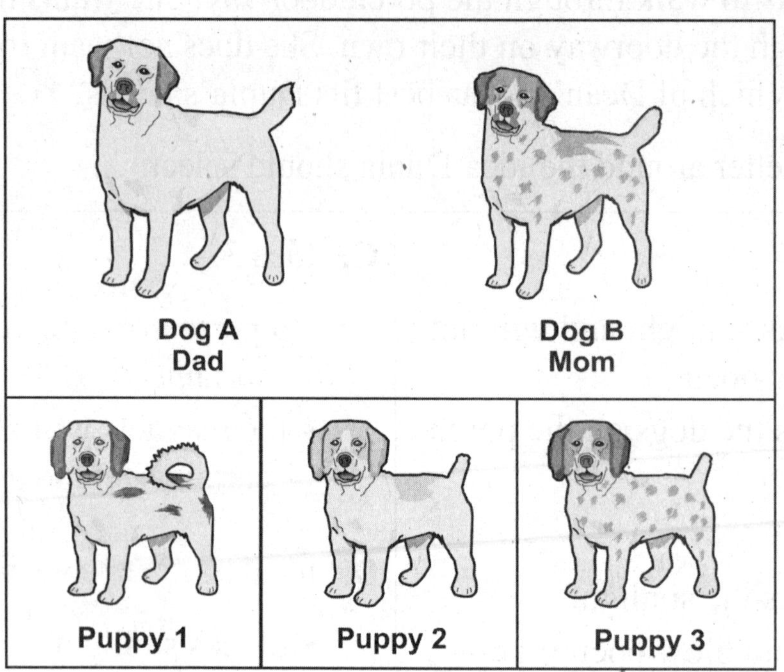

Write one letter in each blank to correctly complete the sentences.

Dogs A and B are the parents of **1.** _________ . This puppy's **2.** _________ is the same as dogs A and B. This puppy got its fur pattern from its **3.** _________ .

1.	2.	3.
A. puppy 1	**D.** fur pattern	**F.** dad
B. puppy 2	**E.** tail length	**G.** mom
C. puppy 3		

25. Picture 1 shows Jing holding a ball. Picture 2 shows that Jing let go of the ball. Picture 3 shows the ball after it hit the floor.

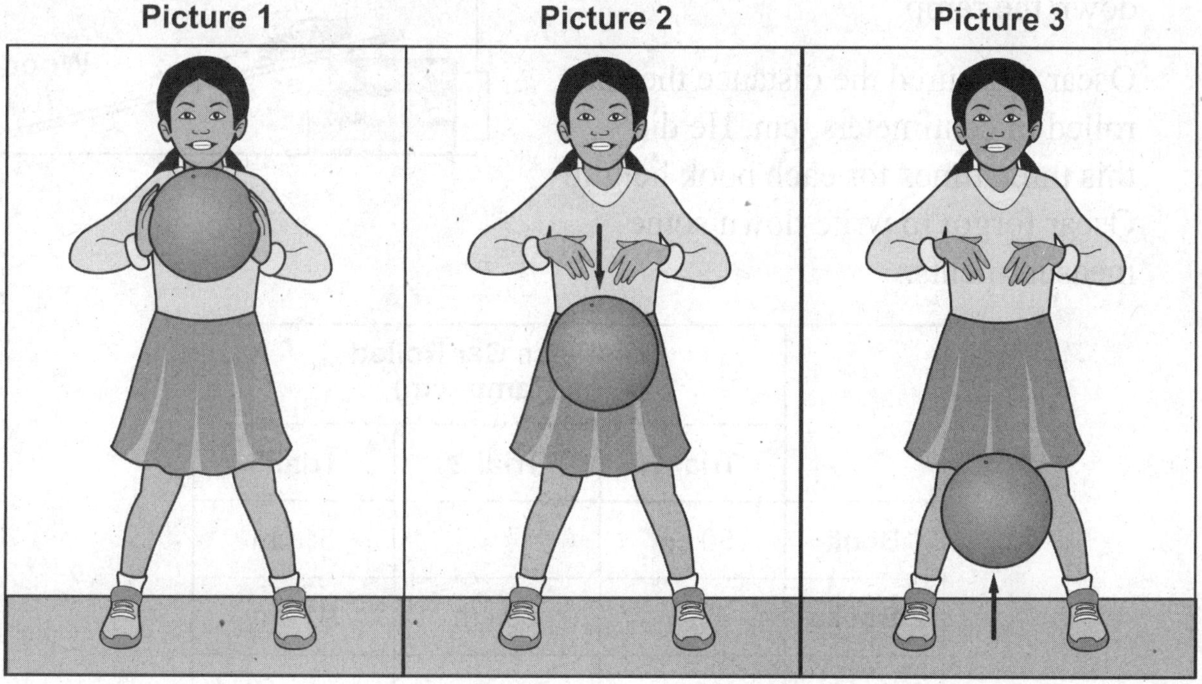

Picture 1   **Picture 2**   **Picture 3**

Read each statement. Write your answer on the lines.

Identify the picture where the forces on the ball are balanced.

____

Identify the two pictures where the forces on the ball are unbalanced.

____

Explain how the force changed when the ball hit the floor.

____

____

26. Oscar made a ramp from a piece of wood and books. He let a toy car roll down the ramp.

Oscar measured the distance the car rolled in centimeters, cm. He did this three times for each book height. Oscar forgot to write down some measurements.

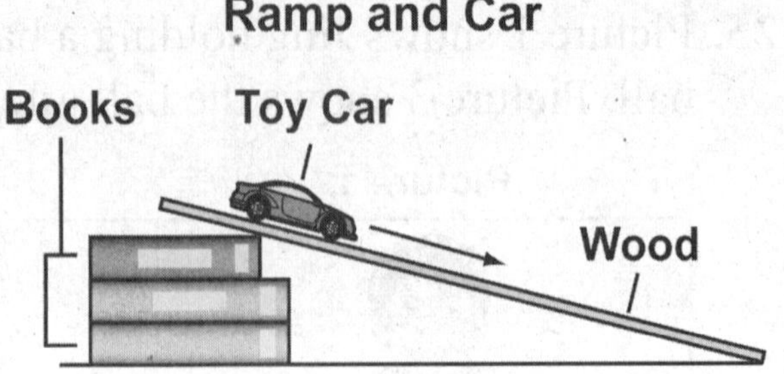

	Distance Car Rolled off Ramp (cm)		
	Trial 1	Trial 2	Trial 3
1 Book	50 cm		51 cm
2 Books		89 cm	91 cm
3 Books	130 cm	131 cm	

Conclusion:

Write the letters for the distance in the table. Write one letter for the conclusion below the table.

Distance	Conclusion
A. 90 cm	**D.** The car will not roll down a short ramp.
B. 129 cm	
C. 52 cm	**E.** The car rolls farther when the ramp is taller.

© Houghton Mifflin Harcourt Publishing Company

27. Ellis held his arm out straight and dropped a tennis ball. The picture shows the ball's motion.

Ellis will drop a rubber ball. Predict the ball's motion.

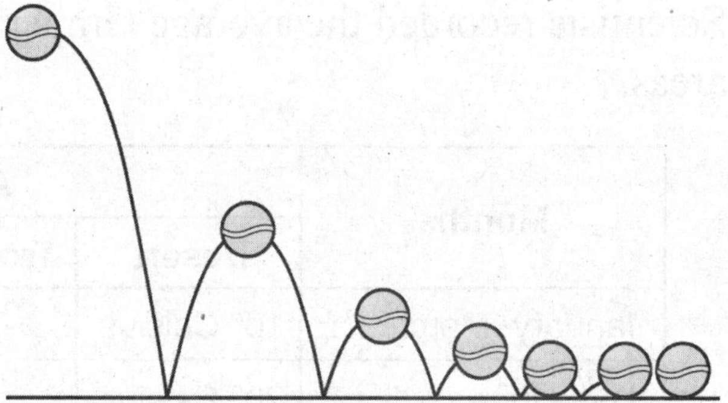

Write numbers 1, 2, and 3 in the boxes to show the order of the ball's motion.

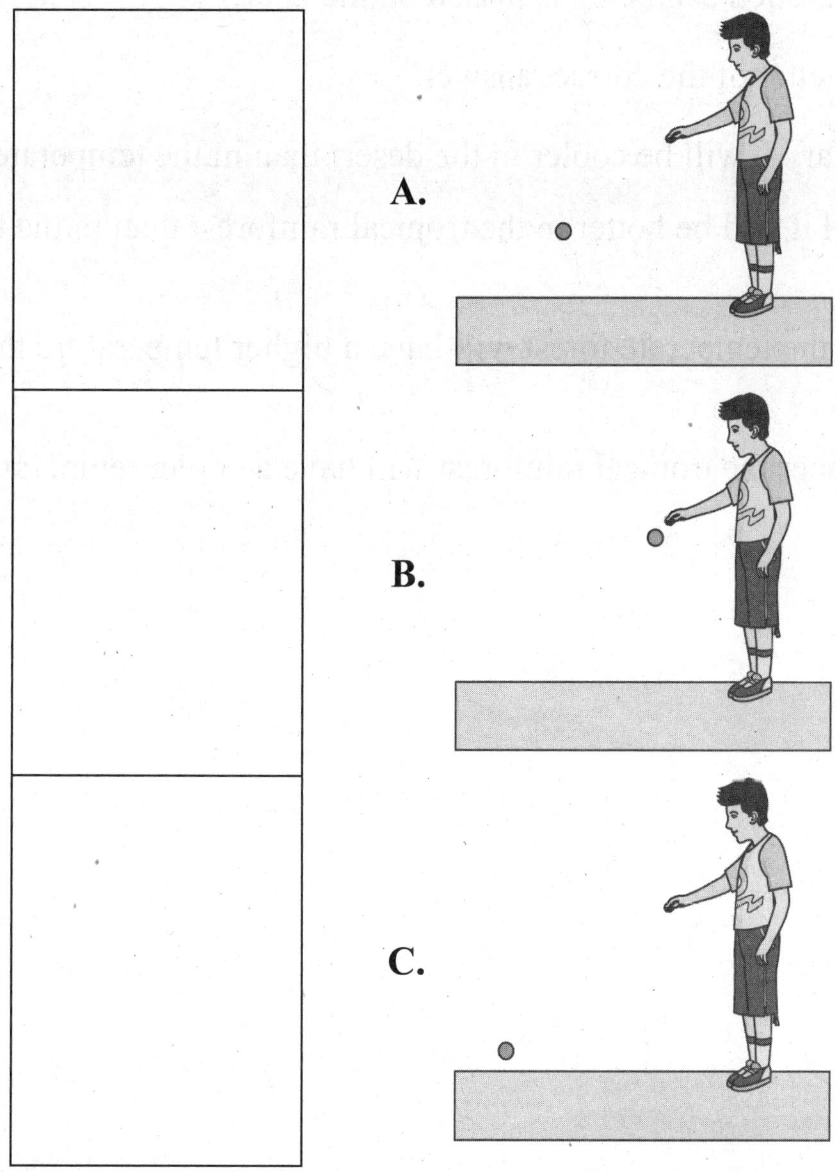

28. Scientists recorded the average temperature each month in three different areas.

Months	Average Temperature		
	Desert	Tropical Rainforest	Temperate Forest
January–March	10° Celsius	20° Celsius	0° Celsius
April–June	20° Celsius	30° Celsius	15° Celsius
July–September	25° Celsius	33° Celsius	20° Celsius
October–December	15° Celsius	20° Celsius	0° Celsius

Which prediction can be made based on the data?

Circle the letter of the correct answer.

A. In January it will be cooler in the desert than in the temperate forest.

B. In April it will be hotter in the tropical rainforest than in the temperate forest.

C. In July the temperate forest will have a higher temperature than the desert.

D. In October the tropical rainforest will have a cooler temperature than the desert.

29. Owen put a toy train engine on a track. The engine traveled 1 lap in 10 seconds, s. Owen added boxcars to the engine and wrote down the time.

Time to Make One Lap

Number of Boxcars Added to Engine	Time to Travel 1 Lap (s)
0	10
1	11
2	12
3	13
4	14

Toy Train Track

How much time will it take the engine if 5 boxcars are added?

Circle the letter of the correct answer.

A. 5 s   **B.** 9 s   **C.** 15 s   **D.** 19 s

30. Nancy wants to build a rack to hold backpacks and coats. The rack must hold at least five backpacks and five coats. It cannot cost more than $75.00. She cannot spend more than five hours building the rack. The table shows information about each design.

Circle the numbers of the two designs Nancy should use.

Coat Rack Designs

Design	Cost to Build	Time to Build	Number of Backpacks	Number of Coats
1	$100.00	2 hours	6	6
2	$50.00	6 hours	4	4
3	$20.00	4 hours	5	6
4	$30.00	3 hours	2	7
5	$60.00	5 hours	6	6

Mid-Year Test

Read each question. Follow the instructions to answer the questions.

1. Tim designs a wagon that waters grass.

   Tim tests the wagon. The water drains out of the wagon too quickly. How could Tim improve his design?

   Circle the letter of the correct answer.

   A. make the holes smaller

   B. make the handle longer

   C. make the wheels larger

2. The picture shows some stages of a chicken's life cycle.

   Birth is the first stage of the life cycle.

   Number the other stages in the correct order, starting with "2" for the second stage.

1	birth
	death
	reproduction
	growth

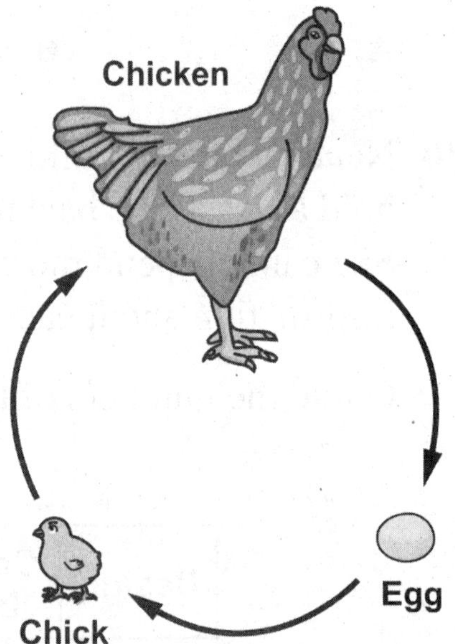

© Houghton Mifflin Harcourt Publishing Company

3. Jo started to group pictures of animals. Finish grouping them.

Write one letter in each box.

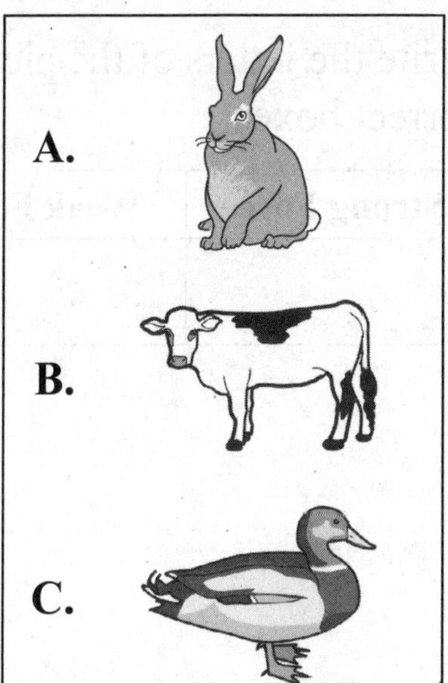

4. Sam wants to show how magnets attract each other. How should she set up the magnets?

Write the letters of the pictures in the correct boxes.

	Magnet 1	Magnet 2
Attract		

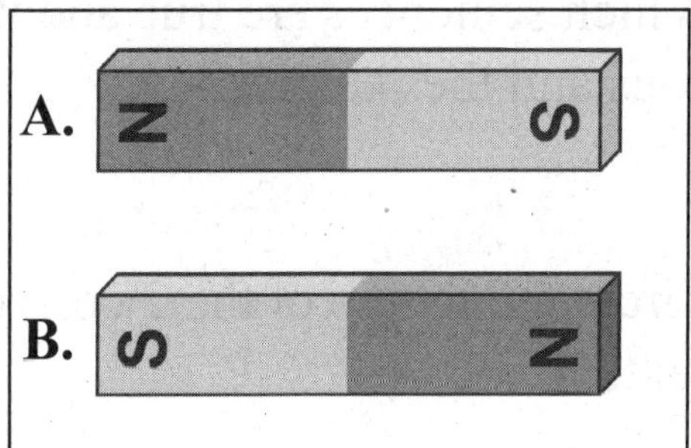

5. Bob is studying static electricity. He holds a glass rod over paper. What happens with the rod and paper?

Write the letters of the pictures in the correct boxes.

Strong Force	Weak Force

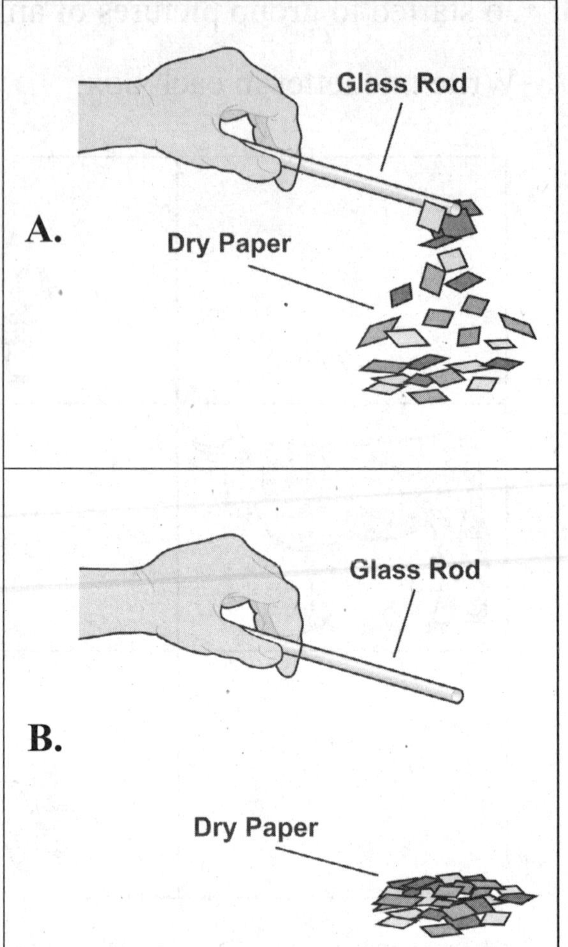

6. Heath saw two adult dogs and their puppies. He wrote down the color of the puppies' fur.

Which sentences are true about the dogs and the puppies?

Circle the letters of the 2 correct sentences.

Puppy Number	Color of Fur
1	Black
2	Brown
3	Black
4	Black
5	Brown
6	Brown

A. The puppies look like their mother but not like their father.

B. Some of the puppies have the same fur color as their father.

C. One parent has brown fur because some of the puppies have brown fur.

7. Jen tied weights onto strings of different lengths. She counted the number of swings until the weights stopped moving.

The 5-centimeter string swung 10 times. The 10-centimeter string swung 45 times.

Make a graph of Jen's data. Use your pencil to draw each bar up to the correct number.

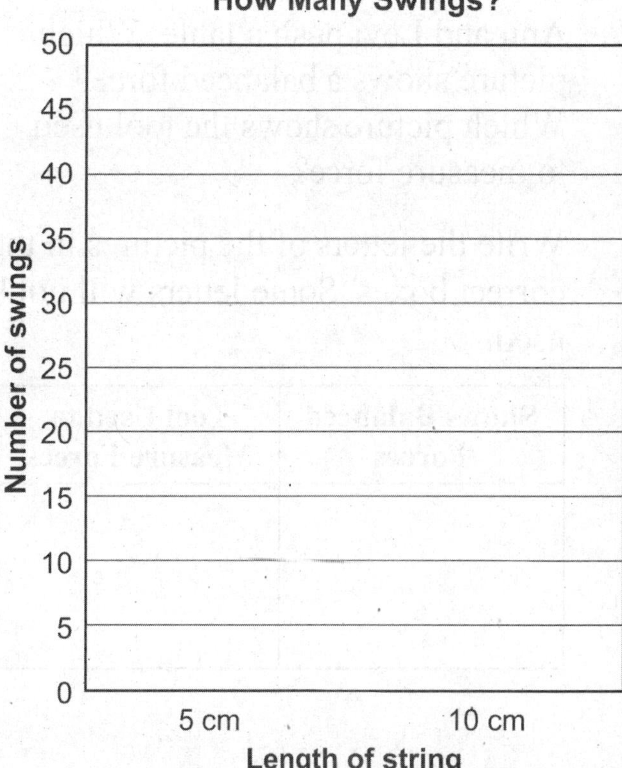

8. The life cycle stages of a frog and a lizard are listed.

Life Cycle Data for Two Animals

Stage in Life Cycle	Frog	Lizard
Birth	Eggs hatch tadpoles in water	Eggs hatch on land
Growth	Lives in water and on land; adults breathe air	Lives on land; adults breathe air
Reproduction	Happens in water	Happens on land

How are the two life cycles alike?

Circle the letter of the correct answer.

A. adults breathe air

B. reproduce on land

C. lay eggs that hatch in water

9. Ann and Levi push a table. Which picture shows a balanced force? Which picture shows the tool used to measure force?

Write the letters of the pictures in the correct boxes. Some letters will not be used.

Shows Balanced Forces	Tool Used to Measure Forces

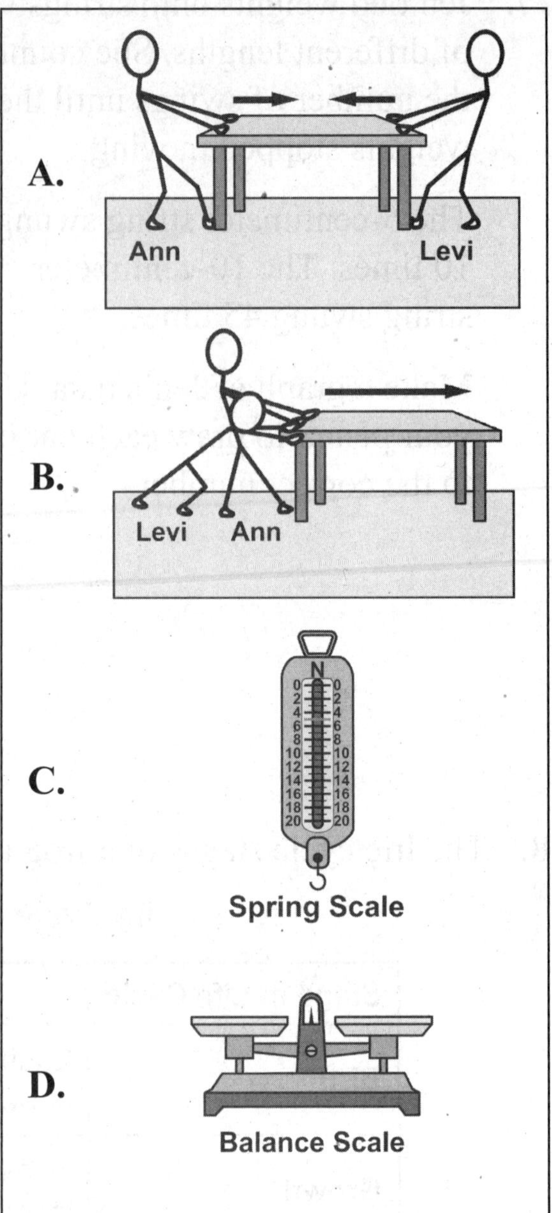

10. Some of the first car tires were very thin. Cars with these tires often slid off wet roads. Thicker tires were designed.

What are the likely reasons for the new tire design?

Early Design Thin Tire   Recent Design Thick Tire

Write one X in the correct box to show whether each statement is a likely reason or not.

Reason	Likely	Not Likely
A. People wanted safer tires.		
B. People wanted tires that could stay on wet roads.		
C. People wanted nicer-looking tires on their cars.		

11. The pictures show the same plant.

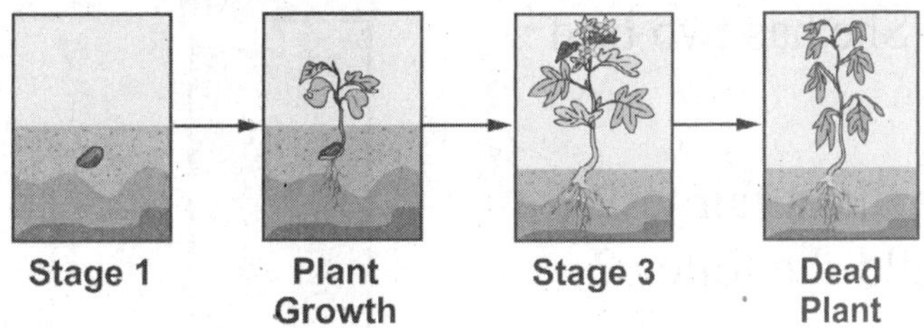

Read each question. Write your answer on the lines.

What is the name of the process shown?

____

What is the name of stage 1?

____

What is the name of stage 3?

____

12. Kim made a data table about magnets. Complete her table.

Write the letters in the empty boxes to correctly complete the table. Some letters will not be used.

Kim's Data Table

Picture of Magnet and Nail	Distance	Force
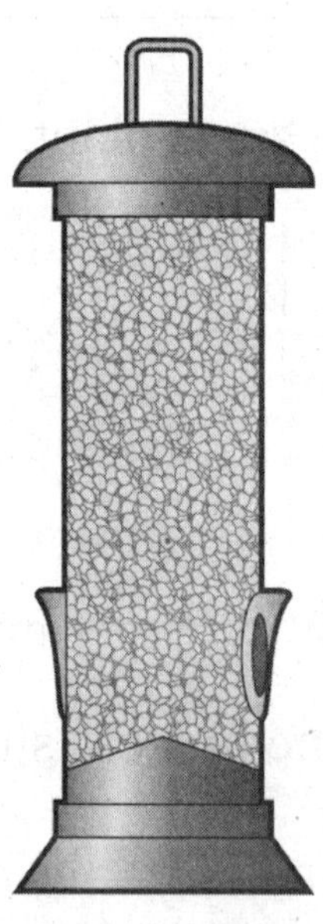		Strongest
	Far apart	

A. Weakest

B. Far apart

C. Close together

D. 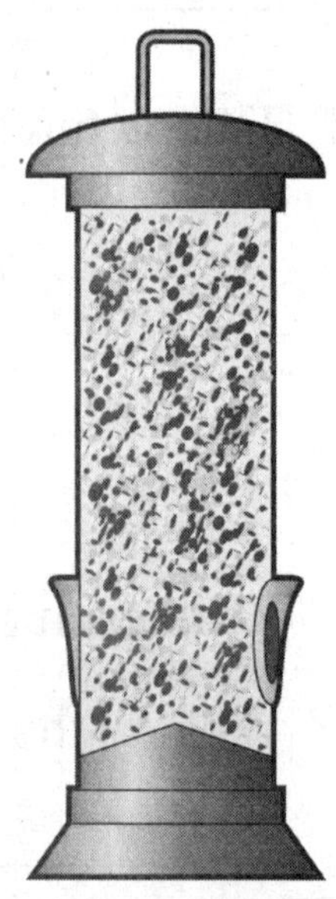

E. 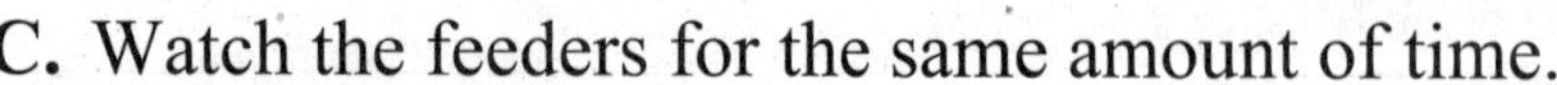

13. Mina wants to know which seed birds like most. She has two bird feeders.

Mina wants to make a fair test. Which step should she follow?

Circle the letter of the correct answer.

A. Look at one feeder only in the morning.

B. Place the feeders far apart from each other.

C. Watch the feeders for the same amount of time.

Bird Feeder 1   **Bird Feeder 2**

14. The pictures show the life cycles of a butterfly and a tree.

Life Cycles of a Butterfly and a Tree

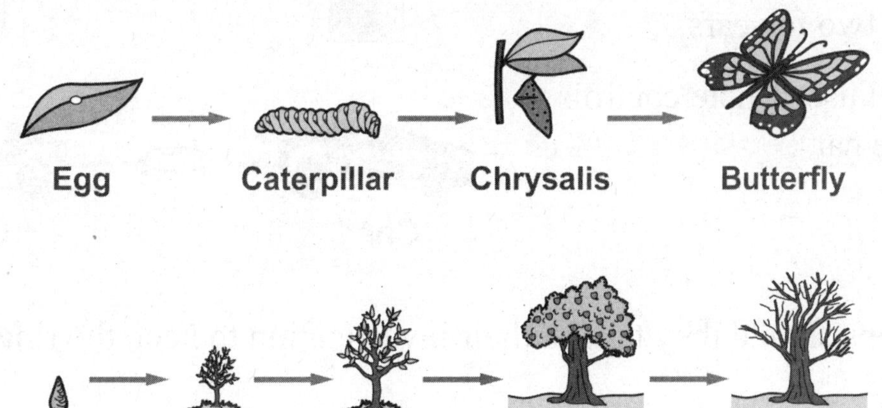

Decide if each sentence is true or false.

Write one X in the box to show whether each statement is true or false.

Statement	True	False
A. The butterfly and tree life cycles are the same.		
B. The caterpillar lays the egg that becomes the butterfly.		
C. The tree grows larger and the caterpillar changes into a butterfly.		

15. Walt put some weights on springs. He measured how far a spring stretched in centimeters, cm. Weight A stretched 22 cm. Weight B stretched 18 cm. Weight C stretched 16 cm.

Write the letter of the weight in the box next to the length that the spring stretched.

Length of Spring	Letter of Weight
16 cm	
18 cm	
22 cm	

A. weight A

B. weight B

C. weight C

16. Leo and Mary want to show that forces can keep an object still. They connect a plastic ring between two toy cars.

They will use remote controls to move the cars.

What steps should they take in their investigation to keep the ring from moving?

Write the letters of the steps for this investigation in the correct order.

Step	Letters for the Step
1	
2	
3	

A. Move Cars 1 and 2 forward at the same time and at the same speed.

B. Watch that the ring remains still.

C. Write down that both cars had equal forces on the ring.

17. The pictures show how some living things are grouped.

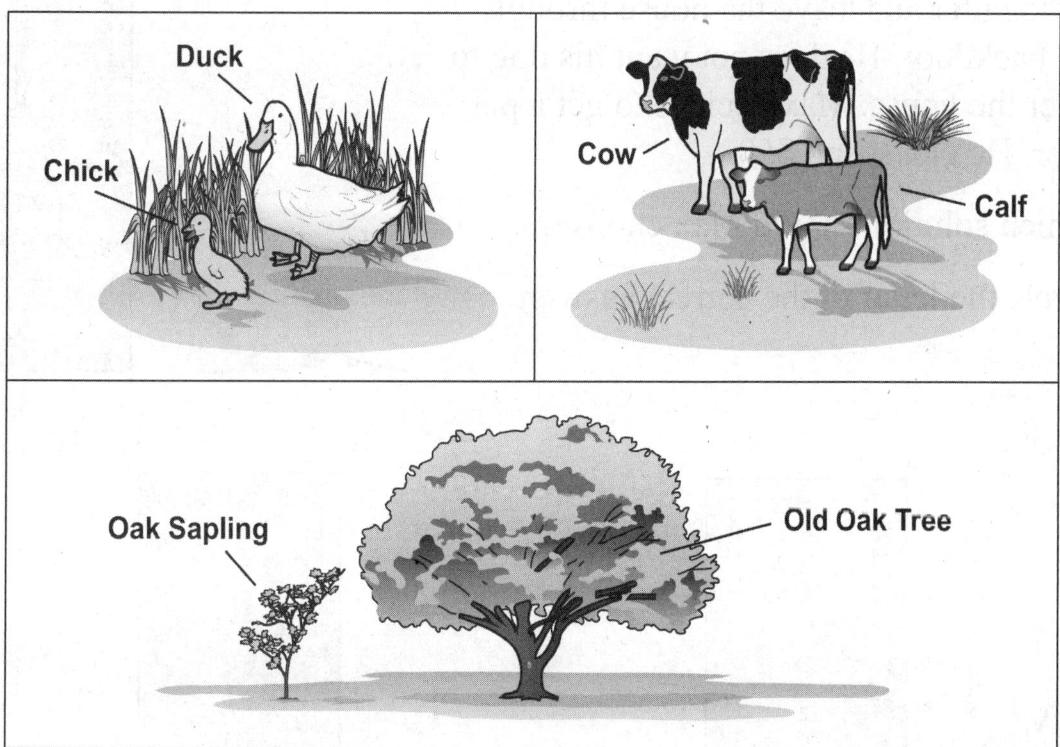

How are living things grouped?

Circle the letter of the correct answer.

A. by how much they eat each day

B. by how similar the young look to the adults

C. by how different the young look from the adults

18. Max has a cat and a dog. He wants his cat to enter and leave the house through the backdoor. He does not want his dog to enter the house. Max decides to get a pet door. He can spend $50.

Which solution should Max choose?

Circle the letter of the correct answer.

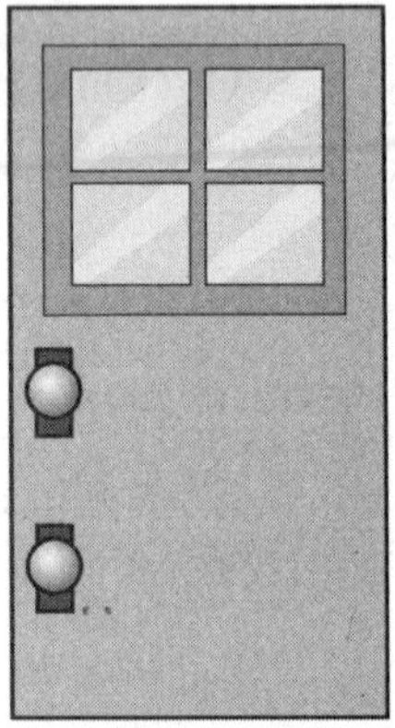

A.

**Cost of Installing New Doorknob
Closer to Ground = $10**

C.

**Cost of Installing Small
Plastic Flap with
Magnetic Closure = $40**

B.

**Cost of Buying New Door
with Built-In Cat Door = $150**

Directions: Read the passage, then answer the questions that follow.

Making the Shade

The sun shines on Dunia's porch. The heat hurts the plants on her porch. She put cloth curtains in the doorway of the porch.

The curtains block the sunlight. But there are downsides. The wind blows the curtains open, letting sunlight into the porch area. Dunia wants to fix the problem but has some requirements.

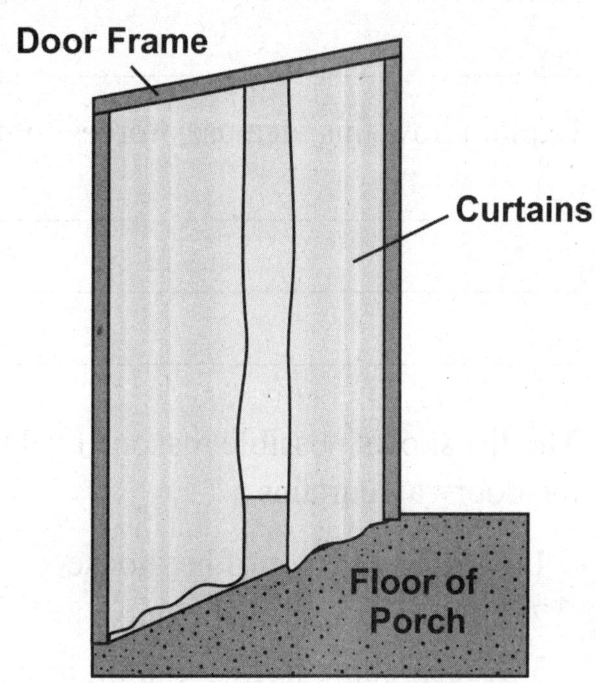

1. She must be able to walk through the doorway.
2. Her dogs must be able to walk through the doorway on their own.
3. The total cost must be $50 or less.

Dunia's friend Dean has helped other people with the same problem. He drew sketches of ideas that have worked for others. Dean wrote down the cost of each idea in a table.

Dean's Idea	Cost
1. Hang doors in doorway.	$100
2. Tie the curtains to the doorframe posts.	$10
3. Put magnets on the curtains to keep the wind from opening.	$5
4. Tie a string in the doorway and twist growing vines on the string.	$20

19. Read Dean's ideas listed in the passage.

Read each statement. Write your answer on the lines.

Which idea works because of forces at different distances?

____

Explain how this idea uses forces to meet Dunia's requirements.

____

____

____

20. The list shows possible reasons for Dunia to make changes to the doorway curtains.

   1. Match the color of her house
   2. Keep heat from her plants
   3. Keep people from breaking into her house

Which reasons match Dunia's requirements?

Circle the letter of the correct answer.

A. 1 only

B. 2 only

C. 1 and 3

21. Dean's third idea uses magnets. Which facts about magnetic force were used in Dean's idea?

Circle the letters of all of the sentences that are correct.

A. Magnets can attract or repel each other.

B. The force of a magnet can move through fabrics.

C. A magnet must touch an object in order to move it.

22. Dunia wants to walk through the porch doorway. She wants her dogs to walk through the doorway on their own. She does not want to spend more than $50. Which of Dean's ideas best fits Dunia's needs?

Circle the letter around the idea Dunia should select.

A. Idea 1:

- blocks sunlight and will not blow open
- keeps the dogs on the porch

B. Idea 2:

- blocks the sunlight
- will not blow open if kept tied down

C. Idea 3:

- a person or a dog can open the curtains
- the magnets will close the curtains behind a person or dog

23. The picture shows Dean's third idea.

What is the position of two magnets when the force is the strongest?

Circle the letter that shows the magnet position when the force is the strongest.

Magnet Positions

A	〇 〇
B	〇 〇
C	〇〇

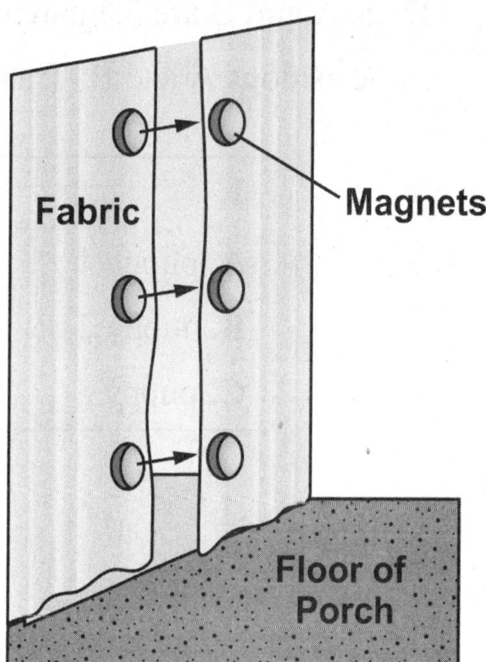

Bottom Part of the Curtain

24. The picture shows two dogs that are parents to one of the puppies.

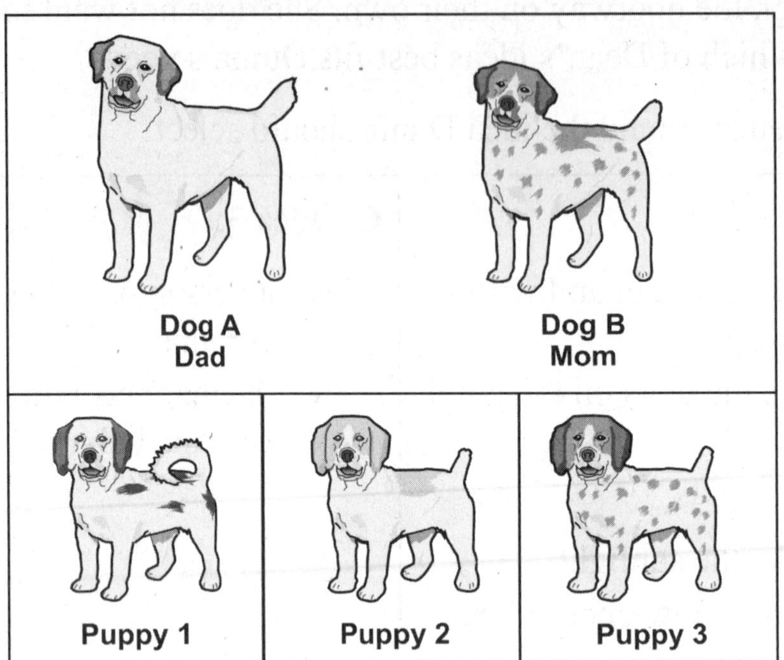

Write one letter in each blank to correctly complete the sentences.

Dogs A and B are the parents of **1.** _________ . This puppy's **2.** _________ is the same as dogs A and B. This puppy got its fur pattern from its **3.** _________ .

1.	2.	3.
A. puppy 1	**D.** fur pattern	**F.** dad
B. puppy 2	**E.** tail length	**G.** mom
C. puppy 3		

25. Picture 1 shows Jing holding a ball. Picture 2 shows that Jing dropped the ball. Picture 3 shows the ball after it hit the floor.

| Picture 1 | Picture 2 | Picture 3 |

Read each statement. Write your answer on the lines.

Identify the picture that shows the forces on the ball are balanced.

____

____

Explain how the force changed when the ball hit the floor.

____

____

____

26. Oscar made a ramp. He let a toy car roll down the ramp.

Oscar measured the distance the car rolled in centimeters (cm). He did this three times for each book height. Oscar wrote some of this data in a table.

Ramp and Car

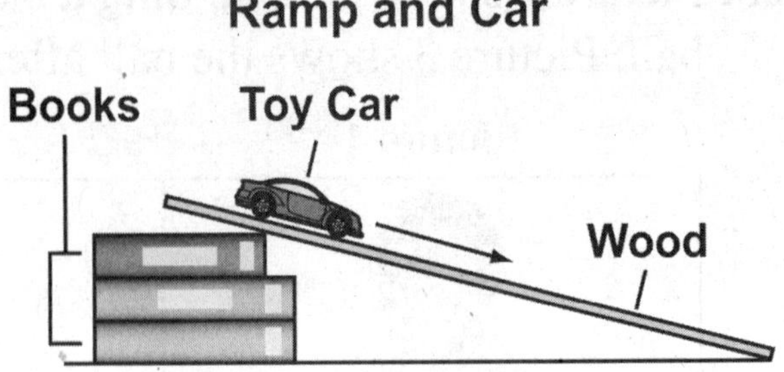

	Distance Car Rolled off Ramp (cm)		
	Trial 1	Trial 2	Trial 3
1 Book	50 cm		51 cm
2 Books		89 cm	91 cm
3 Books	130 cm	131 cm	

Conclusion:

Write the letters for the distance in the table. Write one letter for the conclusion below the table.

Distance	Conclusion
A. 90 cm	**D.** The car will not roll down a short ramp.
B. 129 cm	
C. 52 cm	**E.** The car rolls farther when the ramp is taller.

© Houghton Mifflin Harcourt Publishing Company

27. Ellis held his arm out straight and dropped a tennis ball. The picture shows the ball's motion.

Ellis will drop a rubber ball. Predict the ball's motion.

Write numbers 1, 2, and 3 in the boxes to show the order of the ball's motion.

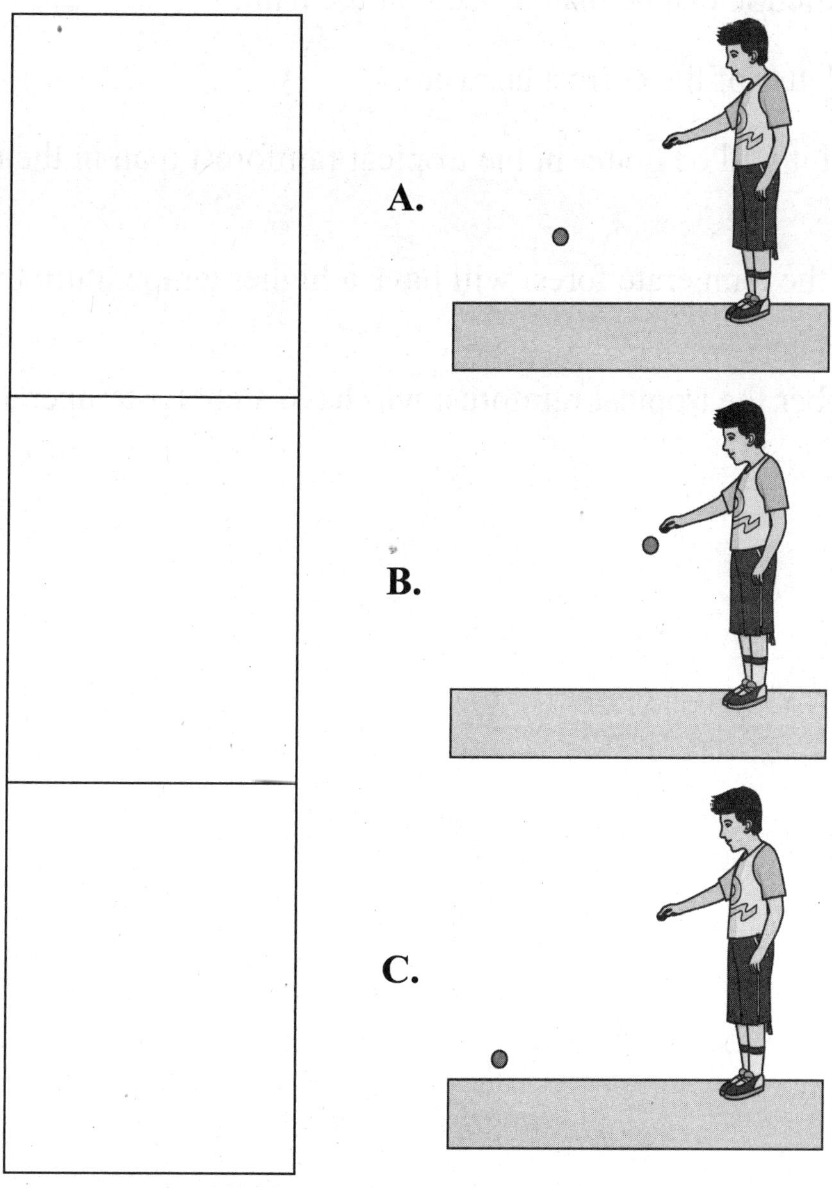

A.

B.

C.

28. Scientists recorded the average temperature each month in three different areas.

Months	Average Temperature		
	Desert	Tropical Rainforest	Temperate Forest
January–March	10° Celsius	20° Celsius	0° Celsius
April–June	20° Celsius	30° Celsius	15° Celsius
July–September	25° Celsius	33° Celsius	20° Celsius
October–December	15° Celsius	20° Celsius	0° Celsius

Which prediction can be made based on the data?

Circle the letter of the correct answer.

A. In April it will be hotter in the tropical rainforest than in the temperate forest.

B. In July the temperate forest will have a higher temperature than the desert.

C. In October the tropical rainforest will have a cooler temperature than the desert.

29. Owen put a toy train engine on a track. The engine traveled 1 lap in 10 seconds, s. Owen added boxcars to the engine and wrote down the time.

Time to Make One Lap

Number of Boxcars Added to Engine	Time to Travel 1 Lap (s)
0	10
1	11
2	12
3	13
4	14

Toy Train Track

How much time will it take to travel 1 lap if 5 boxcars are added?

Circle the letter of the correct answer.

A. 9 s   **B.** 15 s   **C.** 19 s

30. Nancy wants to build a rack. The rack must hold at least five backpacks and five coats. It cannot cost more than $75.00. She cannot spend more than five hours building the rack. The table shows information about each design.

Circle the numbers of the two designs Nancy should use.

Coat Rack Designs

Design	Cost to Build	Time to Build	Number of Backpacks	Number of Coats
1	$100.00	2 hours	6	6
2	$50.00	6 hours	4	4
3	$20.00	4 hours	5	6
4	$30.00	3 hours	2	7
5	$60.00	5 hours	6	6

End-of-Year Test

Read each question. Follow the instructions to answer the questions.

1. Write the letter in the box next to the correct hazard.

lightning	
flooding	
blizzard	

A. causes fires

B. freezes plants

C. brings too much water

2. Alex wants to learn about climate. What should Alex study most?

   Circle the letter of the correct answer.

   A. the number of days without rainfall

   B. the temperature and rainfall for each season

   C. the temperature of the ground during winter

   D. the number of people and animals living in an area

3. Which of these are living things and which are nonliving things?

   Write the correct letters in each box.

Living Things	Nonliving Things

   A. sunlight

   B. deer

   C. tree

   D. air

4. Some animals live in groups. Some groups help animals get food. Other groups help animals stay safe. Which of these are examples of how groups help animals stay safe?

Circle the letters of the 2 correct answers.

A. Wolves hunt in a pack.

B. Many fish swim closely together.

C. Cats brush their hair by licking it.

D. Blackbirds make loud calls when a predator is near.

5. Missy grew potato crops for three years. She wrote down data and took pictures of the potatoes. Sample data for three years are shown.

Year	Total Rain for Year (inches)	Average Temperature for Year (degrees Fahrenheit)	Picture of Plant Above Ground	Picture of Potato
1	20	85°		
2	20	95°		
3	30	90°		

In which way did the weather change the potato plant?

Circle the letter of the correct answer.

A. More rain caused brighter flowers.

B. Lower temperatures made smaller potatoes.

C. Rain and temperature changed what the potatoes looked like.

D. Little rain and high temperatures caused white spots to form on the potatoes.

6. The weather report for Mainville is shown in the picture. The temperature is shown in degrees Fahrenheit (°F).

Day	Wednesday	Thursday	Friday	Saturday	Sunday
Weather	Stormy	Blizzard	Blizzard	Snowy	Rainy
Temperature	33°F	22°F	23°F	23°F	33°F

The people of Mainville want to stay safe. The table lists some actions people might take. Decide which actions a person should follow.

Write an X in the correct box in the table for each statement.

Statement	Yes, follow this action.	No, this action is not needed.
A. Stay inside during the storm.		
B. Check that the smoke detectors are working.		
C. Remove snow from sidewalks and roads after the storm.		

7. A road is being built in an area with a lot of animals. Some people think that the road will hurt the animals. These people suggest a land bridge be built over the road. The picture shows a land bridge.

How could this bridge help the animals?

Circle the letters of the 2 correct statements.

> **A.** Animals can safely search for food.
>
> **B.** Animals will be less likely to be hit by moving cars.
>
> **C.** Animals like natural bridges instead of human-made bridges.

8. The tables list animal behaviors and possible effects. Which behaviors match the effects?

Draw a line from the behavior to the effect that matches it.

Animal Behavior

1	Adult elephants huddling around newborn
2	Prairie dog makes a loud crying noise when hawks fly over
3	Many ants carry dirt in mouth and leave at hole entrance

Effect

A	Helping each other keeps group alive
B	Protects young, smaller member from predators
C	Warns group of danger

9. Which statement describes climate?

Circle the letter of the correct answer.

A. Climate can change each day.

B. Climate is also known as seasons.

C. Climate happens for a short period of time.

D. Climate is weather conditions for a long period of time.

10. A forest is brown, orange, and yellow in the fall. The same forest is mostly white during the winter. The pictures show hares with different-colored fur. Which hares can hide from predators during the fall? Which can hide during the winter?

Write the letters of the pictures in the correct boxes.

Hide From Predators During Fall	Hide From Predators During Winter

 A.

 B.

 C.

 D.

11. Cora studied where different plants and animals live. She studied very hot, dry areas compared with very cold and wet areas. She wrote down what she learned. Finish Cora's table.

Write the letters in the correct boxes to complete the table.

Where Can It Live?

Habitat	Best able to survive	Why able to survive?
Hot and dry		
Cold and wet		

A. polar bear	**C.** stores fat for warmth
B. camel	**D.** stores water for use later

© Houghton Mifflin Harcourt Publishing Company

12. A town has not had rain or snow in a long time. The town's people are making lists of possible solutions to the problem of not having enough water. One possible solution is to find ways for people to use less water.

Write the letter of each solution in the correct box.

Will Help	Will Not Help

A. fix leaky faucets

B. water the yard less often

C. stay inside until it rains

D. water plants more often so they will not die

13. Jamal studies a grass meadow. He makes these notes:

- Bees get food from flowers.
- Flowers need bees to transfer pollen.
- Skunks eat the bees and mice.

A disease has killed several bees. Which changes will likely affect the organisms in this meadow?

Write an X in the box for each possible change. Each possible change may have more than one X.

Possible Change	Bees	Mice	Flowers	Skunks
A. The disease will keep this organism from reproducing.				
B. The disease will prevent skunks from eating this organism.				

14. Some organisms have parts that help them survive. Others behave differently to help them survive. Match the parts and behaviors to how they help the organism survive.

Draw lines from Table 1 to Table 2 to show which letters match the numbers.

Table 1

Letter	Body Part/Behavior That Is Different from Rest of Group
A	Has larger leaves
B	Stores fat in thick layer
C	Fur changes from brown to white in winter

Table 2

Number	How Helps Animal Survive
1	Blends in with color of environment
2	Collects more sunlight
3	Keeps warm during winter

15. Aaron measured the snowfall for three days. He wrote down the amount in centimeters (cm): Monday, 2 cm; Tuesday, 0 cm; Wednesday, 4 cm. Graph the snowfall for the three days.

Use your pencil to draw bars for the correct amount of snowfall. Draw one X for each centimeter of snow, stacked on top of each other to show the total amount of snow on Monday. Do the same for Tuesday and for Wednesday.

Snowfall over Three Days

Monday   Tuesday   Wednesday

Day

16. Travis noticed some things about the weather in his hometown.

- greatest rainfall was in the spring
- rained more in the summer than in the fall
- did not rain or snow much in the winter

Complete Travis's table.

Write the letters in the correct boxes. Some letters may be used more than once or not at all.

Weather Conditions by Season

Season and Pattern	Average Temperature (degrees Celsius)	Average Snow/Rain (centimeters)
Spring	22°	7
Summer	31°	
Fall		4
Winter	12°	
Pattern	The temperature __________ and then __________.	Rainfall __________ with each season.

A. 0°	**C.** 2	**E.** decreased
B. 19°	**D.** 5	**F.** increased

> **Directions:** Read the passage, then answer the questions that follow.

Finding Fossils

Canyon walls can be a good place to find fossils. The rock layers in canyon walls are easy to see. The diagram shows some fossils in four layers of rock from a canyon wall.

Layers of Rock in a Canyon Wall

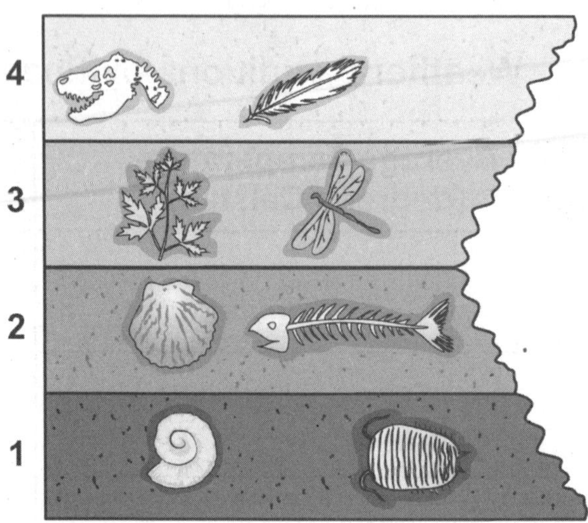

17. Look at the fossils of layer 1 in the passage diagram. Which describes the animals in layer 1?

Circle the letter of the correct answer.

A. They lived at the same time as birds.

B. These kinds of animals are alive today.

C. The animals that made these fossils lived here a few years ago.

D. The animals that made this fossil have not lived in the area for a long time.

18. The pictures show two fossils. Organism 1 is related to modern birds. Organism 2 is related to modern lobsters.

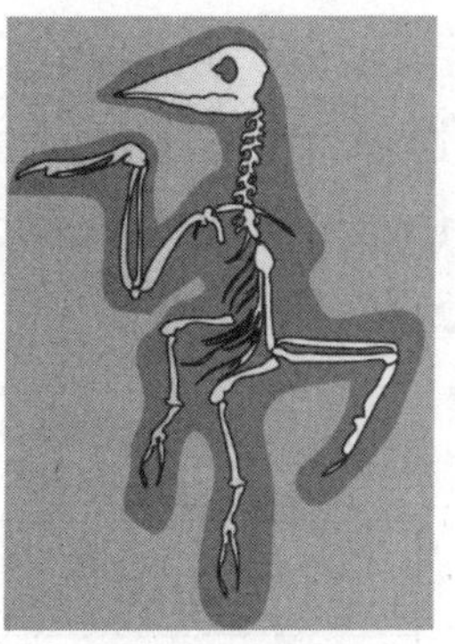 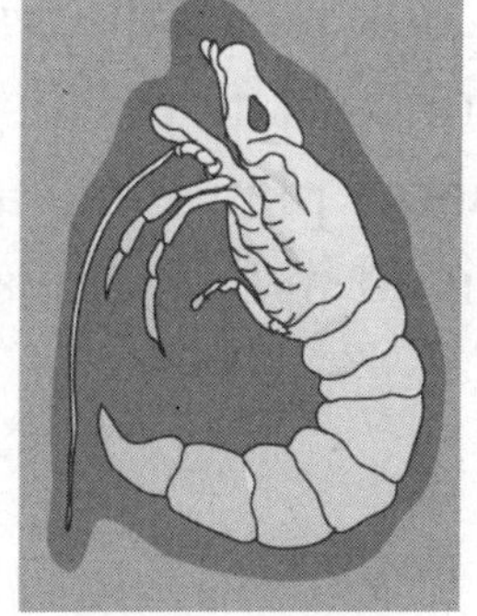

Organism 1   **Organism 2**

Which statements are most likely true about these organisms?

Write the letters in the correct boxes for each organism. Some letters may be used more than once or not at all.

Organism 1	Organism 2

A. had wings and legs

B. probably lived on land

C. probably lived in water

D. had a hard outer shell and legs

19. Look at the diagram in the passage. Layer 3 shows the fossils of a fern and a dragonfly.

Write your answers on the lines.

Identify the fossils in layer 2.

____

Identify the fossils in layer 4

____

Describe how the environment changed from layers 2 to 4.

____

____

____

20. Look at the diagram in the passage. The sea has covered this land at different times. The fossils show plants and animals that lived in the area. Which layers show plants and animals that lived on the land? Which layers show those that lived in the seawater?

Land	Seawater

A. layer 1	**C.** layer 3
B. layer 2	**D.** layer 4

21. Ernie's dog has three puppies that look alike. He names them Astro, Bailey, and Cooper. Ernie gives the puppies to his best friends. The dogs are raised differently.

Astro - eats a lot of food and treats; does not get much exercise

Bailey - does not like the food he is given; does not eat much

Cooper - eats a normal amount of food; goes for walks daily

Which dog is which? Write the letter for each dog beneath the correct picture.

1. _______________ 2. _______________ 3. _______________

A. Astro	**B.** Bailey	**C.** Cooper

22. The list describes squirrels living in a forest.

- make nests in trees
- eat nuts and berries from trees
- eat insects living in grass

Some people want wood from the trees. They want to cut down the trees in the forest. What is likely to happen to the squirrels?

Circle the letters of the 2 correct sentences.

> **A.** Nuts growing in trees will not be available as food.
>
> **B.** The squirrels will not have insects to eat.
>
> **C.** The squirrels will not have trees in which to hide and make nests.

23. These penguins live in groups in Antarctica. It gets very cold and windy in Antarctica. The males huddle with each other and with their chicks. The females leave in search for food.

Dad Penguin and Baby Chick

Penguins Huddled

Read each statement. Write your answer on the lines.

Identify the reason that these penguins huddle.

____

Explain how the huddle helps penguins have more chicks.

____

____

24. The map shows the Arctic habitat above the line. It is a very cold habitat. Some animals can survive well in the Arctic. Some animals will barely survive, and some animals cannot survive in the Arctic.

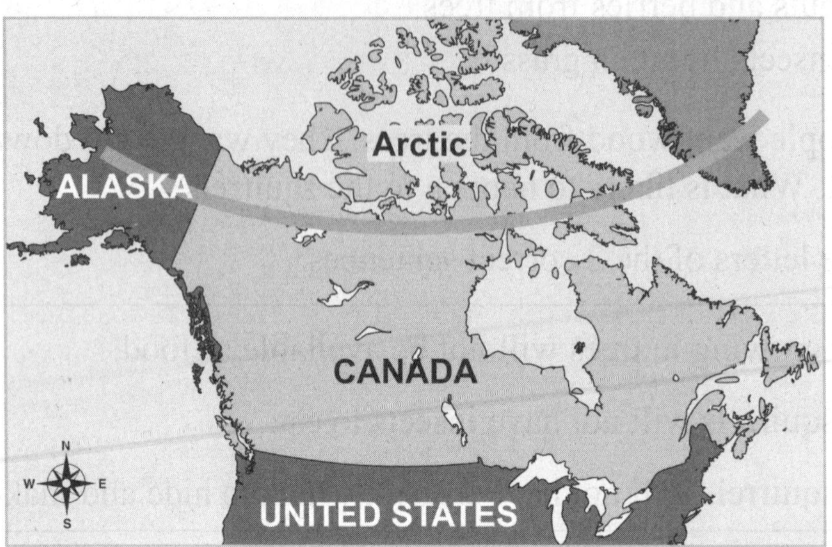

Would the animals in the table survive in the Arctic?

Write the letter for *Yes, Maybe,* or *No* to correctly complete the table.

Animal	Animal Habitat	Will the Animal Survive in Arctic?
Red Fox	Cold areas of U.S.	1.
Reindeer	Cold areas of Alaska and Canada	2.
Rattlesnake	Hot and dry areas of U.S.	3.

A. Yes	**B.** Maybe	**C.** No

25. Reba is studying peacocks, a type of bird that lives in the forest. She wrote down the findings for two groups. Reba thinks that one group is more likely to reproduce. Which numbers should she use to back up her idea?

Circle the numbers that are the reasons that back up Reba's idea.

Group A	Group B
1. Eat plant parts, insects, and lizards.	4. Eat flowers, leaves, insects, and frogs.
2. Females are not interested in males.	5. Females are attracted to males.
3. Females do not lay many eggs.	6. Females lay many eggs.

26. A scientist is studying insects near a pond. He notices that one kind of insect can look light green or dark brown. He writes the number of each color by age.

Number of Insects Near a Pond

Age of Insects	Color of Insects	
	Light Green	Dark Brown
Young Insects	20	21
Older Insects	18	4

What can the scientist conclude about these insects?

Circle the letters of the 2 correct answers.

A. Dark-brown insects are more likely to reproduce.

B. Light-green insects can survive better near the pond.

C. Animals that eat insects can more easily see dark-brown insects near the pond.

D. In this ecosystem, larger insects are more likely to survive than smaller insects.

27. Type Z clams are becoming a problem to pipes and animals. They are poisonous to seabirds. They attach to pipes and other clams. Scientists have found a special metal that the Z clams cannot stick to.

Write your answer on the lines.

Identify one animal that the Z clam hurts.

____

Describe a possible solution for reducing the damage to pipes.

____

____

____

28. Lexa is studying the weather for her hometown. She wrote down weather data for the month of May in degrees Celsius, °C, and centimeters, cm.

Lexa's Weather Data

Year	Temperature (Degrees Celsius)	Rainfall (Centimeters)
Year 1	12	7
Year 2	13	8
Year 3	13	8
Year 4	14	9

What weather should Lexa predict for next May?

Circle the letter of the correct answer.

A. rain each day and temperatures around 8°C

B. cloudy skies with about 14 cm of rain daily

C. temperatures around 13°C and about 8 cm of rain for the month

D. about 8 cm of rain for the month and the hottest temperature around 13°C

29. Elma studied roses, moths, and kiwi birds. She found that there were differences in each group. For example, she noticed that some rose bushes had thorns and others did not. Elma made a table of what she learned. Finish her table.

Write the letters of the descriptions in the correct boxes. Not all of the letters will be used.

Elma's Study of Living Things

Living Thing	Thing That Is Different	Likely Reason for Difference
Rose Bush	**Thorn** Thorns Instead of Smooth Stem	
Moth	Brown Instead of White	
Kiwi Bird	**Beak** Long Beak Instead of Short	

Conclusion:

The thing that makes the living thing different

helps it to [ ].

A. Protects against predators

B. Pokes in the ground for food

C. Blends into tree bark to hide

D. survive

E. lead the group

30. Jack is comparing a type of frog to a type of scorpion. He writes down what he learns.

Jack's Data

Name of Organism	Frog	Scorpion
Appearance		
Diet	Insects, worms, and small animals	Insects, spiders, other scorpions and lizards
Other	Lays eggs in water Needs water to stay moist	Blends in with sand Cannot survive cold temperatures

In what habitat do these organisms live?

Circle the letter of the correct answer.

A. frog – in a wetland
scorpion – in a desert

B. frog – in any location
scorpion – in a forest

C. frog – in the cold habitat
scorpion – in any location

D. frog – in a forest
scorpion – in the cold habitat

End-of-Year Test

Read each question. Follow the instructions to answer the questions.

1. Write the letter in the box next to the correct hazard.

lightning	
flooding	
blizzard	

A. causes fires
B. freezes plants
C. brings too much water

2. Alex wants to learn about the climate where he lives. What should Alex study most?

   Circle the letter of the correct answer.

   A. the number of days without rainfall

   B. the temperature and rainfall for each season

   C. the temperature of the ground during winter

3. Some of the things below are living and some are nonliving. Which of these are living things and which are nonliving things?

   Write the correct letters in each box.

Living Things	Nonliving Things

A. sunlight
B. deer
C. tree
D. air

4. Some animals live in groups. Which of these are examples of ways that groups help animals stay safe?

    Circle the letters of the 2 correct answers.

    A. Many fish swim closely together.

    B. Cats brush their hair by licking it.

    C. Blackbirds make loud calls when a predator is near.

5. Missy grew potatoes for three years. She wrote down data and took pictures of the potatoes. Her findings are in the table.

Year	Total Rain for Year (inches)	Average Temperature for Year (degrees Fahrenheit)	Picture of Plant Above Ground	Picture of Potato
1	20	85°		
2	20	95°		
3	30	90°		

    How did the weather change the potato?

    Circle the letter of the correct answer.

    A. More rain caused brighter flowers.

    B. Lower temperatures made smaller potatoes.

    C. Rain and temperature changed what the potatoes looked like.

6. The weather report for Mainville is shown in the picture.

Day	Wednesday	Thursday	Friday	Saturday	Sunday
Weather	Stormy	Blizzard	Blizzard	Snowy	Rainy
Temperature	33°F	22°F	23°F	23°F	33°F

The people of Mainville want to stay safe. The table lists some actions people might take. Decide which actions the people of Mainville should do to stay safe.

Write an X in the correct box in the table for each statement.

Statement	Yes, follow this action.	No, this action is not needed.
A. Stay inside during the storm.		
B. Check that the smoke detectors are working.		

7. A road is being built in an area with a lot of animals. Some people think that the road will hurt the animals. These people suggest a land bridge be built over the road. The picture shows a land bridge.

How could this bridge help the animals?

Circle the letters of the 2 correct statements.

A. Animals can safely search for food.

B. Animals will be less likely to be hit by moving cars.

C. Animals like natural bridges instead of human-made bridges.

8. The tables list animal behaviors and the effects that the behaviors have. Which behaviors match the effects?

Draw a line from the behavior to the effect that matches it.

Animal Behavior

1	Adult elephants huddling around newborn
2	Prairie dog makes a loud crying noise when hawks fly over
3	Many ants carry dirt in mouth and leave at hole entrance

Effect

A	Helping each other keeps group alive
B	Protects young, smaller member from predators
C	Warns group of danger

9. Which statement best describes climate?

Circle the letter of the correct answer.

A. Climate can change each day.

B. Climate happens for a short period of time.

C. Climate is weather conditions for a long period of time.

10. A forest is brown, orange, and yellow in the fall. The same forest is mostly white during the winter. The pictures show hares with different-colored fur. Which hares can hide from predators during the fall? Which can hide during the winter?

Write the letters of the pictures in the correct boxes.

Hide From Predators During Fall	Hide From Predators During Winter

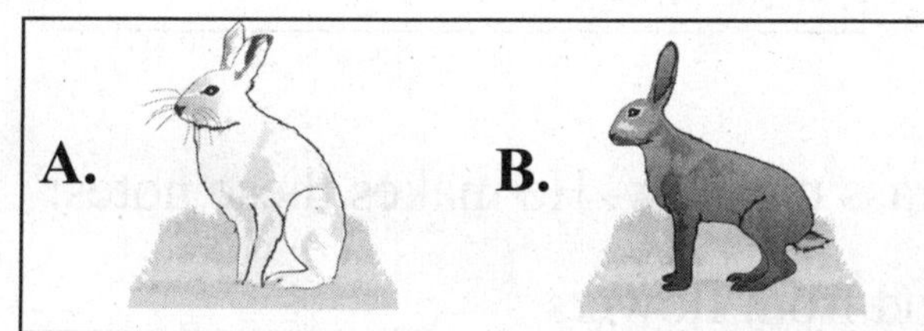

11. Cora studied where different plants and animals live. She studied very hot, dry areas and very cold and wet areas. She wrote down what she learned.

Write the letters in the correct boxes to complete the table.

Where Can It Live?

Habitat	Best able to survive	Why able to survive?
Hot and dry		
Cold and wet		

A. polar bear	C. stores fat for warmth
B. camel	D. stores water for use later

12. A town has not had rain or snow in a long time. People in town are coming up with ways for people to use less water.

Write the letter of each solution in the correct box.

Will Help	Will Not Help

> **A.** fix leaky faucets
>
> **B.** stay inside until it rains

13. Jamal studies a grass meadow. He makes these notes:

- Bees get food from flowers.
- Flowers need bees to transfer pollen.
- Skunks eat the bees and mice.

A disease has killed several bees. Which changes will likely affect the organisms in this meadow?

Write an X in the box for each possible change. Each possible change may have more than one X.

Possible Change	Bees	Flowers
A. The disease will keep this organism from reproducing.		
B. The disease will prevent skunks from eating this organism.		

14. Some organisms have body parts that help them survive. Some organisms behave differently to help them survive. Match the parts and behaviors to how they help the organism survive.

Draw lines from Table 1 to Table 2 to show which letters match the numbers.

Table 1

Letter	Body Part/Behavior That Is Different from Rest of Group
A	Has larger leaves
B	Stores fat in thick layer
C	Fur changes from brown to white in winter

Table 2

Number	How Helps Animal Survive
1	Blends in with color of environment
2	Collects more sunlight
3	Keeps warm during winter

15. Aaron measured the snowfall for two days. He wrote down the amount in centimeters (cm): Monday, 2 cm; Tuesday, 0 cm. Graph the snowfall for the two days.

Use your pencil to draw bars for the correct amount of snowfall.

Snowfall over Two Days

Monday   Tuesday

Day

16. Travis noticed some things about the weather in his hometown.

- greatest rainfall was in the spring
- rained more in the summer than in the fall
- did not rain or snow much in the winter

Complete Travis's table.

Write the letters in the correct boxes. The word "decreased" will be used in two places.

Weather Conditions by Season

Season and Pattern	Average Temperature (degrees Celsius)	Average Snow/Rain (centimeters)
Spring	22°	7
Summer	31°	
Fall		4
Winter	12°	
Pattern	The temperature ___________ and then ___________.	Rainfall ___________ with each season.

A. 19°	**D.** decreased
B. 2	**E.** increased
C. 5	

Directions: Read the passage, then answer the questions that follow.

Finding Fossils

Canyon walls can be a good place to find fossils. The rock layers in canyon walls are easy to see. The diagram shows some fossils in four layers of rock from a canyon wall.

Layers of Rock in a Canyon Wall

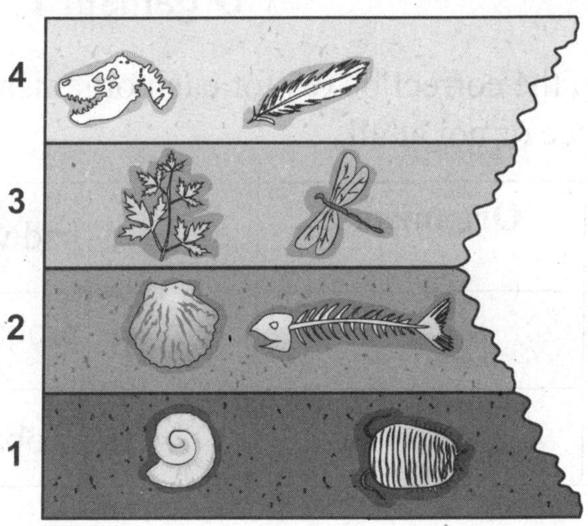

17. Look at the fossils of layer 1 in the picture. Which describes the animals in layer 1?

Circle the letter of the correct answer.

A. These kinds of animals are alive today.

B. The animals that made these fossils lived here a few years ago.

C. The animals that made these fossils have not lived in the area for a long time.

18. The pictures show two fossils.
Organism 1 is related to birds.
Organism 2 is related to lobsters.

Which statements are most likely
true about these organisms?

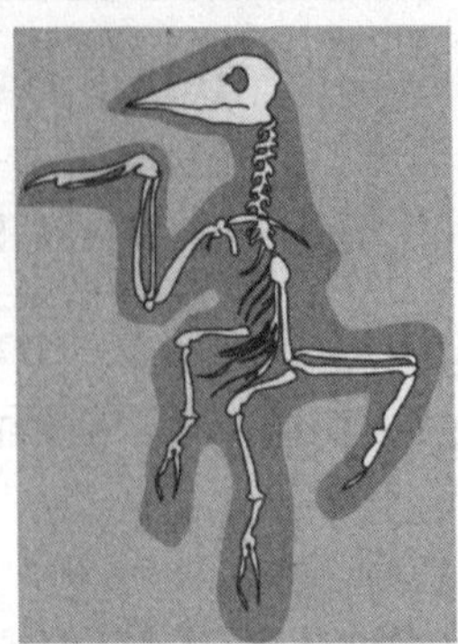 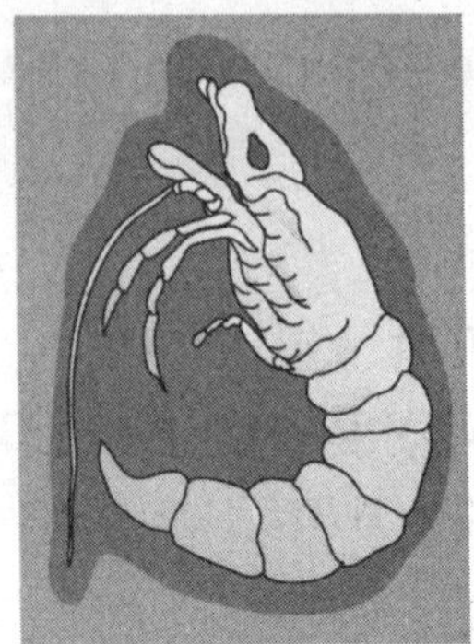

Organism 1   Organism 2

Write the letters in the correct boxes for each organism. Some letters may be
used more than once or not at all.

Organism 1	Organism 2

A.	had wings and legs
B.	probably lived on land
C.	probably lived in water

19. Look at the diagram in the passage. Layer 3 shows fossils of a fern and a
dragonfly.

Write your answers on the lines.

Identify the fossils in layer 2.

____

Identify the fossils in layer 4

____

Describe how the environment changed from layers 2 to 4.

____

____

____

20. Look at the diagram in the passage. This area has been covered by sea and land. The fossils show plants and animals that lived in the area. Which layers show plants and animals that lived on the land? Which layers show those that lived in the seawater?

Write the letters of the numbered layers in the correct boxes.

Land	Seawater

A. layer 1	**C.** layer 3
B. layer 2	**D.** layer 4

21. Ernie's dog has three puppies that look alike. He names them Astro, Bailey, and Cooper. Ernie gives the puppies to his best friends. The dogs are raised in the same neighborhood, but Ernie sees that they are being raised differently.

Astro eats a lot of food and treats and he does not get much exercise.

Bailey does not like the food he is given and he does not eat much.

Cooper eats a normal amount of food and he goes for walks daily.

Which dog is which? Write the letter for each dog beneath the correct picture.

1. _______________   2. _______________   3. _______________

A. Astro	**B.** Bailey	**C.** Cooper

22. The list describes squirrels living in a forest.

- make nests in trees
- eat nuts and berries from trees
- eat insects living in grass

Some people want to cut down the trees in the forest for wood. What is likely to happen to the squirrels?

Circle the letters of the 2 correct sentences.

> **A.** Nuts growing in trees will not be available as food.
>
> **B.** The squirrels will not have insects to eat.
>
> **C.** The squirrels will not have trees in which to hide and make nests.

23. These penguins live in groups in Antarctica. It gets very cold and windy in Antarctica. The males huddle with each other and with their chicks.

Dad Penguin and Baby Chick

Penguins Huddled

Read each statement. Write your answer on the lines.

Identify the reason that these penguins huddle.

____

____

24. The area at the top of the map is the Arctic. It is a very cold habitat. Not all animals can survive in the Artic.

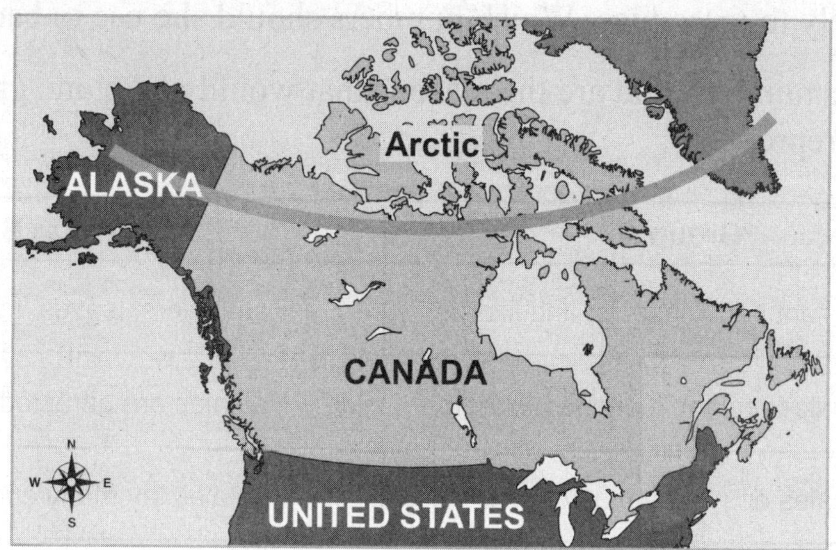

Would the animals in the table survive in the Arctic?

Write the letter for *Yes, Maybe,* or *No* to correctly complete the table.

Animal	Animal Habitat	Will the Animal Survive in Arctic?
Red Fox	Cold areas of U.S.	1.
Reindeer	Cold areas of Alaska and Canada	2.
Rattlesnake	Hot and dry areas of U.S.	3.

A. Yes   **B.** Maybe   **C.** No

25. Reba is studying peacocks, a type of bird that lives in the forest. She studied two groups and wrote down what she found. Reba thinks that one group is more likely to reproduce. Which numbers should she use to back up her idea?

Circle the numbers that are the reasons that would make one group more likely to reproduce.

Group A	Group B
1. Eat plant parts, insects, and lizards.	4. Eat flowers, leaves, insects, and frogs.
2. Females are not interested in males.	5. Females are attracted to males.
3. Females do not lay many eggs.	6. Females lay many eggs.

26. A scientist is studying insects near a pond. He notices that the insects can look either light green or dark brown. He writes the number of each color by age.

Number of Insects Near a Pond

Age of Insects	Color of Insects	
	Light Green	Dark Brown
Young Insects	20	21
Older Insects	18	4

What can the scientist conclude about these insects?

Circle the letters of the 2 correct answers.

A. Dark-brown insects are more likely to reproduce.

B. Light-green insects can survive better near the pond.

C. Animals that eat insects can more easily see dark-brown insects near the pond.

27. Type Z clams are becoming a problem to pipes and animals. They attach to pipes and other clams. Scientists have found a special metal that the Z clams cannot stick to.

Write your answer on the lines.

Identify one animal that the Z clam hurts.

____

Describe one way to reduce the damage to pipes.

____

____

____

28. Lexa is studying the weather where she lives. She wrote down the temperature (in degrees Celsius, °C) and the rainfall (in centimeters, cm) for the month of May.

Lexa's Weather Data

Year	Temperature (Degrees Celsius)	Rainfall (Centimeters)
Year 1	12	7
Year 2	13	8
Year 3	13	8
Year 4	14	9

What weather should Lexa expect for next May?

Circle the letter of the correct answer.

A. rain each day and temperatures around 8°C

B. cloudy skies with about 14 cm of rain daily

C. temperatures around 13°C and about 8 cm of rain for the month

29. Elma studied roses, moths, and kiwi birds. She found that each group had differences. For example, she noticed that some rose bushes had thorns and others did not. Elma made a table of what she learned. Finish her table.

Write the letters of the descriptions in the correct boxes. Not all of the letters will be used.

Elma's Study of Living Things

Living Thing	Thing That Is Different	Likely Reason for Difference
Rose Bush	**Thorn** Thorns Instead of Smooth Stem	
Moth	Brown Instead of White	
Kiwi Bird	**Beak** Long Beak Instead of Short	

Conclusion:

The thing that makes the living thing different

helps it to [________].

A. Protects against predators

B. Pokes in the ground for food

C. Blends into tree bark to hide

D. survive

E. lead the group

© Houghton Mifflin Harcourt Publishing Company

30. Jack is comparing a frog to a scorpion. He writes down what he learns.

Jack's Data

Name of Organism	Frog	Scorpion
Appearance		
Diet	Insects, worms, and small animals	Insects, spiders, other scorpions and lizards
Other	Lays eggs in water Needs water to stay moist	Blends in with sand Cannot survive cold temperatures

What habitats do the frog and the scorpion most likely live in?

Circle the letter of the correct answer.

A. frog – in a wetland
scorpion – in a desert

B. frog – in the cold habitat
scorpion – in any location

C. frog – in a forest
scorpion – in the cold habitat

Beginning-of-Year Test

<table>
<tr><th colspan="3">Item Analysis</th></tr>
<tr><th>Item #</th><th>Standards</th><th>DOK</th></tr>
<tr><td>1</td><td>2-PS1-1, DCI.2-PS1.A.1</td><td>1</td></tr>
<tr><td>2</td><td>K-2-ETS1-1, DCI.K-2-ETS1.A.3</td><td>2</td></tr>
<tr><td>3</td><td>2-ESS2-2, DCI.2-ESS2.B.1, SEP.K-2.B.3</td><td>2</td></tr>
<tr><td>4</td><td>2-ESS1-1, DCI.2-ESS1.C.1</td><td>1</td></tr>
<tr><td>5</td><td>2-PS1-2, DCI.2-PS1.A.2, CCC.STSE.K-2.B.2</td><td>1</td></tr>
<tr><td>6</td><td>2-LS2-2, DCI.2-LS2.A.2</td><td>1</td></tr>
<tr><td>7</td><td>2-ESS2-3, DCI.2-ESS2.C.1</td><td>1</td></tr>
<tr><td>8</td><td>2-LS4-1, DCI.2-LS4.D.1, SEP.K-2.C.3</td><td>1</td></tr>
<tr><td>9</td><td>K-2-ETS1-3, DCI.K-2-ETS1.C.1, SEP.K-2.D.2</td><td>1</td></tr>
<tr><td>10</td><td>2-ESS2-3, DCI.2-ESS2.C.1</td><td>1</td></tr>
<tr><td>11</td><td>2-PS1-4, DCI.2-PS1.B.1, SEP.NOS.K-2.D.1</td><td>2</td></tr>
<tr><td>12</td><td>2-PS1-3, DCI.2-PS1.A.3</td><td>2</td></tr>
<tr><td>13</td><td>2-ESS2-1, DCI.2-ESS2.A.1</td><td>2</td></tr>
<tr><td>14</td><td>2-PS1-1, DCI.2-PS1.A.1</td><td>2</td></tr>
<tr><td>15</td><td>2.K-2-ETS1-1, DCI.K-2-ETS1.A.2, SEP.K-2.A.1</td><td>1</td></tr>
<tr><td>16</td><td>2-LS2-1, DCI.2-LS2.A.1, SEP.K-2.C.2</td><td>2</td></tr>
<tr><td>17</td><td>2-ESS1-1, DCI.2-ESS1.C.1</td><td>2</td></tr>
<tr><td>18</td><td>2-PS1-4, DCI.2-PS1.B.1, SEP.NOS.K-2.D.1</td><td>1</td></tr>
<tr><td>19</td><td>K-2-ETS1-2, DCI.K-2-ETS1.B.1, SEP.K-2.B.2</td><td>2</td></tr>
<tr><td>20</td><td>2-ESS2-2, DCI.2-ESS2.B.1, CCC.K-2.A.1</td><td>1</td></tr>
</table>

1. **A.** This is correct because when heat is added to a plastic spoon, it will start to melt.

   B. This is incorrect because adding heat will not cause a plastic spoon or other object to freeze.

   C. This is incorrect because the heat will start to melt the spoon, and it will not be as strong.

2. **A.** This is correct because the number of jump ropes should be considered to determine the size of the tool or object.

   B. This is incorrect because the cost of the jump ropes does not need to be considered when designing an organizational tool.

   C. This is incorrect because knowing who likes to jump rope does not need to be considered when creating an organizational tool.

   D. This is correct because knowing where the jump ropes are kept will determine the size of the tool and the material it should be made of.

3. **1C.** *Mountain* is correct for this raised landform.

   2F. *River* is correct because it is a long, narrow body of water that flows to the ocean.

   3E. *Ocean* is correct because it is a vast body of water that surrounds land.

   4D. *Lake* is correct because it is a large body of water surrounded by land.

4. **A.** This is correct because glaciers move and displace soil and rocks as they travel.

   B. This is incorrect because an earthquake is a fast change that is not caused by a glacier.

   C. This is incorrect because weathering is caused by breaking down rocks. Glaciers move rocks and soil.

5. **A.** The rocks should not be moved into the box because the rock will not cushion the egg. One of the properties of rocks is that they are hard and heavy. When Liza moves the basket, the rocks could roll into each other and break the egg between the weight of the rocks.

   B. The leaves should be moved into the box because the leaves will cushion the egg. An individual leaf does not have edges that will break something fragile. Many leaves together will displace the weight of an object.

   C. The feathers should be moved into the box because the feathers will cushion the egg. An individual feather is soft and does not have edges that will break something fragile. Many feathers together will displace the weight of an object.

6. **A.** This is incorrect because an animal disperses this type of seed by eating or burying it. There are no burrs to get stuck in animal fur.

   B. This is incorrect because this type of seed is dispersed by the wind.

   C. This is correct. This seed design allows it to easily get stuck in animal fur and can be dispersed.

7. **A.** This description matches the *river*. A river is a flowing body of water.

   B. This description matches the *ocean*. An ocean is a large body of salt water.

   C. This description matches the *pond*. A pond is a small body of water with land on all sides.

8. **A.** *Eagle* belongs in the canopy. It swoops down and uses its claws to grab prey from the treetops.

   B. *Monkey* belongs in the canopy. Its claws and tail allow it to climb, balance, and jump through the canopy treetop. It eats fruit from the canopy.

   C. *Orchid* belongs in the canopy. It grows on a tree without soil and is close to bright sunlight.

   D. *Snake* belongs in the understory. It winds around medium- and low-level branches and camouflages in leaves to hunt.

9. *Test and Improve*, the middle box, is correct. This step of the design process requires that a design be tested, analyzed, and improved if necessary to meet desired criteria.

10. **A.** This is correct because oceans are larger than ponds and rivers.

   B. This is incorrect because ponds are smaller than oceans.

   C. This is incorrect because rivers are smaller than oceans.

11. **A.** *Heat was added* is correct because heat causes a log to burn and turn into ash. Not selecting the button for *It is reversible* is correct because the ash cannot change back into a log.

   B. *Heat was added* is correct because heat causes the raw egg to cook and changes it into a hard-boiled egg. Not selecting the button for *It is reversible* is correct because the hard-boiled egg cannot change back into a raw egg.

   C. *It is reversible* is correct because the frozen ice cream can have heat added to it to cause it to melt and change back to liquid cream.

12. **1B.** *Many small pieces* is correct. The houses were made from the many small pieces, not one big block and not three large pieces.

13. The picture of the sand dunes in the desert is correct. The wind causes erosion by blowing around sand over time. The other three pictures show Earth structures changed primarily by water.

14. **A.** *Soft* belongs in the bottom box. The cotton ball and the feather are soft.

© Houghton Mifflin Harcourt Publishing Company

   B. *Bendable* belongs in the top box. The rope and the belt can bend without breaking, making them very flexible.

   C. *Smooth* belongs in the middle box. The mirror and the satin fabric have no rough spots, so they have a texture that is smooth.

15. **A.** This is incorrect. Digging holes for seeds will not help him design a tool.

   B. This is incorrect because drawing pictures of trees will not help design a tool.

   C. This is correct. In order to design an effective tool he needs information about what needs to be done. This information will help him design a tool and choose materials.

16. **A.** *Height of plant* belongs in the *Things to Measure* box because height is a linear measurement, determined by a ruler.

   B. *How dark the soil is* does not belong in the box because the soil color is viewed by eyes and not counted or measured.

   C. *Number of hours in sunlight* belongs in the *Things to Measure* box because a person must use a clock and count to get this measurement.

   D. *Amount of water given to plant* belongs in the *Things to Measure* box because the amount must be measured with a measuring device, such as a cup or beaker.

17. **A.** *Flood* belongs in the *Minutes or Days* box because flooding occurs quickly.

   B. *Landslide* belongs in the *Minutes or Days* box because a landslide occurs quickly.

   C. *Rock wears away* belongs in the *Many Years* box because erosion of rock can take many years.

   D. *Tree roots break apart rock* belongs in the *Many Years* box because weathering of rock can take many years.

18. **A.** This is incorrect because the treat completely melted. If the stick broke apart the treat, there would be some small solid and frozen pieces.

   B. This is correct because the treat was frozen but melted. Melting occurs when heat is applied to a solid.

   C. This is incorrect because the treat was frozen liquid and was not cooked. In addition, if the treat was cooked for too long, it would have a burned appearance.

19. **A.** The picture of the screwdriver is incorrect. A screwdriver will not grab the toy. It may also damage the toy.

   B. The picture of the wheels is incorrect. Wheels will not grab the toy, and they could make it move farther away.

   C. The picture of the rake head is correct. The rake head can grab the toy, hold it down, and allow it to be pulled out.

20. **A.** This is correct. A map key is a key feature missing from the maps pictured.

   B. This is incorrect. Each map pictured has a title.

   C. This is incorrect. Each map pictured has a compass rose.

Unit 1 Engineering
Unit 1 Pretest

Item Analysis			
Item #	**Key**	**Standards**	**DOK**
1	B	3-5-ETS1-3, DCI.3-5-ETS1.B.4	1
2	D	3-5-ETS1-2, DCI.3-5-ETS1.B.2	1
3	D	3-5-ETS1-1, DCI.3-5-ETS1.A.1	1

© Houghton Mifflin Harcourt Publishing Company

4	A	3-5-ETS1-1, DCI.3-5-ETS1.A.1	1
5	A	3-5-ETS1-2, DCI.3-5-ETS1.B.2	2
6	C	3-5-ETS1-3, DCI.3-5-ETS1.B.4	2
7	A	3-5-ETS1-3, DCI.3-5-ETS1.C.1	2
8	B	3-5-ETS1-1, DCI.3-5-ETS1.A.1	2
9	D	3-5-ETS1-1, DCI.3-5-ETS1.A.1, CCC.STSE.3-5.B.2	2
10	C	3-5-ETS1-2, DCI.3-5-ETS1.B.2	2

Unit 1 Lesson 1

Item Analysis			
Item #	Key	Standards	DOK
1	A	3-5-ETS1-1, DCI.3-5-ETS1.A.1	2
2	D	3-5-ETS1-1, DCI.3-5-ETS1.A.1	2
3	B	3-5-ETS1-1, DCI.3-5-ETS1.A.1	2
4	C	3-5-ETS1-1, DCI.3-5-ETS1.A.1	2
5	B	3-5-ETS1-1, DCI.3-5-ETS1.A.1	2
6	Rubric	3-5-ETS1-1, DCI.3-5-ETS1.A.1, SEP.3-5.A.2	2
7	Rubric	3-5-ETS1-1, DCI.3-5-ETS1.A.1, CCC.STSE.3-5.B.2	3

6. Use the rubric below to evaluate total points earned for this item.

NGSS Constructed Response Answer – 1 Point	
Evidence of Mastery	Sample answer: • Kenji needs to get to school without getting his feet wet. • Kenji could use wood to build a bridge. To receive full credit for this item, students must identify the problem Kenji is trying to solve and list one material that could be used in the solution.

7. Use the rubric below to evaluate total points earned for this item.

NGSS Constructed Response Answer – 1 Point	
Evidence of Mastery	Sample answer: • The design has plenty of roads for traffic flow and it is easy to go from one place to another. But the design does not put a park by the school. To receive full credit for this test item, students must include that the design does provide roads but does not provide a park near the school.

Unit 1 Lesson 2

Item Analysis			
Item #	Key	Standards	DOK
1	B	3-5-ETS1-2, DCI.3-5-ETS1.B.3	2
2	C	3-5-ETS1-2, DCI.3-5-ETS1.B.3	2
3	D	3-5-ETS1-2, DCI.3-5-ETS1.B.2	2

© Houghton Mifflin Harcourt Publishing Company

4	A	3-5-ETS1-2, DCI.3-5-ETS1.B.2, CCC.STSE.3-5.B.1	2
5	B	3-5-ETS1-2, DCI.3-5-ETS1.B.2, SEP.3-5.F.4	3
6	Rubric	3-5-ETS1-2, DCI.3-5-ETS1.B.3	2
7	Rubric	3-5-ETS1-2, DCI.3-5-ETS1.B.2, CCC.STSE.3-5.B.1	3

6. Use the rubric below to evaluate total points earned for this item.

NGSS Constructed Response Answer – 1 Point	
Evidence of Mastery	Sample answers: • The straws under the paper will help keep the bridge from collapsing when cars cross it. • The straws will hold up the paper when a toy car crosses the bridge. To receive full credit for this test item, students must include at least one reasonable argument why straws are good supports for a paper bridge.

7. Use the rubric below to evaluate total points earned for this item.

NGSS Constructed Response Answer – 1 Point	
Evidence of Mastery	Sample answer: • The engineers should think about how well their ideas meet the listed criteria. They should build the design that best fits the criteria. They repeat this process for all designs. To receive full credit for this test item, students must explain that the engineers should compare the solutions based on how well they meet the criteria and constraints of the problem.

Unit 1 Lesson 3

Item Analysis			
Item #	**Key**	**Standards**	**DOK**
1	C	3-5-ETS1-3, DCI.3-5-ETS1.B.4	2
2	B	3-5-ETS1-3, DCI.3-5-ETS1.B.4	2
3	A	3-5-ETS1-3, DCI.3-5-ETS1.B.4	2
4	C	3-5-ETS1-3, DCI.3-5-ETS1.B.4	3
5	D	3-5-ETS1-3, DCI.3-5-ETS1.B.4	3
6	Rubric	3-5-ETS1-3, DCI.3-5-ETS1.C.1	2
7	Rubric	3-5-ETS1-3, DCI.3-5-ETS1.B.1	3

6. Use the rubric below to evaluate total points earned for this item.

NGSS Constructed Response Answer – 1 Point	
Evidence of Mastery	Sample answer: • No, the results were the same for both cups. To receive full credit for this test item, students must indicate that the new material is not better and say that the results were the same for both materials.

Answer Key
© Houghton Mifflin Harcourt Publishing Company

Grade 3 • Assessment Guide

7. Use the rubric below to evaluate total points earned for this item.

NGSS Constructed Response Answer – 1 Point	
Evidence of Mastery	Sample answer: • After testing the prototype, the engineers should evaluate the design to decide whether building a full-scale car is reasonable (or present the design solution using graphs or drawings, etc.). To receive full credit for this test item, students must include a part of the design process that should be done after testing.

Unit 1 Unit Test

Item Analysis		
Item #	**Standards**	**DOK**
1	3-5-ETS1-2, DCI.3-5-ETS1.B.3, SEP.3-5.F.4	2
2	3-5-ETS1-1, DCI.3-5-ETS1.A.1, SEP.3-5.A.2	2
3	3-5-ETS1-1, DCI.3-5-ETS1.A.1	1
4	3-5-ETS1-2, DCI.3-5-ETS1.B.3, CCC.STSE.3-5.B.1	2
5	3-5-ETS1-3, DCI.3-5-ETS1.B.4, SEP.3-5.F.1	3
6	3-5-ETS1-2, DCI.3-5-ETS1.B.1, SEP.3-5.F.4	2
7	3-5-ETS1-2, DCI.3-5-ETS1.B.3, SEP.3-5.F.4, CCC.STSE.3-5.B.1	2
8	3-5-ETS1-1, DCI.3-5-ETS1.A.1, CCC.STSE.3-5.B.2	2
9	3-5-ETS1-3, DCI.3-5-ETS1.B.4, SEP.3-5.C.1	3
10	3-5-ETS1-3, DCI.3-5-ETS1.B.4	1
11	3-5-ETS1-2, DCI.3-5-ETS1.B.1, SEP.3-5.F.4, CCC.STSE.3-5.B.1	3
12	3-5-ETS1-2, DCI.3-5-ETS1.B.1, CCC.STSE.3-5.B.1	2
13	3-5-ETS1-3, DCI.3-5-ETS1.C.1, CCC.STSE.3-5.B.1	2
14	3-5-ETS1-3, DCI.3-5-ETS1.C.1, SEP.3-5.F.1	2
15	3-5-ETS1-1, DCI.3-5-ETS1.A.1, SEP.3-5.A.2	3

1. **A.** This is incorrect because the lamp cord is the same for both girls and the lamp is bolted to the floor; therefore, Quinn's plan will not work.

   B. This is incorrect because the weight of the lamp is not the issue. The girls are working around the criterion that the lamp is bolted to the floor.

   C. This is incorrect because the lamp is bolted to the floor; therefore, it is not easily moved.

   D. This is correct. Lisa's plan will work because the lamp is bolted to the floor. The lamp will have to be plugged in by an extension cord.

2. **A.** This is incorrect because a large brick would likely scratch the wooden floor.

   B. This is incorrect because paper would not have the force to hold a door open.

   C. This is incorrect because cotton balls are soft and would easily move when the door moved.

   D. This is correct because a large rock is heavy enough to hold open a door, and the sock will keep the rock from scratching the floor.

3. **A.** This is incorrect because Ella's criterion was to keep the food from going down the drain, not to have the water be cold.

© Houghton Mifflin Harcourt Publishing Company

B. This is incorrect because Ella's criterion was to keep the food from going down the drain, not to have clean dishes.

C. This is incorrect because Ella's criterion was to keep the food from going down the drain, not to have slow-flowing water.

D. This is correct because when Ella had a problem, her only criterion was that the food not go down the drain.

4. **A.** This is correct because redesigning a shovel to reduce back pain helps her but does not necessarily help others or bring her fame and fortune.

B. This is incorrect because Dori is not seeking fame. She wants to reduce her back pain after shoveling snow.

C. This is incorrect because Dori is not seeking to satisfy the demands of society. She wants to reduce her back pain after shoveling snow.

D. This is incorrect because Dori is not seeking to earn money from her design. She wants to reduce her back pain after shoveling snow.

5. **A.** This is incorrect because both ropes are made of plastic.

B. This is incorrect because though brand Y is thinner, it did not pull as much weight as brand X.

C. This is incorrect because brand Y is thinner, not thicker, than brand X.

D. This is correct because brand X pulled more weight than brand Y. It is the strongest of the two ropes.

6. **A.** This picture belongs in the box because there is a barrier that reduces the direct sunlight from the late afternoon shade is between the plant and the sun.

B. The picture does not belong in the box because it lacks a barrier between the plant and the late afternoon sun.

C. The picture belongs in the box because though there is a barrier, it is not between the plant and the late afternoon sun.

D. This picture does not belong in the box because there is a barrier that reduces the direct sunlight from the late afternoon shade is between the plant and the sun.

7. The numbers should be 1, 5, 4, 3, and 2. The order in which Sam should try to fix his class pencil sharpener is as follows: (1) Find where the sharpener is broken. (2) Ask Jeff for ideas on how to remove the broken pencil lead. (3) Remove the broken pencil lead from the sharpener. (4) Test the sharpener to see if it works again. (5) Redesign and repeat if it doesn't work.

8. **A.** The picture of the computer matches the middle description about sending letters and pictures. The computer uses technology that allows people to send mail electronically without having to leave the home or office.

B. The picture of the microwave oven matches the bottom description about heating food. The microwave oven uses technology to warm small or large amounts of food quickly.

C. The picture of the remote control matches the top description about not having to walk to turn on the television. The remote control uses technology that remotely transfers information from the control to the television.

9. **A.** This description belongs in the third and sixth steps. Sara has observed the wagon with type A tires and also with type B tires.

B. This description for type B tires belongs in step 1 or step 4, depending on which tires Sara places on the wagon first. The tires are the variable being studied. They must be placed on the wagon before testing the wagon.

C. This description for type A tires belongs in step 1 or step 4, depending on which tires Sara places on the wagon first. The tires are the variable being studied. They must be placed on the wagon before testing the wagon.

© Houghton Mifflin Harcourt Publishing Company

D. This description belongs in the second and fifth step. Sara needs to pull the wagon with type A tires and then with type B tires.

10. The student should push on the spot between plants 2 and 3 on the water hose. There is a leak at this location. The leak is forming a small puddle back behind plant 2.

11. Use the rubric below to evaluate total points earned for this item. *[max point: 3]*

DCI, SEP, CCC - 3 points	
Claims	The student is able to: 1. describe the benefits of new technology under a new condition (DCI); and 2. identify the requirements to a problem (SEP); and 3. explain improvements that were made by engineers (CCC).
Evidence of Mastery of Disciplinary Core Ideas	1 point for correctly identifying the criterion **Part 1:** One point is earned for correctly identifying that the new siren needed to be louder than the older siren. The following answer, or an equivalent, is acceptable. • The new siren needs to be louder so more people can hear it.
Evidence of Mastery of Science and Engineering Practices	1 point for correctly explaining the improvements that were made to the new siren **Part 2:** One point is earned for correctly explaining that the new siren had improvements that benefited the community over the old siren. The following answer, or an equivalent, is acceptable. • The new siren has multiple speakers in a circle pointing outward, allowing the sound to travel in all direction.
Evidence of Mastery of Crosscutting Concepts	1 point for correctly describing the benefits of the new siren versus the old siren **Part 3:** One point is earned for correctly describing that the new siren will be heard 360 degrees around the pole, instead of one direction. Therefore, more people will be able to hear the siren. • The new siren can be heard all around the siren instead of the sound traveling in one direction. More people will be able to hear the siren.

12. **A.** This is incorrect because if she plugs the hole in the front it could keep predators out, but then the birds would not get in and out, and it would not be easier to clean.

    B. This is incorrect because the birds could not build a nest inside, and they would fall out. This design could make it easier to clean but would not keep predators out.

    C. This is incorrect because while it would likely be easier to clean, it would allow predators into the birdhouse.

    D. This is correct because a latch can allow Ali to open and close the birdhouse so that she can clean it.

13. The designs shown in the middle picture and the picture on the right meet Ali's requirements. The design shown on the left is unattached and can easily fall out of the tree, injuring the birds inside.

14. **A.** This is incorrect because Ali's research shows that the opening should be 1.5 inches wide, not just 1 inch.

    B. This is incorrect because Ali's research indicates that the birdhouse for a bluebird needs to be at 10 inches tall.

    C. This is incorrect because Ali's research indicates that only one opening is needed.

    D. This is correct because Ali hung the birdhouses 6 feet off the ground, which is a requirement for bluebirds.

© Houghton Mifflin Harcourt Publishing Company

15. Use the rubric below to evaluate total points earned for this item. *[max point: 2]*

DCI, SEP Only - 2 Points	
Claims	The student is able to: • consider the desired features of a solution (DCI); and • consider criteria when recommending how to adjust a design (SEP).
Evidence of Mastery of Disciplinary Core Ideas	1 point for correctly describing one way to adjust Design 1 **Part 1:** One point is earned for describing that the hole in the front is too small for the bird and should be enlarged or that the height of the birdhouse needs to increase to 10 inches. The following response, or an equivalent, is acceptable. • Make the entry hole larger, at least 1.5 inches.
Evidence of Mastery of Science and Engineering Practices	1 point for correctly describing a second way to adjust Design 1 **Part 1:** One point is earned for describing that the hole in the front is too small for the bird and should be enlarged or that the height of the birdhouse needs to increase to 10 inches. The following response, or an equivalent, is acceptable. • Make the bird house taller, at least 10 inches.

Unit 2 Forces
Unit 2 Pretest

Item Analysis			
Item #	**Key**	**Standards**	**DOK**
1	C	3-PS2-4, DCI.3-PS2.B.2, SEP.3-5.A.2	1
2	C	3-PS2-3, DCI.3-PS2.B.2	2
3	D	3-PS2-3, DCI.3-PS2.B.2	1
4	C	3-PS2-3, DCI.3-PS2.B.2, CCC.3-5.B.1	2
5	D	3-PS2-1, DCI.3-PS2.A.1	2
6	B	3-PS2-1, DCI.3-PS2.A.1	2
7	C	3-PS2-3, DCI.3-PS2.B.2	2
8	B	3-PS2-3, DCI.3-PS2.B.2	2
9	A	3-PS2-3, DCI.3-PS2.B.2	2
10	A	3-PS2-1, DCI.3-PS2.A.1	2

Unit 2 Lesson 1

Item Analysis			
Item #	**Key**	**Standards**	**DOK**
1	A	3-PS2-1	1
2	C	3-PS2-1, DCI.3-PS2.A.1	2
3	B	3-PS2-1, DCI.3-PS2.A.1	2
4	D	3-PS2-1, DCI.3-PS2.A.1, SEP.3-5.C.2	2
5	A	3-PS2-1, DCI.3-PS2.A.1, CCC.3-5.A.2	3
6	Rubric	3-PS2-1, DCI.3-PS2.A.1	1
7	Rubric	3-PS2-1, DCI.3-PS2.A.1, SEP.3-5.A.1	3

© Houghton Mifflin Harcourt Publishing Company

6. Use the rubric below to evaluate total points earned for this item.

NGSS Constructed Response Answer – 1 Point	
Evidence of Mastery	Sample answer: • Force is the amount of energy required to move a load. To receive full credit for this test item, students must include an accurate definition of force.

7. Use the rubric below to evaluate total points earned for this item.

NGSS Constructed Response Answer – 1 Point	
Evidence of Mastery	Sample answer: • The forces up and down on it are the same because it is not moving. The book will be pulled to the ground. The downward force will be greater so it will move down to the ground. To receive full credit for this test item, students must describe the balanced forces on the book when Grant is holding it. Then students must predict what will happen to the book when it is released, and they must identifying a force (pull/gravity) and a direction (down, to the ground, etc.).

Unit 2 Lesson 2

Item Analysis			
Item #	**Key**	**Standards**	**DOK**
1	C	3-PS2-1, DCI.3-PS2.A.1	1
2	A	3-PS2-1, DCI.3-PS2.A.1	2
3	C	3-PS2-1, DCI.3-PS2.A.1	1
4	B	3-PS2-1, DCI.3-PS2.A.1	2
5	D	3-PS2-1, DCI.3-PS2.A.1	3
6	Rubric	3-PS2-1, DCI.3-PS2.A.1, CCC.3-5.B.1	2
7	Rubric	3-PS2-1, DCI.3-PS2.A.1, SEP.NOS.3-5.A.1	3

6. Use the rubric below to evaluate total points earned for this item.

NGSS Constructed Response Answer – 1 Point	
Evidence of Mastery	Sample answer: • The forces are balanced. When all the forces are balanced, the object will not move. To receive full credit for this item, students must indicate that when forces are balanced, objects do not move.

7. Use the rubric below to evaluate total points earned for this item.

NGSS Constructed Response Answer – 1 Point	
Evidence of Mastery	Sample answer: • The car in picture B will take less force to pull up the ramp. Because the ramp is not as steep, it takes less force to pull the car up the ramp. To receive full credit for this test item, students must demonstrate an understanding that the car in picture B requires less force to pull up the ramp because the incline is not as steep as the incline in picture A.

© Houghton Mifflin Harcourt Publishing Company

Unit 2 Lesson 3 ~~4~~ quiz

<table>
<tr><th colspan="4">Item Analysis</th></tr>
<tr><th>Item #</th><th>Key</th><th>Standards</th><th>DOK</th></tr>
<tr><td>1</td><td>A</td><td>3-PS2-3, DCI.3-PS2.B.2</td><td>2</td></tr>
<tr><td>2</td><td>B</td><td>3-PS2-3, DCI.3-PS2.B.2, CCC.3-5.B.1</td><td>2</td></tr>
<tr><td>3</td><td>C</td><td>3-PS2-4, DCI.3-PS2.B.2, SEP.3-5.A.2</td><td>2</td></tr>
<tr><td>4</td><td>B</td><td>3-PS2-4, DCI.3-PS2.B.2</td><td>2</td></tr>
<tr><td>5</td><td>D</td><td>3-PS2-3, DCI.3-PS2.B.2, CCC.3-5.B.1</td><td>3</td></tr>
<tr><td>6</td><td>Rubric</td><td>3-PS2-3, DCI.3-PS2.B.2, CCC.3-5.B.1</td><td>2</td></tr>
<tr><td>7</td><td>Rubric</td><td>3-PS2-3, DCI.3-PS2.B.2, CCC.3-5.B.1</td><td>3</td></tr>
</table>

6. Use the rubric below to evaluate total points earned for this item.

<table>
<tr><th colspan="2">NGSS Constructed Response Answer – 1 Point</th></tr>
<tr><td rowspan="2">Evidence of Mastery</td><td>Sample answer:

• The magnets in picture B will repel each other.

• They have the same pole facing each other. Like poles repel.</td></tr>
<tr><td>To receive full credit for this item, students must identify picture B as containing the magnets that will repel each other and indicate that like poles repel.</td></tr>
</table>

7. Use the rubric below to evaluate total points earned for this item.

<table>
<tr><th colspan="2">NGSS Constructed Response Answer – 1 Point</th></tr>
<tr><td rowspan="2">Evidence of Mastery</td><td>Sample answer:

• The rod will repel the balloon with the positive charge because they both have the same charge and like charges repel one another. The rod will attract the balloon with the negative charge because they have opposite charges and unlike charges attract one another. The rod will attract the balloon with no charge because a charged object will attract uncharged objects.</td></tr>
<tr><td>To receive full credit for this test item, students must include the following information: (1) a description of how a charge on the rod affects each balloon, (2) an explanation of why each balloon reacts the way that it does, (3) a statement of what happens to a balloon if it has the same charge as the rod, (4) a statement of what happens to a balloon if it has a different charge than the rod or no charge.</td></tr>
</table>

Unit 2 Unit Test

<table>
<tr><th colspan="3">Item Analysis</th></tr>
<tr><th>Item #</th><th>Standards</th><th>DOK</th></tr>
<tr><td>1</td><td>3-PS2-1, DCI.3-PS2.A.1</td><td>1</td></tr>
<tr><td>2</td><td>3-PS2-3, DCI.3-PS2.B.2, SEP.3-5.A.1</td><td>2</td></tr>
<tr><td>3</td><td>3-PS2-1, DCI.3-PS2.A.1</td><td>1</td></tr>
<tr><td>4</td><td>3-PS2-3, DCI.3-PS2.B.2</td><td>2</td></tr>
<tr><td>5</td><td>3-PS2-4, DCI.3-PS2.B.2, SEP.3-5.A.2</td><td>2</td></tr>
<tr><td>6</td><td>3-PS2-1, DCI.3-PS2.B.1</td><td>1</td></tr>
<tr><td>7</td><td>3-PS2-1, DCI.3-PS2.A.1, SEP.3-5.A.1</td><td>3</td></tr>
<tr><td>8</td><td>3-PS2-1, DCI.3-PS2.A.1, SEP.3-5.C.1</td><td>2</td></tr>
</table>

9	3-PS2-4, DCI.3-PS2.B.2, CCC.STSE.3-5.A.1	3
10	3-PS2-1, DCI.3-PS2.A.1, CCC.3-5.B.1	3
11	3-PS2-2, DCI.3-PS2.A.2, CCC.3-5.A.2	2
12	3-PS2-3, DCI.3-PS2.B.2, CCC.3-5.B.1	2
13	3-PS2-1, DCI.3-PS2.A.1, SEP.NOS.3-5.A.1	2
14	3-PS2-1, DCI.3-PS2.B.1	2
15	3-PS2-1, DCI.3-PS2.A.1, CCC.3-5.B.1	3

1. **A.** This is correct because the book and desk are exerting the same force on each other, resulting in no movement and zero net force.

   B. This is incorrect because the leaf increases speed as it falls from the branch, so the forces are not balanced; there is a downward net force.

   C. This is incorrect because the girl is slowing down on her bike.

   D. This is incorrect because the truck is increasing speed, so the forward force must be greater than the force in the opposing direction. The unbalanced forces mean the net force is not zero.

2. **A.** This is incorrect because the question relates to attractive forces of magnets, not to static electricity.

   B. This is incorrect because the question relates to the attraction of magnets, not to static electricity.

   C. This is correct because it is a question that relates to the study of static electricity.

   D. This is incorrect because, though it relates to static electricity, this is a fact rather than a question.

3. **A.** This is correct because Car 1 and the bike are of different sizes, with Car 1 being larger than the bike, meaning it has the greater force.

   B. This is incorrect because Car 1 and the other car are equal size, meaning that the net force of their movement is zero. This is an example of a balanced force with no car having a greater force.

   C. This is incorrect because though the picture shows an unbalanced force, Car 1 is smaller than the truck and therefore does not have a greater force.

   D. This is incorrect because Car 1 and the other car are equal size, meaning that the net force of their movement is zero. This is an example of a balanced force with no car having a greater force.

4. **A.** This is incorrect because two like poles repel each other, not attract each other.

   B. This is correct because opposite poles are attracted to each other. In addition, the magnets are very close together, indicating a stronger magnetic force.

   C. This is incorrect because although the poles are opposite and do have a magnetic attraction, this attraction is weak.

   D. This is incorrect because the magnets are far apart, indicating a weak magnetic force. In addition, the poles are alike and repel rather than attract.

5. **A.** This is correct because the metal tacks are attracted to a magnet. The magnet can pick up the tacks, and because it is tied to a broomstick, Larry will not have to step on the grass. He can just extend the broom handle over the grass.

   B. This is incorrect because a lawnmower will shorten the grass but will also scatter the tacks. In addition, the cost is above the limit of $20.

   C. This is incorrect because although this solution may allow Larry to pick up the tacks, this solution may cause him to step on a tack. In addition, with this solution some tacks may not be retrieved.

   D. This is incorrect because although the light bulbs may help Larry see the tacks, the circuit does not directly remove the tacks.

© Houghton Mifflin Harcourt Publishing Company

6. **A.** This is correct because the boy is using his arm to move the wagon forward.

   B. This is incorrect because the girl is using her foot to push the ball away from her.

   C. This is incorrect because the person is throwing the ball, which means the ball is pushed forward, out of the person's hand.

   D. This is incorrect because the ball is falling, which is a push down due to gravity.

7. **1A.** This question is something Kori should ask herself before starting the experiment. Knowing whether the chair has wheels will help Kori push the chair, which will help demonstrate an unbalanced force.

   2B. This question does not help with the investigation because knowing the color of the chair will not affect whether or not Kori can push the chair.

   3A. This question is something Kori should ask herself before starting the experiment. Knowing whether the friend weighs more or less will help Kori know if she can overcome the weight difference and actually move the friend. It will be easier for Kori to move a lighter friend than a heavier friend.

8. **A.** This picture matches Step 3 because it shows how blocks of equal size and weight have a balanced force.

   B. This picture does not match any step because it shows two blocks of equal size being unbalanced.

   C. This picture matches Step 1 because it shows how gravity is of equal for both sides of the seesaw, allowing for a balanced force.

   D. This picture matches Step 2 because it shows how blocks of unequal size and weight have an unbalanced force.

9. **A.** This is correct because an electromagnet is attached to the crane. The electricity makes the metal cylinder a magnet, which allows the crane to pick up the car. When the electricity is turned off, the magnet turns off and the crane drops the car.

   B. This is incorrect because the dryer machine produces static electricity, not magnetism.

   C. This is correct because the metal within the name tag is attracted to the magnet, bringing the two together, even through fabric.

   D. This is incorrect because the machine is producing static electricity, not magnetism.

10. Use the rubric below to evaluate total points earned for this item. *[max point: 3]*

DCI, CCC - 3 Points	
Claims	The student is able to: • identify an unbalanced force (DCI); and • explain what caused an unbalanced force (CCC).
Evidence of Mastery of Disciplinary Core Ideas	1 point for correctly identifying the unbalanced force **Part 1:** One point is earned for identifying that the picture of the students pulling on the rope is an example of an unbalanced force. The following response, or an equivalent, is acceptable. • unbalanced
Evidence of Mastery of Crosscutting Concepts	2 points for correctly explaining why the force is an unbalanced force **Part 2:** Two points are earned for explaining that the force is unbalanced because there are three students on the right side and only two on the left side. Because the students appear to be of the same size, there is a greater force being pulled on the right side. The following response, or an equivalent, is acceptable. • There are more kids on one side and they are pulling more.

11. **A.** This is incorrect because all of the toy cars are identical.

   B. This is incorrect because the car itself will not be taller than the other ramps. The ramp will be taller than the other ramps.

© Houghton Mifflin Harcourt Publishing Company

    C. This is incorrect because the taller the ramp, the farther the car will roll. This ramp will have four bricks, making it the tallest of the ramps in Kate's experiment.

    D. This is correct because this new ramp will be taller than the other ramps, meaning that force of gravity will cause the car to accelerate is it moves down the ramp, indicating that more force was applied.

12. A. This is true because opposite charges are attracted to each other. The positive charge of car 1 will be attracted to the negative charge of car 2.

    B. This is true because opposite charges are attracted to each other. The negative charge of car 2 will be attracted to the positive charge of car 1.

    C. This is false because the cars have magnets of opposite charges and will therefore be attracted to each other.

    D. This is false because car 2 has a magnet with a negative charge and will be attracted to the positive magnet on car 1.

13. A. This action belongs in the *Will Not Help Measure* column because weighing the cars will not help Kate know which car moved the fastest or took more time to roll. In addition, the cars are identical and the weight would be the same for each car.

    B. This action belongs in the *Will Help Measure* column because measuring time is a way to know which car moved longer, and therefore farther.

    C. This action belongs in the *Will Help Measure* column because measuring distance is a way to know which car moved farther.

    D. This action belongs in the *Will Not Help Measure* column because taking pictures of the cars will not help Kate know which car moved the fastest or took more time to roll. In addition, the cars are identical and the photos will be the same.

14. A. This is incorrect because both arrows are showing that the ball will roll toward the car.

    B. This is incorrect because both arrows are pointing toward the ramp instead of away from the ramp.

    C. This is incorrect because the first arrow shows that the ball moves toward the car and then the ball moves to the right.

    D. This is correct because the arrows show that the car rolls into the ball and the ball rolls toward the right.

15. Use the rubric below to evaluate total points earned for this item.   *[max point: 3]*

DCI, CCC - 3 Points	
Claims	The student is able to: 1. identify the strength of forces of an object (DCI); and 2. explain the cause-and-effect relationship between force and movement (CCC).
Evidence of Mastery of Disciplinary Core Ideas	1 point for correctly identifying the car with the greatest force pushing on it **Part 1:** One point is earned for identifying that the car on Ramp C had the greatest amount of force. The following response, or an equivalent, is acceptable. • The car on ramp C.
Evidence of Mastery of Crosscutting Concepts	2 points for correctly explaining why the car on ramp C had the greatest force pushing on it **Part 1:** Two points are earned for explaining that the car on Ramp C has the greatest force pushing on it because it rolled the farthest. Because the cars are identical, the only variable that could have made this car roll farther is the height of the ramp. The car started at a higher level, allowing gravity to push it down the ramp, accelerating as it moved. The following response, or an equivalent, is acceptable. • The car on ramp C had the most force because it was on a taller ramp.

© Houghton Mifflin Harcourt Publishing Company

Unit 3 Motion
Unit 3 Pretest

		Item Analysis	
Item #	**Key**	**Standards**	**DOK**
1	D	3-PS2-1, DCI.3-PS2.A.1, SEP.3-5.C.2	1
2	B	3-PS2-1, DCI.3-PS2.A.1	1
3	C	3-PS2-2, DCI.3-PS2.A.2	1
4	B	3-PS2-1, DCI.3-PS2.A.1, SEP.3-5.A.1	1
5	C	3-PS2-1, DCI.3-PS2.A.1	2
6	A	3-PS2-2, DCI.3-PS2.A.2, SEP.NOS.3-5.B.1	2
7	B	3-PS2-2, DCI.3-PS2.A.2, SEP.NOS.3-5.B.1	1
8	D	3-PS2-2, DCI.3-PS2.A.2, SEP.3-5.C.2	2
9	A	3-PS2-1, DCI.3-PS2.A.1, CCC.3-5.B.1	2
10	C	3-PS2-2, DCI.3-PS2.A.2, SEP.NOS.3-5.B.1	3

Unit 3 Lesson 1

		Item Analysis	
Item #	**Key**	**Standards**	**DOK**
1	B	3-PS2-1, DCI.3-PS2.A.1	1
2	D	3-PS2-1, DCI.3-PS2.A.1, CCC.3-5.B.1	1
3	A	3-PS2-1, DCI.3-PS2.A.1	2
4	B	3-PS2-1, DCI.3-PS2.A.1, CCC.3-5.B.1	2
5	C	3-PS2-1, DCI.3-PS2.A.1, SEP.NOS.3-5.A.1	2
6	Rubric	3-PS2-1, DCI.3-PS2.A.1, CCC.3-5.B.1	2
7	Rubric	3-PS2-1, DCI.3-PS2.A.1, CCC.3-5.B.1	2

6. Use the rubric below to evaluate total points earned for this item.

	NGSS Constructed Response Answer – 1 Point
Evidence of Mastery	Sample answer: • Ken's brother weighs less than Ken's dad. With his brother in the wagon, Ken pulls with enough force to move the wagon. However, if Ken uses the same or even more force, it is not enough to move the wagon with his dad in it because his dad weighs more than his little brother. To receive full credit for this test item, students must include the following information: (1) an understanding that Ken's dad weighs more (is bigger than) Ken's brother; (2) an explanation that Ken uses enough force to pull his brother in the wagon, but the same amount of force has less effect when he tries to pull his dad in the wagon.

7. Use the rubric below to evaluate total points earned for this item.

	NGSS Constructed Response Answer – 1 Point
Evidence of Mastery	Sample answer: • The cars are not moving because they are both using the same force and strength. If the engine of the green car was turned off, the yellow car would be pulled because then the strength of the green car would be greater.

© Houghton Mifflin Harcourt Publishing Company

	To get full credit for this test item, students must identify that the reason the cars are not moving is because the forces are balanced (or have the same strength of pull). Students must explain that the effect of the yellow car having a stronger pull/force would make it move the green car if the green car was not using any force.

Unit 3 Lesson 2

Item Analysis			
Item #	Key	Standards	DOK
1	D	3-PS2-2, DCI.3-PS2.A.2, CCC.3-5.A.2	2
2	A	3-PS2-2, DCI.3-PS2.A.2, CCC.3-5.A.2	2
3	C	3-PS2-2, DCI.3-PS2.A.2, SEP.3-5.C.2	2
4	C	3-PS2-2, DCI.3-PS2.A.2	3
5	B	3-PS2-2, DCI.3-PS2.A.2, SEP.NOS.3-5.B.1	2
6	Rubric	3-PS2-2, DCI.3-PS2.A.2, SEP.NOS.3-5.B.1, CCC.3-5.A.2	2
7	Rubric	3-PS2-2, DCI.3-PS2.A.2, SEP.3-5.C.2, CCC.3-5.A.2	3

6. Use the rubric below to evaluate total points earned for this item.

NGSS Constructed Response Answer – 1 Point	
Evidence of Mastery	Sample answer: • The ball will bounce back up to a height of 10 cm. To receive full credit for this test item, students must recognize that the ball will bounce back up and that the height will be more than 0 cm but less than 20 cm.

7. Use the rubric below to evaluate total points earned for this item.

NGSS Constructed Response Answer – 1 Point	
Evidence of Mastery	Sample answer: • She could write down what pole on the pier the water is at or measure the distance from the sidewalk. To receive full credit for this test item, students must include a description of how to use the pier or the sidewalk to measure where the water is at.

Unit 3 Unit Test

Item Analysis		
Item #	Standards	DOK
1	3-PS2-1, DCI.3-PS2.A.1, SEP.3-5.C.1	2
2	3-PS2-2, DCI.3-PS2.A.2, CCC.3-5.B.1	2
3	3-PS2-2, DCI.3-PS2.A.2, SEP.3-5.A.1	2
4	3-PS2-2, DCI.3-PS2.A.2	1
5	3-PS2-2, DCI.3-PS2.A.2	1
6	3-PS2-2, DCI.3-PS2.A.2, CCC.3-5.A.2	2
7	3-PS2-1, DCI.3-PS2.A.1	1
8	3-PS2-2, DCI.3-PS2.A.2, SEP.3-5.H.1	2

© Houghton Mifflin Harcourt Publishing Company

9	3-PS2-2, DCI.3-PS2.A.2, SEP.3-5.C.2	2
10	3-PS2-2, DCI.3-PS2.A.2, SEP.3-5.C.2	2
11	3-PS2-2, DCI.3-PS2.A.2, SEP.3-5.C.2, CCC.3-5.A.2	3
12	3-PS2-2, DCI.3-PS2.A.2, SEP.NOS.3-5.B.1	2
13	3-PS2-2, DCI.3-PS2.A.2, SEP.3-5.G.1	2
14	3-PS2-1, DCI.3-PS2.A.1, CCC.3-5.B.1	2
15	3-PS2-1, DCI.3-PS2.A.1, SEP.3-5.C.1, CCC.3-5.B.1	3

1. **A.** This is incorrect because two larger bricks on Side 2 will cause an unbalanced force.

   B. This is incorrect because a smaller brick on Side 2 is not equal to a larger and a small brick on Side 1. The result would be an unbalanced force.

   C. This is correct because two identical bricks are of equal weight, allowing for balanced force.

   D. This is incorrect because adding a second brick will add more weight to Side 1. To show balanced forces, equal weights should be placed on both sides of the seesaw.

2. **A.** This answer is correct because as Jack travels down the hill his speed will increase with the pull of gravity.

   B. This answer is incorrect because the force of gravity will cause Jack's speed to increase as he travels down the hill.

   C. This answer is incorrect because as gravity pulls Jack down the hill his speed will increase.

   D. This answer is incorrect because gravity will pull Jack downhill, increasing his speed but not making him move side to side.

3. **A.** This answer choice is incorrect because the picture shows the dominoes standing still. The dominoes are not in motion.

   B. This answer is correct because the dominoes have all fallen over. The picture shows what would happen to all of the dominoes after the first one was pushed.

   C. This answer choice is incorrect because the picture shows the dominoes having fallen in the wrong direction, opposite the push of the finger.

   D. This answer choice is incorrect because the picture shows the dominoes have fallen to the right. They would not fall over to the right; they would not tip over the edge to the right and knock into each other, pushing the next over and then the next.

4. **A.** This answer is correct because one cannot predict the movement of a rabbit.

   B. This answer is incorrect because the ceiling fan spins in a continuous circular motion.

   C. This answer is incorrect because the earth spins on its axis in a circular motion continuously.

   D. This answer is incorrect because the gears in the inside of a watch are moving the same way to keep the watch working properly.

5. The picture of the girl on the swing represents a back-and-forth predictable motion. The swing is like a pendulum, moving back and forth in a predictable pattern.

6. **A.** This is correct because if the fan stops moving, there is nothing pushing the fan to move and the blade's motion will stop completely.

   B. This is incorrect because if the fan turns off, there is nothing forcing the fan to continue to move.

   C. This is incorrect because if the speed of the fan decreases, the rate the blue blade goes around will also decrease.

   D. This is correct because if the speed of the fan decreases, the rate the blue blade goes around will also decrease.

© Houghton Mifflin Harcourt Publishing Company

7. Use the rubric below to evaluate total points earned for this item.   *[max point: 1]*

DCI - 1 Point	
Claims	The student is able to identify the direction an object will move based on the location of an added force (DCI).
Evidence of Mastery of Disciplinary Core Ideas	1 point for correctly drawing an arrow to represent the direction of the ball's movement **Part 1:** One point is earned for drawing an arrow leading away from the ball and to the left. The following response, or an equivalent, is acceptable.

8. **1A.** Circular motion is the correct label for the toy car spiraling around a center point.

    2C. Up-and-down motion is the correct label for the yo-yo because the yo-yo moves up and down on the string.

    3B. Zigzag motion is the correct label for the picture of a bee flying in a zigzag pattern because the bee veers right and left alternately in the shape of a z.

9. **A.** *0 swings* does not belong in the table because the pattern shows that if the string is of any length, then it will swing.

    B. *15 swings* belongs in the 90-centimeter column because the pattern shows that the longer the string, the more swings of the pendulum.

    C. *45 swings* belongs in the 30-centimeter column because the pattern shows that the shorter the string, the fewer swings of the pendulum.

10. The bar for the short ramp should be at 1 meter; the bar for the tall ramp should be at 5 meters.

11. Use the rubric below to evaluate total points earned for this item.   *[max point: 3]*

DCI, SEP, CCC - 3 points	
Claims	The student is able to: 1. use past motion to predict future motion (DCI); 2. use measurements as the basis for evidence of a phenomenon (SEP); and 3. describe the pattern of change used to make the prediction (CCC).
Evidence of Mastery of Disciplinary Core Ideas	1 point for correctly predicting how long it will take to travel 4 laps **Part 1:** One point is earned for identifying that it will take 40 minutes. The following response, or an equivalent, is acceptable. • 40
Evidence of Mastery of Science and Engineering Practices	1 point for correctly using the measurements in the table to determine the speed of the car **Part 3:** One point is earned for calculating the speed of the car as 0.1 miles per minute. The following response, or an equivalent, is acceptable. • 0.1
Evidence of Mastery of Crosscutting Concepts	1 point for correctly explaining that each lap takes 10 minutes **Part 3:** One point is earned for explaining that the car takes 10 minutes to travel one lap. The following response, or an equivalent, is acceptable. • Each lap takes 10 minutes.

12. **A.** This is incorrect because Activity 1 shows the student twirling the rope in circles, not moving in a zigzag pattern.

    B. This is correct because when jumping rope, the rope moves in a circular pattern.

    C. This is incorrect because the rope is moving in a circular pattern.

    D. This is incorrect because the rope is moving in a circular pattern.

13. The student should select the ribbon and the marble track. Both have a zigzag pattern as shown in Activity 2 in the passage.

14. **A.** In Activity 1, the forces are *unbalanced*. The direction of motion changes as the ropes are turned around.

    B. In Activity 2, the forces are *unbalanced*. The direction of the rope is changing as it moves.

    C. In Activity 3, the forces are *balanced*. There is no motion shown in the image, and the size and number of students are balanced.

15. Use the rubric below to evaluate total points earned for this item.   *[max point: 3]*

DCI, SEP, CCC - 3 points	
Claims	The student is able to: 1. describe that forces that do not sum to zero can cause changes in an object's speed (DCI); and 2. explain that repeating trials helps to create a fair test (SEP); and 3. use cause-and-effect relationships to explain the changes in motion seen in the investigation (CCC).
Evidence of Mastery of Disciplinary Core Ideas	1 point for correctly identifying how the speed of motion would be affected from trial 2 to 3 **Part 2:** One point is earned for indicating that the speed would increase from trial 2 to 3. The following response, or an equivalent, is acceptable. • They would move faster in three than two.
Evidence of Mastery of Science and Engineering Practices	1 point for correctly explaining what the student should do to check his or her results **Part 3:** One point is earned for explaining that the student should repeat the trials. The following response, or an equivalent, is acceptable. • They should repeat their trials to see if they get the same results.
Evidence of Mastery of Crosscutting Concepts	1 point for correctly explaining the cause and effect that led to the results **Part 1:** One point is earned for explaining that the cause was pulling forces that were balanced or unbalanced that led to the motion or lack of motion seen. The following response, or an equivalent, is acceptable. • They were putting equal forces on both sides in trial 1, and then there was more force in trial 2 on the left side, and even more force on the left in trial 3.

Unit 4 Life Cycles and Inherited Traits
Unit 4 Pretest

Item Analysis			
Item #	**Key**	**Standards**	**DOK**
1	B	3-LS1-1, DCI.3-LS1.B.1	1
2	C	3-LS1-1, DCI.3-LS1.B.1	1
3	C	3-LS1-1, DCI.3-LS1.B.1, CCC.3-5.A.2	1
4	A	3-LS1-1, DCI.3-LS1.B.1	1
5	B	3-LS1-1, DCI.3-LS1.B.1, SEP.NOS.3-5.B.1	1

© Houghton Mifflin Harcourt Publishing Company

6	C	3-LS1-1, DCI.3-LS1.B.1	2
7	D	3-LS1-1, DCI.3-LS1.B.1	1
8	D	3-LS1-1, DCI.3-LS1.B.1	1
9	B	3-LS1-1, DCI.3-LS1.B.1	2
10	A	3-LS1-1, DCI.3-LS1.B.1	2

Unit 4 Lesson 1

Item Analysis			
Item #	Key	Standards	DOK
1	B	3-LS1-1, DCI.3-LS1.B.1, SEP.3-5.B.2	2
2	A	3-LS1-1, DCI.3-LS1.B.1	2
3	A	3-LS1-1, DCI.3-LS1.B.1	2
4	D	3-LS1-1, DCI.3-LS1.B.1	2
5	C	3-LS1-1, DCI.3-LS1.B.1, SEP.3-5.B.2	2
6	Rubric	3-LS1-1, DCI.3-LS1.B.1	3
7	Rubric	3-LS1-1, DCI.3-LS1.B.1, SEP.3-5.B.2, CCC.3-5.A.2	3

6. Use the rubric below to evaluate total points earned for this item.

NGSS Constructed Response Answer – 1 Point	
Evidence of Mastery	Sample answers: • He can watch it grow and see what kind of structures it produces to reproduce. • The structures will tell him if the plant produces seeds or spores. • Flowers and cones are structures that form seeds for reproduction. • Ferns and mosses do not form flowers. Instead, ferns and mosses have other structures that produce spores. To receive full credit for this test item, students must explain that until the young plant grows, Jared cannot tell what kinds of structures it has for reproduction. But once the plant is full grown, flowers and cones produce seeds, and ferns and mosses have structures that produce spores.

7. Use the rubric below to evaluate total points earned for this item.

NGSS Constructed Response Answer – 1 Point	
Evidence of Mastery	Sample answer: • Move the one numbered 2 to the end, after the one numbered 4. To receive full credit for this test item, students must explain how to change the order to make the drawing correct.

Unit 4 Lesson 2

Item Analysis			
Item #	Key	Standards	DOK
1	A	3-LS1-1, DCI.3-LS1.B.1, CCC.3-5.A.2	1
2	B	3-LS1-1, DCI.3-LS1.B.1	3

© Houghton Mifflin Harcourt Publishing Company

3	B	3-LS1-1, DCI.3-LS1.B.1	2
4	D	3-LS1-1, DCI.3-LS1.B.1	1
5	C	3-LS1-1, DCI.3-LS1.B.1	2
6	Rubric	3-LS1-1, DCI.3-LS1.B.1	2
7	Rubric	3-LS1-1, DCI.3-LS1.B.1	3

6. Use the rubric below to evaluate total points earned for this item.

NGSS Constructed Response Answer – 1 Point	
Evidence of Mastery	Sample answer: • An animal is born or hatches from an egg. • The new animal grows and develops into an adult. • The adult animal reproduces to make new animals. • The adult animal dies. To receive full credit for this test item, students must include the four general phases of every animal's life cycle: birth, growth, reproduction by adult animals, and death.

7. Use the rubric below to evaluate total points earned for this item.

NGSS Constructed Response Answer – 1 Point	
Evidence of Mastery	Sample answer: • She can wait for the eggs to hatch and observe the insects as they go through metamorphosis To receive full credit for this test item, students must explain that if Leah observes the metamorphosis of the insects after they hatch, she will get clues about what type of insect she found.

Unit 4 Lesson 3

Item Analysis			
Item #	**Key**	**Standards**	**DOK**
1	D	3-LS3-1, DCI.3-LS3.A.1	1
2	C	3-LS3-1, DCI.3-LS3.A.1	2
3	D	3-LS3-1, DCI.3-LS3.B.1	2
4	B	3-LS3-1, DCI.3-LS3.A.1	3
5	A	3-LS3-1, DCI.3-LS3.A.1	2

6. Use the rubric below to evaluate total points earned for this item.

NGSS Constructed Response Answer – 1 Point	
Evidence of Mastery	Sample answer: • Inherited behaviors: singing, knowing when to migrate, building nests, flying To receive full credit for this test item, students must give one example of an inherited behavior of a bird.

© Houghton Mifflin Harcourt Publishing Company

7. Use the rubric below to evaluate total points earned for this item.

NGSS Constructed Response Answer – 1 Point	
Evidence of Mastery	Sample answer: • The kittens will probably be different sizes and colors. To receive full credit for this test item, students must explain that the kittens will show diversity and must provide examples of this diversity, such as different sizes and colors.

Unit 4 Unit Test

Item Analysis		
Item #	**Standards**	**DOK**
1	3-LS1-1, DCI.3-LS1.B.1, CCC.3-5.A.2	2
2	3-LS1-1, DCI.3-LS1.B.1	1
3	3-LS1-1, DCI.3-LS3.B.1, SEP.NOS.3-5.B.1	2
4	3-LS3-1, DCI.3-LS3.A.1	1
5	3-LS3-1, DCI.3-LS3.B.1, CCC.3-5.A.1	2
6	3-LS1-1, DCI.3-LS3.B.1, SEP.3-5.B.2, CCC.3-5.A.2	2
7	3-LS3-1, DCI.3-LS3.B.1, SEP.3-5.D.2	2
8	3-LS3-1, DCI.3-LS3.B.1, SEP.3-5.D.2, CCC.3-5.A.1	3
9	3-LS3-1, DCI.3-LS3.B.1	1
10	3-LS3-1, DCI.3-LS3.A.1, CCC.3-5.A.1	2
11	3-LS3-1, DCI.3-LS3.A.1, SEP.3-5.D.2, CCC.3-5.A.1	3
12	3-LS3-1, DCI.3-LS3.A.1, SEP.3-5.D.2	2
13	3-LS1-1, DCI.3-LS1.B.1, CCC.3-5.A.2	2
14	3-LS1-1, DCI.3-LS1.B.1, SEP.3-5.B.2	2
15	3-LS1-1, DCI.3-LS1.B.1, SEP.NOS.3-5.B.1, CCC.3-5.A.2	3

1. **A.** This is incorrect because the picture shows an adult tomato plant in the reproduction stage.

   B. This is correct because the picture shows a young plant offspring just beginning to grow, displaying a resemblance to the adult plant.

   C. This is incorrect because the picture shows a seed that has not begun to grow.

   D. This is incorrect because the picture shows the beginning growth of a different type of plant that does not share the same leaf type as the tomato.

2. **A.** This is incorrect because the adult stage is the final stage of the life cycle, which would be a butterfly.

   B. This is incorrect because the egg life stage would look like a ball or oval with an undeveloped organism inside.

   C. This is correct because during the larva stage it becomes a caterpillar.

   D. This is incorrect because pupa is the transformation stage, when it would be a chrysalis before it transforms into an adult.

3. **A.** This is correct because the offspring of the two blue-seed corn plants would result in an all blue corn plant.

   B. This is incorrect because the offspring of the two blue-seed parent plants would result in blue corn, not yellow.

© Houghton Mifflin Harcourt Publishing Company

C. This is incorrect because the offspring of the two blue-seed parent plants would result in only blue corn, not yellow and blue.

D. This is incorrect because the offspring of the two blue-seed parent plants would result in only blue corn, not yellow, blue, and green corn.

4. A. This is correct because pine trees all have needle-like leaves like their parents.

B. This is incorrect because where a plant is located is not an inheritable trait.

C. This is incorrect because how much light it gets is not a trait.

D. This is incorrect because the number of branches will vary based on many external factors; the number of branches on a tree cannot be predicted.

5. A. This answer is incorrect because the picture shows all the same type of organism, evidenced by the same leaves, flower shape, height, etc.

B. This answer is incorrect because the picture shows a group of the same type of plant.

C. This answer is incorrect because the image shows clear similarities and differences between the offspring and the parent.

D. This is correct because the offspring inherits the same leaf colors but not necessarily the same petal color from the parent.

6. A. This picture is incorrect because it shows the wrong order of the stages; the seed should be first, and death last.

B. This picture is incorrect because it does not show the life stages in the correct order. Nothing comes after the death of the plant.

C. This picture is incorrect because it shows the stages in the wrong order; the seed should be first, and death last.

D. This picture is correct because the stages are in the correct order: seed, growth, adult, death.

7. A. This is incorrect because age at death is not an inherited trait.

B. This is incorrect because the data say that clown fish have three stripes, so the young will also have three stripes.

C. This is correct because the paragraph says that clown fish are orange, white, and black. The color of the fish is inherited.

D. This is correct. Average size at adulthood is an inherited trait, so a young clown fish will be smaller than the adult.

8. A. *Spots* belongs in the second blank. The offspring would likely inherit black spots from the parents in set A.

B. *Black* belongs in the first blank. The black tail is an inherited trait from the parents in set A.

C. *Horns* belongs in the third blank. The offspring would likely inherit horns from the parents in set B.

D. *Brown* belongs in the fourth blank. The offspring would likely inherit brown spots from the parents in set B.

9. Use the rubric below to evaluate total points earned for this item.   *[max point: 1]*

DCI - 1 Point	
Claims	The student is able to identify that different organisms vary in how they look because they have different inherited information.
Evidence of Mastery of Disciplinary Core Ideas	1 point for correctly matching the parent to the offspring based on shared traits **Part 1:** One point is earned for drawing a line from the adult falcon to its offspring and from the adult sparrow to its offspring. The following response, or equivalent, is acceptable.

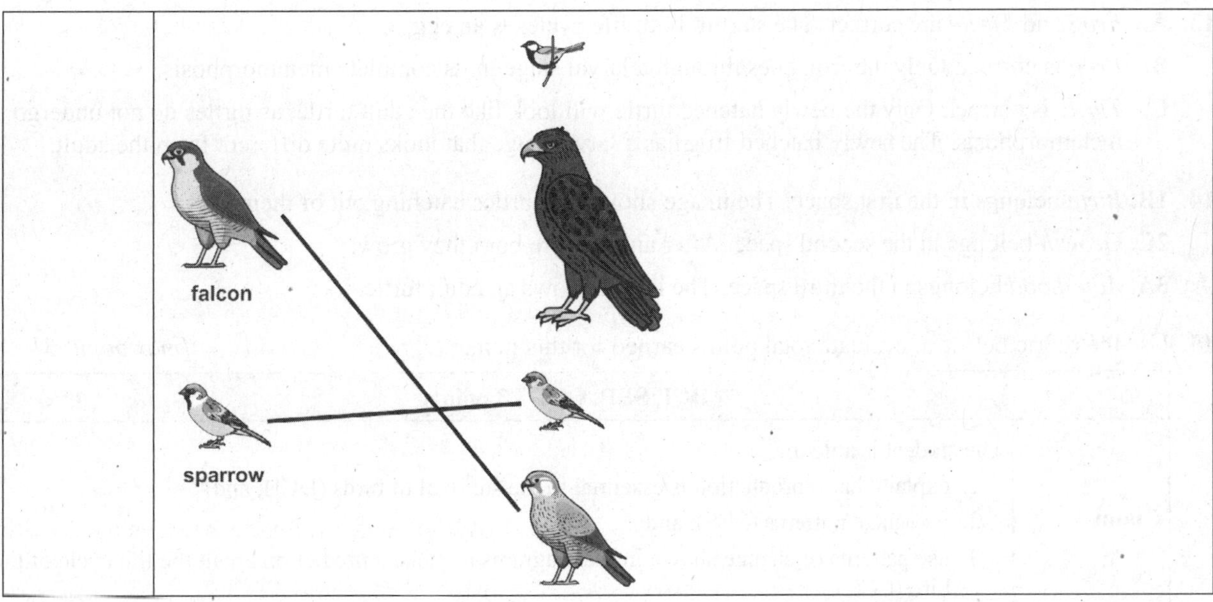

10. **A.** The picture of a palm tree offspring belongs in the second box next to the adult palm tree. The inherited traits are the long wispy palms and thin trunk.

   B. The picture of an oak tree offspring belongs in the third box next to the adult oak tree. The inherited traits are a thick trunk and thick green leaves.

   C. The picture of a cherry tree offspring belongs in the first box next to the adult cherry tree. The inherited trait is the pink blooming flowers on both trees.

11. Use the rubric below to evaluate total points earned for this item. *[max point: 3]*

DCI, SEP, CCC - 3 points	
Claims	The student is able to: 1. recognize what type of traits are inherited (DCI); and 2. analyze and interpret the data to predict the type of oak (SEP); and 3. describe similarities and differences in patterns in the parent and offspring (CCC).
Evidence of Mastery of Disciplinary Core Ideas	1 point for correctly identifying the inherited traits of the oak plants **Part 3:** One point is earned for identifying that a sibling plant would also have acorns and the same type of leaves but could vary in number of branches, leaves, height, etc. The following answer, or an equivalent, is acceptable. • It would have the same type of leaves, but it would have a different number of leaves.
Evidence of Mastery of Science and Engineering Practices	1 point for correctly explaining the type of oak **Part 1:** One point is earned for identifying the type of oak as willow oak because of its size and leaf shape. The following answer, or an equivalent, is acceptable. • willow; it has the same smooth leaves
Evidence of Mastery of Crosscutting Concepts	1 point for recognizing the patterns **Part 2:** One point is earned for explaining that the younger tree is not yet reproducing, or that its size is at the smallest of the ranges. The following answer, or an equivalent, is acceptable. • It does not have acorns yet, but it will when it is fully grown.

12. **A.** This is incorrect because both the turtle and frog inherit the trait of having a tail.

   B. This is correct because only the turtle inherits the trait of having a shell.

   C. This is incorrect because the frog young lives only in water, while the turtle can live in water and on land.

   D. This is incorrect because only the frog inherits the trait of not having legs when it hatches.

© Houghton Mifflin Harcourt Publishing Company

13. A. *Frog* and *Turtle* are correct. The start of both life cycles is an egg.

B. *Frog* is correct. Only the frog goes through a larval stage in its complete metamorphosis.

C. *Turtle* is correct. Only the newly hatched turtle will look like the adult turtle, as turtles do not undergo metamorphosis. The newly hatched frog has a larval stage that looks quite different from the adult.

14. 1B. *Birth* belongs in the first space. The image shows the turtles hatching out of their eggs.

2C. *Growth* belongs in the second space. After animals are born they grow.

3A. *Adulthood* belongs in the third space. The image shows an adult turtle.

15. Use the rubric below to evaluate total points earned for this item. *[max point: 3]*

DCI, SEP, CCC - 3 points	
Claims	The student is able to: 1. explain that reproduction is essential to the survival of birds (DCI); and 2. recognize patterns (SEP); and 3. use patterns of change shown in the diagrams to make a prediction about the life cycle of the bird (CCC).
Evidence of Mastery of Disciplinary Core Ideas	1 point for correctly explaining why birds lay eggs **Part 3:** One point is earned for explaining that laying eggs is how birds reproduce, and reproduction is necessary for birds to survive. The following response, or an equivalent, is acceptable. • They have to lay eggs to start the life cycle over and have more baby birds.
Evidence of Mastery of Science and Engineering Practices	1 point for correctly identifying which other life cycle a bird's life cycle is similar to **Part 1:** One point is earned for identifying the turtle life cycle. The following response, or an equivalent, is acceptable. • turtle
Evidence of Mastery of Crosscutting Concepts	1 point for correctly predicting what stage of the life cycle the bird will enter after the egg stage **Part 2:** One student is earned for predicting the stage after the egg as birth or growth. One of the following, or an equivalent, is acceptable. • The egg will hatch. The bird will grow.

Unit 5 Organisms and Their Environments
Unit 5 Pretest

Item Analysis			
Item #	**Key**	**Standards**	**DOK**
1	B	3-LS3-2, DCI.3-LS3.A.2, SEP.3-5.F.1	1
2	C	3-LS3-2, DCI.3-LS3.B.2, CCC.3-5.B.1	1
3	D	3-LS2-1, DCI.3-LS2.D.1	1
4	C	3-LS4-4, DCI.3-LS4.D.1	2
5	B	3-LS3-2, DCI.3-LS3.B.2	1
6	A	3-LS4-3, DCI.3-LS4.C.1	2
7	D	3-LS4-4, DCI.3-LS2.C.1	2
8	D	3-LS2-1, DCI.3-LS2.D.1	2
9	C	3-LS4-3, DCI.3-LS4.C.1	2
10	A	3-LS4-3, DCI.3-LS4.C.1	2

© Houghton Mifflin Harcourt Publishing Company

Unit 5 Lesson 1

Item Analysis			
Item #	Key	Standards	DOK
1	C	3-LS3-2, DCI.3-LS3.A.2	2
2	B	3-LS3-2, DCI.3-LS3.A.2	1
3	D	3-LS3-2, DCI.3-LS3.B.2	1
4	C	3-LS3-2, DCI.3-LS3.B.2, CCC.3-5.B.1	2
5	A	3-LS3-2, DCI.3-LS3.A.2, SEP.3-5.F.1	2
6	Rubric	3-LS3-2, DCI.3-LS3.A.2, CCC.3-5.B.1	3
7	Rubric	3-LS3-2, DCI.3-LS3.B.2	3

6. Use the rubric below to evaluate total points earned for this item.

	NGSS Constructed Response Answer – 1 Point
Evidence of Mastery	Sample answer: • In the winter the environment is cold and white, and the fox has white fur. In the summer the Arctic fox has brown fur when it is warm. To receive full credit for this test item, the student must address how the environment affects the color of the fox in the winter and summer.

7. Use the rubric below to evaluate total points earned for this item.

	NGSS Constructed Response Answer – 1 Point
Evidence of Mastery	Sample answer: • The color of the cardinal is inherited because cardinals all have the same colors as their moms and dads. • The food the cardinal eats makes it bright or dull red. To get full credit for this test item, the student must explain that the color of an animal is inherited from its parents but that the environment can affect the brightness of the cardinal and that the bird would not be as bright red if it did not have food with the chemical in it to eat.

Unit 5 Lesson 2

Item Analysis			
Item #	Key	Standards	DOK
1	B	3-LS4-3, DCI.3-LS4.C.1	2
2	D	3-LS4-3, DCI.3-LS4.C.1	2
3	C	3-LS4-3, DCI.3-LS4.C.1	2
4	A	3-LS4-3, DCI.3-LS4.C.1, CCC.3-5.B.1	2
5	B	3-LS4-3, DCI.3-LS4.C.1, CCC.3-5.B.1	2
6	Rubric	3-LS4-3, DCI.3-LS4.C.1, CCC.3-5.B.1	3
7	Rubric	3-LS4-3, DCI.3-LS4.C.1	3

© Houghton Mifflin Harcourt Publishing Company

6. Use the rubric below to evaluate total points earned for this item.

NGSS Constructed Response Answer – 1 Point	
Evidence of Mastery	Sample answer: • The wolf will think the possum is dead and is not good to eat. The turtle's shell is hard and the wolf cannot get in it. To receive full credit for this test item, students must describe how the possum and the turtle protect themselves from the wolf.

7. Use the rubric below to evaluate total points earned for this item.

NGSS Constructed Response Answer – 1 Point	
Evidence of Mastery	Sample answers (any two of the following): • thin fur (desert) and thick fur (arctic) • large ears (desert) and small ears (arctic) • long legs (desert) and short legs (arctic) • small in size (desert) and large in size (arctic) To receive full credit for this test item, students must answer with any two of the choices above.

Unit 5 Lesson 3

Item Analysis			
Item #	**Key**	**Standards**	**DOK**
1	D	4-LS1-2, DCI.4.LS1.D.1, SEP.3-5.B.1, CCC.3-5.D.1	2
2	A	4-LS1-2, DCI.4.LS1.D.1	2
3	B	4-LS1-2, DCI.4.LS1.D.1	2
4	C	4-LS1-2, DCI.4.LS1.D.1	2
5	B	4-LS1-2, DCI.4.LS1.D.1, CCC.3-5.D.1	3
6	Rubric	4-LS1-2, DCI.4.LS1.D.1	2
7	Rubric	4-LS1-2, DCI.4.LS1.D.1, CCC.3-5.D.1	2

6. Use the rubric below to evaluate total points earned for this item.

NGSS Constructed Response Answer – 1 Point	
Evidence of Mastery	Sample Answers: • Animals use their hearing so they can hear if predators are coming. • Animals use their taste to help defend themselves; if something tastes bad they don't eat it and then they won't get sick. • Animals use their sense of touch to know when something is hurting them; they can move when something touches them. • They use their sight to see if a predator is coming at them, or to help them know where to claw or bite. • They use their sense of smell; animals can smell other animals coming and hide. To receive full credit for this test item, students must include two senses and how animals use their senses to protect themselves.

© Houghton Mifflin Harcourt Publishing Company

7. Use the rubric below to evaluate total points earned for this item.

NGSS Constructed Response Answer – 1 Point	
Evidence of Mastery	Sample answer: • Tamra's eyes will see the image of the ball and send signals to the brain. The brain will interpret those images. As the ball gets closer, her eyes will continue to relay messages to the brain. The brain will send messages to the leg and arm muscles to block the ball. These messages travel along the nerves to the muscles. The muscles contract and Tamra blocks the ball. To receive full credit for this test item, students must include: • The eyes sense light and send messages to the brain. • The brain processes those messages. • The brain commands the muscles to move. • Those commands travel along nerves to muscles.

Unit 5 Lesson 4

Item Analysis			
Item #	Key	Standards	DOK
1	D	3-LS4-4, DCI.3-LS2.C.1	2
2	A	3-LS4-4, DCI.3-LS2.C.1	3
3	B	3-LS4-4, DCI.3-LS2.C.1	2
4	C	3-LS4-4, DCI.3-LS4.D.1	2
5	A	3-LS4-4, DCI.3-LS4.D.1, CCC.3-5.D.1	2
6	Rubric	3-LS4-4, DCI.3-LS2.C.1	2
7	Rubric	3-LS4-4, DCI.3-LS2.C.1	2

6. Use the rubric below to evaluate total points earned for this item.

NGSS Constructed Response Answer – 1 Point	
Evidence of Mastery	Sample answer: • A flood might injure or kill animals in an ecosystem, decrease their food supply, destroy their homes, or force them to move to other ecosystems. To receive full credit for this item, students must identify at least two ways that a flood may affect an animal.

7. Use the rubric below to evaluate total points earned for this item.

NGSS Constructed Response Answer – 1 Point	
Evidence of Mastery	Sample answers: • If water freezes it may be hard for plants to get water. • Snow might cover plants that animals need for food. • The cold weather may cause plants to die and trees to fall. To receive full credit for this item, students must include at least two ways that a blizzard might affect plants and animals in a forest ecosystem.

© Houghton Mifflin Harcourt Publishing Company

Unit 5 Unit Test

Item Analysis		
Item #	**Standards**	**DOK**
1	3-LS4-3, DCI.3-LS4.C.1, CCC.3-5.B.1	2
2	3-LS4-4, DCI.3-LS2.C.1	2
3	3-LS2-1, DCI.3-LS2.D.1, SEP.3-5.G.1	1
4	3-LS4-2, DCI.3-LS4.B.1, CCC.3-5.B.1	2
5	3-LS4-4, DCI.3-LS4.D.1, CCC.3-5.D.1	1
6	3-LS3-2, DCI.3-LS3.B.2, SEP.3-5.F.1	2
7	3-LS4-2, DCI.3-LS4.B.1	1
8	3-LS4-4, DCI.3-LS4.D.1, CCC.3-5.C.1	2
9	3-LS4-3, DCI.3-LS4.C.1, SEP.3-5.D.2	2
10	3-LS2-1, DCI.3-LS2.D.1, SEP.3-5.G.1, CCC.3-5.B.1	2
11	3-LS3-2, DCI.3-LS3.A.2, SEP.3-5.F.1, CCC.3-5.B.1	3
12	3-LS3-2, DCI.3-LS3.B.2, SEP.3-5.H.1	2
13	3-LS3-2, DCI.3-LS3.A.2, SEP.3-5.B.2	2
14	3-LS4-3, DCI.3-LS4.C.1	1
15	3-LS4-4, DCI.3-LS4.D.1, SEP.3-5.G.2, CCC.3-5.D.1	3

1. **A.** This is incorrect because while air is a nonliving factor in the environment, there is air in all parts of the environment shown.

   B. This is incorrect because birds are a living factor in the environment, and they are not the determining factor to where the plants grow.

   C. This is correct because plants need sunlight to grow. The picture shows that in the shady area near the fence there are fewer plants growing, only grass.

   D. This is incorrect because there is soil in all areas of the yard shown, evidenced by the presence of grass and plant growth. Soil is a nonliving factor, but not the one in this image that determines where the flowers are growing.

2. **A.** This is correct because the extreme temperatures from the lava kill the plants. Plants cannot withstand the extreme heat and being covered with lava.

   B. This is incorrect because plants are not able to move to different habitats. This, however, is what might happen to some of the animals in the area.

   C. This is incorrect because volcanoes do not release oxygen; the heat will burn the plants, and the lava will cover them.

   D. This is incorrect because when lava flows, it forms rock, and plants can't grow in the rock until many years later when the rock has been broken down into soil.

3. **A.** This answer is incorrect because the group hunt is not a social activity done for fun with friends. It is necessary for the species to survive.

   B. This answer is correct because animals often hunt together so that they can take a portion to eat.

   C. This answer is incorrect because only humans work together to grow food.

   D. This answer is incorrect because hyenas hunt together to outsmart their prey. The hyenas gather around their prey so no matter what direction it runs, they can catch it.

© Houghton Mifflin Harcourt Publishing Company

4. **A.** This is incorrect because the stem says that more of the insects are green, so the green color is the advantage.

    B. This is incorrect because katydids are plant-eating insects; they do not have prey.

    C. This is correct because the stem says that more of the green katydid exist, so they have some sort of survival advantage. Since they are plant-eating insects, being green means they blend in with their environment.

    D. This is incorrect because there are fewer pink katydids, so they do not have a survival or reproduction advantage.

5. **A.** This is incorrect because if the krill population began to die off, then the seaweed would probably grow larger because fewer organisms would be around to eat it.

    B. This is incorrect because if the krill population died off, the fish population would not have as large of a food source; therefore, it would begin to decrease as well.

    C. This is incorrect because if the krill population died off, the fish population would not have as much food and the whale population would have less food; therefore, these populations would begin to decrease.

    D. This is correct. If the krill population decreased, the fish would decrease. In turn, this would decrease the whale population.

6. **A.** This is incorrect because water may have an effect on plant color but would not likely affect animal coloration.

    B. This is incorrect because the birds look like they are of similar weight.

    C. This is correct because diet often has an effect on color.

    D. This is incorrect because birds of the same species are likely to live in the same type of climate; also, temperature would be more likely to affect the type or weight of the feathers or the amount of fat the birds store.

7. **A.** This is an *Advantage for Surviving*. Hiding helps protect an animal from predators, but it would not help the animal find a mate.

    B. This is an *Advantage for Attracting a Mate*. Pretty feathers will help an animal stand out in a crowd, which can bring attention to it; they may not help the animal survive, but the feathers would help it attract a mate.

    C. This is an *Advantage for Attracting a Mate*. Singing is a typical behavior animals use to attract mates.

    D. This is an *Advantage for Surviving*. Running can help an animal catch prey or outrun predators.

8. The picture of the desolate pond habitat in the bottom left is the correct answer. The animals either died off or moved due to the lack of rainfall in the area. The grass and trees are browned, some plants died, and the water level is lowest.

9. **A.** *Warmer* belongs in the third box. Black bears can tolerate warm temperatures because their fur is not very thick.

    B. *Cool off* does not belong in any box.

    C. *Climb trees* is not used. The polar bear lives in an area without trees, so it does not use its claws to help it climb trees. Shedding an undercoat does not help the black bear climb trees.

    D. *Grip the ice* belongs in the second box. Having back claws helps the polar bear grip the ice and not slide around as much.

    E. *Cold, harsh* belongs in the first box. Polar bears live in a cold, harsh environment.

10. **A.** *More infants reach adulthood* matches *sperm whales travel in pods*. Traveling together allows the larger adults to protect and hide the young so that more survive.

    B. *A lion sneaks through the grass stalking its prey* matches *antelope travel in groups with more eyes looking out for predators*. Some animals travel in groups so that they can better watch what is around them and warn each other if there is a predator nearby.

© Houghton Mifflin Harcourt Publishing Company

11. Use the rubric below to evaluate total points earned for this item. *[max point: 3]*

DCI, SEP, CCC - 3 points	
Claims	The student is able to: 1. describe how the characteristic of color is a result of interaction with the environment (DCI); and 2. use evidence to construct an explanation of how changing colors helps protect the animal from predators (SEP); and 3. identify the effect of not being able to change colors (CCC).
Evidence of Mastery of Disciplinary Core Ideas	1 point for correctly identifying how the environment affects the animal's traits **Part 1:** One point is earned for identifying that the octopus changes colors based on the colors around it. Any of the following responses, or an equivalent, is acceptable. • The octopus camouflages itself with its surroundings. • The octopus changes colors to look like the environment around it.
Evidence of Mastery of Science and Engineering Practices	1 point for correctly describing how the octopus changing colors helps protect the animal **Part 2:** One point is earned for describing that the octopus changes colors to camouflage itself so that predators do not easily see it. One of the following responses, or an equivalent, is acceptable. • The predators will not see the octopus if it is camouflaged with its surroundings. • The predators will not notice the octopus if it blends into its environment.
Evidence of Mastery of Crosscutting Concepts	1 point for correctly explaining what would happen to the octopus if it did not change colors **Part 3:** One point is earned for explaining that the octopus would be seen if it did not blend into its surroundings. The following response, or an equivalent, is acceptable. • The octopus would likely be seen and/or eaten by the predator if it did not blend into its surroundings.

12. **A.** This is incorrect because roots will continue to grow when there is plenty of rain available.

    B. This is incorrect because plants will continue to grow and develop more leaves.

    C. This is correct because there will be plenty of nutrients and water, which will allow the leaves to generally grow larger.

    D. This is correct because with more rainfall available at the surface there will be more roots growing near the surface.

    E. This is incorrect because needles would never form on a leaf-bearing tree.

13. The leaves will start to fall off when the plant does not have water, and the roots will start to spread out farther searching for more water.

14. **A.** This is incorrect because in a hot, dry environment, plants with short roots and large leaves will die quickly.

    B. This is incorrect because the roots are too short to reach deep groundwater.

    C. This is incorrect because large leaves are not a good adaptation for the desert; they will lose too much water through their leaves.

    D. This is correct because in a dry environment a plant will likely have either long fibrous roots near the surface or a very long taproot. The types of leaves best suited for a desert environment are small leaves that do not have much surface area.

15. Use the rubric below to evaluate total points earned for this item. *[max point: 3]*

DCI, SEP, CCC - 3 points	
Claims	The student is able to: • explain how the change in the environment affects the organisms living there (DCI); and • identify a solution to a problem by citing relevant evidence about how it meets the criteria of the problem (SEP); and • explain the farm ecosystem interactions by explaining how the affected grass would affect the cows (CCC).
Evidence of Mastery of Disciplinary Core Ideas	1 point for correctly explaining how the lack of rain affects the grass **Part 1:** One point is earned for explaining that the grass would probably die. The following response, or an equivalent, is acceptable. • Without rain the grass will probably die.
Evidence of Mastery of Science and Engineering Practices	1 point for correctly describing a solution that will help solve Jan's problem **Part 3:** One point is earned for describing a solution that will provide water to the roots of the grass. The following response, or an equivalent, is acceptable. • She could use sprinkler system that will provide water for the grass so it lives and the cows have food again.
Evidence of Mastery of Crosscutting Concepts	1 point for correctly explaining how the effect on the grass would affect the cows **Part 2:** One point is earned for identifying that the cow depends on the grass, so without the grass the cows might die or need a different food source. The following response, or an equivalent, is acceptable. • The cows would lose a source of food and water from the grass. They will need different food.

Unit 6 Fossils
Unit 6 Pretest

Item Analysis			
Item #	**Key**	**Standards**	**DOK**
1	D	3-LS4-1, DCI.3-LS4.A.1	1
2	C	3-LS4-1, DCI.3-LS4.A.1	1
3	A	3-LS4-1, DCI.3-LS4.A.2	2
4	D	3-LS4-1, DCI.3-LS4.A.2, SEP.3-5.D.2, CCC.NOS.3-5.A.1	1
5	B	3-LS4-1, DCI.3-LS4.A.2, SEP.3-5.D.2	1
6	C	3-LS4-1, DCI.3-LS4.A.2, SEP.3-5.D.2	2
7	B	3-LS4-1, DCI.3-LS4.A.2, CCC.NOS.3-5.A.1	2
8	A	3-LS4-1, DCI.3-LS4.A.1, SEP.3-5.D.2	2
9	C	3-LS4-1, DCI.3-LS4.A.2	1
10	A	3-LS4-1, DCI.3-LS4.A.2	2

© Houghton Mifflin Harcourt Publishing Company

Unit 6 Lesson 1

		Item Analysis	
Item #	Key	Standards	DOK
1	B	3-LS4-1, DCI.3-LS4.A.1	1
2	C	3-LS4-1, DCI.3-LS4.A.2	2
3	A	3-LS4-1, DCI.3-LS4.A.2	2
4	D	3-LS4-1, DCI.3-LS4.A.2	2
5	D	3-LS4-1, DCI.3-LS4.A.2, SEP.3-5.D.2	2
6	Rubric	3-LS4-1, DCI.3-LS4.A.2, SEP.3-5.D.2	2
7	Rubric	3-LS4-1, DCI.3-LS4.A.2	2

6. Use the rubric below to evaluate total points earned for this item.

	NGSS Constructed Response Answer – 1 Point
Evidence of Mastery	Sample answer: • Pictures 1 and 3 are fossils. You can tell because they are part of rocks. The live ones have fur and eyes and leaves and flowers. To receive full credit for this item, the student must indicate which pictures are fossils and provide an explanation to support the answer.

7. Use the rubric below to evaluate total points earned for this item.

	NGSS Constructed Response Answer – 1 Point
Evidence of Mastery	Sample answer: • Soft parts are very easily eaten by predators or decomposed by bacteria. Over time, it is the hard parts that are left behind. To receive full credit for this test item, students must demonstrate understanding that organisms' soft tissues are not as easily preserved as the hard parts are.

Unit 6 Lesson 2

		Item Analysis	
Item #	Key	Standards	DOK
1	B	3-LS4-1, DCI.3-LS4.A.2	2
2	C	3-LS4-1, DCI.3-LS4.A.2	2
3	D	3-LS4-1, DCI.3-LS4.A.2, SEP.3-5.D.2, CCC.NOS.3-5.A.1	2
4	A	3-LS4-1, DCI.3-LS4.A.2	3
5	D	3-LS4-1, DCI.3-LS4.A.1, SEP.3-5.D.2	1
6	Rubric	3-LS4-1, DCI.3-LS4.A.2	3
7	Rubric	3-LS4-1, DCI.3-LS4.A.2, SEP.3-5.D.2, CCC.NOS.3-5.A.1	3

© Houghton Mifflin Harcourt Publishing Company

6. Use the rubric below to evaluate total points earned for this item.

NGSS Constructed Response Answer – 1 Point	
Evidence of Mastery	Sample answer: • The area was once wet enough for plants to grow. To receive full credit for this test item, students must indicate that there used to be more rain in that area.

7. Use the rubric below to evaluate total points earned for this item.

NGSS Constructed Response Answer – 1 Point	
Evidence of Mastery	Sample answer: • Layer C shows water animals and layer D shows feathers, so the water probably dried up and became land. To receive full credit for this item, students must indicate that when the animals in layer C were alive, the area was underwater, and when the animals in layer D were alive, the area was most likely land.

Unit 6 Unit Test

Item Analysis		
Item #	**Standards**	**DOK**
1	3-LS4-1, DCI.3-LS4.A.1, SEP.3-5.D.2, CCC.3-5.C.1	3
2	3-LS4-1, DCI.3-LS4.A.1	2
3	3-LS4-1, DCI.3-LS4.A.1, SEP.3-5.D.2	2
4	3-LS4-1, DCI.3-LS4.A.2, CCC.NOS.3-5.A.1	2
5	3-LS4-1, DCI.3-LS4.A.2	1
6	3-LS4-1, DCI.3-LS4.A.1	2
7	3-LS4-1, DCI.3-LS4.A.2, CCC.3-5.C.1	2
8	3-LS4-1, DCI.3-LS4.A.2, SEP.3-5.D.2, CCC.3-5.C.1	2
9	3-LS4-1, DCI.3-LS4.A.1, CCC.NOS.3-5.A.1	2
10	3-LS4-1, DCI.3-LS4.A.1, SEP.3-5.D.2	1
11	3-LS4-1, DCI.3-LS4.A.2, SEP.3-5.D.2, CCC.NOS.3-5.A.1	3
12	3-LS4-1, DCI.3-LS4.A.2, CCC.3-5.C.1	1
13	3-LS4-1, DCI.3-LS4.A.1, CCC.3-5.C.1	2
14	3-LS4-1, DCI.3-LS4.A.2, SEP.3-5.D.2	2
15	3-LS4-1, DCI.3-LS4.A.1, SEP.3-5.D.2, CCC.NOS.3-5.A.1	3

1. **A.** This is incorrect because the type of teeth indicates that both animals were meat-eaters.

B. This is correct. The scientist can infer based on tooth size that the megalodon was much bigger than the great white shark.

C. This is incorrect because the type of teeth indicates that both animals were meat-eaters.

D. This is incorrect because the scientist would infer based on the teeth that the megalodon was bigger than the great white shark.

2. **A.** This is incorrect because some organisms in very cold places get trapped in cold water that freezes. The organism does not decay because it is frozen, and this is a fossil.

© Houghton Mifflin Harcourt Publishing Company

B. This is incorrect because an organism can get trapped in sticky tree sap that hardens. The organism becomes a fossil and the sap becomes amber.

C. This is correct because organisms that get covered in hot lava burn up and their remains are not preserved.

D. This is incorrect because this is how many fossils are formed; an organism gets buried in sediments that get compacted.

3. **A.** This is incorrect because the fish is about 3 times as long as the quarter, rather than one-third the size of the quarter.

   B. This is incorrect because the quarter and the fish are not the same size.

   C. This is correct because the fish is approximately 3 times the width of the quarter, or 72 millimeters.

   D. This is incorrect because 96 millimeters is 4 times the width of the quarter, and the fish is not that long.

4. **A.** This is incorrect because fish do not have feet or shells.

   B. This is incorrect because while a snail has a shell, it does not have that type of shell; nor does it have feet or a pointed mouth.

   C. This is incorrect because a salamander does not have a shell. The feet of the salamander might look similar to the turtle's, but the salamander skull would not have such a pointed beak.

   D. This is correct because the fossils are those of an *Archelon*, which is consistent with a modern-day turtle.

5. **A.** This is incorrect because the fossil imprint does not give us an exact age of the frog.

   B. This is correct because the fossil shows that the fossil is a frog.

   C. This is incorrect because we would have to know the species of the frog to make judgments about the color. If the species no longer exists, color is only speculation.

   D. This is incorrect because different types of frogs make different sounds; if the species is extinct, the sound it made would only be speculation.

6. **A.** This statement is true because the fossil shows a tail.

   B. This statement is false because this animal is now extinct.

   C. This statement is true because the animal that created this fossil is now extinct.

   D. This statement is true because the animal and many others like it roamed the Earth millions of years ago.

7. The student selects the fish, the picture second from the right. Fish are shown in all of the layers that contain fossils, whereas the other organisms are shown only in some.

8. **A.** *The animal had a tail* matches the bottom fossil. The fossil shows bones that make up a tail.

   B. *The animal ate plants* matches the picture of the jaw fossil with dull teeth (third from top). The dull teeth indicate that the animal was an herbivore.

   C. *The animal ate only meat* matches the picture of the jaw fossil with sharp teeth (second from top). The sharp teeth indicate that the animal was a carnivore.

   D. *The animal may have lived in water* matches the first fossil at the top. The fossil is of a shell of an animal that may have lived in the water.

9. **A.** *A starfish* matches the picture of the star-shaped fossil impression.

   B. *A slug or snail* matches the top picture. This fossil impression was made by an animal that does not have legs.

   C. *A four-legged land animal* matches with the middle picture. The fossil impression shows distinct footprints like a land animal would make.

10. Circling the petrified wood is correct because it is the only fossil. The leaf, acorn, and rock are not fossils.

© Houghton Mifflin Harcourt Publishing Company

11. Use the rubric below to evaluate total points earned for this item.   *[max point: 3]*

DCI, SEP, CCC - 3 points	
Claims	The student is able to: 1. identify in which environment the animals lived by analyzing the fossils (DCI); and 2. analyze the fossils and the text and use logical reasoning to explain how the environment has changed (SEP); and 3. explain that consistent patterns in rock formation indicate that fossils found together in the same layer were likely formed at a similar time in history (CCC).
Evidence of Mastery of Disciplinary Core Ideas	1 point for correctly identifying the environment in which the animals lived **Part 1:** One point is earned for identifying that the environment in which the animals most likely lived was the sea/water/ocean. The following response, or an equivalent, is acceptable. • The animals were most likely found in the sea.
Evidence of Mastery of Science and Engineering Practices	1 point for correctly describing how the environment has changed **Part 3:** One point is earned for describing that the environment in which the animals most likely lived was the sea and is now dry land. The following response, or an equivalent, is acceptable. • The sea has dried up, and now it is dry land because it is a forest.
Evidence of Mastery of Crosscutting Concepts	1 point for correctly explaining why the fossils were found together **Part 2:** One point is earned for explaining that the fossils were found together because they most likely lived during the same time period in the same location. The following response, or an equivalent, is acceptable. • The fossils were found together because the animals lived during the same period.

12. **A.** This is incorrect because the fossil was found in only one of the rock layers.

   B. This is correct because this fossil was found in multiple layers; this indicates that it was found on Earth over a longer time period than any of the fossils found in only one of the layers.

   C. This is incorrect because the fossil was found in only one of the rock layers.

   D. This is incorrect because the fossil was found in only one of the rock layers.

13. **A.** This is correct because compared with the other fossils it is very large and looks like an animal that moved on land.

   B. This is incorrect because it would take millions of years for fossils this deep in the ground to form.

   C. This is correct because it was fossilized millions of years ago when the rock layer formed.

   D. This is incorrect because the fossil had structures that indicate movement on land.

   E. This is incorrect because the large dinosaurs disappeared after a major extinction event.

14. The diagram in the passage shows a monkey, dinosaur, fish, and snail shell. These are all animals, so the animal value should be 4. There are two fossils of a fern and one fossil of a water plant. The value for the plant bar should be 3.

15. Use the rubric below to evaluate total points earned for this item.   *[max point: 3]*

DCI, SEP, CCC - 3 points	
Claims	The student is able to: • explain that some kinds of plants and animals that once lived on Earth are no longer found anywhere (DCI); and • analyze data in a diagram to make sense of phenomena (SEP); and • explain that science assumes the consistent pattern of deepest rock layers having been formed first (longest ago) (CCC).

© Houghton Mifflin Harcourt Publishing Company

	1 point for correctly explaining why the animals found in layers C and D are no longer found on Earth
Evidence of Mastery of Disciplinary Core Ideas	**Part 3:** One point is earned for explaining that those layers formed so long ago that those animals are probably extinct. One of the following responses, or an equivalent, is acceptable. • Most of these animals can no longer be found because something happened during the time layer B was formed. It made them disappear. • These layers formed so long ago that most of the plants and animals from that time have gone extinct.
	1 point for correctly describing the environment in layer D millions of years ago
Evidence of Mastery of Science and Engineering Practices	**Part 1:** One point is earned for describing that layer D was most likely a water environment. The following response, or an equivalent, is acceptable. • The fossil was a fish so it is probably a water environment.
	1 point for correctly explaining why layer D has the oldest fossils
Evidence of Mastery of Crosscutting Concepts	**Part 2:** One point is earned for recognizing that rocks become older as she digs deeper; therefore, the oldest fossils are found in the lower layers of rock. The following response, or an equivalent, is acceptable. • The lowest layers of rock are the first to form. So they have the oldest fossils.

Unit 7 Weather and Patterns
Unit 7 Pretest

		Item Analysis	
Item #	**Key**	**Standards**	**DOK**
1	D	3-ESS3-1, DCI.3-ESS3.B.1	1
2	B	3-ESS2-2, DCI.3-ESS2.D.2	1
3	C	3-ESS2-2, DCI.3-ESS2.D.2	1
4	A	3-ESS3-1, DCI.3-ESS3.B.1	1
5	B	3-ESS2-1, DCI.3-ESS2.D.1	1
6	C	3-ESS2-2, DCI.3-ESS2.D.2	1
7	A	3-ESS3-1, DCI.3-ESS3.B.1	1
8	B	3-ESS3-1, DCI.3-ESS3.B.1	2
9	A	3-ESS2-1, DCI.3-ESS2.D.1, SEP.3-5.D.1	1
10	D	3-ESS2-1, DCI.3-ESS2.D.1	1

Unit 7 Lesson 1

		Item Analysis	
Item #	**Key**	**Standards**	**DOK**
1	D	3-ESS2-1, DCI.3-ESS2.D.1	1
2	C	3-ESS2-1, DCI.3-ESS2.D.1	1
3	A	3-ESS2-1, DCI.3-ESS2.D.1	2
4	B	3-ESS2-1, DCI.3-ESS2.D.1	2
5	C	3-ESS2-1, DCI.3-ESS2.D.1	1

© Houghton Mifflin Harcourt Publishing Company

| 6 | Rubric | 3-ESS2-1, DCI.3-ESS2.D.1 | 2 |
| 7 | Rubric | 3-ESS2-1, DCI.3-ESS2.D.1 | 2 |

6. Use the rubric below to evaluate total points earned for this item.

NGSS Constructed Response Answer – 1 Point	
Evidence of Mastery	Sample answer: • about one-half centimeter To receive full credit for this test item, students must include both the correct amount of rain and the unit of measurement.

7. Use the rubric below to evaluate total points earned for this item.

NGSS Constructed Response Answer – 1 Point	
Evidence of Mastery	Sample answer: • It shows winter because it's snowy everywhere. To receive full credit for this item, students must indicate it is winter and that cold weather or snow is more likely in the winter.

Unit 7 Lesson 2

Item Analysis			
Item #	**Key**	**Standards**	**DOK**
1	D	3-ESS2-1, DCI.3-ESS2.D.1, SEP.3-5.D.1	3
2	B	3-ESS2-1, DCI.3-ESS2.D.1, SEP.3-5.D.1	2
3	A	3-ESS2-1, DCI.3-ESS2.D.1, SEP.3-5.D.1	2
4	D	3-ESS2-1, DCI.3-ESS2.D.1, SEP.3-5.D.1, CCC.3-5.A.2	3
5	C	3-ESS2-1, DCI.3-ESS2.D.1, SEP.3-5.D.1	3
6	Rubric	3-ESS2-1, DCI.3-ESS2.D.1, CCC.3-5.A.2	3
7	Rubric	3-ESS2-1, DCI.3-ESS2.D.1, SEP.3-5.D.1, CCC.3-5.A.2	3

6. Use the rubric below to evaluate total points earned for this item.

NGSS Constructed Response Answer – 1 Point	
Evidence of Mastery	Sample answers: • rainy weather • windy weather To receive full credit for this test item, students must include one type of weather that would occur with thunder and dark skies.

7. Use the rubric below to evaluate total points earned for this item.

NGSS Constructed Response Answer – 1 Point	
Evidence of Mastery	Sample answer: • Winter, because they get the most rain in January and February which are winter months. To receive full credit for this test item, students must indicate winter is the rainiest season and support their answers with data from the table.

© Houghton Mifflin Harcourt Publishing Company

Unit 7 Lesson 3

		Item Analysis	
Item #	**Key**	**Standards**	**DOK**
1	B	3-ESS3-1, DCI.3-ESS3.B.1	1
2	B	3-ESS3-1, DCI.3-ESS3.B.1	1
3	A	3-ESS3-1, DCI.3-ESS3.B.1	1
4	D	3-ESS3-1, DCI.3-ESS3.B.1	2
5	B	3-ESS3-1, DCI.3-ESS3.B.1	2
6	Rubric	3-ESS3-1, DCI.3-ESS3.B.1, CCC.NOS.3-5.B.1	3
7	Rubric	3-ESS3-1, DCI.3-ESS3.B.1, SEP.3-5.G.2, CCC.NOS.3-5.B.1	3

6. Use the rubric below to evaluate total points earned for this item.

	NGSS Constructed Response Answer – 1 Point
Evidence of Mastery	Sample answers: • To be safe in a flood, a family could listen to radio and TV reports when the weather gets bad. • They could have a bag with spare clothes, blankets, and a first aid kit ready in case of a flood. • They could also have a radio and flashlight with spare batteries. • They could pack fresh water and food to take with them if they have to leave the house before a flood. To receive full credit for this test item, students must describe four reasonable things that a family can do to prepare for or do during a flood.

7. Use the rubric below to evaluate total points earned for this item.

	NGSS Constructed Response Answer – 1 Point
Evidence of Mastery	Sample answer: • Meteorologists use radar, satellites, and radios to collect data; computers to analyze the data and make predictions; and the Internet to warn people about approaching storms. • When people know a dangerous storm is coming, they can save their lives by leaving the area. To receive full credit for this test item, students must name at least one way meteorologists use technological aids and explain how early warning saves lives.

Unit 7 Lesson 4

		Item Analysis	
Item #	**Key**	**Standards**	**DOK**
1	C	3-ESS2-2, DCI.3-ESS2.D.2, SEP.3-5.D.1	2
2	C	3-ESS2-2, DCI.3-ESS2.D.2	1
3	D	3-ESS2-2, DCI.3-ESS2.D.1	3
4	C	3-ESS2-2, DCI.3-ESS2.D.2, SEP.3-5.D.1	3
5	C	3-ESS2-1, DCI.3-ESS2.D.1, SEP.3-5.D.1	2
6	Rubric	3-ESS2-2, DCI.3-ESS2.D.2, SEP.3-5.H.1	3
7	Rubric	3-ESS2-1, DCI.3-ESS2.D.1	2

© Houghton Mifflin Harcourt Publishing Company

6. Use the rubric below to evaluate total points earned for this item.

NGSS Constructed Response Answer – 1 Point	
Evidence of Mastery	Sample answer: • Polar is very cold and snowy. • Temperate is mild. To receive full credit for this test item, students must provide a description of both climate zones.

7. Use the rubric below to evaluate total points earned for this item.

NGSS Constructed Response Answer – 1 Point	
Evidence of Mastery	Sample answer: • They could live in different areas of the country. To receive full credit for this test item, students must indicate that Dena and Abram live in different climates.

Unit 7 Unit Test

Item Analysis		
Item #	**Standards**	**DOK**
1	3-ESS2-1, DCI.3-ESS2.D.1	1
2	3-ESS3-1, DCI.3-ESS3.B.1, CCC.NOS.3-5.B.1	1
3	3-ESS2-1, DCI.3-ESS2.D.1, SEP.3-5.H.1	2
4	3-ESS2-1, DCI.3-ESS2.D.1, SEP.3-5.D.1, CCC.3-5.A.2	3
5	3-ESS2-2, DCI.3-ESS2.D.2, CCC.3-5.A.2	2
6	3-ESS2-1, DCI.3-ESS3.B.1, SEP.3-5.G.2, CCC.STSE.3-5.B.1	2
7	3-ESS2-2, DCI.3-ESS2.D.2, SEP.3-5.H.1, CCC.3-5.A.2	2
8	3-ESS3-1, DCI.3-ESS3.B.1, CCC.3-5.B.1	2
9	3-ESS2-1, DCI.3-ESS2.D.1, SEP.3-5.D.1	2
10	3-ESS2-2, DCI.3-ESS2.D.2, CCC.3-5.B.1	2
11	3-ESS2-2, DCI.3-ESS2.D.2, SEP.3-5.H.1	2
12	3-ESS2-2, DCI.3-ESS2.D.2	2
13	3-ESS2-1, DCI.3-ESS2.D.1, CCC.3-5.A.2	1
14	3 ESS3-1, DCI.3-ESS3.B.1, CCC.STSE.3-5.B.1	2
15	3-ESS3-1, DCI.3-ESS3.B.1, SEP.3-5.G.2, CCC.NOS.3-5.B.1	3

1. **A.** This is incorrect because August has one of the lowest amounts of rainfall out of all the months.
   B. This is incorrect because although July's rainfall amount is in the top three highest amounts, it is not the highest.
   C. This is correct because according to the graph, March has the highest amount of rainfall.
   D. This is incorrect because September has one of the lowest amounts of rainfall out of all the months.

2. **A.** This is correct, because depending on the severity of the hurricane, instant evacuation can be mandated.
   B. This is incorrect, because people stay inside for thunderstorms, which do not require people to have to leave home.

C. This is incorrect because people do not have to evacuate because of a sunny day. People tend to go outside and enjoy sunny weather.

D. This is incorrect because a winter storm keeps people inside of the house instead of having them evacuate.

3. **A.** This is incorrect because the data in the table indicate that it will be cloudy and snowy, rather than clear.

   B. This is incorrect because the data in the table indicate that it will cloudy and snowy, rather than foggy.

   C. This is correct because the data in the table indicate that the temperature will be below freezing and snowing.

   D. This is incorrect because the data in the table indicate that it will snow, and the temperature will be below freezing, which is cold.

4. **A.** This is incorrect because the data show that the majority of rain falls during the warmer months.

   B. This is correct because the data show that the majority of rain falls during the warmer months of the year.

   C. This is incorrect because the data show that the majority of rain falls during the middle of the year.

   D. This is incorrect because the data show that the city gets more than 40 inches of rain per year.

5. **A.** This is incorrect because, according to the data, it rains more during the spring in City 1 than it does during the spring in City 2.

   B. This is incorrect because, according to the data, it rains less during the summer in City 2 than during any other time of the year.

   C. This is incorrect because, according to the data, it rains significantly more in City 1 than in City 2 during the winter months.

   D. This is correct because, according to the data, it rains more during the spring in City 1 than it rains all year long in City 2, so it is likely the same pattern will continue.

6. The order of the numbers is 3, 1, 4, and 2. The steps in place that help protect Kerry and her students from lightning while swimming are as follows: (1) Meteorologists study the weather. (2) Meteorologists alert the weather center of lightning and send out an alert. (3) Kerry hears the alert. (4) Everyone gets out of the pool safely.

7. Circling one or more of the tropical areas on the map is correct. Tropical climates are hot and wet.

8. **A.** *Tornado* matches with *Ashley's family* because tornadoes have very high-speed winds, and well-built, underground shelter can protect people from high-speed winds.

   B. *Snowstorm* belongs with *Jason* and big coat and gloves because he is preparing for very cold weather.

   C. *Heavy rain* belongs with *Steve* because rubber boots and umbrella are most useful to protect a person from rain.

9. The order of the numbers is 2, 4, 1 and 3. The months in order from fewest tornadoes to most tornadoes is July, January, November, March.

10. **A.** *They shed their heavy fur in summer* is correct because it shows that they have heavy fur for the winter cold, and lighter fur for the summer heat.

    B *They live in a tropical area that is warm and wet* is incorrect because the area is described as having little water and extreme hot and cold temperatures.

    C. *They store fat in their humps to use for energy and water* is correct because this helps the camel survive in the harsh climate without rain.

© Houghton Mifflin Harcourt Publishing Company

11. Use the rubric below to evaluate total points earned for this item. *[max point: 2]*

DCI, SEP - 2 Points	
Claims	The student is able to: 1. describe an area's typical weather conditions (DCI); and 2. obtain information from a table to explain the phenomena of climate (SEP).
Evidence of Mastery of Disciplinary Core Ideas	1 point for correctly describing the climate of each of the locations **Part 1:** One point is earned for describing that the climate is hotter and dryer where Frank lives. The following response, or an equivalent, is acceptable. • It is hot and dry where Frank lives and colder and wetter where Mary lives.
Evidence of Mastery of Science and Engineering Practices	1 point for correctly explaining how the table was used **Part 2:** One point is earned for explaining how the table is used to support their conclusion for the climate differences. The following response, or an equivalent, is acceptable. • There are more sunny days on the table for Frank and the temperatures there are higher.

12. **A.** This is incorrect because City 1 has one of the higher average precipitation totals per year, and the climate is described as humid and snowy. Deserts are dry and receive little rainfall.

    B. This is correct because City 2 receives the least amount of rain, and the climate description indicates that it is dry with a rainy season, which is typical of a desert climate. The typical hazard of drought is another indicator the climate is desert-like.

    C. This is incorrect because City 3 gets the most rain of the 4, and the climate is described as wet.

    D. This is incorrect because it receives more rain that City 2, and is likely to have severe thunderstorms and get lots of snow.

13. **A.** This is incorrect because City 1 has the lowest average temperatures given in the table.

    B. This is incorrect, because City 2 does not, on average, have the highest temperatures of the cities listed.

    C. This is correct because both the average low and average high temperature are the highest of any of the cities.

    D. This is incorrect because the average temperatures are lower than most of the other cities on the table.

14. **A.** *Lightning rods* belongs with City 4 because lightning is common during severe thunderstorms. The lightning rod could help direct the lightning and hopefully prevent fires.

    B. *Tornado sirens* belongs with *City 3* because tornadoes are common in that area. They provide warnings so people can seek shelter.

    C. *Irrigation systems* belongs with *City 2* because it is likely to have droughts. Droughts are long periods of time without rain, and an irrigation system could help keep the plant life alive in the area.

    D. *Roofs that hold heavy snow* belongs with *City 1* because blizzards drop heavy snow.

15. Use the rubric below to evaluate total points earned for this item. *[max point: 3]*

DCI, SEP, CCC - 3 points	
Claims	The student is able to: 1. describe a natural hazard that results from heavy rain (DCI); and 2. describe the merit of a rain gauge by citing relative evidence about how it meets the criteria and constraints of the problem of flooding (SEP); and 3. explain how science affects everyday life when dealing with natural hazards (CCC).
Evidence of Mastery of Disciplinary Core Ideas	1 point for correctly describing a the common hazard the people are worried about **Part 1:** One point is earned for describing a natural hazard such as flooding that comes from heavy rain. The following response, or an equivalent, is acceptable.

© Houghton Mifflin Harcourt Publishing Company

	• Flooding can take place because of lots of rain.
Evidence of Mastery of Science and Engineering Practices	1 point for correctly explaining how the water gauge would meet people's needs in a flood situation **Part 3:** One point is earned for explaining that a rain gauge warns people of an impending flood so they can evacuate or build barriers. The following response, or an equivalent, is acceptable. • A water gauge will warn people of rising water. This will give people time to move or to use sandbags to build walls.
Evidence of Mastery of Crosscutting Concepts	1 point for correctly explaining how flooding affects people **Part 2:** One point is earned for explaining how flooding affects everyday life by causing damage that forces people to leave their homes or forces people to build barriers in response to the flooding. The following response, or an equivalent, is acceptable. • Flooding can cause damage to homes and make people leave.

Mid-Year Test A

Item Analysis		
Item #	**Standards**	**DOK**
1	3-5-ETS1-3, DCI.3-5-ETS1.B.4	2
2	3-LS1-1, DCI.3-LS1.B.1, CCC.3-5.A.2	1
3	3-LS3-1, DCI.3-LS3.B.1, CCC.3-5.A.1	1
4	3-PS2-3, DCI.3-PS2.B.2	2
5	3-PS2-3, DCI.3-PS2.B.2, CCC.3-5.B.1	2
6	3-LS3-1, DCI.3-LS3.A.1, SEP.3-5.D.2	2
7	3-PS2-2, DCI.3-PS2.A.1, SEP.3-5.C.2	2
8	3-LS1-1, DCI.3-LS1.B.1	3
9	3-PS2-1, DCI.3-PS2.A.1, SEP.NOS.3-5.A.1	2
10	3-5-ETS1-1, DCI.3-5-ETS1.A.1, CCC.STSE.3-5.B.2	2
11	3-LS1-1, DCI.3-LS1.B.1, SEP.3-5.B.2	2
12	3-PS2-3, DCI.3-PS2.B.2, CCC.3-5.B.1	2
13	3-5-ETS1-3, DCI.3-5-ETS1.C.1, SEP.3-5.C.1	2
14	3-LS1-1, DCI.3-LS1.B.1	2
15	3-PS2-2, DCI.3-PS2.A.2, SEP.3-5.C.2	2
16	3-PS2-1, DCI.3-PS2.A.1, SEP.3-5.C.1	2
17	3-LS3-1, DCI.3-LS3.B.1, CCC.3-5.A.1	2
18	3-5-ETS1-1, DCI.3-5-ETS1.A.1, SEP.3-5.A.2	2
19	3-PS2-4, DCI.3-PS2.B.2, SEP.3-5.A.2	3
20	3-5-ETS1-2, DCI.3-5-ETS1.B.2, CCC.STSE.3-5.B.1	2
21	3-PS2-4, DCI.3-PS2.B.2, CCC.STSE.3-5.A.1	2
22	3-5-ETS1-2, DCI.3-5-ETS1.B.3, SEP.3-5.F.4	3
23	3-PS2-4, DCI.3-PS2.B.2	2
24	3-LS3-1, DCI.3-LS3.A.1	2
25	3-PS2-1, DCI.3-PS2.A.1, CCC.3-5.B.1	3

© Houghton Mifflin Harcourt Publishing Company

26	3-PS2-2, DCI.3-PS2.A.2, SEP.NOS.3-5.B.1	3
27	3-PS2-2, DCI.3-PS2.A.2, CCC.3-5.A.2	3
28	3-ESS2-2, DCI.3-ESS2.D.1, CCC.3-5.A.2	3
29	3-PS2-2, DCI.3-PS2.A.2	3
30	3-5-ETS1-1, DCI.3-5-ETS1.A.1	3

1. **A.** This is correct because the best way to make the water drain more slowly is to make the water holes smaller.

   B. This is incorrect because making the handle longer will not make it drain more slowly.

   C. This is incorrect because making the wheels larger will not make the wagon drain more slowly.

   D. This is incorrect because making the wagon smaller will not make it drain more slowly.

2. The steps of a life cycle are repetitive and the same for all organisms. The cycle starts with the birth of the organism. The organism grows and then reproduces and gives birth to an offspring. At some point, the adult organism dies, but the offspring continues on with the life cycle and reproduces. The pattern repeats itself.

3. **A.** The picture of the adult rabbit matches the baby bunny because they have similar traits, such as tall ears, a white tail, and the same body shape.

   B. The picture of penguin does not match any other animal shown. The penguin is a bird that swims, like ducks; however, the penguin's body is taller and narrower than that of a duck.

   C. The picture of the calf matches the adult cow because they have similar traits, such as four legs, a long tail, and the same body shape.

   D. The picture of the adult mallard duck matches the duckling because they have similar traits, such as two feet, one beak, and the same body shape.

4. **A.** This N/S magnet belongs in the *Attract* row for *Magnet 1* only if it is also placed in the *Attract* row for *Magnet 2*. The magnets that have the opposite poles touching each other have an attractive force. This N/S magnet belongs in the *Repel* row for *Magnet 1* only if the S/N magnet is placed in the *Repel* row for Magnet 2. The magnets that have the same poles near each other repel each other.

   B. This S/N magnet belongs in the *Attract* row for *Magnet 1* only if it also placed in the *Attract* row for *Magnet 2*. The magnets that have the opposite poles touching each other have an attractive force. This N/S magnet belongs in the *Repel* row for *Magnet 1* only if the S/N magnet is placed in the *Repel* row for Magnet 2. The magnets that have the same poles near each other repel each other.

   C. *Poles are alike* belongs in the *Repel* row for the *Reason* column because magnets that repel each other have opposite (different) poles.

   D. *Poles are different* belongs in the *Attract* row for the *Reason* column because magnets that are attracted to each other have opposite (different) poles, not poles that are alike.

5. **A.** The picture of the glass rod touching the pieces of paper belongs in the *Strong force* column. Because the two objects are close together, the positively charged glass rod picks up some of the negatively charged paper.

   B. The picture of the glass rod not touching the pieces of paper belongs in the *Weak force* column. The two objects are too far apart for an electric force to be present.

6. **A.** This is incorrect because the puppies do not all look the same so they cannot all look like their mother. Also, offspring inherit traits from both parents.

   B. This is correct because offspring inherit physical traits from their parents. Because the puppies are siblings, one of the parents is likely to have black fur and the other is likely to have brown fur.

   C. This is correct because offspring inherit physical traits from their parents. Because the puppies are siblings, one of the parents is likely to have brown fur and the other is likely to have black fur.

7. The bar for the 5 cm string should be at 10 swings. The bar for the 10 cm string should be at 45 swings.

© Houghton Mifflin Harcourt Publishing Company

8. **A.** This is correct because frogs and lizards both lay eggs and breathe air as adults.

   B. This is incorrect because frogs lay their eggs in water.

   C. This is incorrect because lizards lay their eggs on land.

   D. This is incorrect because lizards live their whole lives on land.

9. **A.** The picture of the two arrows pointing toward each other belongs in the *Shows Balanced Forces* box because the arrows are of equal size and length, meaning that the forces are balanced and the table will not move.

   B. The picture with the single arrow does not belong in either box because the one arrow means the force is unbalanced and the table will move in the direction the arrow is pointed.

   C. The picture of the *Spring Scale* belongs in the *Tool Used to Measure Forces* box because a spring scale measures newtons, a measurement of force.

   D. The picture of the *Balance Scale* does not belong in either box because a balance scale is a tool used to measure mass in grams. The measurement is determined by placing the object in one pan and the mass weights in the other pan.

10. **A.** This is *Likely* because designs are often brought about by people wanting change, in this case, a safer tire.

    B. This is *Likely* because people likely voiced concern about driving safely on wet roads.

    C. This is *Not Likely* because people were more concerned with tire safety than with how the tire looked.

11. Use the rubric below to evaluate total points earned for this item. *[max point: 3]*

DCI, SEP - 3 Points	
Claims	The student is able to: 1. recognize that a plant follows the life cycle (DCI); and 2. use a model to describe phases of a plant life cycle (SEP).
Evidence of Mastery of Disciplinary Core Ideas	1 point for correctly identifying the process shown **Part 1:** One point is earned for identifying that the process shown is the life cycle. The following response, or an equivalent, is acceptable. • the life cycle
Evidence of Mastery of Science and Engineering Practices	2 points for correctly identifying stages 1 and 3 **Part 2:** One point is earned for identifying stage 1 as birth or a seed. Any one of the following responses, or an equivalent, is acceptable. • 1 is birth • It is a seed. **Part 3:** One point is earned for identifying stage 3 as that of an adult. The following response, or an equivalent, is acceptable. • 3 is an adult

12. **A.** *Weakest* belongs in the *Force* column of the bottom row because the farther apart the magnet and nail, the weaker the magnetic force.

    B. *Far apart* does not need to be placed in any column because it is already present to describe the distance of the magnet and nail in the bottom row.

    C. *Close together* belongs in the *Distance* column of the top row because the magnet and nail are close together, modeling the strongest force of those pictured.

    D. This picture does not belong in any column because the nail and magnet are shown closer together than in picture E. Therefore, this picture does not model the weakest force.

    E. This picture belongs in the bottom row of the *Picture of Magnet and Nail* column because the nail is far away from the magnet, which models the weakest force of those pictured.

13. **A.** This is incorrect because watching one bird feeder in the morning would not allow Mina to compare the results with the other bird feeder.

   B. This is incorrect because setting up the feeders in two different locations may make the tests unfair.

   C. This is correct because observing the birds for the same amount of time each day would help ensure fair tests.

   D. This is incorrect because some birds prefer to eat on the ground and some prefer to eat above the ground.

14. **A.** This statement is false because a butterfly goes through metamorphosis, changing from one form to another, while a tree grows larger but remains as a tree.

   B. This statement is false because the picture shows that the butterfly lays the egg that grows into a caterpillar.

   C. This statement is true because a caterpillar weaves a cocoon around itself, emerging as a butterfly, while a tree gets taller and may lose a branch, but otherwise it remains the same.

15. **A.** *Weight A* matches *22 cm* because Walt's data show that A stretched the spring to a length of 22 cm.

   B. *Weight B* matches *18 cm* because Walt's data show that B stretched the spring to a length of 18 cm.

   C. *Weight C* matches *20 cm* because Walt's data show that C stretched the spring to a length of 20 cm.

   D. *Weight D* matches *16 cm* because Walt's data show that D stretched the spring to a length of 16 cm.

16. **A.** This sentence is not used. This step will not keep the ring from moving.

   B. This sentence belongs in Step 1. Application of the same force in opposite directions balances the forces and results in no motion.

   C. This sentence belongs in Step 2 because if there are equal forces on the cars, they should not move.

   D. This sentence is not used. If they are trying to keep the cars from moving, then they should not need to note that the ring and car moved.

   E. This sentence belongs in Step 3. Recording observations would be the next step in this investigation of how to keep the ring from moving.

17. **A.** This is incorrect because the living things are not grouped by size but by appearance.

   B. This is incorrect because the living things are not grouped by how much they eat but by appearance.

   C. This is correct because the living things are grouped by similarities in appearance.

   D. This is incorrect because the living things are grouped by similarities in appearance.

18. **A.** This is incorrect because the opening is large enough for the dog to get through.

   B. This is incorrect because, although the solution costs less than $50, the cat cannot use the doorknob to open the door.

   C. This is incorrect because Max can spend only $50, and the new door costs $150.

   D. This is correct because only the cat can get in and out, and the solution costs less than $50.

19. Use the rubric below to evaluate total points earned for this item.   *[max point: 4]*

DCI, SEP - 4 Points	
Claims	The student is able to: 1. identify that magnets can attract objects from a distance (DCI); and 2. explain a problem that can be solved using magnetic forces that meet given criteria and constraints (SEP).
Evidence of Mastery of Disciplinary Core Ideas	1 point for correctly identifying Dean's idea **Part 1:** One point is earned for identifying that idea 3 uses magnets to function. One of the following responses, or an equivalent, is acceptable. • Idea 3

© Houghton Mifflin Harcourt Publishing Company

	• Putting magnets on the curtains • The one with magnets
Evidence of Mastery of Science and Engineering Practices	3 points for correctly explaining how forces are used **Part 2:** Three points are earned for explaining that magnetic forces keep the curtains closed but are not so strong that a person cannot push through the force. • The magnets on the curtains attract each other to keep it closed. The wind has to be strong to pull apart the magnets. People and dogs can push the magnets apart. When the magnets come close together, their forces pull them back together.

20. **A.** This is incorrect because Dunia does not indicate a need for the design to match her house.

    B. This is correct because Dunia's plants get too hot. The curtain will reduce the heat on the porch.

    C. This is incorrect because reasons 1 and 3 are not indicated in the passage.

    D. This is incorrect because Dunia does not indicate a need to prevent people from breaking into the house.

21. **A.** This is correct because magnets, depending upon their orientation, can attract or repel each other.

    B. This is correct because fabric can be placed between two magnets and the magnets will still attract each other.

    C. This is incorrect because magnetic force is a noncontact force.

22. **A.** This is incorrect because Dunia wants the dogs to be able to move through the doorway freely.

    B. This is incorrect because the dogs will not be able to untie the string that keeps the curtain in place.

    C. This is correct because it will block sunlight, anyone can open it, the wind will not blow it, and it costs less than $50.

    D. This is incorrect because it will not allow people or dogs to move through the doorway.

23. Use the rubric below to evaluate total points earned for this item. *[max point: 1]*

DCI - 1 Point	
Claims	The student is able to identify that the distance between magnets affects the strength of the magnetic force (DCI).
Evidence of Mastery of Disciplinary Core Ideas	1 point for correctly circling the magnet position of the strongest force **Part 1:** One point is earned for circling letter C as showing the magnet positions with the strongest force because the magnets are closest together. The following, or an equivalent, is acceptable. **Magnet Positions** A B (C)

24. **1C.** *Puppy 3* belongs in the first space because it has the most similar traits to Dad and Mom.

    2E. *Tail length* belongs in the second space because puppy 3 has the same length of tail as Mom and Dad.

    3G. *Mom* belongs in the third space because puppy 3 has a coat similar to dog B, Mom.

© Houghton Mifflin Harcourt Publishing Company

25. Use the rubric below to evaluate total points earned for this item.   *[max point: 3]*

	DCI, CCC - 3 Points	
Claims	The student is able to: 1. describe a force by its direction (DCI); and 2. identify an example of balanced and unbalanced forces (CCC).	
Evidence of Mastery of Disciplinary Core Ideas	1 point for correctly explaining how the force changed **Part 3:** One point is earned for explaining that the direction of the force changed after the ball hit the floor. The following response, or an equivalent, is acceptable. • The direction changed.	
Evidence of Mastery of Crosscutting Concepts	2 points for correctly identifying the pictures of balanced and unbalanced forces **Part 1:** Two points are earned for identifying that the forces are balanced in picture 1, when Jing is holding the ball and the ball is not in motion. One of the following responses, or an equivalent, is acceptable. • picture 1 • when the ball is being held	

26. A. *90 cm* belongs in the row for 2 books under the column of *Trial 1*. This distance is the best of those available and is the approximate distance the car rolled in trial 2 and trial 3.

    B. *129 cm* belongs in the row for 3 books under the column of *Trial 3*. This distance is the best of those available and is the approximate distance the car rolled in trial 1 and trial 2.

    C. *52 cm* belongs in the row for 1 book under the column of *Trial 2*. This distance is the best of those available and is the approximate distance the car rolled in trial 1 and trial 3.

    D. This conclusion does not fit the data. Oscar's investigation does not indicate the length of the ramp, and therefore, a conclusion regarding ramp length is unsupported.

    E. This conclusion fits the data. Adding more books to make the ramp taller had a direct effect on the distance the toy car rolled. The taller the ramp height, the greater the distance of the roll.

27. The number 2 belongs in the box next to A. The number 1 belongs in the box next to B. The number 3 belongs in the bottom box next to C. The pictures are ordered by increasing distance away from Ellis and also show that the ball bounced according to the pattern of motion identified in the stem, which is B, A, and then C. Picture B shows the ball close to Ellis's hand. Picture A shows the ball at the second highest point, as if it has just bounced off the ground. Picture C shows the ball the farthest away from Ellis and almost touching the ground, as if it were about to hit the floor with a small bounce.

28. A. This is incorrect because the average temperature for the temperate forest in January is 0 °C, while it is 10 °C in the desert.

    B. This is correct because the average temperature for the tropical rainforest in April is 30 °C, while it is 15 °C in the temperate forest.

    C. This is incorrect because the average temperature for the temperate forest in July is 20 °C, while it is 25 °C in the desert.

    D. This is incorrect because the average temperature for the tropical rainforest in October is 20 °C, while it is 15 °C in the desert.

29. A. This is incorrect because adding 5 boxcars does not reduce the time it takes to make 1 lap.

    B. This is incorrect because adding 5 boxcars increases the number of seconds it takes to make a lap.

    C. This is correct because the pattern shows that for every boxcar added, 1 second is added to the time to make 1 lap.

    D. This is incorrect because each additional boxcar increases the time by 1 second. You do not add the number of boxcars (5) to the number of seconds it took for the last trial (14).

© Houghton Mifflin Harcourt Publishing Company

30. Designs 3 and 5 should be circled because they both hold the required number of backpacks and coats, five each, they take five hours or less to build, and each of them costs less than $75.00.

Mid-Year Test B

Item Analysis		
Item #	**Standards**	**DOK**
1	3-5-ETS1-3, DCI.3-5-ETS1.B.4	2
2	3-LS1-1, DCI.3-LS1.B.1, CCC.3-5.A.2	1
3	3-LS3-1, DCI.3-LS3.B.1, CCC.3-5.A.1	1
4	3-PS2-3, DCI.3-PS2.B.2	2
5	3-PS2-3, DCI.3-PS2.B.2, CCC.3-5.B.1	2
6	3-LS3-1, DCI.3-LS3.A.1, SEP.3-5.D.2	2
7	3-PS2-2, DCI.3-PS2.A.1, SEP.3-5.C.2	2
8	3-LS1-1, DCI.3-LS1.B.1	3
9	3-PS2-1, DCI.3-PS2.A.1, SEP.NOS.3-5.A.1	2
10	3-5-ETS1-1, DCI.3-5-ETS1.A.1, CCC.STSE.3-5.B.2	2
11	3-LS1-1, DCI.3-LS1.B.1, SEP.3-5.B.2	2
12	3-PS2-3, DCI.3-PS2.B.2, CCC.3-5.B.1	2
13	3-5-ETS1-3, DCI.3-5-ETS1.C.1, SEP.3-5.C.1	2
14	3-LS1-1, DCI.3-LS1.B.1	2
15	3-PS2-2, DCI.3-PS2.A.2, SEP.3-5.C.2	2
16	3-PS2-1, DCI.3-PS2.A.1, SEP.3-5.C.1	2
17	3-LS3-1, DCI.3-LS3.B.1, CCC.3-5.A.1	2
18	3-5-ETS1-1, DCI.3-5-ETS1.A.1, SEP.3-5.A.2	2
19	3-PS2-4, DCI.3-PS2.B.2, SEP.3-5.A.2	3
20	3-5-ETS1-2, DCI.3-5-ETS1.B.2, CCC.STSE.3-5.B.1	2
21	3-PS2-4, DCI.3-PS2.B.2, CCC.STSE.3-5.A.1	2
22	3-5-ETS1-2, DCI.3-5-ETS1.B.3, SEP.3-5.F.4	3
23	3-PS2-4, DCI.3-PS2.B.2	2
24	3-LS3-1, DCI.3-LS3.A.1	2
25	3-PS2-1, DCI.3-PS2.A.1, CCC.3-5.B.1	3
26	3-PS2-2, DCI.3-PS2.A.2, SEP.NOS.3-5.B.1	3
27	3-PS2-2, DCI.3-PS2.A.2, CCC.3-5.A.2	3
28	3-ESS2-2, DCI.3-ESS2.D.1, CCC.3-5.A.2	3
29	3-PS2-2, DCI.3-PS2.A.2	3
30	3-5-ETS1-1, DCI.3-5-ETS1.A.1	3

1. **A.** This is correct because the best way to make the water drain more slowly is to make the water holes smaller.

    B. This is incorrect because making the handle longer will not make it drain more slowly.

    C. This is incorrect because making the wheels larger will not make the wagon drain more slowly.

© Houghton Mifflin Harcourt Publishing Company

2. The steps of a life cycle are repetitive and the same for all organisms. The cycle starts with the birth of the organism. The organism grows and then reproduces and gives birth to an offspring. At some point, the adult organism dies, but the offspring continues on with the life cycle and reproduces. The pattern repeats itself.

3. **A.** The picture of the adult rabbit matches the baby bunny because they have similar traits, such as tall ears, a white tail, and the same body shape.

   B. The picture of the calf matches the adult cow because they have similar traits, such as four legs, a long tail, and the same body shape.

   C. The picture of the adult mallard duck matches the duckling because they have similar traits, such as two feet, one beak, and the same body shape.

4. **A.** This N/S magnet belongs in the *Attract* row for *Magnet 1* only if it is also placed in the *Attract* row for *Magnet 2*. The magnets that have the opposite poles touching each other have an attractive force.

   B. This S/N magnet belongs in the *Attract* row for *Magnet 1* only if it also placed in the *Attract* row for *Magnet 2*. The magnets that have the opposite poles touching each other have an attractive force.

5. **A.** The picture of the glass rod touching the pieces of paper belongs in the *Strong force* column. Because the two objects are close together, the positively charged glass rod picks up some of the negatively charged paper.

   B. The picture of the glass rod not touching the pieces of paper belongs in the *Weak force* column. The two objects are too far apart for an electric force to be present.

6. **A.** This is incorrect because the puppies do not all look the same so they cannot all look like their mother. Also, offspring inherit traits from both parents.

   B. This is correct because offspring inherit physical traits from their parents. Because the puppies are siblings, one of the parents is likely to have black fur and the other is likely to have brown fur.

   C. This is correct because offspring inherit physical traits from their parents. Because the puppies are siblings, one of the parents is likely to have brown fur and the other is likely to have black fur.

7. The bar for the 5 cm string should be at 10 swings. The bar for the 10 cm string should be at 45 swings.

8. **A.** This is correct because frogs and lizards both lay eggs and breathe air as adults.

   B. This is incorrect because frogs lay their eggs in water.

   C. This is incorrect because lizards lay their eggs on land.

9. **A.** The picture of the two arrows pointing toward each other belongs in the *Shows Balanced Forces* box because the arrows are of equal size and length, meaning that the forces are balanced and the table will not move.

   B. The picture with the single arrow does not belong in either box because the one arrow means the force is unbalanced and the table will move in the direction the arrow is pointed.

   C. The picture of the *Spring Scale* belongs in the *Tool Used to Measure Forces* box because a spring scale measures newtons, a measurement of force.

   D. The picture of the *Balance Scale* does not belong in either box because a balance scale is a tool used to measure mass in grams. The measurement is determined by placing the object in one pan and the mass weights in the other pan.

10. **A.** This is *Likely* because designs are often brought about by people wanting change, in this case, a safer tire.

   B. This is *Likely* because people likely voiced concern about driving safely on wet roads.

   C. This is *Not Likely* because people were more concerned with tire safety than with how the tire looked.

© Houghton Mifflin Harcourt Publishing Company

11. Use the rubric below to evaluate total points earned for this item. *[max point: 3]*

DCI, SEP - 3 Points	
Claims	The student is able to: 1. recognize that a plant follows the life cycle (DCI); and 2. use a model to describe phases of a plant life cycle (SEP).
Evidence of Mastery of Disciplinary Core Ideas	1 point for correctly identifying the process shown **Part 1:** One point is earned for identifying that the process shown is the life cycle. The following response, or an equivalent, is acceptable. • the life cycle
Evidence of Mastery of Science and Engineering Practices	2 points for correctly identifying stages 1 and 3 **Part 2:** One point is earned for identifying stage 1 as birth. The following response, or an equivalent, is acceptable. • 1 is birth **Part 3:** One point is earned for identifying stage 3. The following response, or an equivalent, is acceptable. • 3 is an adult

12. A. *Weakest* belongs in the *Force* column of the bottom row because the farther apart the magnet and nail, the weaker the magnetic force.

    B. *Far apart* does not need to be placed in any column because it is already present to describe the distance of the magnet and nail in the bottom row.

    C. *Close together* belongs in the *Distance* column of the top row because the magnet and nail are close together, modeling the strongest force of those pictured.

    D. This picture does not belong in any column because the nail and magnet are shown closer together than in picture E. Therefore, this picture does not model the weakest force.

    E. This picture belongs in the bottom row of the *Picture of Magnet and Nail* column because the nail is far away from the magnet, which models the weakest force of those pictured.

13. A. This is incorrect because watching one bird feeder in the morning would not allow Mina to compare the results with the other bird feeder.

    B. This is incorrect because setting up the feeders in two different locations may make the tests unfair.

    C. This is correct because observing the birds for the same amount of time each day would help ensure fair tests.

14. A. This statement is false because a butterfly goes through metamorphosis, changing from one form to another, while a tree grows larger but remains as a tree.

    B. This statement is false because the picture shows that the butterfly lays the egg that grows into a caterpillar.

    C. This statement is true because a caterpillar weaves a cocoon around itself, emerging as a butterfly, while a tree gets taller and may lose a branch, but otherwise it remains the same.

15. A. *Weight A* matches *22 cm* because Walt's data show that A stretched the spring to a length of 22 cm.

    B. *Weight B* matches *18 cm* because Walt's data show that B stretched the spring to a length of 18 cm.

    C. *Weight D* matches *16 cm* because Walt's data show that D stretched the spring to a length of 16 cm.

16. A. This sentence belongs in Step 1. Application of the same force in opposite directions balances the forces and results in no motion.

    B. This sentence belongs in Step 2 because if there are equal forces on the cars, they should not move.

    C. This sentence belongs in Step 3. Recording observations would be the next step in this investigation of how to keep the ring from moving.

© Houghton Mifflin Harcourt Publishing Company

17. **A.** This is incorrect because the living things are not grouped by how much they eat but by appearance.

   B. This is correct because the living things are grouped by similarities in appearance.

   C. This is incorrect because the living things are grouped by similarities in appearance.

18. **A.** This is incorrect because, although the solution costs less than $50, the cat cannot use the doorknob to open the door.

   B. This is incorrect because Max can spend only $50, and the new door costs $150.

   C. This is correct because only the cat can get in and out, and the solution costs less than $50.

19. Use the rubric below to evaluate total points earned for this item.   *[max point: 4]*

DCI, SEP - 4 Points	
Claims	The student is able to: 1. identify that magnets can attract objects from a distance (DCI); and 2. explain a problem that can be solved using magnetic forces that meet given criteria and constraints (SEP).
Evidence of Mastery of Disciplinary Core Ideas	1 point for correctly identifying Dean's idea **Part 1:** One point is earned for identifying that idea 3 uses magnets to function. One of the following responses, or an equivalent, is acceptable. • Idea 3 • Putting magnets on the curtains • The one with magnets
Evidence of Mastery of Science and Engineering Practices	3 points for correctly explaining how forces are used **Part 2:** Three points are earned for explaining that magnetic forces keep the curtains closed but are not so strong that a person cannot push through the force. • The magnets on the curtains attract each other to keep it closed. The wind has to be strong to pull apart the magnets. People and dogs can push the magnets apart. When the magnets come close together, their forces pull them back together.

20. **A.** This is incorrect because Dunia does not indicate a need for the design to match her house.

   B. This is correct because Dunia's plants get too hot. The curtain will reduce the heat on the porch.

   C. This is incorrect because reasons 1 and 3 are not indicated in the passage.

21. **A.** This is correct because magnets, depending upon their orientation, can attract or repel each other.

   B. This is correct because fabric can be placed between two magnets and the magnets will still attract each other.

   C. This is incorrect because magnetic force is a noncontact force.

22. **A.** This is incorrect because Dunia wants the dogs to be able to move through the doorway freely.

   B. This is incorrect because the dogs will not be able to untie the string that keeps the curtain in place.

   C. This is correct because it will block sunlight, anyone can open it, the wind will not blow it, and it costs less than $50.

23. Use the rubric below to evaluate total points earned for this item.   *[max point: 1]*

DCI - 1 Point	
Claims	The student is able to identify that the distance between magnets affects the strength of the magnetic force (DCI).
Evidence of Mastery of	1 point for correctly circling the magnet position of the strongest force

© Houghton Mifflin Harcourt Publishing Company

Disciplinary Core Ideas	**Part 1:** One point is earned for circling letter C as showing the magnet positions with the strongest force because the magnets are closest together. The following, or an equivalent, is acceptable.

Magnet Positions

A	◗ ◗
B	◗ ◗
(**C**)	◗◗◗

24. **1C.** *Puppy 3* belongs in the first space because it has the most similar traits to Dad and Mom.

    2E. *Tail length* belongs in the second space because puppy 3 has the same length of tail as Mom and Dad.

    3G. *Mom* belongs in the third space because puppy 3 has a coat similar to dog B, Mom.

25. Use the rubric below to evaluate total points earned for this item.   *[max point: 3]*

	DCI, CCC - 3 Points
Claims	The student is able to: 1. describe a force by its direction (DCI); and 2. identify an example of balanced and unbalanced forces (CCC).
Evidence of Mastery of Disciplinary Core Ideas	1 point for correctly explaining how the force changed **Part 3:** One point is earned for explaining that the direction of the force changed after the ball hit the floor. The following response, or an equivalent, is acceptable. • The direction changed.
Evidence of Mastery of Crosscutting Concepts	2 points for correctly identifying the pictures of balanced and unbalanced forces **Part 1:** One point is earned for identifying that the forces are balanced in picture 1, when Jing is holding the ball and the ball is not in motion. One of the following responses, or an equivalent, is acceptable. • picture 1 • when the ball is being held **Part 2:** One point is earned for identifying that the forces are unbalanced in pictures 2 and/or 3, when the ball is in motion. One of the following responses, or an equivalent, is acceptable. • picture 2 or picture 3 • The pictures that show the ball is in motion.

26. **A.** *90 cm* belongs in the row for 2 books under the column of *Trial 1*. This distance is the best of those available and is the approximate distance the car rolled in trial 2 and trial 3.

    B. *129 cm* belongs in the row for 3 books under the column of *Trial 3*. This distance is the best of those available and is the approximate distance the car rolled in trial 1 and trial 2.

    C. *52 cm* belongs in the row for 1 book under the column of *Trial 2*. This distance is the best of those available and is the approximate distance the car rolled in trial 1 and trial 3.

    D. This conclusion does not fit the data. Oscar's investigation does not indicate the length of the ramp, and therefore, a conclusion regarding ramp length is unsupported.

    E. This conclusion fits the data. Adding more books to make the ramp taller had a direct effect on the distance the toy car rolled. The taller the ramp height, the greater the distance of the roll.

© Houghton Mifflin Harcourt Publishing Company

27. The number 2 belongs in the box next to A. The number 1 belongs in the box next to B. The number 3 belongs in the bottom box next to C. The pictures are ordered by increasing distance away from Ellis and also show that the ball bounced according to the pattern of motion identified in the stem. Picture B shows the ball close to Ellis's hand. Picture A shows the ball at the second highest point, as if it has just bounced off the ground. Picture C shows the ball the farthest away from Ellis and almost touching the ground, as if it were about to hit the floor with a small bounce.

28. **A.** This is correct because the average temperature for the tropical rainforest in April is 30 °C, while it is 15 °C in the temperate forest.

   B. This is incorrect because the average temperature for the temperate forest in July is 20 °C, while it is 25 °C in the desert.

   C. This is incorrect because the average temperature for the tropical rainforest in October is 20 °C, while it is 15 °C in the desert.

29. **A.** This is incorrect because adding 5 boxcars increases, not decreases, the number of seconds it takes to make a lap.

   B. This is correct because the pattern shows that for every boxcar added, 1 second is added to the time to make 1 lap.

   C. This is incorrect because each additional boxcar increases the time by 1 second. You do not add the number of boxcars (5) to the number of seconds it took for the last trial (14).

30. Designs 3 and 5 should be circled because they both hold the required number of backpacks and coats, five each, they take five hours or less to build, and each of them costs less than $75.00.

End-of-Year Test A

Item Analysis		
Item #	**Standards**	**DOK**
1	3-ESS3-1, DCI.3-ESS3.B.1, CCC.NOS.3-5.B.1	1
2	3-ESS2-2, DCI.3-ESS2.D.2, SEP.3-5.H.1	2
3	3-LS4-4, DCI.3-LS2.C.1, CCC.3-5.D.1	1
4	3-LS2-1, DCI.3-LS2.D.1	2
5	3-LS3-2, DCI.3-LS3.A.2, SEP.3-5.F.1	2
6	3-ESS3-1, DCI.3-ESS3.B.1	2
7	3-LS4-4, DCI.3-LS4.D.1, SEP.3-5.G.2	2
8	3-LS2-1, DCI.3-LS2.D.1, CCC.3-5.B.1	2
9	3-ESS2-2, DCI.3-ESS2.D.2	2
10	3-LS4-2, DCI.3-LS4.B.1	1
11	3-LS4-3, DCI.3-LS4.C.1	2
12	3-ESS3-1, DCI.3-ESS3.B.1, SEP.3-5.G.2	2
13	3-LS4-4, DCI.3-LS2.C.1	2
14	3-LS4-3, DCI.3-LS4.C.1, CCC.3-5.B.1	2
15	3-ESS2-1, DCI.3-ESS2.D.1, SEP.3-5.D.1, CCC.3-5.A.2	2
16	3-ESS2-1, DCI.3-ESS2.D.1	3
17	3-LS4-1, DCI.3-LS4.A.1	2
18	3-LS4-1, DCI.3-LS4.A.2, SEP.3-5.D.2	3
19	3-LS4-1, DCI.3-LS4.A.2, CCC.NOS.3-5.A.1	3

© Houghton Mifflin Harcourt Publishing Company

20	3-LS4-1, DCI.3-LS4.A.2	2
21	3-LS3-2, DCI.3-LS3.B.2, CCC.3-5.B.1	2
22	3-LS4-4, DCI.3-LS4.D.1	2
23	3-LS2-1, DCI.3-LS2.D.1	3
24	3-LS4-3, DCI.3-LS4.C.1	3
25	3-LS4-2, DCI.3-LS4.B.1, CCC.3-5.B.1	3
26	3-LS4-2, DCI.3-LS4.B.1, SEP.3-5.F.1	3
27	3-LS4-4, DCI.3-LS4.D.1, CCC.STSE.3-5.A.2	3
28	3-ESS2-1, DCI.3-ESS2.D.1, CCC.3-5.A.2	3
29	3-LS4-2, DCI.3-LS4.B.1	3
30	3-LS4-3, DCI.3-LS4.C.1, SEP.3-5.G.1	3

1. **A.** *Causes fires* matches *lightning* because lightning is electricity that can strike objects, causing the objects to catch fire.

   B. *Freezes plants* matches *blizzard* because a blizzard brings very cold temperatures that can freeze the water in plants.

   C. *Brings too much water* matches *flooding* because landslides caused from heavy rainfall can loosen soil and cause land from cliffs or hillsides to fall to the lowest point, which could be the road.

2. **A.** This is incorrect because climate is most determined by rainfall and temperature for each season, not by rainfall alone.

   B. This is correct because temperature and precipitation together during different seasons are most associated with climate.

   C. This is incorrect because climate is determined most by rainfall and air temperature for each season, not by ground temperature during winter.

   D. This is incorrect because climate is most determined by rainfall and temperature for each season, not by the population size of animals and people in an area.

3. **A.** *Sunlight* belongs in the *Nonliving Things* column because it does not grow, reproduce or die.

   B. A *deer* belongs in the *Living Things* column because it is an animal that grows, reproduces, and dies.

   C. A *tree* belongs in the *Living Things* column because it is a plant that grows, reproduces, and dies.

   D. *Air* belongs in the *Nonliving Things* column because it does not grow, reproduce or die.

4. **A.** This is incorrect because wolves hunting in a pack is an example of a group behavior used to obtain food.

   B. This is correct because fish swimming closely together is a behavior that helps fish stay safe.

   C. This is incorrect because cats licking their hair is an example of grooming, not an example of a way that group behavior can help animals stay safe from predators.

   D. This is correct because vocalizing when a predator is near is an example of a group behavior that helps animals stay safe from predators.

5. **A.** This is incorrect because the data show that the greatest amount of rain was in year 3, where there were no flowers.

   B. This is incorrect because the lower temperatures made normal-sized potatoes.

   C. This is correct because the data show that environmental conditions affected the appearance of the potato plant and its tuber.

   D. This is incorrect because the white spots formed the year with the greatest amount of rain.

6. **A.** Following this action is correct because staying inside during a storm is a good way to remain safe.

© Houghton Mifflin Harcourt Publishing Company

B. Following this action is incorrect because checking smoke detectors does not help with being safe during a storm.

C. Following this action is correct because removing snow from sidewalks and roads will help keep the snow out of people's way and will likely help avoid an accident from happening.

7. **A.** This is correct because the land bridge allows animals to search for food on the other side of the road without getting onto the road surface.

    B. This is correct because animals will be less likely to cross the road and be hit by cars.

    C. This is incorrect because the land bridge is made by people.

8. Use the rubric below to evaluate total points earned for this item. *[max point: 1]*

CCC - 1 point	
Claims	The student is able to compare group behaviors and identify the consequent effect of the behavior (CCC).
Evidence of Mastery of Crosscutting Concepts	1 point for correctly matching the behavior (cause) to its outcome (effect) **Part 1:** One point is earned for matching the behavior to the outcome. The student should match 1 and B, 2 and C, 3 and A. The following response, or an equivalent, is acceptable.

Animal Behavior

		Effect
1	Adult elephants huddling around newborn	**A** Helping each other keeps group alive
2	Prairie dog makes a loud crying noise when hawks fly over	**B** Protects young, smaller member from predators
3	Many ants carry dirt in mouth and leave at hole entrance	**C** Warns group of danger

9. **A.** This is incorrect because climate describes weather for a long period. Weather can change daily.

    B. This is incorrect because climate is not the same concept as seasons. Depending on the area on Earth, an area can experience four seasons. Climate is a summary of the weather in an area and is also dependent on the location of the land on Earth. Climate also includes the weather during each season.

    C. This is incorrect because climate is the type of weather for a large area for a long period of time. Weather happens only for a short period of time.

    D. This is correct because climate is the type of weather for a large area for a long period of time.

10. **A.** The brown hare with very long ears and a flat back belongs in the *Hide From Predator During Fall* box. The brown hare will blend in with the brown and orange colors of the fall season.

    B. The white hare with light-brown patches belongs in the *Hide From Predator During Winter* box. The white hare will blend in with the white snow of the winter season.

    C. The dark brown hare with light-brown hair on the underside of the tail belongs in the *Hide From Predator During Fall* box. The brown hare will blend in with the brown and orange colors of the fall season.

    D. The white hare belongs in the *Hide From Predator During Winter* box. The white hare will blend in with the white snow of the winter season.

11. **A.** The polar bear belongs in the *Cold and wet* row. Polar bears have physical adaptations, including storing fat for warmth, that allow them to better survive an Arctic-like environment.

    B. The camel belongs in the *Hot and dry* row. Camels have physical adaptations, including storing water, that allow them to better survive living in a desert-like environment.

© Houghton Mifflin Harcourt Publishing Company

C. *Stores fat for warmth* belongs in the *Cold and Wet* row under the *Why able to survive* heading. Organisms that can survive a very cold environment have adaptations that allow them to conserve heat, such as storing energy as fat to be used as insulation.

D. *Stores water for use later* belongs in the *Hot and dry* row under the *Why able to survive* heading. Organisms that can survive a desert-like environment have adaptions that allow them to conserve water, such as storing excess water for use later.

12. A. *Fix leaky faucets* belongs in the *Will Help* column because it reduces the amount of wasted water.

    B. *Water the yard less often* belongs in the *Will Help* column because it will still allow a person to water the lawn, just not as often. This will allow more water to be available for drinking.

    C. *Stay inside until it rains* belongs in the *Will Not Help* column because this action will not conserve current or future water resources.

    D. *Water plants more often so they will not die* belongs in the *Will Not Help* column because this action does not reduce water use.

13. A. This possible change is correct for *Bees* and *Flowers*. Bees are dying. There will not be any left to reproduce. Flowers need the bees to move the pollen, but without the bees, the flowers will have difficulty reproducing.

    B. This possible change is correct for *Bees*. Skunks eat the bees, and disease is reducing the number of bees.

14. Use the rubric below to evaluate total points earned for this item.   *[max point: 1]*

<table>
<tr><td colspan="2">CCC - 1 point</td></tr>
<tr><td>Claims</td><td>The student is able to compare traits and behaviors of different organisms and identify their consequent effects (CCC).</td></tr>
<tr><td rowspan="2">Evidence of Mastery of Crosscutting Concepts</td><td>1 point for correctly matching the traits and behaviors to the effect

Part 1: One point is earned for drawing lines between the traits and behaviors (Table 1) and the effect of how this trait/behavior assists the organisms (Table 2). One of the following, or an equivalent, is acceptable.</td></tr>
<tr><td>

Table 1

Letter	Body Part/Behavior That Is Different from Rest of Group
A	Has larger leaves
B	Stores fat in thick layer
C	Fur changes from brown to white in winter

Table 2

Number	How Helps Animal Survive
1	Blends in with color of environment
2	Collects more sunlight
3	Keeps warm during winter

</td></tr>
</table>

15. There should be two Xs for Monday to represent 2 cm, no Xs for Tuesday, and four Xs for Wednesday.

16. A. The temperature of *0°* does not belong in the table. The temperature for winter is already listed as 12°. No other season should have an average temperature lower than winter's temperature.

    B. The temperature of *19°* belongs in fall's average temperature. The temperature for fall should be less than summer's but greater than winter's.

    C. The amount of *2 centimeters* belongs in the precipitation column for winter. Travis noticed that it did not rain or snow much in the winter. Fall had 4 cm of precipitation, which means winter had to have 2 cm.

    D. The amount of *5 centimeters* belongs in the precipitation column for summer. Travis noticed that it rained more in the summer than in the fall but the most in spring.

© Houghton Mifflin Harcourt Publishing Company

E. *Decreased* is correct for the second blank in the *Average Temperature* column in the *Pattern* row. The pattern for the average temperature shows that there was an increase and then a decrease (22, 31, 19, and 12 degrees). *Decreased* is also correct for the average snow/rain pattern.

F. *Increased* is correct for the first blank in the *Average Temperature* column in the *Pattern* row. The pattern for the average temperature shows that there was an increase and then a decrease (22, 31, 19, and 12 degrees).

17. **A.** This is incorrect because birds are not found in layer 1 with these organisms.

    B. This is incorrect because these fossils did not appear in recent layers of rock.

    C. This is incorrect because layer 1 is on the bottom of several other layers. The youngest layers are toward the top, closer to layer 4. Layer 1 appears to be the oldest layer.

    D. This correct because these organisms did not appear in any rock layer more recent than layer 1.

18. **A.** *Had wings and legs* belongs in the box for *Organism 1* because the organism's fossil appears to have had legs, and the head appears to be that of a bird, which indicates it was likely to have wings too.

    B. *Probably lived on land* belongs in the box for *Organism 1* because the organism appears to have had legs and wings, which could resemble some sort of bird; birds live on land.

    C. *Probably lived in water* belongs in the box for *Organism 2* because lobsters today live in water and they probably did in the past, too.

    D. *Had a hard outer shell and legs* belongs in the box for *Organism 2* because lobsters today have hard outer shells and their legs are also hard.

19. Use the rubric below to evaluate total points earned for this item. *[max point: 3]*

DCI, CCC - 3 Points	
Claims	The student is able to: 1. identify fossils (DCI); and 2. use patterns in given data to describe the type of environment in which an organism lived long ago (CCC).
Evidence of Mastery of Disciplinary Core Ideas	2 points for correctly identifying the fossils **Part 1:** One point is earned for identifying the fossils in layer 2 as that from a mollusk (shell) and a fish. One of the following, or an equivalent, is acceptable. • clams and fish • mollusks and fish • things that lived in shells and animals that swam **Part 2:** One point is earned for identifying the fossils in layer 4 as a dinosaur and a bird. One of the following, or an equivalent, is acceptable. • dinosaur and bird • reptile and animal that flew
Evidence of Mastery of Crosscutting Concepts	1 point for correctly describing how the environment changed **Part 3:** One point is earned for describing that the environment changed from a water environment in layer 2 to a land environment in layer 4. One of the following, or an equivalent, is acceptable. • Layer 2 was covered with water and layer 4 was not. • The sea covered the area when layer 1 was around.

20. **A.** *Layer 1* belongs in the *Seawater* column because the fossilized shells indicate that mollusks and trilobites lived in the area. These organisms reside in seawater. The sea must have covered the area when layer 1 was formed.

    B. *Layer 2* belongs in the *Seawater* column because the clams and fish reside in seawater. The sea must have covered the area when layer 1 was formed.

© Houghton Mifflin Harcourt Publishing Company

C. *Layer 3* belongs in the *Land* column because trees and dragonflies live mainly on the land. The sea must not have been covering the area when layer 2 was formed.

D. *Layer 4* belongs in the *Land* column because dinosaurs and birds are land animals. There are no fossil remains of organisms that lived in the sea. The sea must not have been covering the area when layer 4 was formed.

21. **1B.** The first dog is too thin. This dog probably does not eat enough. This matches the description of Bailey.

   2C. The second dog's weight seems ideal. He probably eats a healthy amount of food and gets enough exercise. This matches the description of Cooper.

   3A. The third dog is overweight. This dog probably eats too much and doesn't get enough exercise. This matches the description of Astro.

22. **A.** This is correct because cutting down a tree that grows nuts can reduce the squirrel's source of food.

   B. This is incorrect because insects will not disappear in the absences of trees.

   C. This is correct because squirrels use trees to hide from predators; they also make nests in trees.

23. Use the rubric below to evaluate total points earned for this item.   *[max point: 2]*

DCI Only - 2 Points	
Claims	The student is able to explain how being a part of a group helps animals cope with changes (DCI).
Evidence of Mastery of Disciplinary Core Ideas	1 point for correctly identifying the reason for huddling **Part 1:** One point is earned for identifying that these penguins huddle in order to conserve heat and stay warm. The following response, or an equivalent, is acceptable. • The penguins huddle to stay warm. 1 point for correctly explaining how the entire group benefits from huddling **Part 2:** One point is earned for explaining that the group of penguins can keep the wind from entering the center of the huddle, keeping temperatures higher. As more penguins survive the brutal Antarctic winter, more chicks will hatch and live to adulthood, keeping group numbers steady. The following response, or an equivalent, is acceptable. • The penguins block the cold and keep each other warm. This keeps more penguins alive so they can have more chicks.

24. **1B.** *Maybe* belongs in the box for the red fox. The red fox is accustomed to the cold environment of the U.S. The red fox would not die immediately in the Arctic, nor would it survive well. It would barely survive the Arctic.

   2A. *Yes* belongs in the box for the reindeer. The reindeer is accustomed to the cold environment of Alaska and Canada. The reindeer would survive well in the Arctic.

   3C. *No* belongs in the box for the rattlesnake. The rattlesnake is accustomed to the warm environment closer to the equator. The rattlesnake would die very quickly in the Arctic environment.

25. Use the rubric below to evaluate total points earned for this item.   *[max point: 1]*

CCC - 1 point	
Claims	The student is able to identify the cause-and-effect relationship within variation of the same type of organism that allows some to reproduce, while a similar group does not (CCC).
Evidence of Mastery of Crosscutting Concepts	1 point for correctly identifying the numbers **Part 1:** One point is earned for circling numbers 5 and 6 as evidence to support Reba's claim that one group, group B, is more likely to reproduce. The following response, or an equivalent, is acceptable.

© Houghton Mifflin Harcourt Publishing Company

<table>
<tr><th colspan="2">Group A</th><th colspan="2">Group B</th></tr>
<tr><td>1.</td><td>Eat plant parts, insects, and lizards.</td><td>4.</td><td>Eat flowers, leaves, insects, and frogs.</td></tr>
<tr><td>2.</td><td>Females are not interested in males.</td><td>(5.)</td><td>Females are attracted to males.</td></tr>
<tr><td>3.</td><td>Females do not lay many eggs.</td><td>(6.)</td><td>Females lay many eggs.</td></tr>
</table>

26. A. This is incorrect. The evidence presented in the table makes one assume that dark-brown insects are less likely to reproduce because they do not survive as long as light-green insects.

B. This is correct because light-green insects live longer; the light-green color can be an advantage for these insects.

C. This is correct because the dark-brown color would be more obvious to animals than a light-green color, which could potentially blend in with the environment.

D. This is incorrect because there is no evidence presented about the size of the insects.

27. Use the rubric below to evaluate total points earned for this item. *[max point: 3]*

DCI, CCC - 3 Points	
Claims	The student is able to: 1. describe how one or more organisms within that habitat will be adversely affected by the change (DCI); and 2. describe how humans are able to prevent/reduce the effects of environmental change through technology and/or engineering (CCC).
Evidence of Mastery of Disciplinary Core Ideas	1 point for correctly identifying how a Z clam hurts another animal **Part 1:** One point is earned for identifying the negative effects of a Z clam on other organisms. The response may include that the Z is poisonous to birds, and attaches to other clams. One of the following, or an equivalent, is acceptable. • Poisons seabirds • Grows on other clams
Evidence of Mastery of Crosscutting Concepts	2 points for describing a solution **Part 2:** Two points are earned for describing that using pipes with the special metal will prevent the clams from clogging the pipes. The following, or an equivalent, is acceptable. • The Z clams do not like the special metal. They will not stick to it and clog it.

28. A. This is incorrect because the data do not show daily rainfall, and the daily temperature is likely to be around 13°C, not 8°C.

B. This is incorrect because the data do not show cloud coverage, and the rainfall is likely to be about 8 cm monthly, not 14 cm daily.

C. This is correct because the data for temperature range from 12°C to 14°C, and the rainfall ranges from 7 cm to 9 cm.

D. This is incorrect because the data do not show the hottest temperature for the month of May.

29. A. *Protects against predators* belongs in the *Rose Bush* row because thorns deter animals that may otherwise eat the plant.

B. *Pokes in the ground for food* belongs in the *Kiwi Bird* row because the long beak allows the bird to search for worms and other insects in the ground.

C. *Blends into tree bark to survive* belongs in the *Moth* row because the brown wings will camouflage the moth protecting it from predators.

© Houghton Mifflin Harcourt Publishing Company

   D. *Survive* belongs as the last word of the conclusion. The differences help the animals survive in their environments.

   E. *Lead the group* does not belong in any row. The differences stated would not necessarily create a leader, and plants don't have a leader.

30. A. This is correct because a wetland has everything that is essential for a frog's survival such as water to lay eggs and stay moist, and food such as insects and worms. A desert is perfect for a scorpion because it has the food the scorpion eats, and an environment the scorpion can blend in with, and typically has hot temperatures.

   B. This is incorrect because any location would not be suitable for a frog to live in; a scorpion appears to need sand to blend in with, and it is not common to find sand in a forest.

   C. This is incorrect because a frog would freeze in a cold habitat and there is nothing there for it to survive on; a scorpion cannot live in any location because some locations are not suitable for a scorpion to live in.

   D. This is incorrect because although a forest could have what a frog needs to survive, it is not the essential habitat. A scorpion would not be found in the cold habitat due to scorpions not being able to survive cold temperatures.

End-of-Year Test B

Item Analysis		
Item #	**Standards**	**DOK**
1	3-ESS3-1, DCI.3-ESS3.B.1, CCC.NOS.3-5.B.1	1
2	3-ESS2-2, DCI.3-ESS2.D.2, SEP.3-5.H.1	2
3	3-LS4-4, DCI.3-LS2.C.1, CCC.3-5.D.1	1
4	3-LS2-1, DCI.3-LS2.D.1	2
5	3-LS3-2, DCI.3-LS3.A.2, SEP.3-5.F.1	2
6	3-ESS3-1, DCI.3-ESS3.B.1	2
7	3-LS4-4, DCI.3-LS4.D.1, SEP.3-5.G.2	2
8	3-LS2-1, DCI.3-LS2.D.1, CCC.3-5.B.1	2
9	3-ESS2-2, DCI.3-ESS2.D.2	2
10	3-LS4-2, DCI.3-LS4.B.1	1
11	3-LS4-3, DCI.3-LS4.C.1	2
12	3-ESS3-1, DCI.3-ESS3.B.1, SEP.3-5.G.2	2
13	3-LS4-4, DCI.3-LS2.C.1	2
14	3-LS4-3, DCI.3-LS4.C.1, CCC.3-5.B.1	2
15	3-ESS2-1, DCI.3-ESS2.D.1, SEP.3-5.D.1, CCC.3-5.A.2	2
16	3-ESS2-1, DCI.3-ESS2.D.1	3
17	3-LS4-1, DCI.3-LS4.A.1	2
18	3-LS4-1, DCI.3-LS4.A.2, SEP.3-5.D.2	3
19	3-LS4-1, DCI.3-LS4.A.2, CCC.NOS.3-5.A.1	3
20	3-LS4-1, DCI.3-LS4.A.2	2
21	3-LS3-2, DCI.3-LS3.B.2, CCC.3-5.B.1	2
22	3-LS4-4, DCI.3-LS4.D.1	2
23	3-LS2-1, DCI.3-LS2.D.1	3

© Houghton Mifflin Harcourt Publishing Company

24	3-LS4-3, DCI.3-LS4.C.1	3
25	3-LS4-2, DCI.3-LS4.B.1, CCC.3-5.B.1	3
26	3-LS4-2, DCI.3-LS4.B.1, SEP.3-5.F.1	3
27	3-LS4-4, DCI.3-LS4.D.1, CCC.STSE.3-5.A.2	3
28	3-ESS2-1, DCI.3-ESS2.D.1, CCC.3-5.A.2	3
29	3-LS4-2, DCI.3-LS4.B.1	3
30	3-LS4-3, DCI.3-LS4.C.1, SEP.3-5.G.1	3

1. **A.** *Causes fires* matches *lightning* because lightning is electricity that can strike objects, causing the objects to catch fire.

   B. *Freezes plants* matches *blizzard* because a blizzard brings very cold temperatures that can freeze the water in plants.

   C. *Brings too much water* matches *flooding* because landslides caused from heavy rainfall can loosen soil and cause land from cliffs or hillsides to fall to the lowest point, which could be the road.

2. **A.** This is incorrect because climate is most determined by rainfall and temperature for each season, not by rainfall alone.

   B. This is correct because temperature and precipitation together during different seasons are most associated with climate.

   C. This is incorrect because climate is determined most by rainfall and air temperature for each season, not by ground temperature during winter.

3. **A.** *Sunlight* belongs in the *Nonliving Things* column because it does not grow, reproduce or die.

   B. A *deer* belongs in the *Living Things* column because it is an animal that grows, reproduces, and dies.

   C. A *tree* belongs in the *Living Things* column because it is a plant that grows, reproduces, and dies.

   D. *Air* belongs in the *Nonliving Things* column because it does not grow, reproduce or die.

4. **A.** This is correct because fish swimming closely together is a behavior that helps fish stay safe.

   B. This is incorrect because cats licking their hair is an example of grooming, not an example of a way that group behavior can help animals stay safe from predators.

   C. This is correct because vocalizing when a predator is near is an example of a group behavior that helps animals stay safe from predators.

5. **A.** This is incorrect because the data show that the greatest amount of rain was in year 3, where there were no flowers.

   B. This is incorrect because the lower temperatures made normal-sized potatoes.

   C. This is correct because the data show that environmental conditions affected the appearance of the potato plant and its tuber.

6. **A.** Following this action is correct because staying inside during a storm is a good way to remain safe.

   B. Following this action is incorrect because checking smoke detectors does not help with being safe during a storm.

7. **A.** This is correct because the land bridge allows animals to search for food on the other side of the road without getting onto the road surface.

   B. This is correct because animals will be less likely to cross the road and be hit by cars.

   C. This is incorrect because the land bridge is made by people.

8. Use the rubric below to evaluate total points earned for this item.   *[max point: 1]*

© Houghton Mifflin Harcourt Publishing Company

CCC - 1 point		
Claims	The student is able to compare group behaviors and identify the consequent effect of the behavior (CCC).	
Evidence of Mastery of Crosscutting Concepts	1 point for correctly matching the behavior (cause) to its outcome (effect) **Part 1:** One point is earned for matching the behavior to the outcome. The student should match 1 and B, 2 and C, 3 and A. The following response, or an equivalent, is acceptable.	

Animal Behavior → **Effect**

Animal Behavior		Effect	
1	Adult elephants huddling around newborn	A	Helping each other keeps group alive
2	Prairie dog makes a loud crying noise when hawks fly over	B	Protects young, smaller member from predators
3	Many ants carry dirt in mouth and leave at hole entrance	C	Warns group of danger

(Matches: 1–B, 2–C, 3–A)

9. **A.** This is incorrect because climate describes weather for a long period. Weather can change daily.

    B. This is incorrect because climate is the type of weather for a large area for a long period of time. Weather happens only for a short period of time.

    C. This is correct because climate is the type of weather for a large area for a long period of time.

10. **A.** The picture of the white hare belongs in the *Hide From Predator During Winter* box. The white hare will blend in with the white snow of the winter season.

    B. The picture of the dark brown hare belongs in the *Hide From Predator During Fall* box. The brown hare will blend in with the brown and orange colors of the fall season.

11. **A.** The polar bear belongs in the *Cold and wet* row. Polar bears have physical adaptations, including storing fat for warmth, that allow them to better survive an Arctic-like environment.

    B. The camel belongs in the *Hot and dry* row. Camels have physical adaptations, including storing water, that allow them to better survive living in a desert-like environment.

    C. *Stores fat for warmth* belongs in the *Cold and Wet* row under the *Why able to survive* heading. Organisms that can survive a very cold environment have adaptations that allow them to conserve heat, such as storing energy as fat to be used as insulation.

    D. *Stores water for use later* belongs in the *Hot and dry* row under the *Why able to survive* heading. Organisms that can survive a desert-like environment have adaptions that allow them to conserve water, such as storing excess water for use later.

12. **A.** *Fix leaky faucets* belongs in the *Will Help* column because it reduces the amount of wasted water.

    B. *Stay inside until it rains* belongs in the *Will Not Help* column because this action will not conserve current or future water resources.

13. **A.** This possible change is correct for *Bees* and *Flowers*. Bees are dying. There will not be any left to reproduce. Flowers need the bees to move the pollen, but without the bees, the flowers will have difficulty reproducing.

    B. This possible change is correct for *Bees*. Skunks eat the bees, and disease is reducing the number of bees.

© Houghton Mifflin Harcourt Publishing Company

14. Use the rubric below to evaluate total points earned for this item.   *[max point: 1]*

CCC - 1 point	
Claims	The student is able to compare traits and behaviors of different organisms and identify their consequent effects (CCC).
Evidence of Mastery of Crosscutting Concepts	1 point for correctly matching the traits and behaviors to the effect **Part 1:** One point is earned for drawing lines between the traits and behaviors (Table 1) and the effect of how this trait/behavior assists the organisms (Table 2). One of the following, or an equivalent, is acceptable.

Table 1

Letter	Body Part/Behavior That Is Different from Rest of Group
A	Has larger leaves
B	Stores fat in thick layer
C	Fur changes from brown to white in winter

Table 2

Number	How Helps Animal Survive
1	Blends in with color of environment
2	Collects more sunlight
3	Keeps warm during winter

15. There should be two Xs for Monday to represent 2 cm, no Xs for Tuesday, and four Xs for Wednesday.

16. A. The temperature of *19°* belongs in fall's average temperature. The temperature for fall should be less than summer's but greater than winter's.

  B. The amount of *2* centimeters belongs in the precipitation column for winter. Travis noticed that it did not rain or snow much in the winter. Fall had 4 cm of precipitation, which means winter had to have 2 cm.

  C. The amount of *5* centimeters belongs in the precipitation column for summer. Travis noticed that it rained more in the summer than in the fall but the most in spring.

  D. *Decreased* is correct for the second blank in the *Average Temperature* column in the *Pattern* row. The pattern for the average temperature shows that there was an increase and then a decrease (22, 31, 19, and 12 degrees). *Decreased* is also correct for the average snow/rain pattern.

  E. *Increased* is correct for the first blank in the *Average Temperature* column in the *Pattern* row. The pattern for the average temperature shows that there was an increase and then a decrease (22, 31, 19, and 12 degrees).

17. A. This is incorrect because these fossils did not appear in recent layers of rock.

  B. This is incorrect because layer 1 is on the bottom of several other layers. The youngest layers are toward the top, closer to layer 4. Layer 1 appears to be the oldest layer.

  C. This correct because these organisms did not appear in any rock layer more recent than layer 1.

18. A. *Had wings and legs* belongs in the box for *Organism 1* because the organism's fossil appears to have had legs, and the head appears to be that of a bird, which indicates it was likely to have wings too.

  B. *Probably lived on land* belongs in the box for *Organism 1* because the organism appears to have had legs and wings, which could resemble some sort of bird; birds live on land.

  C. *Probably lived in water* belongs in the box for *Organism 2* because lobsters today live in water and they probably did in the past, too.

19. Use the rubric below to evaluate total points earned for this item.   *[max point: 3]*

DCI, CCC - 3 Points	
Claims	The student is able to: 1. identify fossils (DCI); and 2. use patterns in given data to describe the type of environment in which an organism lived long ago (CCC).

© Houghton Mifflin Harcourt Publishing Company

Evidence of Mastery of Disciplinary Core Ideas	2 points for correctly identifying the fossils **Part 1:** One point is earned for identifying the fossils in layer 2 as that from a mollusk (shell) and a fish. One of the following, or an equivalent, is acceptable. • clams and fish • mollusks and fish • things that lived in shells and animals that swam **Part 2:** One point is earned for identifying the fossils in layer 4 as a dinosaur and a bird. One of the following, or an equivalent, is acceptable. • dinosaur and bird • reptile and animal that flew
Evidence of Mastery of Crosscutting Concepts	1 point for correctly describing how the environment changed **Part 3:** One point is earned for describing that the environment changed from a water environment in layer 2 to a land environment in layer 4. One of the following, or an equivalent, is acceptable. • Layer 2 was covered with water and layer 4 was not. • The sea covered the area when layer 1 was around.

20. **A.** *Layer 1* belongs in the *Seawater* column because the fossilized shells indicate that mollusks and trilobites lived in the area. These organisms reside in seawater. The sea must have covered the area when layer 1 was formed.

    B. *Layer 2* belongs in the *Seawater* column because the clams and fish reside in seawater. The sea must have covered the area when layer 1 was formed.

    C. *Layer 3* belongs in the *Land* column because trees and dragonflies live mainly on the land. The sea must not have been covering the area when layer 2 was formed.

    D. *Layer 4* belongs in the *Land* column because dinosaurs and birds are land animals. There are no fossil remains of organisms that lived in the sea. The sea must not have been covering the area when layer 4 was formed.

21. **1B.** The first dog is too thin. This dog probably does not eat enough. This matches the description of Bailey.

    2C. The second dog's weight seems ideal. He probably eats a healthy amount of food and gets enough exercise. This matches the description of Cooper.

    3A. The third dog is overweight. This dog probably eats too much and doesn't get enough exercise. This matches the description of Astro.

22. **A.** This is correct because cutting down a tree that grows nuts can reduce the squirrel's source of food.

    B. This is incorrect because insects will not disappear in the absences of trees.

    C. This is correct because squirrels use trees to hide from predators; they also make nests in trees.

23. Use the rubric below to evaluate total points earned for this item.   *[max point: 2]*

DCI Only - 2 Points	
Claims	The student is able to explain how being a part of a group helps animals cope with changes (DCI).
Evidence of Mastery of Disciplinary Core Ideas	2 points for correctly identifying the reason for huddling **Part 1:** Two points are earned for identifying that these penguins huddle in order to conserve heat and stay warm. The following response, or an equivalent, is acceptable. • The penguins huddle to stay warm.

© Houghton Mifflin Harcourt Publishing Company

24. **1B.** *Maybe* belongs in the box for the red fox. The red fox is accustomed to the cold environment of the U.S. The red fox would not die immediately in the Arctic, nor would it survive well. It would barely survive the Arctic.

   2A. *Yes* belongs in the box for the reindeer. The reindeer is accustomed to the cold environment of Alaska and Canada. The reindeer would survive well in the Arctic.

   3C. *No* belongs in the box for the rattlesnake. The rattlesnake is accustomed to the warm environment closer to the equator. The rattlesnake would die very quickly in the Arctic environment.

25. Use the rubric below to evaluate total points earned for this item. *[max point: 1]*

CCC - 1 point	
Claims	The student is able to identify the cause-and-effect relationship within variation of the same type of organism that allows some to reproduce, while a similar group does not (CCC).
Evidence of Mastery of Crosscutting Concepts	1 point for correctly identifying the numbers **Part 1:** One point is earned for circling numbers 5 and 6 as evidence to support Reba's claim that one group, group B, is more likely to reproduce. The following response, or an equivalent, is acceptable. <table><tr><th>Group A</th><th>Group B</th></tr><tr><td>1. Eat plant parts, insects, and lizards.</td><td>4. Eat flowers, leaves, insects, and frogs.</td></tr><tr><td>2. Females are not interested in males.</td><td>(5.) Females are attracted to males.</td></tr><tr><td>3. Females do not lay many eggs.</td><td>(6.) Females lay many eggs.</td></tr></table>

26. **A.** This is incorrect. The evidence presented in the table makes one assume that dark-brown insects are less likely to reproduce because they do not survive as long as light-green insects.

   B. This is correct because light-green insects live longer; the light-green color can be an advantage for these insects.

   C. This is correct because the dark-brown color would be more obvious to animals than a light-green color, which could potentially blend in with the environment.

27. Use the rubric below to evaluate total points earned for this item. *[max point: 3]*

DCI, CCC - 3 Points	
Claims	The student is able to: 1. describe how one or more organisms within that habitat will be adversely affected by the change (DCI); and 2. describe how humans are able to prevent/reduce the effects of environmental change through technology and/or engineering (CCC).
Evidence of Mastery of Disciplinary Core Ideas	1 point for correctly identifying how a Z clam hurts another animal **Part 1:** One point is earned for identifying the negative effects of a Z clam on other organisms. The response may include that the Z is poisonous to birds, and attaches to other clams. One of the following, or an equivalent, is acceptable. • Poisons seabirds • Grows on other clams
Evidence of Mastery of Crosscutting Concepts	2 points for describing a solution **Part 2:** Two points are earned for describing that using pipes with the special metal will prevent the clams from clogging the pipes. The following, or an equivalent, is acceptable. • The Z clams do not like the special metal. They will not stick to it and clog it.

© Houghton Mifflin Harcourt Publishing Company

28. A. This is incorrect because the data do not show daily rainfall, and the daily temperature is likely to be around 13°C, not 8°C.

   B. This is incorrect because the data do not show cloud coverage, and the rainfall is likely to be about 8 cm monthly, not 14 cm daily.

   C. This is correct because the data for temperature range from 12°C to 14°C and the rainfall ranges from 7 cm to 9 cm.

29. A. *Protects against predators* belongs in the *Rose Bush* row because thorns deter animals that may otherwise eat the plant.

   B. *Pokes in the ground for food* belongs in the *Kiwi Bird* row because the long beak allows the bird to search for worms and other insects in the ground.

   C. *Blends into tree bark to survive* belongs in the *Moth* row because the brown wings will camouflage the moth protecting it from predators.

   D. *Survive* belongs as the last word of the conclusion. The differences help the animals survive in their environments.

   E. *Lead the group* does not belong in any row. The differences stated would not necessarily create a leader, and plants don't have a leader.

30. A. This is correct because a wetland has everything that is essential for a frog's survival such as water to lay eggs and stay moist, and food such as insects and worms. A desert is perfect for a scorpion because it has the food the scorpion eats, and an environment the scorpion can blend in with, and typically has hot temperatures.

   B. This is incorrect because a frog would freeze in a cold habitat and there is nothing there for it to survive on; a scorpion cannot live in any location because some locations are not suitable for a scorpion to live in.

   C. This is incorrect because although a forest could have what a frog needs to survive, it is not the essential habitat. A scorpion would not be found in the cold habitat due to scorpions not being able to survive cold temperatures.

© Houghton Mifflin Harcourt Publishing Company